Managing Information Risks

Managing Information Risks

Threats, Vulnerabilities, and Responses

William Saffady

ROWMAN & LITTLEFIELD
Lanham • Boulder • New York • London

Published by Rowman & Littlefield
An imprint of The Rowman & Littlefield Publishing Group, Inc.
4501 Forbes Boulevard, Suite 200, Lanham, Maryland 20706
www.rowman.com

6 Tinworth Street, London SE11 5AL, United Kingdom

British Library Cataloguing in Publication Information Available

Library of Congress Cataloging-in-Publication Data

Names: Saffady, William, 1944– author.
Title: Managing information risks : threats, vulnerabilities, and responses / William Saffady.
Description: Lanham : Rowman & Littlefield, 2020. | Includes bibliographical references and index. |
    Summary: "Written by one of the foremost records and information management leaders in the
    world, this book provides a clear explanation and analysis of the fundamental principles associat-
    ed with information risk, which is broadly defined as a combination of threats, vulnerabilities,
    and consequences related to use of an organization's information assets."—Provided by publish-
    er.
Identifiers: LCCN 2020000882 (print) | LCCN 2020000883 (ebook) | ISBN 9781538135488 (cloth) |
    ISBN 9781538135495 (paperback) | ISBN 9781538135501 (epub)
Subjects: LCSH: Data protection. | Computer security. | Records—Management. | Database manage-
    ment. | Risk management.
Classification: LCC HF5548.37 .S24 2020 (print) | LCC HF5548.37 (ebook) | DDC 658.4/038—dc23
LC record available at https://lccn.loc.gov/2020000882
LC ebook record available at https://lccn.loc.gov/2020000883

♾ ™ The paper used in this publication meets the minimum requirements of American
National Standard for Information Sciences Permanence of Paper for Printed Library
Materials, ANSI/NISO Z39.48-1992.

Contents

Preface   vii

1   Risk Terms and Concepts   1

2   Creation and Collection of Information   25

3   Loss of Information   61

4   Retention of Information   97

5   Retrieval and Disclosure of Information   141

6   Ownership of Information   189

Index   231

About the Author   245

Preface

Information risk is an important topic at the nexus of risk management and information governance, two disciplines with closely aligned objectives. Risk management is responsible for identifying, analyzing, and controlling threats to an organization's assets. Information governance supports this responsibility by developing effective strategies, policies, and initiatives to identify, assess, and address risks associated with an organization's information assets. The two disciplines have a complementary relationship, and they must work together to fulfill their responsibilities.

This book is intended for risk managers, information governance specialists, compliance officers, attorneys, records managers, data scientists, archivists, librarians, and other decision-makers, managers, and analysts who are involved in or need to be aware of risk management initiatives related to their organizations' information assets. The book can also be used as a textbook by colleges and universities that offer courses in risk management, information governance, or related topics at the graduate or advanced undergraduate level. In particular, the book may be useful for a curriculum that combines risk management with records management, knowledge management, information science, health informatics, information system design, data protection, and other information-related subjects.

Google Trends, a website that analyzes the popularity of Google searches, shows a steady level of worldwide search activity over the past five years for the phrase *information risk*, with most of the searches originating in the United States and United Kingdom. The level of search activity is higher and the range of geographic interest is broader for the terms *information* and *risk* searched together in a Boolean expression rather than as a phrase. For the same period, a Google Scholar search for the phrase *information risk* retrieved approximately 11,500 citations, while a search of the two terms in a Boolean expression retrieved over 1.3 million citations.

Google search results suggest that information risk is strongly associated with information technology in general and cybersecurity in particular, but information risk is not limited to computer data. It encompasses organizational information assets of any type in any format, including paper and photographic records as well as digital content stored on premises or by cloud service providers. Reflecting this broader view, this book discusses risks related to creation, collection, storage, retention, retrieval, disclosure, and ownership of information in organizations of all types and sizes. Chapter 1 provides an introduction to risk terms and concepts that are essential for understanding, assessing, and controlling information risk. Taking a taxonomic approach, the remaining chapters identify and categorize threats and discuss vulnerabilities and risk responses related to the following topics:

- Chapter 2 deals with risks associated with creation and collection of information, including failure to collect information required by laws and regulations; unauthorized collection of personal information; illegal collection of nonpublic information; creation or collection of information with objectionable, defamatory, or private content; and creation or collection of poor-quality information.
- Chapter 3 discusses loss of information due to natural disasters, malicious human actions, accidents, and fire.
- Chapter 4 identifies risks associated with retention and destruction of information, including noncompliance with laws and regulations that require retention, preservation, or destruction of information; retaining information longer than necessary; destroying information that needs to be kept; and media instability and obsolescence problems that affect the usability of information.
- Chapter 5 discusses risks associated with information retrieval and disclosure, including retrieval failures, metadata mining, noncompliance with laws and regulations that mandate information disclosure, failure to prevent unauthorized disclosure of information, prohibitions on cross-border transfer of information, and noncompliance with data breach notification laws.
- Chapter 6 deals with risks associated with ownership of information, including infringement of intellectual property rights, the impact of the work-for-hire doctrine, loss of ownership of trade secrets, and data portability laws and regulations that affect ownership of personal information.

Each chapter begins with a brief overview that summarizes key risks related to the topic at hand, followed by a detailed explanation of each threat, an assessment of vulnerabilities that the threat can exploit, and a review of available options to address the threat and its associated vulnerabilities. Chapters 2 through 6 are self-contained and can be read in any order, but reference is occasionally made to related points that are discussed in other chapters.

Individual chapters include extensive endnotes that cite publications to support specific points and provide suggestions for further reading about risk related topics. Some endnotes also include comments or additional details about matters discussed in the text. Links are provided to the full text of cited publications if they are available via a reliable web site that is likely to be accessible for the foreseeable future. Otherwise, a digital object identifier (DOI) or other persistent identifier is cited for a given publication where available.

International standards that provide authoritative guidance about risk management are cited at appropriate points in the text, as are laws and regulations that impact information risk. The cited standards, which are identified by number and title, are issued by the International Organization for Standardization (www.iso.org). The full text of a law or regulation can be retrieved by doing a web search based on the title or the abbreviated reference, which is cited in a commonly used format.

As the endnotes to each chapter indicate, this book draws on a large and growing body of ideas from a variety of disciplines, including business process management, insurance, law, financial analysis, information science, librarianship, records management, and archival administration. While the book's coverage of risk related topics is supported by scholarly research, the treatment is practical rather than theoretical. Risk is a pervasive and inevitable aspect of information-related initiatives and activities, but it is often underestimated or overlooked. Risk related thinking must be incorporated into the planning and implementation process for every project, system, or service that creates, collects, stores, retrieves, or discloses information. To support this objective, this book focuses on knowledge and recommendations that readers can use to heighten risk awareness within their organizations, identify threats and their associated consequences, assess vulnerabilities, evaluate risk mitigation options, define risk related responsibilities, and align information-related initiatives and activities with their organizations' risk management strategies and policies.

Chapter One

Risk Terms and Concepts

As defined in ISO 55000:2014, *Asset Management—Overview, Principles, and Terminology*, assets are items or entities that have actual or potential value to an organization. Risk assessment and control are important components of an organization's asset-management strategy. According to ISO 55002:2018, *Asset Management—Management Systems—Guidelines for the Application of ISO 55001*, risk management processes must be aligned with and integrated into the design and execution of an organization's asset-management plan. This principle applies to all organizational assets, including information assets. For many organizations, strategic plans, financial data, product formulations, technical specifications, customer lists, supplier data, trade secrets, and other information contained in databases, documents, and other records are more valuable than equipment, inventory, and physical assets.[1] The following sections define and discuss concepts and principles that are relevant for identification, assessment, and control of risks that endanger an organization's information assets.

DEFINITIONS

Risk is a complex concept that does not have a universally accepted definition.[2] Citing usage from the seventeenth century, the *Oxford English Dictionary* defines *risk* as exposure to "the possibility of loss, injury, or other adverse or unwelcome circumstance" or "a chance or situation involving such a possibility." Other dictionary definitions likewise equate risk with exposure to danger.[3] According to ISO Guide 73:2009, *Risk Management—Vocabulary*, which defines terms used by international risk management standards, *risk* is "the effect of uncertainty on objectives," where uncertainty is a "deficiency of information" related to a particular matter and the effect is

1

a "deviation from the expected."[4] The ISO definition notes that risk may have a positive or negative connotation. Positive risk creates opportunities. Negative risk undermines an organization's objective and activities. Positive risk is sometimes characterized as speculative risk because it involves the possibility of a gain as well as a loss, while negative risk is considered pure risk because it only involves the possibility of a loss.[5]

Definitions presented in most academic and business publications emphasize the negative aspect of risk.[6] Reflecting the interdisciplinary nature of risk concepts and a variety of viewpoints, *risk* is variously defined as the possibility of an unfortunate occurrence with potential for unwanted, negative consequences;[7] the result of a threat with adverse effects to a vulnerable system;[8] the potential for damage or loss of an asset, which includes anything that has a positive value to its owner;[9] an expression of the likelihood that a specific vulnerability will be exploited by a defined threat to cause a given consequence;[10] the probability and severity of a future loss, disaster, or other adverse outcome;[11] and a quantitative measure of hazard consequences that can be expressed as conditional probabilities of experiencing harm.[12]

Drawing on these definitions, this book defines *information risk* as a combination of threats, vulnerabilities, and consequences related to creation, collection, ownership, retention, retrieval, and disclosure of information. A threat is a circumstance, action, or event that poses a danger to an organization's information assets or that otherwise impairs an organization's ability to achieve information-dependent objectives. A vulnerability is a weakness that a threat can exploit to damage or compromise an information asset. A consequence is a negative outcome that results when such exploitation occurs. Taken together, these risk components address three questions that are implicit in all definitions of risk: What can go wrong? What can cause it to go wrong? What are the consequences if it does go wrong?[13]

Because future events and outcomes cannot be predicted with complete confidence, uncertainty is an inherent characteristic of all threats, vulnerabilities, and consequences. As previously cited, uncertainty is a component of the definition of *risk* presented in ISO Guide 73:2009, but some researchers differentiate risk, where the possible outcomes of a situation or event are known, from uncertainty, where the possibilities cannot be determined.[14] The probability of a negative outcome, which is mentioned in some definitions of *risk*, is reflected in the likelihood of occurrence of a given threat and the level of an organization's vulnerability should the threat occur. Probability is sometimes expressed as an annualized loss expectancy or another statistical measure derived from empirical or historical data that are not readily available for most instances of information risk. With few exceptions, probability estimates and management decisions related to threats, vulnerabilities, and consequences discussed in this book are based on subjective rather than quantitative analysis. The subjective approach, which is more common than measurable evaluations in practice, seeks a reasonable assessment of the danger to information assets in a given situation. Threats are evaluated and prioritized by informed decision-makers who are familiar with specific business processes and information assets.[15]

The threats discussed in this book range from low-probability events with a limited negative impact to high-impact events with a high probability of occurrence. Reflecting the link between information risk and uncertainty, most threats to information assets have a variable rate of occurrence and a variable impact on information assets that can only be evaluated in specific contexts. Certain extreme threats, such as destructive weather, have a low probability of occurrence but can cause massive damage to information assets.

ENTERPRISE RISK MANAGEMENT

As defined in the previously cited ISO Guide 73:2009, risk management consists of "coordinated activities to direct and control an organization with regard to risk." The earliest risk management initiatives focused on insurance risks and financial risks. Since the 1990s, their scope has broadened to address all types of organizational risks.[16] An organization-wide approach that treats risk management as a component of organizational governance and business strategy is termed enterprise risk management (ERM) to differentiate it from risk management initiatives of limited scope, such as investment risk management, flood risk management, epidemiological risk management, supply chain risk management, or cybersecurity risk management.[17] Because information risk affects all organizational processes, operations, and activities, information risk management is an important component of enterprise risk management.

An ERM framework establishes the foundation and organizational arrangements for developing, implementing, and monitoring a risk management program. The most influential risk management frameworks are delineated in ISO 31000:2018 (*Risk Management—Guidelines*) and ISO 31010:2019 (*Risk Management—Risk Assessment Techniques*) and in the Enterprise Risk Management—Integrated Framework developed by the Committee of Sponsoring Organizations (COSO) of the Treadway Commission. As defined by COSO, a risk management framework is "designed to identify potential events that may affect the entity, and manage risks to be within its risk appetite, to provide reasonable assurance regarding the achievement of entity objectives."[18]

To fulfill its purpose, an ERM framework provides a coordinated set of risk management principles, policies, objectives, roles, and processes:

- Risk oversight is widely recognized as the responsibility of an organization's governing body, which must understand and be committed to risk management principles and objectives.[19] Some organizations have established board-level risk committees that review risk-management policies and processes to ensure that they are aligned with the organization's strategies, business objectives, and internal controls.[20]
- An organization's executive management must approve and articulate a risk management program's objectives; integrate risk awareness into the organization's strategies and operations at every level; and create an environment for effective implementation of risk related initiatives.
- An ERM framework must assign risk management authority, define risk responsibilities, and allocate resources required for development and implementation of a risk management program. Since the 1990s, some large organizations have appointed a chief risk officer (CRO) to coordinate, direct, and monitor their risk management processes.[21] Alternatively, risk management responsibility may be assigned to an organization's general counsel, chief financial officer, or other senior executive who works closely with internal auditors and a governing board's audit committee. This is typically the case in small and medium-size organizations.
- Department heads and other key stakeholders have primary responsibility for managing risks related to their operations and activities on a day-to-day basis. They must comply with risk management policies; promote risk awareness within their business units; and incorporate risk considerations into the planning, prioritization, review, and approval process for projects, investments, and other organizational initiatives. Project managers must likewise incorporate risk management concepts into every stage of their work.
- An enterprise risk management program must provide accountability, monitoring, and review mechanisms to ensure compliance and respond to changing conditions. In some organizations, the internal audit function is responsible for evaluating risk management processes for compliance and effectiveness and for preparing audit reports with recommendation for corrective actions to address deficiencies to ensure that risks are managed appropriately. Because internal audit is concerned with compliance and internal controls, its objectives are closely aligned with those of risk management, but its status as an independent function increases the likelihood of an objective evaluation of programmatic objectives.[22]

Various maturity models are available to help an organization evaluate the current status of its enterprise risk management program, identify gaps that must be addressed, and track the progress of ongoing improvements.[23] Designed as self-assessment tools, these maturity models typically define five to seven levels that represent a hierarchy of formalization and effectiveness for enterprise risk management.[24] For programs at the lowest level in the hierarchy, formalization is limited or nonexistent, risk management objectives and responsibilities are poorly defined, and risk management policies and practices, where they exist at all, are developed and applied on an ad hoc basis. The highest level is characterized by optimized performance based on clearly articulated, well-tested risk management policies and processes with a focus on continuous improvement. In a fully developed ERM program, which is more likely to exist in textbooks than in practice, risk management is aligned with and fully integrated into an organization's strategic objectives and is a recognized contributor to cost containment, client services, and competitive advantage. Intermediate levels in the maturity hierarchy represent progressively more effective stages between the two extremes. The third level typically represents a functioning risk management program with effective leadership and an acceptable but not optimal degree of formalization. Stakeholder's risk management responsibilities are defined and accepted. Risks associated with specific business processes, operations, and initiatives are identified, assessed, prioritized, and addressed based on agreed-upon criteria. A risk management program's performance improves as it moves up the levels, but the highest level may not be attainable in every situation. For some organizations, the third or fourth level in a five-step maturity model represents an acceptable balance of formalization, effort, and cost.

The effectiveness of risk management is most clearly demonstrated when an adverse event is successfully addressed. Otherwise, the business case for risk management is based on measurable and intangible benefits that presumably outweigh the cost of a risk management program. Frequently cited advantages include improved corporate governance, more informed decisions, greater management consensus about risk related matters, improved management accountability, better oversight of manager's risk related behavior, reduced fines and penalties for compliance violations, lower legal costs for civil litigation and regulatory enforcement actions, and, in rare instances, avoidance of criminal prosecution.[25] A number of empirical studies have examined the impact of risk management programs on company valuations, but the evidence is mixed.[26] Some researchers found higher stock prices and lower volatility for both stock prices and earnings for companies that have a risk management program when compared to companies in the same industry that do not have such a program. Perhaps a risk management program increases the confidence of investors and rating agencies, but these research findings are correlations that do not necessary imply causation.

GOVERNANCE, RISK, AND COMPLIANCE (GRC)

Governance is the system by which an organization is directed and controlled.[27] Compliance is concerned with an organization's adherence to applicable laws and regulations to avoid civil and criminal liability.[28] In some organizations, enterprise risk management is aligned with and integrated into an organization's governance and compliance initiatives. This umbrella approach, known as a GRC framework, is designed to coordinate risk related initiatives and promote sharing of information about enterprise risks across all three functions.[29] OCEG, a nonprofit organization originally founded as the Open Compliance and Ethics Group, equates GRC with "principled performance," which it defines as the ability to "reliably achieve objectives (governance) while addressing uncertainty (risk management) and acting with integrity (compliance)."[30] As discussed in subsequent chapters, compliance violations expose an organization to fines, penalties, and other disciplinary actions that are costly, disrupt specific business operations, and expose an organization to increased regulatory scrutiny and, in extreme cases, criminal prosecution. A GRC capability model developed by OCEG defines characteristics that enable an organization to achieve its objectives while addressing uncertainty and integrity issues.[31]

In a GRC context, some sources substitute the phrase *risk governance* for *risk management* to more closely identify risk related initiatives with corporate governance and, in the case of information risk, information governance.[32] This usage highlights the difference between governance and management. Governance is concerned with vision and purpose; management is responsible for operations and performance. As defined by the International Risk Governance Council (IRGC), a not-for-profit organization dedicated to understanding and managing risks, risk governance is a focused aspect of organizational governance. It applies governance concepts to the identification, categorization, assessment, management, evaluation, and communication of threats and vulnerabilities.[33] The IRGC has developed a risk governance framework that includes the following components:

- preassessment to define and clarify a risk related problem;
- appraisal based on a risk's measurable characteristics, such as the probability of occurrence and the financial impact of adverse effects;
- evaluation to determine whether a risk is acceptable, tolerable with mitigation, or intolerable;
- management action to accept, reduce, transfer, or avoid a specific risk; and
- communication to inform stakeholders affected by risk.

This risk governance framework enables organizational governance to fulfill its responsibility for prudent stewardship of assets, which may be adversely affected by risk.[34] Risk governance strongly supports organizational governance's responsibility for understanding, assessing, and monitoring internal controls, including policies and processes for financial controls and disclosure controls. The COSO framework, which was mentioned above, defines *internal controls* as ongoing tasks and activities that are "designed to provide reasonable assurance regarding the achievement of objectives relating to operations, reporting, and compliance."[35] As one of the principle components of the COSO framework, risk governance requires an organization's governing body and management to identify and analyze threats and vulnerabilities and to take action to mitigate their negative impact.

Risk governance also helps an organization address the so-called "principal-agent problem" in which the actions of a department, subsidiary, or other organizational unit (the agent) are not aligned with the interests of the organization as a whole (the principal).[36] This lack of alignment can squander assets, obstruct operations, and prevent an organization from capitalizing on opportunities. To prevent this from occurring, risk governance uses policy and oversight to align local operations and activities with enterprise-wide risk strategies and priorities.

As a GRC component, risk governance affects and is affected by other organizational governance initiatives, including data governance, information technology governance, information security governance, process governance, and project governance. As it relates to information risk, risk governance is responsible for identifying, assessing, and monitoring the threats and vulnerabilities discussed in this book within the broad framework of governance principles that apply to an organization's information assets. Definitions of *information governance* specifically mention risk as a component. According to ISO/TR 11633-1, *Health Informatics—Information Security Management for Remote Maintenance of Medical Devices and Medical Information Systems—Part 1: Requirements and Risk Analysis*, for example, information governance is the "processes by which an organization obtains assurance that the risks to its information, and thereby the operational capabilities and integrity of the organization, are effectively identified and managed." The Sedona Conference, a research and educational institute that focuses on law and policy issues, cites information risk as a key issue for information governance. The Information Governance Initiative, a cross-disciplinary consortium, defines *information governance* as "the activities and technologies that organizations employ to maximize the value of their information while minimizing associated risks and costs."[37]

THREATS AND VULNERABILITIES

A coherent risk management framework enables an organization to develop effective risk strategies and responses. A risk management process must identify and describe threats and consequences, identify and evaluate vulnerabilities, and assess options for risk response. Because unrecognized risks cannot be managed, an effective risk management process begins with identification of potential threats, which are sometimes described as threat agents or risk sources.[38]

A threat agent has the potential to harm organizational assets. Threat agents may be internal, such as employee errors, or external, such as destructive weather, civil unrest, or computer hackers. Threats may arise from natural or human sources. The latter may involve individuals or groups. A threat agent's actions may be malicious or accidental. Where human threat agents are involved, a malicious action is a function of the threat agent's motivation (monetary gain, disruption of business operations, political or social agenda, or other reasons to harm a specific asset), capability (the knowledge, skill, software tools, or other resources needed to cause damage), and opportunity (appropriate access to the asset).[39]

Threats vary in their likelihood of occurrence. Some threat agents are readily identifiable, well understood, and predictable within limits; others may arise from extremely unlikely events that are not anticipated—so-called "black swans"—or from emerging risk sources that were previously unrecognized or underestimated. The probability of a given threat must be balanced against the consequences, which may likewise vary in severity from negligible to catastrophic. Risk management is generally concerned with monetary consequences resulting from lost revenue caused by business disruption or imposition of fines for regulatory noncompliance, but noneconomic consequences, such as breach of duty, may also be considered.

A threat poses no harm in the absence of vulnerability, which is the basis for an organization's risk exposure. As defined by the Open Group, which develops technology standards and certifications, vulnerability is the probability that a particular threat exceeds an organization's ability to resist it.[40] As part of the risk management process, vulnerabilities associated with specific threat agents must be identified and assessed. With reference to a given threat agent, the key factors for vulnerability assessment are susceptibility (openness to attack by the threat agent) and exposure (opportunity for attack by the threat agent). Vulnerability assessment may be based on qualitative, quantitative, or hybrid approaches.[41] Vulnerabilities may be natural or caused by human action or inaction. The latter may reflect a lack of required capabilities, such as unqualified staff; defects in organizational processes, such as inadequate employee training or supervision; flawed system components, such as unreliable software; or external factors, such as an organization's geographical location.

RISK RESPONSE

Risk response, sometimes termed risk treatment or risk mitigation, is the process of reducing, eliminating, or otherwise reacting to threats and their associated vulnerabilities. An organization's risk appetite determines its approach to risk mitigation. As defined in the previously cited ISO Guide 73:2009, risk appetite is the amount and type of risk an organization is willing to pursue or retain.[42] The four basic risk responses are acceptance, avoidance, transfer, and limitation:

- Risk acceptance is based on an informed decision to accept the consequences associated with a given threat or vulnerability. It is the only risk mitigation option that does not reduce threats or vulnerabilities. Acceptance may be the preferred approach for threats with a low probability of occurrence or low level of severity, situations where a particular threat or vulnerability cannot be eliminated, or situations where the cost of other mitigation options is greater than the adverse economic consequences posed by a threat or vulnerability. Risk acceptance criteria define the level of risk that an organization is willing to tolerate in a given set of circumstances. Beyond that level, other mitigation actions must be taken.[43]
- Risk avoidance is an extreme form of risk aversion, which attempts to reduce uncertainty in decision-making. Risk avoidance eliminates an unacceptable threat by discontinuing the business operation or activity with which the threat is associated or by restructuring the operation or activity to eliminate vulnerabilities. Risk avoidance may also be a factor in an organization's decision not to begin a new initiative that involves unacceptable threats or unavoidable vulnerabilities. Risk avoidance based on discontinuation is not a viable mitigation strategy for business operations that are mission-critical or mandated by laws or regulations, but a business process might be modified to eliminate specific vulnerabilities. Where a risky business operation cannot be eliminated, an organization might be able to outsource it to shift the risk to a contractor or other third party, a mitigation approach that combines risk avoidance and risk transfer.
- In risk transfer, an organization or individual deliberately transfers a threat under contract to a willing third party, usually an insurance company, which accepts the potentially adverse consequences in return for an agreed-upon payment. An insurance policy covers monetary damages or financial losses associated with designated risks within specified limits. Alternatively, some contracts include an indemnification clause or hold-

harmless agreement that transfers specified risks to the contracting party. These noninsurance risk transfer mechanisms require one contracting party to assume certain legal liabilities of the other party, which may purchase insurance to cover the contractually agreed risk. A warranty is a form of contractual risk transfer that shifts the threat of malfunction, defective workmanship, or other problems to the manufacturer or supplier of a product or service.

- Risk limitation, the most common mitigation option, involves actions that address specific vulnerabilities to minimize the adverse consequences associated with a given threat. To prevent vandalism of its buildings, for example, an organization might upgrade its alarm system and hire security guards for nighttime hours and on weekends. To reduce costly data entry errors, an organization might increase staff training, pay more to hire more-skilled personnel, or utilize double-keying of critical data values. A risk limitation strategy typically avoids some threats while accepting a lower degree of harm for others. This risk mitigation option requires comprehensive identification and analysis of both threats and vulnerabilities.

Taken together, these risk responses will reduce an organization's exposure to the negative consequences of events that would otherwise disrupt its business operations and cause financial distress. Risk response can successfully address many threats and vulnerabilities, but it may not eliminate them completely. Inherent risk is the level of risk before risk response. Residual risk is the level of risk that remains after mitigation. The goal of risk response is to attain a tolerable level of residual risk for a given operation or activity.

RISK TAXONOMY

This book takes a taxonomic approach to information risk. A risk taxonomy is an organized categorization of risk events that can have a negative impact on an organization's objectives or operations. As its principle benefit, a risk taxonomy facilitates the identification and assessment of threats and vulnerabilities. Taxonomic categorization is typically based on a historical review of risk events that have actually occurred, supplemented where possible by informed predictions of adverse events that may occur in the future. Some risk management software provides preformulated lists of common and unusual risks from which an organization can select those that are relevant to its operations and activities.

Although there is no standard taxonomy of risk, various risk taxonomies have been developed for specific purposes and disciplines.[44] These specialized taxonomies identify and categorize threats and vulnerabilities by the activity or discipline to which they relate. Examples include construction project risk, manufacturing risk, design risk, workplace safety risk, cybersecurity risk, software development risk, and medical treatment risk.[45] Alternatively, risk may be categorized broadly as business or nonbusiness (personal) risk. The latter has been widely studied by psychologists, social scientists, and others but is out of scope for this book.

Business risk may be further categorized as financial or general. Financial risk, which is out of scope for this book, is concerned with threats and vulnerabilities related to monetary assets, securities, interest rates, currency exchange rates, inflation, liquidity, and other matters that affect organizational and individual investors.[46] General business risk includes operational threats and vulnerabilities related to an organization's day-to-day business processes and activities; economic threats and vulnerabilities related to changes in economic conditions; legal threats and vulnerabilities related to civil litigation or criminal prosecution; compliance threats and vulnerabilities related to fines or penalties for regulatory violations; technological threats and vulnerabilities related to an organization's computer systems and networks; and reputational threats and vulnerabilities related to defective products, poor customer service, dishonest business practices, or other issues. These threats and vulnerabilities apply to information risk, which is a type of general business risk.

The risk taxonomy presented in this book identifies twenty-four significant threats that can damage or destroy an organization's information assets or expose the organization to negative consequences that directly impact its operations or activities. As discussed in the preface, the taxonomy groups threats into five categories: (1) creation and collection of information, (2) loss of information, (3) retention of information, (4) retrieval and disclosure of information, and (5) ownership of information. Fourteen of the twenty-four threats expose an organization to fines or other monetary penalties for failure to comply with information-related laws and regulations. Thirteen threats expose an organization to civil litigation related to ownership, collection, or disclosure of information.

Human agents, including employee errors and malicious actions, are involved in twenty-two of the twenty-four threats. Many human-induced threats originate from internal risk sources, particularly action or inaction by an organization's own employees. Such threats are usually controllable. An appropriate risk response can limit or eliminate their destructive potential. Some human-induced threats originate from external risk sources, such as technological malfunctions, criminal behavior, and civil unrest. These threats are difficult to control. Just two threats are caused by natural threat agents, but both have significant destructive potential and are generally uncontrollable. One of the threat agents involves meteorological, geological, and hydrological hazards. The other involves time-dependent deterioration of media on which information is recorded.

Whether they have human or natural causes, threats to an organization's information assets exploit commonly encountered vulnerabilities. The following chapters explain the threats listed in the information risk taxonomy and identify over 120 vulnerabilities that may affect organizations of all types and sizes. Depending on the circumstances, a given vulnerability may result from limited risk awareness, lack of appropriate risk policies, risk prone business processes, inadequate training, ineffective supervision, poor decision-making, negligence, or other factors that can be successfully addressed. In a few cases, vulnerability results from uncontrollable factors, such as an organization's geographic location, political disruption, or unpreventable accidents.

Actions that an organization can take to limit risk by addressing specific vulnerabilities are recommended for every threat discussed in the following chapters. Risk transfer through insurance is possible for about half of the threats, but insurance cannot completely eliminate all negative consequences of a given threat. Insurance is not available for threats associated with non-compliance with information-related laws or regulations. Risk avoidance, within limits, is possible for about half of the threats, but complete risk avoidance is rarely possible. Some measure of risk acceptance is necessary for threats that are unavoidable or uncontrollable.

SUMMARY OF MAJOR POINTS

- Risk is a combination of threats, vulnerabilities, and consequences. Taken together, these risk components address three questions that are implicit in all definitions of risk: What can go wrong? What can cause it to go wrong? What are the consequences if it does go wrong?
- An enterprise risk management (ERM) program provides a coherent framework of policies and processes that enables an organization to develop effective risk strategies and responses. An ERM program assigns risk management authority, defines risk responsibilities, and allocates resources required for development and implementation of effective risk management.
- Risk oversight is widely recognized as the responsibility of an organization's governing body. An organization's executive management must approve and articulate a risk management program's objectives; integrate risk awareness into the organization's strategies and operations at every level; and create an environment for effective implementation of risk related initiatives. Department heads and other key stakeholders have primary responsibility for managing risk related to their operations and activities on a day-to-day basis.

- In some organizations, enterprise risk management is aligned with and integrated into an organization's governance and compliance initiatives. This umbrella approach, known as a GRC framework, is designed to coordinate risk related initiatives and promote sharing of information about enterprise risks across all three functions.

- Because unrecognized risks cannot be managed, an effective risk management process begins with identification of threat agents that have the potential to harm organizational assets, but threat agents pose no harm in the absence of vulnerability, which is the basis for an organization's risk exposure. Vulnerability is a weakness that a threat agent can exploit.

- Risk response, sometimes termed *risk treatment* or *risk mitigation*, is the process of reducing, eliminating, or otherwise reacting to threats and their associated vulnerabilities. The four basic risk responses are acceptance, avoidance, transfer, and limitation.

- A risk taxonomy is an organized categorization of risk events that can have a negative impact on an organization's objectives or operations. As its principle benefit, a risk taxonomy facilitates the identification and assessment of threats and their associated vulnerabilities. The risk taxonomy presented in this book identifies twenty-four significant threats that can damage or destroy an organization's information assets or expose the organization to negative consequences that directly impact its operations or activities.

NOTES

1. The Hawley Committee, a group of high-level executives from the financial, retail, and security industries in the United Kingdom, was among the first authorities to characterize information as an asset. The committee was chaired by Dr. Robert Hawley, the chief executive of Nuclear Power plc. The committee's report, which was issued in 1995, cited types of information that have value as assets, including customer information, product information, specialist knowledge, business process information, management information on which decisions are based, human resources information, supplier information, and legal and regulatory information. Hawley Committee, *Information as an Asset: The Board Agenda—A Consultative Report* (London: KPMG IMPACT Programme, 1995). See also C. Oppenheim et al., "Studies on Information as an Asset I: Definitions," *Journal of Information Science* 29, no. 3 (2003): 159–66, https://doi.org/10.1177/01655515030293003; R. Wilson and J. Stenson, "Valuation of Information Assets on the Balance Sheet: The Recognition and Approaches to the Valuation of Intangible Assets," *Business Information Review* 25, no. 3 (2008): 167–82, https://doi.org/ 10.1177/0266382108095039; S. Ward and D. Carter, "Information as an Asset—Today's Board Agenda: The Value of Rediscovering Gold," *Business Information Review* 36, no. 2 (2019): 53–59, https://doi.org/10.1177/0266382119844639; N. Silburn and J. Ezingeard, "Treating an Organization's Information as Valuable: Exploratory Research," in *Proceedings of the 11th IFIP TC 11.1 Working Conference on Information Security Management*, ed. P. Dowland and S. Furnell (Plymouth, UK: International Federation for Information Processing, 2008), 46–58. According to the 2018 revision of the Conceptual Framework for Financial Reporting, issued by the International Accounting Standards Board, information is properly considered an asset: it is controlled by the organization that owns it and is capable of producing

economic benefits through sale or use; www.ifrs.org/issued-standards/list-of-standards/conceptual-framework.

2. On the complicated nature of risk, see S. Hansson, "Philosophical Perspectives on Risk," *Techne* 8, no. 1 (2004): 10–35, https://scholar.lib.vt.edu/ejournals/SPT/v8n1/pdf/hansson.pdf; B. Fischhoff et al., "Defining Risk," *Policy Sciences* 17, no. 2 (1984): 123–39, https://doi.org/10.1007/BF00146924; S. Hansson, *The Ethics of Risk: Ethical Analysis in an Uncertain World* (Basingstoke, UK: Palgrave Macmillan, 2013).

3. For example, *Merriam-Webster*: "something that creates or suggests a hazard"; *American Heritage Dictionary of the English Language*: "the possibility of suffering harm or loss"; *Cambridge Dictionary*: "danger, or the possibility of danger, defeat, or loss"; *Macmillan Dictionary*: "the possibility that something unpleasant or dangerous might happen." For a history of risk, see P. Bernstein, *Against the Gods: The Remarkable Story of Risk* (New York: Wiley, 1996).

4. For a discussion of ISO Guide 73, see T. Aven, "On the New ISO Guide on Risk Management Terminology," *Reliability Engineering & System Safety* 96, no. 7 (2011): 719–26, https://doi.org/10.1016/j.ress.2010.12.020. On uncertainty about an event or outcome as an essential characteristics of risk, see T. Aven and O. Renn, "On Risk Defined as an Event Where the Outcome is Uncertain," *Journal of Risk Research* 12, no. 1 (2009): 1–11, https://doi.org/10.1080/13669870802488883; T. Aven, "On How to Define, Understand and Describe Risk," *Reliability Engineering & System Safety* 95, no. 6 (2010): 623–31, https://doi.org/10.1016/j.ress.2010.01.011; T. Aven, *Misconceptions of Risk* (Chichester, UK: Wiley, 2010); T. Aven et al., *Uncertainty in Risk Assessment: The Representation and Treatment of Uncertainties by Probabilistic and Non-Probabilistic Methods* (Chichester, UK: Wiley, 2014); H. Kumamoto and E. Henley, *Probabilistic Risk Assessment and Management for Engineers and Scientists,* 2nd ed. (Piscataway, NJ: IEEE Press, 1996).

5. R. MacMinn, "Risk and Choice: A Perspective on the Integration of Finance and Insurance," *Risk Management and Insurance Review* 3, no. 1 (2000): 69–79, https://doi.org/10.1111/j.1540-6296.2000.tb00017.x; R. Ferrer and N. Mallari, "Speculative and Pure Risks: Their Impact on Firms' Earnings Per Share," *Journal of International Business Research* 10, no. 1 (2011): 115–36, www.abacademies.org/articles/jibrvol10nosi12011.pdf - page=121; C. Williams Jr., "Attitudes toward Speculative Risks as an Indicator of Attitudes toward Pure Risks," *Journal of Risk and Insurance* 33, no. 4 (1966): 577–86, https://doi.org/10.2307/251231.

6. T. Aven, "The Risk Concept—Historical and Recent Development Trends," *Reliability Engineering and System Safety* 99, no 1 (2012): 33–44, https://doi.org/10.1016/j.ress.2011.11.006; T. Aven, "Risk Assessment and Risk Management: Review of Recent Advances on Their Foundation," *European Journal of Operational Research* 253, no. 1 (2016): 1–13, https://doi.org/10.1016/j.ejor.2015.12.023; D. Spiegelhalter and H. Riesch, "Don't Know, Can't Know: Embracing Deeper Uncertainties When Analyzing Risks," *Philosophical Transactions of the Royal Society A: Mathematical, Physical and Engineering Sciences* 396, no. 1956 (2011): 4730–50, https://doi.org/10.1098/rsta.2011.0113; M. Boholm et al., "The Concepts of Risk, Safety, and Security: Applications in Everyday Language," *Risk Analysis* 36, no. 2 (2016): 320–38, https://doi.org/10.1111/risa.12464; M. Boholm, "How Do Swedish Government Agencies Define Risk?," *Journal of Risk Research* 22, no. 6 (2019): 717–34, https://doi.org/10.1080/13669877.2017.1422782.

7. Society for Risk Analysis Glossary (August 2018), https://sra.org/sites/default/files/pdf/SRA Glossary - FINAL.pdf.

8. Y. Haimes, "On the Definition of Vulnerabilities in Measuring Risks to Infrastructures," *Risk Analysis* 26, no. 2 (2006): 293–96, https://doi.org/10.1111/j.1539-6924.2006.00755.x; Y. Haimes, *Risk Modeling, Assessment, and Management*, 2nd ed. (Hoboken, NJ: Wiley, 2009);

9. C. Roper, *Risk Management for Security Professionals* (Burlington, MA: Butterworth Heinemann, 1999); R. Kates and J. Kasperson, "Comparative Risk Analysis of Technological Hazards (a Review)," *Proceedings of the National Academy of Sciences, Part 2: Physical Sciences* 80, no. 22 (1983): 7027–48, https://doi.org/ 10.1073/pnas.80.22.7027.

10. *Guidelines for Analyzing and Managing the Security Vulnerabilities of Fixed Chemical Sites* (New York: Center for Chemical Process Safety of the American Institute of Chemical

Engineers, 2003), https://doi.org/10.1002/9780470925003; *Security Vulnerability Assessment Methodology for the Petroleum and Petrochemical Industries* (Washington, DC: American Petroleum Institution and National Petrochemical & Refiners Association, 2003), www.nrc.gov/docs/ML0502/ML050260624.pdf.

11. W. Lawrence, *Of Acceptable Risk: Science and the Determination of Safety* (Los Altos, CA: William Kaufmann, 1976); D. Hubbard, *The Failure of Risk Management: Why It's Broken and How to Fix It* (Hoboken, NJ: Wiley, 2009); B. Fischhoff and J. Kadvany, *Risk: A Very Short Introduction* (Oxford: Oxford University Press, 2011); J. Graham and J. Wiener, "Confronting Risk Tradeoffs," in *Risk Versus Risk*, ed. J. Graham and J. Wiener (Cambridge, MA: Harvard University Press, 1995), 1–41; B. Ale, *Risk: An Introduction: The Concepts of Risk, Danger and Chance* (London: Routledge, 2009); R. Wilson and E. Crouch, *Risk-Benefit Analysis: Second Edition* (Cambridge, MA: Harvard University Press, 2001); J. Freund and J. Jones, *Measuring and Managing Information Risk: A FAIR Approach* (Waltham, MA: Butterworth-Heinemann, 2015); Y. Haimes, "On the Complex Definition of Risk: A Systems-Based Approach," *Risk Analysis* 29, no. 12 (2009): 1647–54, https://doi.org/10.1111/j.1539-6924.2009.01310.x.

12. C. Hohenemser et al., "The Nature of Technological Hazard," *Science* 220, no. 4495 (1983): 378–94, https://doi.org/10.1126/science.6836279; C. Hehensemser et al., "Methods for Analyzing and Comparing Technological Hazards," in *Risk Evaluation and Management*, ed. V. Covello et al. (New York: Plenum Press, 1986), 249–74. These publications address the difference between hazards, which are "threats to humans and what they value," and risks, which are "quantitative measures of hazard consequences that can be expressed as conditional probabilities of experiencing harm." On the limitations of mathematical risk calculations, see L. Cox Jr., "Some Limitations of 'Risk = Threat × Vulnerability × Consequence' for Risk Analysis of Terrorist Attacks," *Risk Analysis* 28, no. 6 (2008): 1749–61, https://doi.org/10.1111/j.1539-6924.2008.01142.x; H. Willis, "Guiding Resource Allocations Based on Terrorism Risk," *Risk Analysis* 27, no. 3 (2007): 597–606, https://doi.org/10.1111/j.1539-6924.2007.00909.x; B. Ezell et al., "Probabilistic Risk Analysis and Terrorism Risk," *Risk Analysis* 30, no. 4, 575–89, https://doi.org/10.1111/j.1539-6924.2010.01401.x.

13. These are variations of questions posed in S. Kaplan and B. Garrick, "On the Quantitative Definition of Risk," *Risk Analysis* 1, no. 1 (1981): 11–27, https://doi.org/10.1111/j.1539-6924.1981.tb01350.x.

14. On the often ambiguous relationship between risk and uncertainty, see F. Knight, *Risk, Uncertainty, and Profit* (Boston, MA: Houghton Mifflin, 1921), https://oll.libertyfund.org/titles/knight-risk-uncertainty-and-profit; D. Ellsberg, "Risk, Ambiguity, and the Savage Axioms," *Quarterly Journal of Economics* 75, no. 4 (1961): https://doi.org/10.2307/1884324; G. Bammer and M. Smithson, eds., *Uncertainty and Risk: Multidisciplinary Perspectives* (London: Earthscan, 2008); A. Tversky and C. Fox, "Weighing Risk and Uncertainty," *Psychological Review* 102, no. 2 (1995): 269–83, https://doi.org/10.1037/0033-295X.102.2.269; O. Perminova et al., "Defining Uncertainty in Projects—a New Perspective," *International Journal of Project Management* 26, no. 1 (2008): 73–79, https://doi.org/10.1016/j.ijproman.2007.08.005; M. Van Asselt, "The Complex Significance of Uncertainty in a Risk Era: Logics, Manners and Strategies in Use," *International Journal of Risk Assessment and Management* 5, nos. 2–4 (2005): 125–58, https://doi.org/10.1504/IJRAM.2005.007164.

15. J. March and Z. Shapira, "Managerial Perspectives on Risk and Risk Taking," *Management Science* 33, no. 11 (1987): 1367–509, https://doi.org/10.1287/mnsc.33.11.1404, found that management decision-making is insensitive to estimated probabilities of possible outcomes. For a survey of risk assessment methods, see J. Kouns and D. Minioli, *Information Technology Risk Management in Enterprise Environments: A Review of Industry Practices and a Practical Guide to Risk Management Teams* (Hoboken, NJ: Wiley, 2010). On subjective risk evaluation, see *Guide for Conducting Risk Assessments, NIST Special Publication 800-30* (Gaithersburg, MD: National Institute of Standards and Technology, 2012), https://csrc.nist.gov/publications/detail/sp/800-30/rev-1/final, which notes that "risk assessments are often not precise instruments of measurement." On failure mode and effects analysis (FMEA), a subjective risk assessment method used in a wide range of industries, see H. Liu et al., "Risk Evaluation Approaches in Failure Mode and Effects Analysis: A Literature Review," *Expert*

Systems with Applications 40, no. 2 (2013): 828–38, https://doi.org/10.1016/j.eswa.2012.08.010. On the complementary nature of subjective and quantitative risk assessment, see G. Apostolakis, "How Useful Is Quantitative Risk Assessment?" *Risk Analysis* 24, no. 3 (2004): 515–20, https://doi.org/10.1111/j.0272-4332.2004.00455.x.

16. G. Dickinson, "Enterprise Risk Management: Its Origins and Conceptual Foundation," *Geneva Papers on Risk and Insurance* 26, no. 3 (2001): 360–66, www.jstor.org/stable/41952578; G. Crockford, "The Bibliography and History of Risk Management: Some Preliminary Observations," *Geneva Papers on Risk and Insurance* 7, no. 23 (1982): 169–79, www.jstor.org/stable/41950036; M. Beasley et al., "Enterprise Risk Management: An Empirical Analysis of Factors Associated with the Extent of Implementation," *Journal of Accounting and Public Policy* 24, no. 6 (2005): 521–31, https://doi.org/10.1016/j.jaccpubpol.2005.10.001; M. Arena et al., "The Organizational Dynamics of Enterprise Risk Management," *Accounting, Organizations and Society* 35, no. 7 (2010): 659–75, https://doi.org/10.1016/j.aos.2010.07.003; P. Bromiley et al., "Enterprise Risk Management: Review, Critique, and Research Directions," *Long Range Planning* 48, no. 4 (2015): 265–76, https://doi.org/10.1016/j.lrp.2014.07.005; M. McShane, "Enterprise Risk Management: History and Design Science Proposal," *Journal of Risk Finance* 19, no. 2 (2018): 137–53, https://doi.org/10.1108/JRF-03-2017-0048; J. Kallman and R. Maric, "A Refined Risk Management Paradigm," *Risk Management: An International Journal* 6, no. 3 (2004): 57–68, https://link.springer.com/article/10.1057/palgrave.rm.8240190.

17. Examples of the many books on enterprise risk management include R. Chapman, *Simple Tools and Techniques for Enterprise Risk Management* (Chichester, UK: Wiley, 2011); T. Coleman, *A Practical Guide to Risk Management* (Charlottesville, VA: Research Foundation of CFA Institute, 2011); M. Crouhy et al., *The Essentials of Risk Management*, 2nd ed. (New York: McGraw Hill, 2014); J. Fraser and B. Simkins, eds., *Enterprise Risk Management: Today's Leading Research and Best Practices for Tomorrow's Executives* (Hoboken, NJ: Wiley, 2010); J. Fraser et al., eds., *Implementing Enterprise Risk Management: Case Studies and Best Practices* (Hoboken, NJ: Wiley, 2015); P. Green, *Enterprise Risk Management: A Common Framework for the Entire Organization* (Waltham, MA: Butterworth-Heinemann, 2016); J. Hampton, *Fundamentals of Enterprise Risk Management: How Top Companies Assess Risk, Manage Exposures, and Seize Opportunities* (New York: AMACON, 2009); D. Hillson, ed., *The Risk Management Handbook: A Practical Guide to Managing the Multiple Dimensions of Risk* (London: Kogan Page, 2016); P. Hopkin, *Fundamentals of Risk Management: Understanding, Evaluating and Implementing Effective Risk Management*, 5th ed. (London: Kogan Page, 2018); J. Lam, *Implementing Enterprise Risk Management: From Methods to Applications* (Hoboken, NJ: Wiley, 2017); N. Marks and M. Herman, *World-Class Risk Management for Nonprofits* (Leesburg, VA: Nonprofit Risk Management Center, 2017); D. Olson and D. Wu, *Enterprise Risk Management Models*, 2nd ed. (Berlin: Springer-Verlag, 2017); C. Pritchard, *Risk Management: Concepts and Guidance*, 5th ed. (Boca Raton, FL: CRC Press, 2015); S. Segal, *Corporate Value of Enterprise Risk Management* (Hoboken, NJ: Wiley, 2011); M. Woods, *Risk Management in Organizations: An Integrated Case Study Approach* (Abingdon, UK: Routledge, 2011).

18. www.coso.org/Pages/erm-integratedframework.aspx. For a discussion of these risk management frameworks, see M. Frigo and R. Anderson, "Risk Management Frameworks: Adapt, Don't Adopt: Here's a Primer on Two Well-Known Approaches," *Strategic Finance* 95, no. 7 (2014): 49–53, https://go.galegroup.com/ps/anonymous?id=GALE|A355777959&sid=googleScholar&v=2.1&it=r&linkaccess=abs&issn=1524833X&p=AONE&sw=w; C. Lalonde and O. Boiral, "Managing Risks through ISO 31000: A Critical Analysis," *Risk Management* 14, no. 4 (2012): 272–300, www.jstor.org/stable/23351513; G. Purdy, "ISO 31000:2009—Setting a New Standard for Risk Management," *Risk Analysis* 30, no. 6 (2010): 881–86, https://doi.org/10.1111/j.1539-6924.2010.01442.x; M. Leitch, "ISO 31000:2009—the New International Standard on Risk Management," *Risk Analysis* 30, no. 6 (2010): 887–92, https://doi.org/10.1111/j.1539-6924.2010.01397.x; Gjerdrum and M. Peter, "The New International Standard on the Practice of Risk Management: A Comparison of ISO 31000:2009 and the COSO ERM Framework," *Risk Management*, no. 31 (2011): 8–13, www.soa.org/globalassets/assets/library/newsletters/risk-management-newsletter/2011/march/jrm-2011-iss21-gjerdrum.pdf; N. Baker, "Managing the Complexity of Risk: The ISO 31000 Framework Aims to

Provide a Foundation for Effective Risk Management within the Organization," *Internal Auditor: Journal of the Institute of Internal Auditors* 68, no. 2 (2011): 35–40, https://go.gale.com/ps/anonymous?id=GALE|A258242604&sid=googleScholar&v=2.1&it=r&linkaccess=abs&issn=00205745&p=AONE&sw=w.

19. C. Ittner and T. Keusch, *The Influence of Board of Directors' Risk Oversight on Risk Management Maturity and Firm Risk-Taking* (August 2015), https://sites.insead.edu/facultyresearch/research/file.cfm?fid=56764. As discussed in a 2009 report by the National Association of Corporate Directors (NACD), a governing body must understand, evaluate, and monitor an organization's risk exposure. *Report of the NACD Blue Ribbon Commission on Risk Governance: Balancing Risk and Reward* (Washington, DC: National Association of Corporate Directors, 2009), www.nacdonline.org/insights/publications.cfm?ItemNumber=675. The Financial Reporting Council, which maintains the United Kingdom's corporate governance and stewardship codes, emphatically states that a governing body "has responsibility for an organization's overall approach to risk management." *Guidance on Risk Management, Internal Control and Related Financial and Business Reporting* (London: Financial Reporting Council, 2014), www.frc.org.uk/getattachment/d672c107-b1fb-4051-84b0-f5b83a1b93f6/Guidance-on-Risk-Management-Internal-Control-and-Related-Reporting.pdf.

20. Examples of the large and growing literature on risk committees include W. Atkinson, "Board-Level Risk Committees," *Risk Management* 55, no. 6 (2008): 42–45, https://search.proquest.com/openview/e65ee66c1d33c5df148a2703aaa2e419/1?pq-origsite=gscholar&cbl=47271; N. Tao and M. Hutchinson, "Corporate Governance and Risk Management: The Role of Risk Management and Compensation Committees," *Journal of Contemporary Accounting & Economics* 9, no. 1 (2013): 83–99, https://doi.org/10.1016/j.jcae.2013.03.003; N. Subramaniam, "Corporate Governance, Firm Characteristics and Risk Management Committee Formation in Australian Companies," *Managerial Auditing Journal* 24, no. 4 (2009): 316–39, https://doi.org/10.1108/02686900910948170; A. Abubakar et al., "The Effect of Risk Management Committee Attributes and Board Financial Knowledge on the Financial Performance of Listed Banks in Nigeria," *American International Journal of Business Management* 1, no. 5 (2018): 7–13, www.aijbm.com/wp-content/uploads/2018/12/B150713.pdf; I. Brown et al., "Risk Management in Corporate Governance: A Review and Proposal," *Corporate Governance* 17, no. 5 (2009): 546–58, https://doi.org/10.1111/j.1467-8683.2009.00763.x; C. Hines and G. Peters, "Voluntary Risk Management Committee Formation: Determinants and Short-Term Outcomes," *Journal of Accounting and Public Policy* 34, no. 3 (2015): 267–90, https://doi.org/10.1016/j.jaccpubpol.2015.02.001; P. Yatim, "Board Structures and the Establishment of a Risk Committee by Malaysian Listed Firms," *Journal of Management & Governance* 14, no. 1 (2010): 17–36, https://doi.org/10.1007/s10997-009-9089-6.

21. J. Lam and B. Kawamoto, "Emergence of the Chief Risk Officer," *Risk Management* 44, no. 9 (1997): 30–35, https://search.proquest.com/openview/538524217dc9d9e07539341a615b5cbf/1?pq-origsite=gscholar&cbl=47271; T. Aabo et al., "The Rise and Evolution of the Chief Risk Officer: Enterprise Risk Management at Hydro One," *Journal of Applied Corporate Finance* 17, no. 3 (2005): 62–75, https://doi.org/10.1111/j.1745-6622.2005.00045.x; E. Karanja and M. Rosso, "The Chief Risk Officer: A Study of Roles and Responsibilities," *Risk Management* 19, no. 2 (2017): 103–30, https://link.springer.com/article/10.1057/s41283-017-0014-z, M. Power, "Organizational Responses to Risk: The Rise of the Chief Risk Officer," in *Organizational Encounters with Risk*, ed. B. Hutter and M. Power (Cambridge: Cambridge University Press, 2005), 132–49; W. Daud et al., "The Effect of the Chief Risk Officer (CRO) on Enterprise Risk Management (ERM) Practices: Evidence from Malaysia," *International Business & Economics Research Journal* 9, no. 11 (2010): 55–64, https://doi.org/10.19030/iber.v9i11.30; A. Liebenberg and R. Hoyt, "The Determinants of Enterprise Risk Management: Evidence from the Appointment of Chief Risk Officers," *Risk Management and Insurance Review* 6, no. 1 (2003): 37–52, https://doi.org/10.1111/1098-1616.00019; D. Pagach and R. Warr, "The Characteristics of Firms That Hire Chief Risk Officers," *Journal of Risk and Insurance* 78, no. 1 (2011): 185–211, https://doi.org/10.1111/j.1539-6975.2010.01378.x; E. Karanja, "Does the Hiring of Chief Risk Officers Align with the COSO/ISO Enterprise Risk Management Frameworks?" *International Journal of Accounting*

& *Information Management* 25, no. 3 (2017): 274–95, https://doi.org/10.1108/IJAIM-04-2016-0037.

22. See *IIA Position Paper: The Role of Internal Auditing in Enterprise-Wide Risk Management* (Lake Mary, FL: Institute of Internal Auditors, 2009), https://na.theiia.org/standards-guidance/Public Documents/PP The Role of Internal Auditing in Enterprise Risk Management.pdf; L. Spira and M. Page, "Risk Management: The Reinvention of Internal Control and the Changing Role of Internal Audit," *Accounting, Auditing & Accountability Journal* 16, no. 4 (2003): 640–61, https://doi.org/10.1108/09513570310492335; L. de Zwaan and N. Subramaniam, "Internal Audit Involvement in Enterprise Risk Management," *Managerial Auditing Journal* 26, no. 7 (2011): 586–604, https://doi.org/10.1108/02686901111151323; M. Beasley et al., "The Impact of Enterprise Risk Management on the Internal Audit Function," *Journal of Forensic Accounting* 9, no. 1 (2006): 1–20, https://digitalcommons.kennesaw.edu/facpubs/1349; G. Selim and D. McNamee, "Risk Management and Internal Auditing: What are the Essential Building Blocks for a Successful Paradigm Change?" *International Journal of Auditing* 3, no. 2 (1999): 147–55, https://doi.org/10.1111/1099-1123.00055.

23. An online assessment tool developed by the Risk Management Society (RIMS) defines attributes and competency drivers for risk management programs at five levels of maturity: www.rims.org/resources/strategic-enterprise-risk-center/risk-maturity-model. For other examples, see D. Proenca et al., "Risk Management: A Maturity Model Based on ISO 31000," in *Proceedings—2017 IEEE 19th Conference on Business Informatics*, ed. B. Theodoulidis et al. (Piscataway, NJ: Institute of Electrical and Electronics Engineers, 2017), 99–108, https://novaresearch.unl.pt/en/publications/risk-management-a-maturity-model-based-on-iso-31000; F. Oliva, "A Maturity Model for Enterprise Risk Management," *International Journal of Production Economics* 173 (2016): 66–79, https://doi.org/10.1016/j.ijpe.2015.12.007; D. Antonucci, *Risk Maturity Models: How to Assess Risk Management Effectiveness* (Philadelphia: Kogan Page, 2016); M. Hopkinson, *The Project Risk Maturity Model: Measuring and Improving Risk Management Capability* (Surrey, England: Gower, 2010); M. Elmaallam et al., "A Maturity Model for Assessing IS Risk Management Activity Considering the Dependencies between Its Elements," *Computer and Information Science* 12, no. 1 (2019): 98–111, https://doi.org/10.5539/cis.v12n1p98; M. Wieczorek-Kosmala, "Risk Management Practices from Risk Maturity Models Perspective," *Journal of East European Management Studies* 19, no. 2 (2014): 133–59, www.jstor.org/stable/24330969; K. Yeo and Y. Ren, "Risk Management Capability Maturity Model for Complex Product Systems (CoPS) Projects," *Systems Engineering* 12, no. 4 (2009): 275–94, https://doi.org/10.1002/sys.20123; R. Batenburg et al., "A Maturity Model for Governance, Risk Management, and Compliance in Hospitals," *Journal of Hospital Administration* 3, no. 4 (2–12): 43–52, http://dx.doi.org/10.5430/jha.v3n4p43; G. Coetzee and D. Lubbe, "The Risk Maturity of South African Private and Public Sector Organizations," *Southern African Journal of Accountability and Auditing Research* 14, no. 1 (2013): 45–56, http://hdl.handle.net/2263/21393; C. Mauelshagen et al., "Risk Management Pervasiveness and Organizational Maturity: A Critical Review," *International Journal of Business Continuity and Risk Management* 2, no. 4 (2011): 305–23, https://doi.org/10.1504/IJBCRM.2011.044405; R. Chapman, "Exploring the Value of Risk Management for Projects: Improving Capability through the Deployment of a Maturity Model," *IEEE Engineering Management Review* 47, no. 1 (2019): 126–43, https://doi.org/10.1109/EMR.2019.2891494.

24. As defined in ISO/IEC/IEEE 24765:2017, *Systems and Software Engineering—Vocabulary,* a maturity model "describes an evolutionary improvement path from ad hoc, immature processes to disciplined, mature processes with improved quality and effectiveness." Most maturity models are patterned after the Capability Maturity Model (CMM), which was developed for the U.S. Department of Defense by Carnegie Mellon University's Software Engineering Institute (SEI) in the 1980s. The applicable standard is ISO/IEC 21827:2008, *Information Technology—Security Techniques—Systems Security Engineering—Capability Maturity Model (SSE-CMM).* Some researchers trace the maturity model concept to the five-level hierarchy of needs defined in A. Maslow, *Motivation and Personality* (New York: Harper Brothers, 1954). Maturity model developers adopted Maslow's view that satisfaction of lower-level needs is a precondition for moving up the hierarchy.

25. B. Nocco and R, Stulz, "Enterprise Risk Management: Theory and Practice," *Journal of Applied Corporate Finance* 18, no. 4 (2006): 8–20, https://doi.org/10.1111/j.1745-6622.2006.00106.x; R. Baxter et al., "Enterprise Risk Management Program Quality: Determinants, Value Relevance, and the Financial Crisis," *Contemporary Accounting Research* 30, no. 4 (2013): 1264–95, https://doi.org/10.1111/j.1911-3846.2012.01194.x; S. Gates, "Incorporating Strategic Risk into Enterprise Risk Management: A Survey of Current Corporate Practice," *Journal of Applied Corporate Finance* 18, no. 4 (2006), https://doi.org/10.1111/j.1745-6622.2006.00114.x; S. Gates et al., "Enterprise Risk Management: A Process for Enhanced Management and Improved Performance," *Management Accounting Quarterly* 13, no. 3 (2012): 28–38, https://hal.archives-ouvertes.fr/hal-00857435; M. Grace et al., "The Value of Investing in Enterprise Risk Management," *Journal of Risk and Insurance* 82, no. 2 (2015): 289–316, https://doi.org/10.1111/jori.12022.

26. R. Hoyt and A. Liebenberg, "The Value of Enterprise Risk Management," *Journal of Risk and Insurance* 78, no. 4 (2011): 795–822, https://doi.org/10.1111/j.1539-6975.2011.01413.x; A. Bohnert et al., "The Drivers and Value of Enterprise Risk Management: Evidence from ERM Ratings," *European Journal of Finance* 25, no. 3 (2019): 234–55, https://doi.org/10.1080/1351847X.2018.1514314; P. Lechner and N. Gatzert, "Determinants and Value of Enterprise Risk Management: Empirical Evidence from Germany," *The European Journal of Finance* 24, no. 10 (2018): 867–87, https://doi.org/10.1080/1351847X.2017.1347100; M. Beasley et al., "Information Conveyed in Hiring Announcements of Senior Executives Overseeing Enterprise-Wide Risk Management Processes," *Journal of Accounting, Auditing, & Finance* 23, no. 3 (2008): 311–32, https://doi.org/10.1177/0148558X0802300303; D. Pagach and R. Warr, *The Effects of Enterprise Risk Management on Firm Performance* (Raleigh: Jenkins Graduate School of Management, North Carolina State University, 2010), https://pdfs.semanticscholar.org/f68b/4373f08bdfccc967e47eb612b8ff51b6c35a.pdf; I. Iswajuni et al., "The Effect of Enterprise Risk Management (ERM) on Firm Value in Manufacturing Companies Listed on Indonesian Stock Exchange Year 2010–2013," *Asian Journal of Accounting Research* 3, no. 2 (2018): 224–35, https://doi.org/10.1108/AJAR-06-2018-0006; L. Gordon et al., "Enterprise Risk Management and Firm Performance: A Contingency Perspective," *Journal of Accounting and Public Policy* 28, no. 4 (2009): 301–27, https://doi.org/10.1016/j.jaccpubpol.2009.06.006; M. McShane et al., "Does Enterprise Risk Management Increase Firm Value?" *Journal of Accounting, Auditing, & Finance* 26, no. 4 (2011): 641–58, https://doi.org/10.1177/0148558X11409160; V. Aebi et al., "Risk Management, Corporate Governance, and Bank Performance in the Financial Crisis," *Journal of Banking & Finance* 36, no. 12 (2012): 3213–26, https://doi.org/10.1016/j.jbankfin.2011.10.020; M. Farrell and R. Gallagher, "The Valuation Implications of Enterprise Risk Management Maturity," *Journal of Risk and Insurance* 82, no. 3 (2015): 625–57, https://doi.org/10.1111/jori.12035; J. Fraser and B. Simkins, "Ten Common Misconceptions about Enterprise Risk Management," *Journal of Applied Corporate Finance* 19, no. 4 (2007): 75–81, https://doi.org/10.1111/j.1745-6622.2007.00161.x.

27. This is the widely accepted definition presented in the *Report of the Committee on Financial Aspects of Corporate Governance,* the so-called Cadbury Report, which was issued in the United Kingdom in 1992 by a committee chaired by Sir Adrian Cadbury, a former Chairman of Cadbury Schweppes and a director of the Bank of England. The report is available at www.ecgi.org/codes/documents/cadbury.pdf.

28. According to chapter 8 of the *2018 Guidelines Manual* issued by the U.S. Sentencing Commission, the purpose of an organization's compliance program is to prevent and detect criminal conduct: www.ussc.gov/sites/default/files/pdf/guidelines-manual/2018/GLMFull.pdf. D. Murphy, "The Federal Sentencing Guidelines for Organizations: A Decade of Promoting Compliance and Ethics," *Iowa Law Review* 87, no. 2 (2002): 697–719, www.ussc.gov/sites/default/files/pdf/training/organizational-guidelines/selected-articles/Murphy1.pdf; J. Fatino, "Corporate Compliance Programs: An Approach to Avoid or Minimize Criminal and Civil Liability," *Drake Law Review* 51, no. 1 (2002): 81–104, https://lawreview-drake.files.wordpress.com/2015/04/fatino.pdf; P. Wellner, "Effective Compliance Programs and Corporate Criminal Prosecutions," *Cardozo Law Review* 27, no. 1 (2005): 497–528, www.friedfrank.com/sitefiles/publications/cdb6714353b1b712d3a5db85f508483e.pdf; S. Kowal, "Corporate Compliance Programs: A Shield against Criminal Liability," *Food and*

Drug Law Journal 53, no. 3 (1998): 517–25, www.ncbi.nlm.nih.gov/pubmed/10346724; D. Webb et al., "Understanding and Avoiding Corporate and Executive Criminal Liability," *The Business Lawyer* 49, no. 2 (1994): 617–68, www.jstor.org/stable/40687471. A compliance program also aligns an organization's business needs with professional and ethical standards. See *G20/OECD Principles of Corporate Governance* (Paris: OECD, 2015), http://dx.doi.org/10.1787/9789264236882-en; J. Weber and D. Wasieleski, "Corporate Ethics and Compliance Programs," *Journal of Business Ethics* 112, no. 4 (2013): 609–26, https://link.springer.com/article/10.1007/s10551-012-1561-6.

29. R. Steinberg, *Governance, Risk Management, and Compliance: It Can't Happen to Us—Avoiding Corporate Disaster while Driving Success* (Hoboken, NJ: Wiley, 2011); A. Tarantino, ed., *Governance, Risk, and Compliance Handbook* (Hoboken, NJ: Wiley, 2008); G. Miller, *The Law of Governance, Risk Management, and Compliance* (New York: Wolters, Kluwer, 2019).

30. Various maturity models for compliance and risk management have been developed by consulting firms, academic researchers, healthcare organizations, and others. See, for example, C. Switzer and S. Mitchell, *GRC Capability Model (Red Book), Version 3.0* (Phoenix, AZ: OCEG, 2017), https://go.oceg.org/grc-capability-model-red-book; S. Mitchell, "GRC360: A Framework to Help Organizations Drive Principled Performance," *International Journal of Disclosure and Governance* 4, no. 4 (2007): 279–96, https://doi.org/10.1057/palgrave.jdg.2050066.

31. www.oceg.org/resources/red-book-3.

32. M. van Asselt and O. Renn, "Risk Governance," *Journal of Risk Research* 14, no. 4 (2011): 431–49, https://doi.org/10.1080/13669877.2011.553730; O. Renn, *Risk Governance: Coping with Uncertainty in a Complex World* (London: Earthscan, 2008); A. Boholm et al., "The Practice of Risk Governance: Lessons from the Field," *Journal of Risk Research* 15, no. 1 (2012): 1–20, https://doi.org/10.1080/13669877.2011.587886; S. Lundqvist, "Why Firms Implement Risk Governance—Stepping beyond Traditional Risk Management to Enterprise Risk Management," *Journal of Accounting and Public Policy* 34, no. 5 (2015): 441–66, https://doi.org/10.1016/j.jaccpubpol.2015.05.002; *The Sedona Conference Commentary on Information Governance*, 2nd ed. (Phoenix, AZ: The Sedona Conference, 2019), https://thesedonaconference.org/publication/Commentary_on_Information_Governance.

33. On the risk management framework developed by the International Risk Governance Council, see O. Renn and K. Walker, eds., *Global Risk Governance: Concept and Practice Using the IRGC Framework* (Dordrecht, The Netherlands: Springer, 2008), and F. Bouder et al., *The Tolerability of Risk: A New Framework for Risk Management* (London: Earthscan, 2007).

34. Governance's responsibility for stewardship of assets is forcefully stated in *Corpus Juris Secundum* (St. Paul, MN: West Publishing, 2003–present, updated annually), a multi-volume legal encyclopedia that presents the principles of US law as derived from legislation and reported cases. According to volume 19, section 491, an organization's officers have a duty "to be vigilant and to exercise ordinary or reasonable care and diligence and the utmost good faith and fidelity to conserve the corporate property; and, if a loss or depletion of assets results from their willful or negligent failure to perform their duties, or to a willful or fraudulent abuse of their trust, they are liable, provided such losses were the natural and necessary consequences of omission on their part."

35. *Internal Control—Integrated Framework: Executive Summary* (Durham, NC: American Institute of Certified Public Accountants, 2013), https://na.theiia.org/standards-guidance/topics/Documents/Executive_Summary.pdf. See also R. Moeller, *COCO Enterprise Risk Management: Understanding the New Integrated Framework* (Hoboken, NJ: Wiley, 2007); H. Cendrowski and W. Mair, *Enterprise Risk Management and COSO: A Guide for Directors, Executives, and Practitioners* (Hoboken, NJ: Wiley, 2009); C. Hayne and C. Free, "Hybridized Professional Groups and Institutional Work: COSO and the Rise of Enterprise Risk Management," *Accounting, Organizations and Society* 39, no. 5 (2014): 309–30, https://doi.org/10.1016/j.aos.2014.05.002; D. Williamson, "The COSO ERM Framework: A Critique from Systems Theory of Management Control," *International Journal of Risk Assessment and Management* 7, no. 8 (2007): 1089–119, https://doi.org/10.1504/IJRAM.2007.015296; L. Paape and

R. Spekle, "The Adoption and Design of Enterprise Risk Management Practices: An Empirical Study," *European Accounting Review* 21, no. 3 (2012): 533–64, https://doi.org/10.1080/09638180.2012.661937; B. Klamm and M. Watson, "SOX 404 Reported Internal Control Weaknesses: A Test of COSO Framework Components and Information Technology," *Journal of Information Systems* 23, no. 2 (2009): 1–23, https://doi.org/10.2308/jis.2009.23.2.1; D. Janvrin et al., "The Updated COSO Internal Control-Integrated Framework: Recommendations and Opportunities for Future Research," *Journal of Information Systems* 26, no. 2 (2012): 189–213, https://doi.org/10.2308/isys-50255.

36. S. Ross, "The Economic Theory of Agency: The Principal's Problem," *The American Economic Review* 63, no. 2 (1973): 134–39, www.jstor.org/stable/1817064.

37. *The Sedona Conference Commentary on Information Governance*, 2nd ed. (Phoenix, AZ: The Sedona Conference, 2019), https://thesedonaconference.org/publication/Commentary_on_Information_Governance; *Information Governance Initiative: Annual Report 2015–2016*, http://iginitiative.com/wp-content/uploads/2015_IGI-Annual-Report_Final-digital-use.pdf. On risk awareness as a component of information governance initiatives, see P. Tallon et al., "The Evolution of Information Governance at Intel," *MIS Quarterly Executive* 12, no. 4 (2013): 189–98, www.researchgate.net/profile/Paul_Tallon/publication/289680549_The_Evolution_of_Information_Governance_at_Intel/links/574306ef08ae9ace8418be3b/The-Evolution-of-Information-Governance-at-Intel.pdf; A. MacLennan, *Information Governance and Assurance: Reducing Risk, Promoting Policy* (London: Facet, 2014).

38. E. O'Donnell, "Enterprise Risk Management: A Systems-Thinking Framework for the Event Identification Phase," *International Journal of Accounting Information Systems* 6, no. 3 (2005): 177–95, https://doi.org/10.1016/j.accinf.2005.05.002; T. Casey et al., "Threat Agents: A Necessary Component of Threat Analysis," in *CSIIRW '10: Proceedings of the Sixth Annual Workshop on Cyber Security and Information Intelligence Research*, ed. F. Sheldon et al. (New York: ACM, 2010), article no. 56, https://doi.org/10.1145/1852666.1852728. Taxonomies that identify, categorize, and describe threat agents have been developed for specific situations. For example, B. Narwal et al., "Towards a Taxonomy of Cyber Threats against Target Applications," *Journal of Statistics and Management Systems* 22, no. 2 (2019): 301–25, https://doi.org/10.1080/09720510.2019.1580907; K. Desouza, "Weaponizing Information Systems for Political Disruption: The Actor, Lever, Effects, and Response Taxonomy (ALERT)," *Computers & Security* 88 (2020): Article 101606, https://doi.org/10.1016/j.cose.2019.101606; A. Rea-Guaman et al., "Systematic Review: Cybersecurity Risk Taxonomy," in J. Mejia et al., eds., *Trends and Applications in Software Engineering: CIMPS 2017, Advances in Intelligent Systems and Computing* (Cham, Switzerland: Springer, 2017), 137–46, https://doi.org/10.1007/978-3-319-69341-5_13; S. Babar, "Proposed Security Model and Threat Taxonomy for the Internet of Things (IoT)," in *Recent Trends in Network Security and Applications: CNSA 2010*, ed. N. Meghanathan et al. (Berlin: Springer, 2010), 420–29, https://doi.org/10.1007/978-3-642-14478-3_42; H. Lutijif and A. Neiuwenhuijs, "Extensible Threat Taxonomy for Critical Infrastructures," *International Journal of Critical Infrastructures* 4, no. 4 (2008): 409–17, https://doi.org/10.1504/IJCIS.2008.020159; A. Uzunov and E. Fernandez, "An Extensible Pattern-Based Library and Taxonomy of Security Threats for Distributed Systems," *Computer Standards & Interfaces* 36, no. 4 (2014): 734–47, https://doi.org/10.1016/j.csi.2013.12.008; N. Juliadotter and K. Choo, "Cloud Attack and Risk Assessment Taxonomy," *IEEE Cloud Computing* 2, no. 1 (2015): 14–20, https://doi.org/10.1109/MCC.2015.2.

39. C. Pfleeger and S. Pfleeger, *Computer Security: A Threat, Vulnerability, Countermeasure Approach* (Upper Saddle River, NJ: Prentice Hall, 2012), esp. 28–29; S. Vidalis and A. Jones, *Analyzing Threat Agents & Their Attributes* (Pontyclun, Wales: Geo-Bureau Ltd., 2005), http://citeseerx.ist.psu.edu/viewdoc/download?doi=10.1.1.104.6908&rep=rep1&type=pdf; T. Casey et al., "Defining Threat Agents: Towards a More Complete Threat Analysis," in *ISSE 2010 Securing Electronic Business Processes*, ed. N. Pholmann et al. (Wiesbaden, Germany: Vieweg+Teubner, 2011), 214–25, https://doi.org/10.1007/978-3-8348-9788-6; S. Kumar and S. Padapriya, "A Survey on Cloud Computing Security Threats and Vulnerabilities," *International Journal of Innovative Research in Electrical, Electronics, Instrumentation and Control*

Engineering 2, no. 1 (2014): 622–25, https://pdfs.semanticscholar.org/d707/9ca424002a3dffdb4c725b111d2b0863263f.pdf.

40. The Open Group, *Risk Management: The Open Group Guide* ('s-Hertogenbosch, The Netherlands: Van Haren, 2011), https://media.standaardboekhandel.be/-/media/mdm/tolinomedia/product/DT0222/9789087539009/PREVIEW/9789087539009_preview.pdf.

41. On the advantages and limitations of specific methods, see A. Shameli-Sendi et al., "Taxonomy of Information Security Risk Assessment (ISRA)," *Computers & Security* 57, no. 1 (2016): 14–30, https://doi.org/10.1016/j.cose.2015.11.001.

42. On the relationship of risk appetite and risk management, see T. Aven, "On the Meaning and Use of the Risk Appetite Concept," *Risk Analysis* 33, no. 3 (2013): 462–68, https://doi.org/10.1111/j.1539-6924.2012.01887.x; D. Hillson and R. Murray-Webster, *A Short Guide to Risk Appetite* (London: Routledge, 2016).

43. According to the risk homeostasis theory (RHT), a target level of acceptable risk is based on four factors: the expected benefits of risky alternatives, the expected cost of risky alternatives, the expected benefits of safe alternatives, and the expected cost of safe alternatives. Risk decisions involve comparing perceived risk to the target level. Risk homeostasis theory is based on traffic safety research, but it is considered applicable to a broad range of risk decisions. G. S. Wilde, "Risk Homeostasis Theory: An Overview," *Injury Prevention* 4, no. 2 (1998): 89–91, www.ncbi.nlm.nih.gov/pmc/articles/PMC1730348/pdf/v004p00089.pdf; R. Trimpop, "Risk Homeostasis Theory: Problems of the Past and Promises for the Future," *Safety Science* 22, nos. 1–3 (1996): 119–30, https://doi.org/10.1016/0925-7535(96)00010-0; W. Janssen and E. Tenkink, "Risk Hemostasis Theory and Its Critics: Time for an Agreement," *Ergonomics* 31, no. 4 (1988): 429–33, https://doi.org/10.1080/00140138808966689; T. Hoyes, "Risk Homeostasis Theory—Beyond Transportational Research," *Safety Science* 17, no. 2 (1994): 77–89, https://doi.org/10.1016/0925-7535(94)90002-7.

44. The many examples that might be cited include M. Carr et al., *Taxonomy-Based Risk Identification* (Pittsburgh, PA: Software Engineering Institute, Carnegie Mellon University, 1993), https://apps.dtic.mil/docs/citations/ADA266992; B. Bahli and Y. Benslimane, "An Exploration of Wireless Computing Risks," *Information Management & Computer Security* 12, no. 3 (2004): 245–54, https://doi.org/10.1108/09685220410542606; K. Hurtado et al., "Construction Risk Taxonomy: An International Convergence of Academic and Industry Perspectives," *American Journal of Applied Sciences* 10, no. 7 (2013): 706–13, https://doi.org/10.3844/ajassp.2013.706.713; A. Shameli-Sendi et al., "Taxonomy of Intrusion Risk Assessment and Response System," *Computers & Security* 45, no. 6 (2014): 1–16, https://doi.org/10.1016/j.cose.2014.04.009; A. Sutcliffe and G. Rugg, "A Taxonomy of Error Types for Failure Analysis and Risk Assessment," *International Journal of Human-Computer Interaction* 10, no. 4 (1998): 381–405, https://doi.org/10.1207/s15327590ijhc1004_5; B. Gallagher et al., *A Taxonomy of Operational Risks* (Pittsburgh, PA: Software Engineering Institute, Carnegie Mellon University, 2005), https://apps.dtic.mil/docs/citations/ADA441289; J. Cebula and L. Young, *A Taxonomy of Operational Cyber Security Risks* (Pittsburgh, PA: Software Engineering Institute, Carnegie Mellon University, 2010), https://apps.dtic.mil/docs/citations/ADA537111; M. Cohen, "Economic Dimensions of Environmental and Technological Risk Events: Toward a Tenable Taxonomy," *Industrial & Environmental Crisis Quarterly* 9, no. 4 (1996): 448–81, https://doi.org/10.1177/108602669600900402; M. Coccia, "A New Taxonomy of Country Performance and Risk Based on Economic and Technological Indicators," *Journal of Applied Economics* 10, no. 1 (2007): 29–42, https://doi.org/10.1080/15140326.2007.12040480; P. Han et al., "Varieties of Uncertainty in Health Care: A Conceptual Taxonomy," *Medical Decision Making* 31, no. 6 (2011): 828–38, https://doi.org/10.1177/0272989X10393976; *NASA Risk Management Handbook, NASA/SP-2011-3422* (Washington, DC: National Aeronautics and Space Administration, 2011), especially 106–11, https://ntrs.nasa.gov/archive/nasa/casi.ntrs.nasa.gov/20120000033.pdf.

45. K. Hurtado et al., "Construction Risk Taxonomy: An International Convergence of Academic and Industry Perspectives," *American Journal of Applied Sciences* 10, no. 7 (2013): 706–13, https://doi.org/10.3844/ajassp.2013.706.713; J. Cabecas, "Taxonomy to Characterize Occupational Hazards (Risk Factors) at the Workplace Level," *Work* 51, no. 4 (2013): 703–13, https://doi.org/10.3233/WOR-152023; A. Rea-Guaman et al., "Systematic Review: Cyberse-

curity Risk Taxonomy," in *Trends and Applications in Software Engineering: Proceedings of the Sixth International Conference on Software Process Improvement*, ed. J. Mejia et al. (Cham, Switzerland: Springer International, 2017), 137–46, https://doi.org/10.1007/978-3-319-69341-5_13; R. Kendall et al., *A Proposed Taxonomy for Software Development Risks for High-Performance Computing (HPC) Scientific/Engineering Applications, CMU/SEI-2006-TN-039* (Pittsburgh, PA: Software Engineering Institute, Carnegie Mellon University, 2007), https://resources.sei.cmu.edu/library/asset-view.cfm?assetid=8013; P. Han et al., "Varieties of Uncertainty in Health Care: A Conceptual Taxonomy," *Medical Decision Making* 31, no. 6 (2011): 828–38, https://doi.org/ 10.1177/0272989x11393976.

46. A specialized form of information risk is associated with financial risk. It denotes the threat of a material misstatement, mistaken auditor's opinion, or other incorrect or incomplete information that may be used to value an investment. See F. Ecker, *Information Risk and Long-Run Performance of Initial Public Offerings* (Wiesbaden, Germany: Gabler, 2008). This form of information risk typically arises when financial statements or other information provided by a company do not accurately represent its financial condition. In this context, information risk is related to information asymmetry, a situation in which one party has relevant information about an investment that others do not have.

Chapter Two

Creation and Collection of Information

In the course of their work, companies, government agencies, and not-for-profit organizations create and collect information related to their operations, programs, initiatives, activities, transactions, and other matters. This chapter identifies and discusses risks associated with the following aspects of information creation and collection:

- failure to collect information that is mandated by laws and regulations;
- unauthorized or excessive collection of personal information;
- illegal collection of nonpublic information;
- creation or collection of information with objectionable content;
- creation or collection of information with defamatory or private content; and
- creation or collection of poor quality information.

As discussed in the following sections, these risks expose an organization to regulatory fines and penalties, civil litigation, and, in some cases, criminal prosecution. They have a negative impact on planning, decision-making, transaction processing, marketing, customer service, and other business operations and activities. They also pose downstream risks related to disclosure, use, protection, and retention of information.

The risks listed above are associated with creation or collection of information in all formats and media, including databases, digital documents, paper records, photographs, and social media content. While they are less widely publicized than some other matters discussed in this book, risks associated with creation and collection of information have a high probability of occurrence. The risks discussed in the following sections are generally unacceptable and, for the most part, unavoidable, but their adverse effects can be prevented, limited, or, in some cases, transferred.

MANDATORY INFORMATION COLLECTION

Thousands of laws and regulations mandate the collection of specific information for submission to government agencies. These legal mandates are sometimes termed *data collection requirements*, but they are not limited to computer data. They apply to information in all formats.

In the United States, the Office of Management and Budget (OMB) estimated that the public would spend approximately 11.33 billion person-hours in 2019 responding to information-collection requests required by federal regulations.[1] This total represents an increase of 15.7 percent from the 9.8 billon person-hours estimated by OMB in 2009. Of the 2019 estimate, 8.1 billion person-hours—approximately 70 percent—involved information requested by the Department of the Treasury; over 99 percent of that information, totaling 8.06 billion person-hours of effort, was requested by the Internal Revenue Service. Among other federal agencies, information requested by the Department of Health and Human Services accounted for 1.36 billion person-hours of effort, information requested by the Securities and Exchange Commission accounted for 248 million person-hours, information requested by the Department of Transportation accounted for 192 million person-hours, information requested by the Environmental Protection Agency accounted for 169 million person-hours, and information requested by the Department of Labor accounted for 165 million person-hours.

Federal laws and regulations specify the types of information to be collected about specific activities and operations, the government agencies to which the information must be reported, and the method and frequency of reporting. Federal laws and regulations may also provide severe penalties for failure to collect and submit the required information. Among the many examples that might be cited:

- 31 C.F.R. § 1020.220 requires banks, savings associations, credit unions, and other financial institutions to collect and retain sufficient information to identify their customers. For individuals, the information to be collected includes the customer's name, date of birth, address, a taxpayer identification number or other numeric identifier, and the type, identifying number, and other descriptions of the documents that were examined to verify a customer's identity. For corporations, partnerships, or other legal entities, the customer due diligence rule issued by the Financial Crimes Enforcement Network (FinCEN) requires financial institutions to collect and verify information about all beneficial owners. The civil penalty for noncompliance with these information-collection requirements is $25,000 per day for each office, branch, or other place of business where a violation occurs.

- According to 42 C.F.R. § 438.242, state Medicaid agencies must require their authorized managed care organizations to collect and report information about their providers and enrollees, including encounter data relating to Medicaid services provided to enrollees. As an enforcement mechanism, a state Medicaid agency may penalize managed care organizations that fail to comply with this data collection requirement. Depending on the circumstances, civil penalties can total 1.5 percent of Medicaid premiums. Penalties imposed on a Medicaid managed care organization may flow down to their providers. As specified in 42 C.F.R. § 422.310, Medicare Advantage organizations must likewise collect encounter data from their providers, subject to civil penalties for noncompliance.

- As specified in 21 C.F.R. § 312.62, a physician or other qualified clinical investigator working for a pharmaceutical company or other sponsor of a drug trial must create and collect case report forms, signed consent forms, physicians' progress notes, nurses' notes, and other medical information for each individual to whom an investigational drug is administered or who is employed as a control subject in an investigation. 21 C.F.R. § 812.140 specifies similar requirements for creation and collection of information related to clinical trials that involve investigational medical devices. Repeated or deliberate noncompliance will result in disqualification of a clinical investigator or, in extreme cases, termination of a clinical trial.

- Under the Physician Payments Sunshine Act (42 U.S.C. § 1320a-7h), which is part of the Affordable Care Act, manufacturers of drugs, medical devices, and biologicals that participate in US federal healthcare programs must collect and report information about certain payments and items of value, such as travel and meals, given to physicians and teaching hospitals in the United States. As specified in 42 C.F.R. § 403.912, noncompliant manufacturers are subject to civil penalties up to $150,000 per year.

- According to 41 C.F.R. § 60-741.44, federal government contractors must collect information about the number of job applicants with disabilities in a given year, the total number of job openings filled, the total number of applicants for all jobs, the number of applicants with disabilities hired, and the total number of applicants hired. As specified in 41 C.F.R. § 60-741.66, penalties for failure to comply include withholding of payments, termination of a contract, and debarment from future contracts.

- As specified in 45 C.F.R. § 1356.82 et seq., state government agencies responsible for child welfare must collect over four dozen items of personal, demographic, educational, and other information about children in foster care. Depending on the circumstances, this information is obtained from city or county social services agencies, which may, in turn, obtain it from community-based organizations, not-for-profit entities, or other foster care providers. According to 45 C.F.R. § 1356.85, the data must be reported to the U.S. Department of Health and Human Services in a timely manner, in the correct format, and 100-percent error free. Penalties for noncompliance may equal up to 5 percent of the total funds allocated to the state agency for the development of foster care independence programs under Title IV-E of the Social Security Act (42 U.S.C. 677).

- As specified in 42 C.F.R. § Part 40, the U.S. Department of Transportation requires data collection and annual reporting related to drug and alcohol testing of employees with safety-sensitive duties and applicants for safety-sensitive positions in companies and other organizations regulated by federal transportation agencies. Regulated entities that fail to comply with data collection and -reporting requirements are subject to civil penalties that vary from agency to agency. As an example, the Federal Railroad Administration imposes fines of $2,500 to $5,000 per violation for failure to collect and submit required data. The Federal Aviation Administration penalizes air carriers and commercial operators up to $30,000 per violation for failure to comply with data collection and -reporting requirements. The Federal Motor Carrier Safety Administration selects a group of motor carriers to report their drug and alcohol testing information in a given year. Nonrespondents are subject to a penalty of up to $1,000 per day for failure to comply. Motor carriers not selected must collect and retain the testing information.

Additional information-collection requirements apply to industries and activities that are regulated at the state level. State insurance regulators, for example, require annual collection and reporting of financial and statistical data by insurance companies, which are solely chartered and regulated by states. Alternatively, data collection requirements specified in state regulations may provide an additional level of oversight for federally regulated industries and activities. State banking regulations specify information-collection and -reporting requirements that may differ from their federal counterparts. In some states, healthcare providers must collect and report information about certain diseases, schools must collect and report information about special education students, social services agencies must collect and report information about children in foster care, nursing homes must collect and report information about mistreatment of residents, operators of licensed vessels must collect and report information about commercial fishing activity, utility companies must collect and report information about customer disconnections, and licensed firearms dealers must collect and report information about the theft of firearms in their possession.

Laws and regulations that mandate information collection with significant penalties for noncompliance are not unique to the United States. Many countries have anti-money-laundering and anti-terrorism laws that require collection of customer information. In Canada, for example, customer identification rules issued by the Financial Transactions and Reports Analysis Centre (FINTRAC) apply to banks, securities dealers, life insurance companies, accountants, real estate companies, and other financial services entities. Violations are subject to penalties up to $500,000 and imprisonment for up to five years. The Australian Transaction Reports and Analysis Center (AUS-TRAC) has similar requirements for customer identification with significant penalties for noncompliance. EU Directive 2015/849, the European Union's money laundering directive, specifies customer due diligence and data collection requirements that member states must transpose into national legislation. Penalties for noncompliance can exceed €100,000.

Among hundreds of other sector-specific laws that mandate information collection, Loi Bertrand, the French version of the Physician Payments Sunshine Act, is more expansive than its US counterpart. It requires health products companies to collect and report information related to direct and indirect gifts or other benefits to pharmacists, nurses, medical students, and healthcare associations as well as to physicians and teaching hospitals. Violations are subject to sanctions and fines up to €45,000. According to EU Directive 2016/681, air carriers must collect certain passenger information for flights between EU member states and other countries. Penalties for noncompliance vary with national legislation but may be as high as €50,000. As specified in Regulation (EC) No. 223/2999, commonly known as the European Statistical Law, legal entities and individuals in EU member states are required to collect and report certain statistical data. Penalties for noncompliance, which are defined by national statistical authorities in member states, may exceed €2,500 per offense.

Vulnerability Assessment

The following vulnerabilities contribute to the risk of noncompliance with information-collection mandates specified in laws and regulations:

- A regulated entity may not be aware of information-collection requirements. An organization's compliance officer or legal department is typically responsible for identifying laws and regulations that affect specific business operations, but some organizations do not have in-house compliance expertise. Even for those that do, it can be difficult to keep informed about all applicable legal and regulatory requirements, especially in multinational and transnational organizations that operate in multiple political jurisdictions.

- A regulated entity may not correctly interpret information-collection requirements. Laws and regulations can be voluminous, complicated, poorly written, and difficult to understand. Amendments may add complexity and confusion. It may be difficult to determine the specific types of information that must be collected about specific matters.

- A regulated entity's business processes and practices may not be conducive to information collection. Information required by laws and regulations may not be maintained in a single, easily accessible repository. It may be managed by multiple applications, saved in multiple formats, recorded in multiple languages, and scattered in multiple locations. If the information is not available in-house, it must be obtained from external sources through time-consuming surveys, interviews, or other methods.

- Departments and other organizational units responsible for information collection may not be able to complete their work in the required timeframe due to lack of clear instructions, inadequate staffing, insufficient training, or ineffective supervision. The progress of compliance initiatives can be particularly difficult to monitor in large enterprises with complex organizational structures and geographically dispersed business operations.

- Collection efforts may be impeded by missing, damaged, outdated, unreliable, irrelevant, and poorly organized information. Inconsistent information from different sources can be difficult to integrate. Format conversion can introduce errors that were not present in the original sources.

Risk Response

While federal information-collection requirements are labor-intensive and time-consuming, noncompliance can have significant adverse consequences. Risk mitigation options are limited. Risk acceptance based on a conscious business decision not to comply fully with legal and regulatory requirements is not an effective mitigation strategy. The consequences of that approach range from damaging to catastrophic. Fines for failing to collect required information can add up for repeated noncompliance, and some regulations impose greater penalties for willful violations. Monetary penalties aside, regulatory noncompliance exposes an organization to additional risks that can have an adverse impact on the organization's objectives and performance. Noncompliance may raise the level of regulatory scrutiny, leading to audits and inspections that can be time-consuming, will likely result in high legal costs, and may reveal additional problems that require corrective action. In extreme cases, regulatory noncompliance may force an organization to suspend specific operations until violations are corrected or to shut down permanently. Noncompliance also poses risks to an organization's reputation, which can damage business relationships, erode the confidence of investors and other stakeholders, lead to loss of revenue, and make it difficult to recruit and keep qualified employees.

Risk avoidance is only possible if the regulated activity that is subject to information collection is eliminated. This is not a viable mitigation strategy where the regulated activity is a core component of an organization's business. A bank cannot eliminate customers to avoid customer-identification regulations. A managed-care organization cannot eliminate providers and enrollees to avoid collecting information about them. A clinical investigator cannot stop treating patients in order to avoid collecting case report forms and supporting documentation. An airline cannot eliminate pilots to avoid collecting drug and alcohol information.

Risk transfer through insurance is generally not an option for criminal violations. Most insurance policies exclude coverage for civil fines and penalties resulting from illegal activity, although insurance coverage may be available for legal fees and other costs associated with government investigations and litigation. In some situations, risk transfer may be possible (but not necessarily advisable) by increasing prices or fees to offset damage resulting from failure to collect required information. Thus, a bank might charge a fee for collection of customer information when an account is opened, or a managed-care organization might impose a fee on providers and enrollees.

A risk limitation plan that directly addresses the vulnerabilities discussed in the preceding section is the only viable mitigation strategy for regulatory risks associated with information-collection requirements. An effective limitation plan depends on thorough preparation and systematic execution to reduce the likelihood of risk events:

- An organization's senior management and key stakeholders must be committed to regulatory compliance. They must understand the importance, purpose, and scope of legal requirements and authorize the necessary resources for fully compliant information collection.
- Ignorance of or confusion about information-collection requirements is not an acceptable defense for noncompliance. A qualified organizational unit must be responsible for identifying, analyzing, and interpreting laws and regulations, including any amendments and supplemental guidance documents, that mandate information collection. This must be done for all national and subnational jurisdictions where an organization operates. If necessary, external compliance specialists should be hired to supplement internal expertise.
- Information collection must be a managed initiative. A qualified employee must be designated as project manager with full responsibility for planning, organizing, executing, and controlling the information-collection process. The project manager must be familiar with the business activities and operations to which the information relates. The project manager will

determine the staffing, technology support, consulting expertise, and other resources needed to fulfill the information-collection mandate within the required timeframe.

- To ensure compliance and achieve a manageable focus, the scope and intended outcome of an information-collection initiative must be clearly defined. The specific information needed to satisfy legal and regulatory requirements must be determined, and collection efforts should be strictly limited to that information. Irrelevant or unnecessary information must be excluded.

- Databases, document repositories, and other records that may contain required information, and their associated business processes, must be identified and evaluated for relevance, reliability, accessibility, and usability. To the extent possible, concerns about data formats, legacy applications, information stored offsite, and other matters should be anticipated, assessed, and addressed.

- Organizational units that have relevant information in their custody or under their supervisory control must be made aware of regulatory requirements and compliance initiatives. Their advice and assistance will be needed to address questions and problems that arise during the information-collection process.

- If required information is not available within the organization, a plan and timetable must be developed to obtain it from external sources.

- Staff assigned to an information-collection initiative must be trained to perform the work correctly and completely. Clearly written specifications and operating procedures must be prepared for use as training materials. The operating procedures must include instructions about problems—such as missing, poorly organized, or unusable data—that may arise during the collection process. Staff should be given a due-diligence checklist or similar quality-control mechanism to ensure that all information-collection tasks have been properly completed.

- Project oversight is essential for quality control. Collected information must be carefully reviewed for correctness and completeness prior to submission to regulatory authorities.

COLLECTION OF PERSONAL INFORMATION

Many countries have laws and regulations that restrict or prohibit the collection of personal information, which is broadly defined as any information that can be used to distinguish or trace an individual's identity, either by itself or in combination with other information.[2] The individual to whom the information pertains is termed the *data subject*. A name and unique numeric identifier are obvious examples of information that can directly identify a data subject, but there are many other possibilities, including a mailing address, email address, telephone number, date of birth, job title, distinctive physical characteristics, and information about personally owned property, such as vehicle registration numbers.

The General Data Protection Regulation (GDPR) is the most widely cited law governing the collection of personal information.[3] Officially titled Regulation (EU) 2016/679, it became effective in all member states of the European Union in May 2018. The GDPR regulates collection of personal information about EU citizens, regardless of their place of residence; EU residents who are not EU citizens, such as persons with EU work permits and residence permits; and visitors to the EU to the extent that they obtain products or services that are provided in the EU. According to the GDPR's data minimization principle, which is articulated in Article 5(1), collection of personal information must be limited to the minimum amount necessary for a specific, explicit, and legitimate purpose. This restriction applies to personal information that is collected directly from a data subject or obtained from other sources.

Under Article 13 of the GDPR, a data subject must be informed about the purpose for which personal information is being collected, but the data subject does not have the option of withholding information that is needed for a valid purpose. According to GDPR Recital 60, however, the data subject should be informed of the consequences of not providing personal information. Violations of the GDPR's restrictions on collection of personal information are subject to administrative fines and other civil or criminal penalties that are specified by national laws. Fines for infringement of GDPR Article 5, which states general principles for processing of personal data, can range up to €20 million or 4 percent of the offending organization's worldwide revenue for the prior financial year.

The GDPR has a broad territorial scope. It applies to organizations that are established within an EU member state, whether or not the actual collection of personal information takes place in the European Union. It also applies to collection of personal information by organizations established elsewhere that provide goods and services to, or monitor the behavior of, EU data subjects. Other countries have adopted data protection and privacy laws that are based on the GDPR or its predecessor, Directive 95/46/EC of the European Parliament. Those national laws prohibit indiscriminate or excessive collection of personal information with significant penalties for violations.[4]

While the United States does not have comprehensive data protection or privacy laws, limited collection of personal information is one of the Fair Information Practice Principles (FIPPS) adopted by federal government agencies.[5] The FIPPS provide a standard for assessing privacy impacts and developing risk mitigation plans. According to the principles, personal information collected by federal agencies must be relevant and necessary for a legally authorized purpose.[6]

Sector-specific data protection and privacy legislation typically focuses on unauthorized disclosure, but some federal laws restrict the collection of personal information by nongovernmental entities in certain circumstances. As an example, the Children's Online Privacy Protection Act (COPPA), which is codified at 15 U.S.C. §§ 6501-6508, requires operators of commercial websites and online services to obtain verifiable parental consent before collecting personal information from a child under age 13. The Federal Trade Commission, which is responsible for enforcement, defines *online services* broadly to include social networking apps, Internet-enabled location services, voice over Internet protocol services, and Internet-of-things devices. Violations of the COPPA Rule specified in 16 C.F.R. Part 312 are subject to fines up to $40,000, but some settlements have involved larger amounts.[7]

Financial institutions subject to the Financial Services Modernization Act of 1999, also known as the Gramm-Leach Bliley Act (GLBA), must comply with data collection requirements specified in the Financial Privacy Rule specified in 16 C.F.R. Part 313. They must notify consumers periodically about the categories of nonpublic personal information they collect from customers. Noncompliance is punishable by fines up to $100,000 per violation, and officers and directors of the institution may be personally subject to imprisonment for up to five years and fines up to $10,000 per violation.

Various state laws restrict the collection of personal information about consumers, students, and others. Among widely publicized examples:

- The California Consumer Privacy Act of 2018 (Cal. Civ. Code §§ 1798.100 et seq.) requires certain businesses to inform consumers about the categories of personal information to be collected from them and prohibits the collection of additional categories unless the consumer is notified.
- Section 49076.7 of the California Education Code prohibits school districts, county education offices, and charter schools from collecting social security numbers or the last four digits of social security numbers unless otherwise required by state or federal law. Section 53E-9-304 of the Utah Code contains a similar prohibition.
- According to Section 17852 of the California Welfare and Institutions Code, government agencies and hospital districts are prohibited from collecting personal information that is not required to assess eligibility or administer public services or programs.
- According to Fla. Stat. § 1002.222, schools and educational agencies are prohibited from collecting information about political affiliations, voting history, religious affiliation, or biometric data from a student, parent, or sibling. Laws in other states impose similar restrictions.

- A number of states have introduced legislation that prohibits telecommunication and information service providers from collecting web browsing history, app usage data, geolocation data, and certain other personal information without affirmative consent.

Rather than specifying monetary penalties for violations, these state laws create a private right of civil action by an aggrieved data subject.

Vulnerability Assessment

Data minimization is a critical aspect of data protection and privacy legislation, but excessive collection of personal information is commonplace in many organizations. In the absence of privacy awareness, it is rarely faulted. The following vulnerabilities contribute to risk associated with excessive collection of personal information:

- When developing job applications, employee information forms, contractor qualification forms, college applications, patient intake sheets, opinion surveys, questionnaires, website inquiry forms, and other data collection instruments, organizations may solicit personal information that is not absolutely necessary for the task at hand. This may occur because information requirements associated with a given task have not been carefully determined.
- Some personal information may be collected in anticipation of future uses that are not clearly defined and may never occur. This is a violation of the GDPR and national data protection laws.
- Data minimization requirements are easily misunderstood and misinterpreted. Laws and regulations that incorporate data minimization principles rarely specify the types of personal information that should not be collected. The GDPR allows data collection in the "legitimate interest" of an organization, but appropriate limits can only be determined in the context of specific situations.
- Some researchers and data analysts have noted that the data minimization principle is incompatible with big data initiatives, which process large data sets to reveal patterns, trends, and associations related to personal information.[8] Data protection and privacy laws generally prohibit such secondary uses, although exceptions may be made for scientific, statistical, and historical research subject to appropriate safeguards that protect the identity of data subjects.
- Where data minimization is prescribed by data protection and privacy laws, collection of unnecessary personal information exposes an organization to monetary penalties. Given the GDPR's broad territorial scope, this risk extends to countries, like the United States, that do not have omnibus

data protection or privacy legislation. In some situations, it can be difficult to determine whether and to what extent an organization outside of the European Union is subject to GDPR's extra-territorial requirements.

- Data minimization violations are difficult to conceal. In many cases, the unnecessary personal information is collected directly from the data subject, who must be told why specific personal information is needed and the consequences of not providing it. Where personal information is obtained from an external source, the data subject has the right to be told about the categories of information involved.
- Excessive collection of personal information poses downstream risks related to high storage costs and unauthorized disclosure, which will be discussed in subsequent chapters.

Risk Response

Data protection and privacy laws do not prohibit the collection of personal information for a valid purpose that is clearly articulated at the time the information is collected. The benefits of collecting additional personal information for secondary uses, such as big data analysis, must be weighed against potentially negative impacts, taking applicable legal restrictions into account.

In the United States and other countries that do not have comprehensive data protection or privacy legislation, an organization may choose to accept the risks associated with excessive collection of personal information. Given the monetary penalties involved, however, risk acceptance is not an effective strategy where laws and regulations restrict the collection of personal information. Historically, such restrictions have been limited to specific political jurisdictions or industries, but the broad territorial scope of the GDPR extends data minimization requirements to many organizations that might not otherwise be subject to restrictions on collection of personal information.

Where data minimization is mandated by laws or regulations, risk avoidance is only possible if collection of personal information is discontinued or severely curtailed. Whenever personal information is requested from data subjects, excessive collection is always a possibility. Personal information obtained from an external source, such as a purchased database or a video recording produced by a surveillance camera, is highly likely to have content that is unnecessary and possibly illegal for an organization to collect.

Risk transfer through insurance is generally not possible for criminal violation of data protection or privacy laws. In most countries, insurance policies also exclude coverage for fines and penalties for civil infractions of data minimization requirements, but insurance coverage may be available for legal fees associated with litigation, regulatory investigation, public relations expenses, or the cost to notify or compensate data subjects affected by excessive collection of personal information. Insurance claims are typically excluded for willful or negligent violations of data minimization requirements.

For collection of personal information, the only viable mitigation strategy is a risk limitation plan that directly addresses data minimization requirements:

- An organization's top management and key stakeholders must understand and be committed to compliance with data protection and privacy laws in general and data minimization requirements in particular.
- A qualified organizational unit must be responsible for identifying, analyzing, and interpreting data collection laws and regulations, including amendments and supplemental guidance documents. This must be done for all national and subnational jurisdictions where an organization operates. If necessary, external data protection specialists should be hired to supplement internal expertise.
- Organizational units and employees involved in the collection of personal information must understand the importance, purpose, and scope of data minimization. Taking a proactive "privacy by design" approach,[9] data minimization principles must be built into an organization's business processes, information systems, and technology infrastructure.
- Operational objectives and processing requirements must be carefully defined and explicitly articulated when collection of personal information is planned. The organization must be able to respond clearly and fully to a data subject's question about the purpose for which specific information is requested.
- A compliance officer, privacy officer, or another knowledgeable employee must review surveys, questionnaires, web forms, and other data collection instruments to ensure that personal information requested is relevant, legally authorized, and necessary for the defined purpose. Questionable data elements must be highlighted, evaluated, and revised or eliminated as necessary. The review should consider whether the objectives of data collection can be achieved without the questionable data elements.
- Where personal information is obtained from a source other than the data subject, it must be examined to identify and expunge unnecessary content before processing begins.
- If additional personal information is collected for secondary uses, it must be clearly marked as optional. The data subject must not be adversely affected by a refusal to provide the requested information. Proposed secondary uses of personal information must be reviewed by a compliance officer, privacy officer, or another knowledgeable employee to ensure that they are legally permissible.
- Where personal information will be used for big data initiatives, scientific research, statistical analysis, or similar purposes, an anonymization or

pseudonymization process must separate personal identifiers from other information. Anonymization irreversibly obliterates the identity of a data subject, while pseudonymization is a reversible process that substitutes a token for information that might identify a data subject. [10]

DATA THEFT

Data theft is defined as the unauthorized collection of nonpublic information from an organization or individual. The phrase is usually applied to hacking of a computer system in order to obtain access to confidential information, but it broadly denotes collection of information in any format by any means from any unauthorized source. Depending on the circumstances, the stolen information may be copied, memorized for transcription at a later time, or removed outright from its original location. The information may be stolen directly from its owner or obtained from a third party who has obtained it legally or illegally. In any case, the information ends up in the possession of someone who is not authorized to have it.

If personal information is involved, data theft is sometimes characterized as identity theft, which is often perpetrated by individual hackers working alone or in small groups with criminal intent. More important for this discussion, personal information about a competitor's customers and employees may be stolen to obtain a business advantage rather than for identity fraud. Non-identity theft may involve a competitor's financial reports, strategic plans, marketing plans, new product specifications and formulas, unpatented inventions, computer algorithms, business processes, or manufacturing techniques. [11] Collectively, such nonpublic information is considered a trade secret.

Tangentially related to data theft, an organization may obtain trade secrets or other proprietary information about a competitor's business plans through a breach of a non-disclosure agreement (NDA) or other restrictive covenant. The information may come from a current or former employee of the organization that owns the information, from a consultant or contractor who encountered the information during the course of their work for the organization, from a job applicant who learned of the information during an interview, or from another informant.

Various laws impose significant penalties for unlawful collection of trade secrets or other nonpublic information.

- Under the Economic Espionage Act of 1996 (18 U.S.C. § 1832), it is illegal to use deception to collect proprietary information that a competitor has taken active measures to protect where such information collection causes harm to the competitor. Violations are punishable by fines up to $5 million for domestic business infractions or $10 million if a foreign country benefits from the unlawful collection.

- Many states have adopted a version of the Uniform Trade Secrets Act, which prohibits the acquisition of trade secrets by improper means. Penalties for violations are specified in state laws. Section 499c of the California Penal Code, for example, treats misappropriation of trade secrets as a form of larceny, which is punishable by fines up to $5,000 and imprisonment for up to one year. In addition to fines and criminal prosecution, unlawful collection of trade secrets can lead to costly civil litigation and court-ordered payments to the aggrieved party.

- The Defend Trade Secrets Act of 2016 (18 U.S.C. § 1836) and various state laws allow the owner of a trade secret to initiate civil actions for misappropriation of nonpublic information. In the European Union, comparable recourse is provided by EU Directive 2016/943, which prohibits unlawful acquisition of trade secrets in EU member states. Penalties, which may include fines and imprisonment, are specified by national laws.

- Data theft may be committed by an employee, contractor, consultant, intern, volunteer, or other workplace participant acting without an organization's knowledge or approval, but the organization is ultimately accountable for stolen information that is maintained in its offices or on its computer systems. Under the National Stolen Property Act (18 U.S.C. § 2315), it is a federal crime to receive, possess, or store goods valued at more than $5,000, but it is not clear whether this statute applies to stolen information.[12] Other countries have similar laws that criminalize possession of stolen property.[13]

- Several statutes criminalize the possession of stolen information in specific circumstances. Under 18 U.S.C. § 641, for example, it is a crime to receive or retain records stolen from US government agencies or records made under contract for US government agencies. Under the Computer Fraud and Abuse Act (18 U.S.C. § 1030), it is a crime to knowingly access or obtain information from a government computer or financial records from a financial institution without proper authorization.

- Addressing a variant form of data theft, anti-trust laws prohibit the collection of nonpublic information about a competitor's marketing plans, customers, suppliers, prices, discount practices, future product offerings, expansion plans, or other commercially sensitive matters. This prohibition applies to direct collection of information from any nonpublic source, including a competitor's customers, employees, former employees, consultants, contractors, or informants who may have themselves obtained the information by illegal means. The prohibition also applies to the cooperative exchange of non-public information between competing companies for purposes of price fixing, limiting production, market allocation, bid rigging, or other practices that unreasonably restrain trade.[14] In the United

States, the Sherman Act of 1890 (15 U.S.C. §§ 1 et seq.) imposes penalties up to $100 million and ten years in prison for anti-trust violations. Over one hundred other countries have laws that prohibit and penalize anti-competitive business practices. Examples include the Canadian Competition Act, the Australian Competition and Consumer Act 2010, the New Zealand Commerce Act 1986, the Indian Competition Act 2002, the Singapore Competition Act, and Article 102 of the Treaty on the Functioning of the European Union, which prohibits anti-competitive business practices in EU member states.

Vulnerability Assessment

An organization might be in possession of nonpublic information that is collected from competitors or other external sources. Such information may be obtained without an organization's knowledge or authorization in a variety of ways. The following vulnerabilities contribute to risk associated with collection of nonpublic information:

- Nonpublic information may be offered unsolicited, and perhaps anonymously, by a disgruntled employee or former employee of a competitor as an act of retribution for unfair dismissal or perceived mistreatment. Acting without authorization, an employee may receive this stolen information and keep it in an organization's office or computer storage.
- As an adjunct to data gathering, market research, and other legal forms of competitive intelligence, one or more employees acting with their employer's authorization may engage in industrial espionage to obtain trade secrets, customer records, supplier data, marketing plans, bid responses, or other proprietary information from competitors in order to obtain a business advantage. This may be accomplished by infiltrating a competitor's computer systems, intercepting text messages, wiretapping telephone lines, eavesdropping on a competitor's conversations, trespassing on the competitor's property to obtain files, bribing a competitor's employees to provide documents or data, posing as a job applicant to learn about a competitor's business plans, or other illegal or unethical means. Information collected by these unauthorized methods may be saved in project files, planning files, email messages, or other paper or electronic files.
- Newly hired employees may have copies of nonpublic documents or data taken from their former employers, even though they were forbidden by non-disclosure agreements or company policy to take such copies. Employees may bring this proprietary information to their new workplace where it is stored in office areas or on computer systems.[15]
- A newly hired employee may have unwritten knowledge of a former employer's trade secrets, proprietary business processes, strategic plans, pric-

ing practices, or other matters. This knowledge, which may confer a competitive advantage, is typically covered by non-disclosure agreements. Intentionally or inadvertently, the knowledge may be incorporated into email messages, reports, spreadsheets, presentations, or other written records that the employee creates in the course of assigned duties. These documents will be saved in an organization's office areas or on its computer systems.

- Consultants or contractors, who are often hired for their experience with similar organizations in a given industry, may draw on confidential reports, data compilations, or other information obtained during prior engagements with competitors. Trade secrets and other proprietary information from these records may be incorporated, intentionally or inadvertently, into work prepared for new clients.

Risk Response

Unauthorized collection of nonpublic information can be difficult to monitor. Stolen information maintained in an organization's offices or stored on its computer systems without its knowledge or approval can be difficult to detect in the ordinary course of business, but it may be discovered during audits, investigations, discovery for litigation, or other activities that involve a detailed review of an organization's records. If nonpublic information is found, the organization may be exposed to fines, civil litigation, or criminal prosecution. Risk acceptance is a possible mitigation strategy in not-for-profit organizations or in noncompetitive industries where data theft to obtain a business advantage is unlikely. Risk transfer through insurance coverage is generally not possible for risks associated with illegal collection of information.

In competitive industries, some measure of risk avoidance can be achieved by refusing to hire the former employees of competitors, which may deprive the organization of needed expertise, or by not giving such employees assignments that draw on information obtained in previous employment, which forfeits any experience that the new employee brings to the job. Despite their limitations, those risk avoidance practices can be included in a risk limitation plan that imposes significant restrictions on unauthorized collection of nonpublic information maintained by external entities:

- Many organizations have a code of conduct or comparable policy that prohibits illegal activities as well as unethical actions that may harm a competitor. Employees must understand that this prohibition applies to unauthorized collection of proprietary data, confidential documents, and other nonpublic information, either directly or through intermediaries.

- An organization's code of conduct must prohibit verbal or written exchange of nonpublic information with competitors. The prohibition must apply to strategic plans, marketing plans, customers, suppliers, prices, discount practices, future product offerings, expansion plans, or other data or documents that deal with commercially sensitive matters.
- When hiring a current or former employee of a competitor, an organization must know the full scope of the employee's work for the competitor, including whether and to what extent the employee has knowledge of the competitor's trade secrets, proprietary business processes, strategic plans, and other nonpublic information.
- An organization must be aware of any non-disclosure agreements, non-compete clauses, nonsolicitation agreements, and other restrictive covenants and legal obligations imposed on an employee by a previous employer. The organization should obtain a written statement from the employee acknowledging these restrictions.
- An organization must obtain a written agreement that an employee will not share or use a former employer's trade secrets or proprietary information for as long as legal restrictions are in effect. This agreement is necessary to demonstrate that the organization does not tolerate data theft and will not receive stolen information.
- Employees must be advised that nonpublic information obtained from former employers, competitors, or other external entities is prohibited in the workplace. Such information must not be stored in the organization's offices or saved on its computer systems. This prohibition must extend to home offices that are authorized by the organization.
- Consultants and contractors must be strongly cautioned against the inclusion of trade secrets or other proprietary information in reports, presentations, strategic plans, or other materials that they prepare for the organization.

OBJECTIONABLE CONTENT

Objectionable content consists of documents, data, messages, social media posts, photographs, video recordings, or other materials that contain cruel, insensitive, threatening, inflammatory, insulting, obscene, or otherwise offensive statements or graphic depictions related to a person's race, ethnicity, national origin, immigration status, religious affiliation, sex, gender identity, sexual orientation, age, health, physical appearance, or other characteristics. Employees, consultants, contractors, and other workplace participants may create or collect such materials in the course of their assigned duties, although such duties would themselves be considered objectionable and possibly illegal. More likely, workplace participants may use an organization's facilities, computer systems, equipment, supplies, or other resources to create and collect objectionable content that is solely related to their personal affairs.

An organization that allows or tolerates the creation or collection of documents or other records with objectionable content may violate laws that prohibit workplace harassment as a form of employment discrimination:

- In the United States, Title VII of the Civil Rights Act of 1964 (42 U.S.C. § 2000e-2), the Age Discrimination in Employment Act of 1967 (29 U.S.C. §§ 621-634), and the Americans with Disabilities Act of 1990 (42 U.S.C. §§ 12101 et seq.) prohibit employment discrimination based on race, color, religion, sex, national origin, age, disability, or genetic information. Many state and local governments have enacted similar laws.[16]
- Examples of laws that prohibit employment discrimination in other countries include the Canadian Human Rights Act (R.S.C, 1985, C. H-6) , the various equality directives issued by the European Union, and the Australian Age Discrimination Act 2004, Disability Discrimination Act 1992, Racial Discrimination Act 1975, and Sex Discrimination Act 1984.
- While these laws do not specifically reference objectionable content, a harassment claim may be supported by the presence of such content in the workplace.[17] An employee in a protected class can claim that by allowing workplace participants to create or collect racist, sexist, homophobic, pornographic, or otherwise objectionable content, an organization promotes a hostile work environment—a situation that is sufficiently intimidating, offensive, pervasive, and ongoing to affect the terms and conditions of employment.[18] An employer can be held liable for failing to prohibit the creation and collection of objectionable content that contributes to a hostile work environment.
- In addition to monetary penalties and litigation costs, employers who tolerate objectionable content in the workplace may suffer reputational harm and lose valued employees who prefer a more hospitable and ethical work environment. At a minimum, objectionable content distracts workers, undermines morale, and degrades productivity.

Vulnerability Assessment

Workplace harassment is too pervasive to ignore. In a 2017 survey by Harvard Medical School, UCLA, and the RAND Corporation, one in five workers reported being recently subjected to abusive behavior, humiliation, or unwanted sexual attention from an employer or co-worker.[19] A 2018 survey of five hundred US full-time employees conducted by Wakefield Research for Hiscox, a global specialist insurer, found that 35 percent of all workers and 41 percent of female respondents reported being harassed by a current or former employer.[20] No work environment or discipline is immune. In a 2014 survey of trainee field scientists, 71 percent of women and 41 percent of men reported experiencing sexual harassment.[21] In a 2016 survey of medical clinician-researchers, 30 percent of women reported experiencing sexual harassment.[22]

Objectionable content that exposes an organization to charges of workplace harassment may be created or collected in any work setting. This risk has a high likelihood of occurrence. An employee, consultant, contractor, intern, volunteer, or other workplace participant may send or receive an instant message that contains homophobic statements or racist epithets, write an email that disparages a co-worker as too old to perform effectively, circulate jokes that disparage women or specific ethnic groups, use an office computer to download images or videos from pornographic web sites, post suggestive photos of a co-worker on a social media site, keep sexually explicit photographs in office locations where they might be viewed by others, or otherwise create or collect offensive or intimidating materials that could be construed as contributing to a hostile workplace. These and other examples of information with objectionable content could be scattered in multiple locations. Few organizations rigorously monitor computer files, email systems, Internet usage, social media posts, cloud-based servers, mobile devices, office files, or archival collections to detect objectionable content.

Risk Response

Acceptance of risky practices for creation and collection of information is not an option in the United States and other countries where workplace harassment is prohibited by law. An organization must exercise reasonable care to prevent, detect, and promptly deal with objectionable content that is created or collected by workplace participants. Risk avoidance may be possible in organizations that rely entirely on contractors, consultants, and interns rather than employees—an inadvisable business practice that may be legally questionable—but some laws extend protection from harassment to nonemployees.[23]

A more effective mitigation strategy combines risk transfer with a risk limitation plan. Some measure of risk transfer is possible through employment practices liability insurance (EPLI), which provides coverage for various types of employment litigation, including workplace harassment. A typical EPLI policy covers the cost of defending a lawsuit as well as settlements and judgments, but it will not pay for fines or punitive damages. The cost of an EPLI policy depends on the type and organization, the number of employees, the amount of total coverage, and risk factors, such as the organization's litigation history and policies and practices that affect employment discrimination and workplace harassment.

In litigation, penalties may be reduced or cases dismissed if an employer has taken reasonable actions to prevent and correct harassment. As an adjunct to insurance coverage, an organization should adopt a risk limitation plan that includes the following components related to creation or collection of objectionable content:

- An organization's top management must issue a strong statement that strictly prohibits the creation or collection of objectionable content. This statement can be issued as a separate policy or included in a code of conduct, employee handbook, or comparable document that presents the organization's core values, ethical principles, and approved practices. The statement must include a clear definition of objectionable content. The statement must assert the organization's right to monitor the creation and collection of information to detect objectionable content.
- Workforce participants must receive training to ensure that they are aware of and understand the organization's policy on objectionable content and workplace harassment. Managers must receive appropriate training to enable them to monitor compliance with the policy.
- The prohibition against creation and collection of objectionable content must be enforced. Reports of objectionable content must be investigated promptly, and appropriate corrective action must be taken.
- Objectionable content may be sent or received through an organization's email system. Creation and collection of such content can be minimized by prohibiting the use of an organization's email system for personal communications. Where employees are allowed to use workplace computers, tablets, or smartphones to access personal email accounts, downloading of messages or attachments to those devices should be prohibited.
- Internet filtering software can identify and block access to web sites that are likely to contain objectionable content that might be inadvertently viewed by co-workers or downloaded onto workplace computers.
- Surveillance software uses artificial intelligence technology and other methods to search an organization's email and computer files for potentially offensive words and images. In some jurisdictions, workplace privacy laws require an organization to notify employees in advance about electronic monitoring, but exceptions are typically made for suspected misconduct that creates a hostile work environment.

DEFAMATORY OR PRIVATE CONTENT

Defamation is a false statement presented as a fact. If a defamatory statement is made in writing, it may be libelous. The subject of a libelous statement may be a person—such as a co-worker, former employee, or manager—or an organization—a supplier, business partner, or competitor, for example. To be considered libelous, the statement must be intentionally false and communicated to others with harmful intent.

Most countries have laws that prohibit and penalize libel. While it may be a crime in some circumstances, libel is generally considered a civil wrong. Litigation is possible if the libeled party's reputation is damaged by the false statement. If the libeled party is a person, the damages may be economic (lost present or future earnings, lost business opportunity, or lost employment benefits) or noneconomic (pain and suffering in the form of emotional distress, stress-induced illness, or personal humiliation). If the libeled party is a business or not-for-profit entity, the damages typically involve loss of reputation, which has measurable economic consequences.

Litigation risk is not limited to false statements. It also applies to true statements that contain factual information about a person that is not generally known and that would damage the person's reputation if made public. Examples of private content include information about a person's health, criminal background, family troubles, financial problems, sexual activity, or other details about the person's private life. Disclosure of such information exposes an organization to civil litigation for "publication of private facts," which is considered an invasion of privacy. The disclosure must be made to a large enough group that the private facts become private knowledge. The private content must be offensive to a reasonable person of ordinary sensibilities, and the facts disclosed must not be of legitimate public interest. Damage claims are typically based on loss of reputation or community status.

Vulnerability Assessment

The following vulnerabilities expose an organization to risks associated with collection of libelous or private information:

- The most widely publicized instances of libelous communications or publication of private facts have involved publishing and broadcasting companies, but employees and other workplace participants in any organization or industry may create email messages, reports, social media posts, or other data or documents with libelous or private content.
- Such content may ultimately be communicated to third parties, but until disclosure occurs, creation of defamatory or private information can be very difficult to detect. Few organizations rigorously monitor their computer files, email systems, Internet usage, social media posts, cloud-based servers, mobile devices, or office files to identify libelous or private content, which may be scattered in multiple locations and combined with other information that is true and publicly available.

- Collecting defamatory information created by others poses a related litigation risk if the information is communicated to others verbally by an employee or other representative of the organization that collected it. Verbal disclosure of defamatory information is termed *slander*, even if the defamatory content was collected from others rather than created by the person making the disclosure.
- Collection of defamatory information also poses the risk that an employee or other representative of an organization might incorporate the defamatory content into a written statement, thereby committing libel. The same risks apply to collection of data or documents with private content.
- In some circumstances, the risk window for litigation is long. While laws that prohibit defamation and publication of private facts specify relatively short time periods for initiation of litigation, the limitation period begins when the harmful disclosure occurs, not when the information was created. If libelous or private content finds its way into archival collections, it may not be disclosed for many years after it was created, although the risk window for defamation and invasion of privacy claims is ultimately limited by the life span of the aggrieved party.

Risk Response

Acceptance may be an effective mitigation strategy for litigation risks associated with creation or collection of libelous or private content, especially for an organization that is confident about the legality of its information-handling practices. Cases that allege defamation or disclosure of private information can be difficult for plaintiffs to win. Various defenses are available to the accused party. Damages for reputational risk may be capped in some jurisdictions, and punitive damages are rarely awarded. On the other hand, a lawsuit for defamation or invasion of privacy can involve significant legal costs, even if the claim is settled or dismissed at an early stage.

In a lawsuit for defamation or invasion of privacy, the aggrieved party must demonstrate that harmful content was disclosed to a third party or that private content was made publicly available. An email message or reference letter sent to one recipient may be enough to damage someone's reputation, but many cases of libel or invasion of privacy involve wider distribution of defamatory or private content. Broad dissemination is most likely to involve content that is linked to communication technologies. Email messages may be sent to a wide audience, but content submitted to blogs and social media sites, which may consist of comments that are hastily written or ill-considered, pose the greatest risk. For risk avoidance, an organization can discontinue or sharply curtail the submission of content to blogs and social media sites, but that mitigation strategy might conflict with marketing campaigns or other publicity initiatives that capitalize on a social media presence.

Insurance provides a transfer option for litigation risks related to libelous or private content. Commercial liability policies typically include coverage for legal expenses associated with litigation where the insured party's false statement or publication of private facts was done unknowingly or inadvertently without negligence or recklessness.[24] Some policies may cover settlement costs, but not punitive damages, up to a specified limit. Most policies exclude coverage for defamation of a competitor.

Litigation is triggered by harmful communication of libelous or private content, but the risk begins when defamatory or private information is created or collected; if such content is not created or collected, it cannot be disclosed. The most effective mitigation strategy addresses the creation and collection of data or documents with problematic content:

• By definition, a true statement cannot be defamatory. Creators of email messages, social media posts, reference letters, and other communications must thoroughly review all factual statements for accuracy and provability. Rumor, innuendo, and speculation that might harm the reputation of an individual or organization must be avoided. Any statements of opinion must be clearly identified as such.

• Email messages, social media posts, correspondence, and other communications must be thoroughly reviewed for private information about named individuals. Any information about a person's private life must be avoided in a communication unless it is already known to the recipient of the communication.

• Employees and other workplace participants must avoid collecting information that contains libelous or private information to minimize the possibility of incorporating false statements or private facts into communications.

• An organization must avoid creating detailed reference letters that evaluate a current or former employee's performance. To the extent that they are permitted at all, such letters should be limited to verifiable facts.

INFORMATION QUALITY

Adapting an idea from quality control of manufacturing processes, academic researchers and operations management specialists define *information quality* pragmatically as "fitness for purpose."[25] This definition views information as raw material for the production of databases, documents, and other records. *Fitness for purpose* is determined subjectively by the intended user who may be an employee, a customer, a healthcare provider, a patient, an attorney, an auditor, a manager, an engineer, a researcher, a student, or any other person who needs to access the information for a given task. As in manufacturing, the information must satisfy the consumer's requirements.[26] Quality is an attribute of information that meets or exceeds the intended consumer's expectations. Measured in this way, information quality is a relative concept.[27] The same information may be useful for one purpose and unacceptable for another. Some disciplines—such as financial auditing, medicine, scientific research, cartography, and engineering—set a very high bar for information quality.

Information quality is sometimes equated with data quality. The two concepts are closely aligned, but they are not interchangeable. Adapting a general definition presented in ISO 9000:2015, *Quality Management Systems— Fundamentals and Vocabulary*, the ISO 8000-2:2018 standard, *Data Quality—Part 2: Vocabulary* defines *data quality* as the "degree to which a set of inherent characteristics of data fulfills requirements," which are defined as needs or expectations that are "stated, generally implied or obligatory." But data quality is typically concerned with database content, while the quality concerns discussed in this section apply to information of all types in all formats. In this respect, data quality is properly considered a subset of information quality. The same quality assessment concepts apply in both cases, but data quality initiatives typically focus on identification and correction of errors and inconsistencies in database content. Information quality, by contrast, addresses a broader range of issues, including objectivity, reliability, precision, and verifiability of information.[28]

Quality information is essential for decision-making, accounting, transaction processing, customer service, product development, marketing, and other operations and activities. Within the framework of fitness for purpose, academic researchers have identified various attributes of quality information:[29] With respect to creation or collection, information must be accurate, complete, up to date, relevant, unbiased, appropriately detailed, consistent, and verifiable. Risk increases when one or more of these quality attributes are compromised or absent:

- The adverse consequences of poor-quality information include higher operating costs, lower revenue, missed business opportunities, delayed product launches, reduced cash flow, slower transaction processing, supply chain disruptions, erroneous product shipments, increased product returns, reduced customer satisfaction, tarnished reputation, decreased employee productivity, and wasted resources spent detecting and correcting errors.
- In information-dependent activities, defective content leads to defective work. In specialized fields like medical care, epidemiology, social services, food inspection, drug testing, environmental protection, civil engineering, and law enforcement, information-quality problems can endanger public health, welfare, and safety.

- Laws and regulations that mandate the collection of specific information for submission to government, as discussed above, also require that the information be accurate and complete. This requirement is stated in some cases[30] and implied in others. Failure to comply exposes an organization to fines and other penalties.[31]
- Apart from compliance failures, the adverse economic impact of information-quality problems can only be quantified in the context of specific business operations, but it can be substantial. One source cites three proprietary studies of unidentified companies that estimate the cost of data quality errors at 8 to 12 percent of revenue.[32]
- The negative effects of poor-quality information can cascade through multiple operations and activities. If a company overstates its inventory information, for example, its cost of goods sold will be understated, which will cause an overstatement of gross profit, net income, and the value of assets. These accounting errors will be carried over into financial statements that are consulted by business decision-makers, current shareholders, prospective investors, current and prospective business partners, and government regulators. When the errors are discovered, the company will be forced to restate its earnings, which will damage its reputation. If intentional misinformation is suspected, the company may be subject to regulatory investigation and criminal prosecution.

Vulnerability Assessment

Over the last quarter century, published reports have documented the prevalence of information-quality problems in a varied range of work environments and disciplines.[33] In a 2016 survey of two hundred information technology executives in North American companies with five hundred or more employees, 81 percent of respondents said that their organizations believe their data quality is better than it really is, and 94 percent said that business value was lost because of poor data quality.[34] A 2017 summary of data quality measurements by seventy-five executives over a three-year period found that 47 percent of newly created records had at least one work-impacting error.[35] In any given organization, it is highly likely that employees, consultants, contractors, and other workplace participants are creating or collecting information that is inaccurate, obsolete, insufficiently detailed, obtained from unreliable sources, difficult to verify, confusing, redundant, irrelevant, or otherwise unfit for its intended purpose.[36] Unacceptable information quality may result from carelessness, inadequate training, misinterpretation, or negligence.

Database records, the focus of data quality concerns, may contain typographical errors as well as missing, obsolete, misspelled, inconsistent, or meaningless information about an organization's employees, customers, suppliers, products, inventory, orders, accounting transactions, or other matters. Rounded numbers or estimates may be substituted for precise values. Errors, duplication, and inconsistencies may be introduced when database content is imported from external sources or when application-specific databases are merged. Multiple application-specific databases may have different billing addresses, shipping addresses, or contact information for the same customer. Complexity increases in organizations that maintain information in multiple countries and multiple languages. These problems are widely recognized by quality-control specialists, technology managers, database administrators, and business unit employees whose work is affected by them.

The quality of information in reports, email messages, presentations, and other unstructured business documents has received less attention than database content, but it is no less commonplace or problematic. Business documents may contain unjustified assumptions, false statements, inadequately documented claims, speculation presented as fact, quotes taken out of context, statistics from unreliable sources, or other misinformation that renders the documents unfit for planning, decision-making, or other purposes. This misleading content may be incorporated into web pages, social media posts, promotional materials, or other publicly available resources. These concerns are not limited to textual information. Photographs, video recordings, audio recordings, and other media may be altered, incorrectly identified, or presented out of context. Problems of scale, formatting, positional accuracy, and age can render geographic information system (GIS) data unfit for use, as can intentional alteration to reduce the amount of detail in a cartographic data set. Some commercially available GIS datasets intentionally include nonexistent streets, phantom towns, or other false information to expose copyright violations.

Risk Response

Information-quality problems are endemic and inevitable in organizations of all types and sizes. All organizations create and collect some information that is unfit for its intended purpose. Risk avoidance is not possible. Risk transfer through insurance is not an option for most information-quality problems. Errors and omissions coverage is typically limited to professionals and technology companies that provide advice or services. An effective mitigation strategy must combine risk acceptance with a risk limitation plan.

Because perfect information is unachievable, acceptance of information-quality problems is a necessary component of an organization's risk mitigation strategy, but there are no published standards or guidelines that specify a reasonable percentage of quality problems for a given use case. User expectations, the measure of quality, are context-specific. Every organization must define acceptable information-quality levels for specific types of information and the tasks they support. For a database created for a drug trial, for example, a clinical investigator might require a 95 percent quality level for patient information that is key-entered from case report forms or imported from electronic sources. By contrast, a charitable organization might be satisfied with an 85 percent quality level for names, street addresses, and email addresses in a purchased mailing list that will be used for donor solicitations, recognizing that 15 percent of the solicitations will be undeliverable. Acceptable quality levels for reports, presentations, web pages, and other documents are more difficult to determine. The quality level for a report submitted to a regulatory agency should be as close to 100 percent as possible, but a company may be satisfied with a 75 percent or lower quality level for an analysis of a competitor's likely future plans for product development. Such an analysis may combine facts with speculation that may be interesting but useless. Isolated quality issues related to information from unattributed sources or insufficiently detailed content may be inconsequential, but flawed information can have an adverse impact on an organization's strategic plans and business decisions. As noted above, reports, web pages, and other documents may contain misinformation that is completely unacceptable and unfit for any purpose.

As discussed in ISO 9001:2015, *Quality Management Systems—Requirements*, effective quality management depends on risk based thinking that emphasizes preventive actions. According to the widely adopted 1-10-100 rule developed by Total Quality Management (TQM) specialists, it costs ten times more to correct a quality problem than to prevent it and one hundred times more if the problem is uncorrectable.[37] In line with this concept, an effective risk mitigation strategy must incorporate quality concepts into the information-creation and -collection process:

- Quality-management specialists emphasize the importance of building organizational awareness through top management commitment, goal setting, training, and progress assessment. Line managers must understand and take responsibility for the quality of information created or collected by employees and other workplace participants. System planners must work with users to establish attainable quality expectations for information-dependent business processes. Workplace participants involved in creation or collection of information must receive appropriate training.
- An ongoing audit program must identify information-quality problems, determine their causes, and develop improvement plans, but organizations should focus on building quality into their information-creation and -collection activities so that problem-correction requirements are minimized.
- In research, marketing, product development, customer service, program evaluation, and other activities, database content is often derived from information obtained through questionnaires, surveys, and web forms.

These data collection instruments, whether self-administered or intended for use by trained staff, must be reviewed for reading level, clarity, completeness, and suitability for data tabulation and analysis. Questions must be straightforward and designed to elicit responses that will be fit for purpose. Instructions must be concise, understandable, and easy to follow. Data collection instruments should be pretested on a pilot sample before they are rolled out to all respondents. [38]

- Data entry errors can have an adverse impact on a database's fitness for purpose. To address this significant aspect of database quality, data entry procedures and expectations should be clearly defined, strictly enforced, and closely monitored. Double data entry—in which all data is typed twice, either by the same operator or a different one—should be used for mission-critical data values. [39] Text-to-speech programs can also be used to confirm correct data entry.

- For information exported from external sources or for databases created in the past, data cleaning—also known as data cleansing or data scrubbing— can detect and correct typographical errors, invalid or inconsistent data values, improperly formatted data values, out-of-range values, duplicate data, missing data values, and other quality problems in database records. Data warehouses, federated databases, and other decision-support technologies that aggregate information from a variety of sources must have an effective method of identifying and removing these irregularities. Data cleaning is also important for data mining, machine learning, data modeling, and data visualization. Data cleaning software tools are available from a number of suppliers. These tools can detect errors, inconsistencies, and other anomalies in a given collection of data and make and verify corrections, but some remediation work may require manual intervention. [40]

- To address inconsistent and redundant content in application-specific databases, master data management (MDM) software creates a master data hub that collects and consolidates existing information about a specific matter. A master data hub may contain information about customers, products, suppliers, materials, facilities, or employees, for example. The master data hub is an authoritative, up-to-date reference resource for information that is processed by multiple applications. MDM implementations typically utilize data cleaning tools that identify conflicting data, missing data elements, improperly formatted data, misspellings, inconsistent abbreviations, and other problems. Some MDM software validates data against external information sources, such as a postal reference file or a database of standard abbreviations. MDM software can also identify and remove duplicate data.

- Because quality content begins at the source, collection of information for inclusion in reports, email messages, and other documents should be limited to reliable sources. The accuracy and completeness of a given source will have a significant impact on a document's fitness for purpose. For information derived from observation, interviews, focus groups, or self-administered surveys, the reliability of the persons who provided the information should be verified.

- To the extent possible, preference should be given to information that can be confirmed by observation, that comes from a reputable source with proven expertise and credibility, or that is reported by multiple sources, assuming that all of the sources are trustworthy. Decision-makers must verify the reliability of information before using it.

SUMMARY OF MAJOR POINTS

- Many laws and regulations mandate the collection of specific information for submission to government agencies. Failure to comply with these information-collection requirements exposes an organization to fines and other penalties.
- Many countries have data protection and privacy laws and regulations that restrict or prohibit the collection of personal information. Data minimization is the underlying principle for these laws and regulations. Collection of personal information must be limited to the minimum amount necessary for a specific, explicit, and legitimate purpose. Failure to comply with data minimization requirements exposes an organization to civil and criminal penalties.
- Various laws prohibit unauthorized collection of trade secrets or other nonpublic information from competitors or other sources. While such information may be obtained without an organization's knowledge or authorization, its possession is illegal in most countries.
- An organization that approves or tolerates the creation or collection of documents or other records with objectionable content may violate laws that prohibit workplace harassment as a form of employment discrimination.
- Creation or collection of defamatory or private information exposes an organization to significant litigation risks.
- Information must be accurate, complete, up to date, relevant, unbiased, appropriately detailed, and verifiable. Risk increases when one or more of these quality attributes are compromised or absent. The adverse consequences of poor-quality information include higher operating costs, lower revenue, and diminished productivity.

NOTES

1. Government-wide OMB estimates for active information collections are updated regularly at www.reginfo.gov/public/do/PRAReport?operation=11. Agency-specific estimates are available at www.reginfo.gov/public/do/PRAMain.

2. This is the definition of personally identifiable information (PII) presented in 2 C.F.R. § 200.79, OMB Memorandum M-07-16 issued by the Office of Management and Budget (www.whitehouse.gov/sites/whitehouse.gov/files/omb/memoranda/2007/m07-16.pdf), Report GAO-08-343 issued by the Government Accountability Office (www.gao.gov/new.items/d08343.pdf), and other US government sources. ISO /IEC 29100:2011, *Information Technology—Security Techniques—Privacy Framework* defines *personally identifiable information* as any information that can be directly or indirectly linked to a PII principal—that is, to a "natural person" to whom the PII relates.

3. The official text of the regulation and its recitals, which provide additional details about the specific requirements, are available at https://gdpr-info.eu.

4. Examples of publications that survey national privacy and data protection laws include W. Leichter and D. Berman, *Global Guide to Data Protection Laws: Understanding Privacy and Compliance Requirements in More than 80 Countries* (San Jose, CA: CipherCloud, 2018); G. Greenleaf, *Global Privacy Laws 017: 120 National Data Privacy Laws, Including Indonesia and Turkey* (Sydney, Australia: University of New South Wales, 2017), https://papers.ssrn.com/sol3/papers.cfm?abstract_id=2993035; G. Greenleaf, *Asian Data Privacy Laws: Trade & Human Rights Perspectives* (Oxford: Oxford University Press, 2014); L. Bygrave, *Data Privacy Law: An International Perspective* (Oxford: Oxford University Press, 2014); D. Banisar and S. Davies, "Global Trends in Privacy Protection: an International Survey of Privacy, Data Protection, and Surveillance Laws and Developments," *John Marshall Journal of Information Technology & Privacy Law* 18, no. 1 (1999): 1–111, https://repository.jmls.edu/cgi/viewcontent.cgi?article=1174&context=jitpl.

5. The Fair Information Practice Principles were initially proposed by a federal advisory committee in 1973 as the Code of Fair Information Practice, which formed the basis for the Privacy Act of 1974 (5 U.S.C. § 552a). The principles were subsequently expanded for inclusion in the *OECD Guidelines on the Protection of Privacy and Transborder Flows of Personal Data*, which were issued by the Organization for Economic Cooperation and Development in 1980 (www.oecd.org/internet/ieconomy/oecdguidelinesontheprotectionofprivacyandtransborderflowsofpersonaldata.htm).

6. In keeping with the Fair Information Practice Principles, the USA FREEDOM Act of 2015 (Pub. Law 114-23), the successor to the USA PATRIOT Act, limited the National Security Agency's authority to collect information about private telephone calls, a practice that was revealed in 2013 by Edward J. Snowden, a former intelligence contractor. See *Transparency Report: The USA FREEDOM Act Business Records FISA Implementation* issued by the NSA Civil Liberties and Privacy Office in January 2016. (www.nsa.gov/Portals/70/documents/about/civil-liberties/reports/UFA_Civil_Liberties_and_Privacy_Report.pdf).

7. In 2013, Hershey's and Mrs. Fields Original Cookies agreed to civil penalties of $85,000 and $100,000, respectively, for collecting children's personal information without appropriate parental consent. In 2014, Yelp agreed to a civil penalty of $400,000 for alleged COPPA violations, while TinyCo, a developer of mobile apps targeted at children, was fined $300,000. In 2019, TikTok, developers of an app for creating and sharing short videos, agreed to pay $5.7 million, the largest civil penalty in a children's privacy case, to settle accusations that it had failed to obtain parental consent for users under age 13. A study found that many free children's apps collect personal information in a manner that violates COPPA. See I. Reyes et al., "Won't Somebody Think of the Children? Examining COPPA Compliance at Scale," *Proceedings on Privacy Enhancing Technologies* 2018, no. 3 (2018): 63–83, https://petsymposium.org/2018/files/papers/issue3/popets-2018-0021.pdf.

8. See, for example, N. Richards and W. Hartzog, "Trusting Big Data Research," *DePaul Law Review* 66, no. 2 (2017): 579–90, https://via.library.depaul.edu/cgi/viewcontent.cgi?article=4022&context=law-review; I. Rubinstein, "Big Data: The End of Privacy or a New Beginning," *International Data Privacy Laws* 3, no. 2 (2013): 74–87, https://

papers.ssrn.com/sol3/papers.cfm?abstract_id=2157659; T. Zarsky, "Incompatible: The GDPR in the Age of Big Data," *Seton Hall Law Review* 47, no. 4 (2017): 995–1020, https://scholarship.shu.edu/shlr/vol47/iss4/2/; E. Gray and J. Thorpe, "Comparative Effectiveness Research and Big Data: Balancing Potential with Legal and Ethical Considerations," *Journal of Comparative Effectiveness Research* 4, no. 1 (2015): 61–74, www.ncbi.nlm.nih.gov/pubmed/25565069.

9. Privacy by Design (PbD) concepts and principles originated in Canada in the 1990s. See A. Cavoukian, *Operationalizing Privacy by Design: A Guide to Implementing Strong Privacy Practices* (Toronto: Information and Privacy Commissioner, Ontario, Canada, 2012), www.ontla.on.ca/library/repository/mon/26012/320221.pdf.

10. The significance of these processes for GDPR compliance is discussed in many publications. See, for example, S. Stalla-Bourdillon and A. Knight, "Anonymous Data v. Personal Data—A False Debate: An EU Perspective on Anonymization, Pseudonymization and Personal Data," *Wisconsin International Law Journal* 34, no. 2 (2017): 285–322, http://hosted.law.wisc.edu/wordpress/wilj/files/2017/12/Stalla-Bourdillon_Final.pdf; L. Bolognini and C. Bistolfi, "Pseudonymization and Impacts of Big (Personal/Anonymous) Data Processing in the Transition from the Directive 95/46/EC to the New EU General Data Protection Regulation," *Computer Law & Security Review* 33, no. 2 (2017): 171–81, www.sciencedirect.com/science/article/pii/S0267364916302151; and M. Hintze, "Viewing the GDPR through a De-Identification Lens: A Tool for Clarification and Compliance," *International Data Privacy Law* 8, no. 1 (2018): 86–101, https://academic.oup.com/idpl/article-abstract/8/1/86/4763693?redirectedFrom=fulltext.

11. A Wyoming law deals with an unusual form of data theft. WY Sta. §§ 6-3-414 and 40-27-101 prohibits the collection of "resource data" when such collection involves trespassing on private lands, even if the trespass is unintentional or incidental to the collection. *Resource data* is defined as information relating to land or land use, including agriculture, minerals, geology, history, cultural artifacts, archeology, vegetation, or animal species. The law defines *collection* broadly to encompass acquisition of information in any form. Violations are punishable by imprisonment for up to one year and fines ranging from $1,000 to $5,000. The owner of the property can also bring a civil action against a trespasser for consequential and economic damages caused by illegal collection of resource data.

12. Conflicting opinions are presented in two widely publicized legal cases involving journalists. In 1969, the U.S. Court of Appeals for the District of Columbia Circuit held that Drew Pearson and Jack Anderson, two popular syndicated columnists, were not liable for receiving office records, letters from constituents, and other nonpublic information about Connecticut Senator Thomas Dodd even though they knew that the information had been stolen by the senator's staff. On the other hand, Chief Justice Warren Berger's 1971 dissent in the Pentagon Papers case said that the *New York Times* should be held liable for receiving and publishing stolen property. See K. Middleton et al., *The Law of Public Communication: 2017 Update to the Ninth Edition* (New York: Routledge, 2017), 202–3.

13. The chairman of Pirelli, a tire manufacturer, was found guilty in 2013 for receiving stolen information when he was the head of Telecom Italia. The information, which was delivered to Telecom Italia's headquarters on a DVD in a package without a return address, had been stolen in 2004 from a security agency in Brazil that was allegedly spying on Telecom Italia. Even though the defendant immediately turned the information over to Brazilian and Italian judicial authorities, he received a twenty-month suspended jail sentence and was ordered to pay €900,000. In a related development, the former head of security at Telecom Italia received a prison sentence for collecting private information about prominent Italians. For other examples, see S. Becker, "Discovery of Information and Documents from a Litigant's Former Employees: Synergy and Synthesis of Civil Rules, Ethical Standards, Privilege Doctrines, and Common Law Principles," *Nebraska Law Review* 81, no. 3 (2002/2003): 869–1007, https://digitalcommons.unl.edu/cgi/viewcontent.cgi?article=1345&context=nlr.

14. Insider trading laws restrict or prohibit investment decisions that are based on nonpublic information, but such laws are concerned with the use of nonpublic information rather than its collection and possession.

15. In one of the most widely publicized industrial espionage cases, a former General Motors executive was accused of transferring proprietary information to Volkswagen, his new employer, in 1993. He allegedly began collecting the information in anticipation of changing jobs and used Volkswagen's corporate aircraft to ship seventy boxes of GM documents containing product plans and pricing information from Detroit to Germany, where they were input directly into Volkswagen's computers. To settle the resulting civil suit, Volkswagen agreed to pay General Motors $100 million and to buy $1 billion of GM parts.

16. As an example, the New York State Human Rights Law §296 prohibits employment discrimination based on age, race, creed, color, national origin, sexual orientation, gender identity or expression, military status, sex, disability, predisposing genetic characteristics, family status, marital status, or domestic violence status. The New York City Human Rights Law (Title 8 of the Administrative Code of the City of New York) contains similar prohibitions.

17. In 1995, Chevron Corporation agreed to pay $2.2 million to settle sexual harassment charges by four employees who were the targets of disparaging sexual comments, offensive jokes, and pornography sent through the company's email system. (*Nardinelli et al v. Chevron*, No. 945302, Superior Court, California, 1995). The defendant had an anti-harassment policy that required training for all employees, but compliance was not monitored. In 1998, Morgan Stanley settled a lawsuit filed by two African American employees who claimed they were subject to a hostile work environment after complaining about an internal email that contained racist jokes (*Owens et al. v. Morgan Stanley et al.*, No. 96 Civ. 9747 [DLC], SD NY, settlement Feb. 10, 1998).

18. In 2017, an African American employee sued a New York City hotel for creating a hostile workplace when a co-worker sent a group email with an attached video that contained racial epithets, but the court concluded a single incident of racial harassment was not sufficiently pervasive to constitute a hostile work environment (*Cromwell-Gibbs v. Staybridge Suite Times Square*, No. 16 CIV. 5169 [KPF], WL 2684063 [S.D.N.Y. June 20, 2017]).

19. N. Maestas et al., *How Americans Perceive the Workplace: Results from the American Working Conditions Survey* (Santa Monica, CA: RAND Corporation, 2017), https://doi.org/10.7249/RB9972.

20. www.hiscox.com/documents/2018-Hiscox-Workplace-Harassment-Study.pdf.

21. K. Clancy et al., "Survey of Academic Field Experiences (SAFE): Trainees Report Harassment and Assault," *PLoS ONE* 9, no. 7 (2014): e102172, https://doi.org/10.1371/journal.pone.0102172.

22. R. Jagsi et al., "Sexual Harassment and Discrimination Experiences of Academic Medical Faculty," *Journal of the American Medical Association* 315, no. 19 (2016): 2120–21, https://jamanetwork.com/journals/jama/fullarticle/2521958?appId=scweb.

23. New York State Human Rights Law, § 296-C, for example, prohibits "unwelcome harassment" that creates "an intimidating, hostile, or offensive working environment" for unpaid interns. According to § 296-D, an organization may be held liable for sexual harassment of contractors, subcontractors, vendors, and consultants if appropriate corrective action is not taken immediately.

24. Media liability insurance is a specialized type of business liability insurance that covers defamation and invasion of privacy claims against authors, bloggers, publishers, broadcasters, public speakers, advertising agencies, public relations agencies, and other media professionals.

25. ISO 9000:2015, *Quality Management Systems—Fundamentals and Vocabulary*, defines *quality* as the degree to which a set of inherent characteristics of an object fulfills requirements. This quality concept applies to both goods and services. See J. Juran, "Attaining Superior Results through Quality," in *Juran's Quality Handbook: The Complete Guide*, 6th ed., ed. J. Juran and J. Defeo (New York: McGraw-Hill, 2010), 5: "To be fit for purpose, every good and service must have the right features to satisfy customer needs and must be delivered with few failures."

26. This consumer-centric perspective is in keeping with W. Edwards Deming's quality management dictum that "the consumer is the most import part of the production line." See J. Orsini, ed., *The Essential Deming: Leadership Principles from the Father of Quality Control* (New York: McGraw Hill, 2013), 176–78. On the implications of Deming's approach to total quality management for information quality, see L. English, *Information Quality Applied: Best*

Practices for Improving Business Information, Processes, and Systems (Indianapolis: Wiley Publishing, 2009), 32–41. On the concept of information as a product, see R. Wang et al., "Manage Your Information as a Product," *Sloan Management Review* 39, no. 4 (1998), 95–105.

27. Guidelines developed by the Federal Trade Commission for the Data Quality Act, which amended the Paperwork Reduction Act (44 U.S.C. 3501 et seq.), cite usefulness as one of the three essential characteristics of quality information. The other two are objectivity, which means that the information is clear and complete, and integrity, which means that the information has not been corrupted or falsified. The guidelines have been adopted by other agencies. www.ftc.gov/data-quality-act/guidelines-for-ensuring.

28. In popular speech, the terms *information* and *data* have been used interchangeably since the nineteenth century, as evidenced by Sherlock Holmes's impatient statement in *The Adventure of the Copper Beeches*: "Data! Data! Data! . . . I can't make bricks without clay." The previously cited ISO 8000-2 standard, however, differentiates *data*, which it defines as a "reinterpretable representation of information in a formalized manner suitable for communication, interpretation, or processing" from *information*, which it defines as "knowledge concerning objects, such as facts, events, things, processes, or ideas, including concepts, that within a certain context has a particular meaning." Mirroring the manufacturing analogy noted above, these definitions treat information as processed data. As in manufacturing, quality input is necessary for a satisfactory product.

29. See, for example, Y. Huh et al., "Data Quality," *Information and Software Technology* 32, no. 8 (1990), 559–65, https://doi.org/10.1016/0950-5849(90)90146-I; R. Wang and D. Strong, "Beyond Accuracy: What Data Quality Means to Data Consumers," *Journal of Management Information Systems* 12, no. 4 (1996): 5–33, http://mitiq.mit.edu/Documents/Publications/TDQMpub/14_Beyond_Accuracy.pdf; M. Eppler and D. Wittig, "Conceptualizing Information Quality: A Review of Information Quality Frameworks for the Last Ten Years," in *Proceedings of the 2000 International Conference on Information Quality* (Cambridge, MA: MIT Information Quality Program, 2000), 83–96, http://mitiq.mit.edu/ICIQ/Documents/IQ%20Conference%202000/Papers/ConceptIQaReviewofIQFramework.pdf; B. Kahn et al., "Information Quality Benchmarks: Product and Service Performance," *Communications of the ACM* 45, no. 4 (2002): 184–92, https://dl.acm.org/citation.cfm?doid=505248.506007; L. Pipino et al., "Data Quality Assessment," *Communications of the ACM*, 45, no. 4, (2002): 211–18, http://0374288.netsolhost.com/pdf/MIT-pipleewang.pdf; S. Knight and J. Burn, "Developing a Framework for Assessing Information Quality on the World Wide Web," *Informing Science Journal* 8 (2005): 159–72, https://doi.org/10.28945/493; R. Nelson et al., "Antecedents of Information and System Quality: An Empirical Examination within the Context of Data Warehousing," *Journal of Management Information Systems* 21, no. 4 (2005): 199–235, https://doi.org/10.1080/07421222.2005.11045823, S. Madnick et al., "Overview and Framework for Data and Information Quality Research," *ACM Journal on Data and Information Quality* 1, no. 1 (2009): article no. 2, https://dl.acm.org/citation.cfm?doid=1515693.1516680; J. Kandari et al., "Information Quality on the World Wide Web: A Framework to Measure Its Validation," in *IMCIC 2011—Second International Multi-Conference on Complexity, Informatics and Cybernetics, Proceedings, Volume 2* (Winter Garden, FL: International Institution of Informatics and Systematics, 2011), 204–9.

30. As specified in 21 C.F.R. 211.194, for example, good manufacturing practices for finished pharmaceuticals require accurate, complete records of all laboratory test processes and data. According to 21 C.F.R. 11.10, pharmaceutical companies must validate the accuracy and completeness of electronic records associated with regulated activities. As specified in 49 C.F.R. 107, subpart D, appendix A, the Pipeline and Hazardous Materials Safety Administration, a unit of the U.S. Department of Transportation, levies fines ranging from $1,200 to $3,700 for inaccurate or incomplete testing records. A study of FDA inspections of clinical trials over a thirty-two-year period found that inadequate or inaccurate records accounted for 27 percent of deficiencies. See S. K. Morgan-Linnell et al., "U.S. Food and Drug Administration Inspections of Clinical Investigators: Overview of Results from 1977 to 2009," *Clinical Cancer Research* 20, no. 13 (2014): 3364–70, http://clincancerres.aacrjournals.org/content/early/2014/04/15/1078-0432.CCR-13-3206.

31. As an example, CVS Pharmacy Inc. was fined $535,000 by the Department of Justice in 2019 for filing invalid prescriptions for Percocet, a narcotic, in violation of the Controlled Substances Act (www.justice.gov/usao-ri/pr/cvs-pay-535000-filling-invalid-prescriptions). In 2013, CVS agreed to pay $11 million to settle recordkeeping violations involving errors in prescription data and other matters (www.dea.gov/press-releases/2013/04/03/cvs-pay-11-million-settle-civil-penalty-claims-involving-violations-0).

32. T. C. Redman, "The Impact of Poor Data Quality on the Typical Enterprise," *Communications of the ACM* 41, no. 2 (1998): 79–82 (February 1998). Recent sources are even more pessimistic. A widely cited survey by Gartner Inc. estimates the average annual cost of poor data quality at $15 million due to poor decision-making, missed opportunities, and reputational losses (S. Moore, "How to Create a Business Case for Data Quality Improvement," June 19, 2018, www.gartner.com/smarterwithgartner/how-to-create-a-business-case-for-data-quality-improvement). In Gartner's 2015 survey, respondents estimated their average annual losses at $8.8 million. T. Redman, "Bad Data Costs the U.S. $3 Trillion Per Year," *Harvard Business Review* (web site), September 22, 2016 (https://hbr.org/2016/09/bad-data-costs-the-u-s-3-trillion-per-year), cites an estimate by IBM, but no calculations or supporting documentation are provided. Comments appended to the article dispute the IBM estimate.

33. Among the many examples that might be cited, a 1994 medical study found that 2.4 percent of the data collected in a multicenter field trial had significant errors that affected the study's decisions. (S. Arndt et al., "Effects of Errors in a Multicenter Medical Study: Preventing Misinterpreted Data," *Journal of Psychiatric Research* 28, no. 5, (1994): 447–59, https://doi.org/10.1016/0022-3956(94)90003-5. In a 1997 study, 50 to 85 percent of computerized criminal records in the United States were found to be inaccurate, incomplete, or ambiguous (D. Strong et al., "Data Quality in Context," *Communications of the ACM* 40, no. 55 (1997): 103–10, https://dl.acm.org/citation.cfm?id=253804). A 1998 study found that the error rate for birth certificate information ranged from 10 to 60 percent. (D. Green et al., "Are We Underestimating Rates of Vaginal Birth after Previous Cesarean Birth? The Validity of Delivery Methods from Birth Certificates," *American Journal of Epidemiology* 147, no. 6 (1998): 581–86, www.ncbi.nlm.nih.gov/pubmed/9521185. A study by the U.S. Department of Health and Human Services found that 48 percent of records for Medicare-enrolled providers in the National Plan and Provider Enumeration System and 58 percent of records in the Provider Enrollment, Chain, and Ownership System were inaccurate. Most of the errors related to addresses, which are essential for contacting providers and identifying fraud, waste, and abuse. See Department of the Inspector General, *Improvements Needed to Ensure Provider Enumeration and Medicare Enrollment Data Are Accurate, Complete, and Consistent*, OEI-07-09-00440 (Washington, DC: Department of Health and Human Services, May 2013), 17–22, https://oig.hhs.gov/oei/reports/oei-07-09-00440.pdf.

34. C. Lehman et al., *The State of Enterprise Data Quality: 2016—Perception, Reality and the Future of DQM.* (New York: 451 Research, 2016), https://siliconangle.com/files/2016/01/Blazent_State_of_Data_Quality_Management_2016.pdf.

35. T. Nagle et al., "Only 3% of Companies' Data Meets Basic Quality Standards," *Harvard Business Review* web site, September 11, 2017, https://hbr.org/2017/09/only-3-of-companies-data-meets-basic-quality-standards; T. Nagle et al., "Waking Up to Data Quality," *European Business Review* web site, May 12, 2018, www.europeanbusinessreview.com/waking-up-to-data-quality.

36. One of the earliest and most frequently cited discussions of information quality questions the assumption that relevant information improves management decision-making, noting that rather than lacking relevant information, most managers "suffer more from an overabundance of irrelevant information." R. Ackoff, "Management Misinformation Systems," *Management Sciences* 14, no. 4 (1967): 147–49, https://doi.org/10.1287/mnsc.14.4.B147.

37. This rule is mentioned in many quality-management publications. See, for example, Y. Chang, "Models for Assessing the Cost of Quality—Theory and Practice in the United States," in *Total Quality Measurement in the Oil Industry*, ed. J. Symonds (Dordrecht: Springer, 1994), https://doi.org/10.1007/978-94-011-1320-5_3. In a variation, S. Teli, "Cost of Quality in Automotive Industry and Essence of Knowledge Management," *JM International Journal of Management Research* 2, no. 3 (2012): 192–99, states that the cost to correct an error is ten times

the cost to do the work correctly, while the cost to correct an error detected by a customer is one hundred times more than the cost to do the work correctly and the cost will be a one thousand times more if a dissatisfied customer's experience is shared with others, www.researchgate.net/profile/S_Teli/publication/317428339_Cost_of_Quality_in_Automotive_Industry_Essence_of_Knowledge_Management/links/5947f53f0f7e9b1d9b230393/Cost-of-Quality-in-Automotive-Industry-Essence-of-Knowledge-Management.pdf.

38. For useful ideas about data collection instruments, see D. Vannette and J. Krosnick, eds., *The Palgrave Handbook of Survey Research* (London: Palgrave Macmillan, 2018).

39. The advantages and limitations of double-keying for scientific and medical research projects, which depend on accurate data entry, are discussed in various studies. Examples include S. Day et al., "Double Data Entry: What Value, What Price?" *Controlled Clinical Trials* 19, no. 1 (1998): 15–24, https://doi.org/10.1016/S0197-2456(97)00096-2; M. Kawado, "A Comparison of Error Detection Rates between the Reading Aloud Method and the Double Data Entry Method," *Controlled Clinical Trials* 24, no. 5 (2003): 560–69, https://doi.org/10.1016/S0197-2456(03)00089-8; K. Barchard and L. Pace, "Preventing Human Error: The Impact of Data Entry Methods on Data Accuracy and Statistical Results," *Computers in Human Behavior* 27, no. 5 (2011): 1834–39, https://doi.org/10.1016/j.chb.2011.04.004; C. Johnson et al., "An Evaluation of Data Entry Error and Proofing Methods for Fisheries Data," *Transactions of the American Fisheries Society*, 138, no. 3 (2009): 593–601, https://doi.org/10.1577/T08-075.1; H. Rieder and J. Lauritsen, "Quality Assurance of Data: Ensuring That Numbers Reflect Operational Definitions and Contain Real Measurements," *International Journal of Tuberculosis and Lung Disease* 15, no. 3 (2011): 296–304, www.ingentaconnect.com/content/iuatld/ijtld/2011/00000015/00000003/art00003#; A. Paulsen et al., "Quality of Data Entry Using Single Entry, Double Entry and Automated Forms Processing—An Example Based on a Study of Patient-Reported Outcomes," *PLoS ONE* 7, no. 4 (2012): e35087, https://doi.org/10.1371/journal.pone.0035087.

40. For an overview, see H. Wickham, "Tidy Data," *Journal of Statistical Software* 59, no. 10 (2014): 1–23, www.jstatsoft.org/article/view/v059i10; J. Osborne, *Best Practices in Data Cleaning*, (Thousand Oaks, CA: SAGE, 2013); J. Maletic and A. Marcus, "Data Cleansing: A Prelude to Knowledge Discovery," in *Data Mining and Knowledge Discovery Handbook*, ed. O. Maimon and L. Rokach (New York: Springer, 2005): 19–32; T. Dasu and T. Johnson, *Exploratory Data Mining and Data Cleaning* (Hoboken, NJ: Wiley-Interscience, 2003); E. Rahm and H. Do, "Data Cleaning: Problems and Current Approaches," *Bulletin of the Technical Committee on Data Engineering* 23, no. 4 (2000): 3–13, http://sites.computer.org/debull/A00dec/DecA00-a4final.ps.

Chapter Three

Loss of Information

Loss of information, sometimes termed *data loss*, occurs when information is destroyed, damaged, altered, or otherwise rendered unavailable or unusable before its useful life has elapsed. Various sources identify and categorize threatening events and situations that can damage or destroy information.[1] International standards recognize prevention of information loss and recovery of lost information as essential for business continuity.[2] Loss of information can have an adverse impact on mission-critical business operations, and in extreme circumstances, it threatens an organization's continued viability. In some cases, loss of information with unique content can have a more significant effect on an organization's mission than the loss of physical property, inventory, raw materials, and other physical assets, which are often replaceable. Information loss can also expose an organization to regulatory fines and penalties for failure to comply with legally mandated recordkeeping requirements. Unintentional information loss is not an acceptable excuse for failing to have records that are required by laws and regulations. For archival agencies, manuscript libraries, and other downstream repositories that receive data and documents from external sources, information loss by an originating entity affects the future availability of scholarly resources.

This chapter identifies and discusses risks associated with four significant threats to information:

- natural disasters, which are caused by forces beyond human control;
- malicious human actions, including malicious software that destroys or damages information, geopolitical events that may damage information in the course of destructive activities, vandalism that results in destruction of information, and theft of information;

- accidents, which may result from human error or technological malfunction; and
- fire, which is related to and may be the result of other destructive events.

As discussed in the following sections, information loss associated with these threats may be intentional or incidental. While some of the threats have a low likelihood of occurrence, their consequences for information-dependent operations, activities, and initiatives can be devastating. For the most part, the threats listed above are uncontrollable, unpredictable, unacceptable and unavoidable, but their adverse effects can be limited or transferred. This chapter does not discuss storage-related information loss that is attributable to environmental conditions, time-dependent degradation of storage media, and file format obsolescence. Those threats will be covered in the next chapter.

NATURAL DISASTERS

Broadly defined, a natural disaster is a serious adverse event caused by natural forces.[3] Disasters that threaten information may result from meteorological, geological, hydrological, climatological, or extraterrestrial hazards:

- The most important and frequently cited meteorological hazards are hurricanes, tropical cyclones, nontropical wind storms, tornadoes, ice storms, and hail storms.
- Geological hazards include earthquakes, volcanic eruptions, landslides, rockslides, mudslides, snow avalanches, and sinkholes.
- Hydrological hazards include river flooding resulting from sustained rainfall, snow melting, or ice melting; tsunamis, which are usually linked to earthquakes or other geological events; and storm surges caused by cyclones or nontropical storms.
- Climatological hazards include extreme heat, extreme cold, extreme humidity, and drought.
- Biological hazards include insect infestations, molds, fungi, and rodents.
- Extraterrestrial hazards include solar storms and high-velocity impact by asteroids, comets, or other extraterrestrial objects in earth-crossing orbits.

Widely cited scales measure the damage potential of these natural hazards,[4] while insurance statistics confirm their destructiveness. According to Munich Re Group, one of the world's largest reinsurers, 848 natural disasters accounted for approximately $180 billion in global losses in 2018.[5] For the period from 1960 through 2009, total monetary losses attributable to natural disasters exceeded $2 trillion in the United States alone.[6]

The role of natural disasters in destruction of information has been widely recognized for decades.[7] Meteorological, geological, and hydrological hazards, which accounted for over 93 percent of natural disasters in 2018, threaten information by destroying offices, data centers, record storage facilities, and other property where information is housed or by damaging electrical transmission lines and disrupting communication networks that are necessary to operate computer systems and access information. Windstorms, earthquakes, flooding, and other disastrous events can bring accounting, order processing, customer service, and other information-dependent business operations to an immediate standstill that may last for days, weeks, or longer. Loss of electrical power may put computer systems out of service or make cloud-based computer services inaccessible. Some business operations may be suspended indefinitely.[8]

Natural disasters can damage or destroy information that is needed to comply with legal and regulatory recordkeeping requirements, including preservation orders for information considered relevant for litigation, government investigations, or other legal proceedings. By destroying information or rendering computer systems inoperable, a natural disaster can disrupt transaction processing, customer service, marketing, project management, and other business operations. Information that exists in a single copy may be lost permanently, in which case an organization may be exposed to litigation for failing to properly protect information that is needed by clients, patients, students, shareholders, or others. A survey of US companies affected by meteorological, geological, and hydrological disasters in 2016 and 2017 found that 96 percent had revenue losses.[9] Compared to larger organizations, small businesses are less likely to survive a natural disaster. According to data collected by the Federal Emergency Management Agency and U.S. Department of Labor in 2014, 40 percent of small businesses damaged by a hurricane never reopen, and 25 percent will close within one year.[10] Some small businesses may not qualify for disaster-relief loans because the required financial records were destroyed.

Compared to meteorological, geological, and hydrological events, the harmful effects of climatological hazards on information are less immediate and more difficult to quantify, but extreme heat and drought conditions exacerbate wildfires, which can destroy buildings and computer systems that store information.[11] Over a longer timeframe, extreme temperatures and high humidity can adversely affect the operation of computer systems and damage paper records and electronic media. Mold, fungi, vermin, and other biological hazards pose similar problems that will be discussed in chapter 4.[12] While extraterrestrial hazards are not commonplace, solar storms generate radiation and high-energy particles that can cause computer system and network failures. Solar storms can also damage communication satellites and terrestrial communication links that are essential for transmission of information.[13]

Extraterrestrial objects have collided with the earth but are not known to have damaged information.

Vulnerability Assessment

An organization's vulnerability to information loss from a natural disaster depends on two factors: the likelihood of occurrence of the disaster, which varies with geography and the type of disaster, and the ability to recover the lost information after the disaster occurs. The likelihood of occurrence of a given natural disaster in a specific location in any given year is based on the disaster's return period, which is the estimated time interval between natural disasters of a given type in that location; the shorter the return period, the higher the risk of occurrence. [14] A natural disaster with a return period of one hundred years, for example, has a 1 in 100 (1 percent) chance of occurring in a given location in any given year, while a disaster with a return period of ten years in the same location is ten times more likely to occur in a given year.

Estimated return periods are based on historical data for a specific location and type of disaster, but the average annual frequency of occurrence is not the same as probability of occurrence within a given time frame. Statistically, a natural disaster with a 100-year return period has a 9.6 percent chance of occurring within a ten-year period, a 26 percent chance of occurring within a thirty-year period, and a 39.5 chance of occurring within a fifty-year period. [15] As a complicating factor, natural disasters with long return periods may recur at shorter intervals. A destructive storm with a return period of ten years might recur multiple times within that time frame, but this does not invalidate the return period, which is an average value estimated over a longer span of time. A natural disaster with a return period of ten years is unlikely to occur more than ten times in a century. A natural disaster with a return period of one hundred years is unlikely to occur more than ten times in a millennium.

Hurricanes and tropical cyclones pose significant risks for information that is maintained in coastal areas. The National Oceanic and Atmospheric Administration estimates return periods ranging from five years to fifty years for hurricanes with sustained winds of seventy-four miles per hour (category 1) or greater in US coastal locations along the Gulf of Mexico and the Atlantic Ocean. [16] Many government agencies, companies, and not-for-profit organizations store information in offices, data centers, and record storage facilities in those areas. The locations with the shortest return periods and highest risk of a hurricane measuring category 1 or greater are along the coast of south Florida and North Carolina, where the chance of occurrence in any given year ranges from 14 to 20 percent. The longest return periods and lowest risk are for coastal locations along the north Atlantic Ocean from Massachusetts to Maine, where the chance of occurrence in any given year is just 2 to 3 percent. Return periods are longer and probability estimates are lower for more severe storms. For a category 3 hurricane, which is capable of producing devastating damage, return periods range from sixteen to eighteen years along the south Florida and North Carolina coasts to 170 to 290 years for the upper New England coast.[17]

In the late twentieth century, the Global Seismic Hazard Assessment Program, a United Nations initiative, identified the geographic locations that are at greatest risk for earthquakes.[18] Most earthquakes and volcanic eruptions have occurred along the so-called "ring of fire," a horseshoe-shaped area measuring 25,000 miles that stretches along the edges of the Pacific Ocean from New Zealand along the eastern edge of Asia then across the Aleutian Island through Alaska and down the western coasts of North America and South America.[19] Recurrence periods are difficult to calculate for earthquakes, which can vary in intensity and duration.[20] National seismic hazard maps prepared by the U.S. Geological Survey estimate the likelihood of ground shaking events of a given magnitude in a specific US location in a given time frame.[21] The most vulnerable areas for high magnitude earthquakes are the coast of Alaska, which is sparsely populated, and the coast of California, which has information-rich metropolitan areas. Locations in Oklahoma, Missouri, Arkansas, Tennessee, and other parts of the central United States may experience minor ground shaking that can cause minor damage. In seismically active areas, earthquake-resistant construction may limit damage to information maintained in offices, data centers, record storage facilities, and other repositories.

Tornadoes occur more frequently than hurricanes and earthquakes, but the estimated return period for a given location is longer. In the United States, over 1,200 tornadoes of varying intensity occur annually, but many of these measure EF0 or EF1 (minor or moderate damage) on the Enhanced Fujita scale. Less than 1 percent have severe damage potential, and successive storms in the same location occur at long intervals.[22] The return period at a given location for a storm measuring EF2 (significant damage) or greater in the most tornado-prone parts of the United States is four thousand to ten thousand years. For the most destructive tornadoes (EF4 or EF5), the estimated return interval is too long to calculate reliably.[23] While tornadoes might form in any geographic location, most occur in the central part of the North America from northern Texas to southern Canada, in the southeastern United States, and less commonly in the upper Midwest.[24] Outside of those areas, the risk of a destructive tornado is low.

Flooding poses significant risks for information that is maintained in ground-floor or sub-grade areas in office buildings, data centers, record storage facilities, or other structures adjacent to coastlines, rivers, streams, estuaries, harbors, canals, or other bodies of water that might overflow their banks. Information stored below grade level can also be damaged by surface runoff during periods of heavy rainfall. Flood-prone locations—so-called flood plans—are often characterized by the estimated time interval between inundations. Widely used numbers range from ten years to five hundred years. The Federal Emergency Management Agency has mapped flood zones in all US locations. Areas in the 100-year flood plan have a 1 percent annual likelihood of flooding with average depths of one to three feet or a 26 percent chance of such flooding within a thirty-year period. As with other natural disasters, however, a less devastating incident—water seeping into a basement following a heavy rainstorm, for example—is more likely to occur than pervasive flooding.

The ability to recover lost information following a natural disaster depends on the availability of backup copies. Systematic preparation of backup copies of databases, computer files, email messages, and other electronic information is a well-established disaster-recovery practice in government agencies, companies, and not-for-profit organizations. In some circumstances, backup operations are mandated by government regulations.[25] An organization can create backup copies by online transmission of information to a remote server, which may be operated by the organization itself or by a cloud-based service provider. Alternatively, backup copies can be produced at regular intervals on magnetic tapes or other physical media, which may be sent to a storage facility operated by a commercial provider.

While these backup practices permit recovery of information that is damaged or destroyed by natural disasters, vulnerabilities remain in the following areas:

- In many organizations, full backup copies produced weekly are supplemented by incremental backup copies, which are produced nightly or at other predetermined intervals for information that has changed since the last full backup operation. This method allows recovery of information up to the point of the last backup operation—at the close of business on the previous day, for example—but customer orders, accounting transactions, database updates, email messages, and other information that is created, collected, or processed between backup intervals will be lost.
- While data backup procedures are well established in large organizations with well-staffed information technology units, surveys indicate that small and medium businesses are not as diligent about backing up their data.[26]
- Some organizations keep their backup copies on premises or at a nearby location, such as a commercial storage facility, for easy access when needed. This practice exposes the backup copies to the same natural disasters as the originals.[27]
- While many business operations have been computerized for half a century, government agencies, companies, and not-for-profit organizations continue to maintain mission-critical information in paper files that are not

backed up. Examples include property records, birth and death records, court records, legal case files, social welfare files, student transcripts, healthcare files, and other older records that predate computerization but may still be needed to fulfill legal obligations, support ongoing business operations, or protect the rights and interests of property owners, clients, students, patients, or other data subjects.

Risk Response

The meteorological, geological, hydrological, and climatological disasters discussed in preceding sections result from natural process that are beyond human control. Acceptance—a conscious management decision to take no action to mitigate the risk of information loss due to natural disaster—may be a viable strategy for organizations that are located in areas where natural hazards are rare or infrequent as measured by the estimated return period for a given disaster, but risk acceptance without backup protection for mission-critical information is not advisable, given the human-induced threats discussed elsewhere in this chapter. As discussed below, backup copies are a necessary component of any risk mitigation strategy, but an organization may be willing to accept the loss of information that is created, collected, or processed between backup intervals.

For an organization located in a disaster-prone area, risk avoidance is only possible by relocating the organization's databases, computer files, email system, paper records, and other information resources to an area that is not subject to destructive weather, seismic instability, or other natural hazards. Even if such an area could be found,[28] a mitigation strategy based on geographic relocation may not be practical or possible for organizations with established business operations in a hazard-prone area. Relocation of mission-critical electronic information may be possible, however, by moving selected computer applications from an in-house data center to a cloud-based provider—provided, of course, that the cloud-based operation is located in a low-hazard area.

Risk transfer through insurance is possible for information loss resulting from natural disasters. Some property and casualty insurance policies provide limited coverage for recovery or reconstruction of electronic data that is damaged or destroyed by specified disasters. Additional coverage can be purchased separately through electronic data loss insurance. Insurance coverage is also available, within limits, for business losses associated with disruption of computer operations due to natural disaster. Property and casualty insurance policies do not cover paper records, but valuable papers and records insurance can be purchased for reconstruction or restoration of office files, engineering drawings, and other paper documents that are damaged or destroyed by natural disasters. A blanket limit is typically specified for restoration or reconstruction of replaceable paper records. Coverage for historically significant documents and other irreplaceable records is typically based on their appraised value.

Where an organization maintains information on behalf of others, most commercial liability policies specifically exclude destruction of electronic data from property damage liability coverage. The exclusion is based on a definition of electronic data as intangible property, but electronic data liability coverage can be purchased separately. To be covered, damage to electronic data that an organization maintains on behalf of others must be accompanied by damage to tangible property—that is, the computers on which the data is processed and stored must be damaged or destroyed, which is likely in a natural disaster.

Natural disasters cannot be prevented, but their information-related risks can be minimized. As noted above, backup copies are an essential component of any mitigation strategy for restoration or recovery of lost information due to natural disasters. In most organizations, the information technology operation produces backup copies of electronic information on a regular schedule. Building on that foundation, an organization should consider the following points to further reduce the potential for information loss:

- Backup copies must be stored at a sufficient distance from the original information so as not to be affected by the same natural disasters. While there is no standard for the minimum safe distance, fifty to seventy-five miles offers a reasonable balance between protection from the same disasters and accessibility of backup copies when needed.[29] Where backup copies are maintained on servers rather than on magnetic tapes, greater distances are feasible.
- Real-time backup, also known as continuous data protection, creates a backup copy of every addition, deletion, or other modification to a database, computer file, or other electronic information at the time the modification occurs. The backup copy is saved on a remote computer, which is presumably sufficiently distant from the computer on which the original information is stored.
- Mission-critical office records, engineering drawings, and other hardcopy documents should be scanned and backup copies of the electronic versions saved in a remote location. Microfilming, once the preferred backup method for paper records, has been steadily displaced by digitization, which is an easier, less costly reproduction process. In many organizations, backup protection for mission-critical paper records is a self-limiting problem. Progressive computerization of essential business processes has eliminated many paper records. Where they exist at all, newer mission-critical paper records are often digitized for electronic storage and online access

soon after their creation or collection. Older paper records—once considered indispensable— tend to become less important as time passes.

MALICIOUS INFORMATION LOSS

Malicious information loss is caused by wrongful acts. Unlike other threats discussed in this chapter, the actions that lead to information loss are invariably initiated by humans. In most cases, information loss is the wrongful act's intended outcome. Less commonly, information loss is the incidental result of a wrongful act that has a different objective—the destruction of property that stores information, for example. The most common sources of malicious information loss are malicious software, geopolitical risk, vandalism and sabotage, and theft of information.

Malicious software exploits security defects in a computer's operating system or application software. Examples of malicious software include computer viruses, computer worms, trojan horses, and ransomware. Commonly termed *malware*, malicious software infiltrates a computer system or network for purposes of disrupting computer operations by damaging, destroying, altering, stealing, copying, or interfering with information.[30] The various types of malware are designed to wreak havoc in different ways. A computer virus, the most widely publicized type of destructive software, is a self-replicating program that attaches itself to a computer's operating system, applications, or files. The virus is executed when an infected application or file is opened by an authorized user. By contrast, a computer worm is a standalone, self-replicating program that automatically executes itself without human intervention. A worm can spread itself quickly throughout a computer network, consuming bandwidth, degrading performance, and damaging or destroying information. A trojan horse is a nonreplicating program that appears legitimate but contains malicious code that can destroy or steal information. A trojan horse may infiltrate a computer system through an infected email attachment or content downloaded from a web site. A keylogger is a malicious application that collects users' keystrokes, which may include personal information and sign-on credentials. Ransomware is a form of malware that blocks authorized access to an infected computer or that threatens to disseminate information that the computer stores unless a ransom is paid. Ransomware may enter a computer system through an unsolicited email message that includes an infected attachment or a link to a malicious web site or through a so-called "malvertisement," an infected advertisement that is unknowingly incorporated into a web site.

Broadly defined, *geopolitical risk* encompasses political acts and tensions that adversely affect international relations between sovereign nations.[31] Aspects of geopolitical risk that may result in information loss include civil disorder, armed conflict, and terrorism. As defined in 18 U.S.C. § 232, *civil disorder* encompasses "any public disturbance involving acts of violence by three or more persons, which causes an immediate danger of or results in damage or injury to the property or person of another individual." This definition excludes peaceful demonstrations or group protests that are protected by the constitutional right of assembly. Civil disorder always involves intentional and aggressive noncompliance with a law or regulation. Forms of civil disorder include unlawful assembly, unlawful obstruction, rioting, looting, and other disruptive and potentially destructive events within a given political jurisdiction. Armed conflict includes declared war or other fighting that involves two or more sovereign entities as well as civil war, resistance to alien occupation, or resistance to colonial domination, which may be viewed as extreme forms of civil disorder in which a sovereign entity fights one or more armed groups within its own territory.[32] Terrorism, a widely publicized form of geopolitical risk, is the use of violence or threat of violence for political or ideological objectives.[33] Definitions presented in 18 U.S.C. § 2331 include "mass destruction" as one of the attributes of international and domestic terrorism. Terrorist acts share this attribute with armed conflict and civil disorder, but terrorist acts are not committed by sovereign entities (although terrorism may be supported by sovereign states).

Vandalism and sabotage are willful destructive acts committed by an individual or a small group. Unlike terrorist acts, which may be aimed at people, vandalism and sabotage focus on damage to or destruction of property. Vandalism and sabotage differ in intent. Sabotage involves premeditated, planned damage or destruction of property to achieve a political, strategic, or military objective or benefit. In this respect, sabotage and terrorism are closely aligned, but acts of sabotage are designed to harm a specific opponent rather than spread fear.[34] Barring mental illness, vandalism does not have a political, strategic, or ideological objective, nor does the perpetrator anticipate specific benefits from his or her destructive actions. If vandalism is intended to send a message, it is one of revenge for a perceived wrong. Vandalism may be committed by an angry employee, an aggrieved former employee, a dissatisfied customer, or another person with a vindictive motive. Tampering, a form of either vandalism or sabotage, involves the unauthorized alteration of data or documents. This may be accomplished through malicious software or by conventional means, such as manually editing documents saved on a shared drive. Information is rarely the direct target of other forms of vandalism, which may damage or destroy information incidentally in the course of damaging or destroying buildings or other property.

Information theft, also termed *data theft*, is the physical removal of data or documents without the consent of the rightful owner and without the intention of returning the information to the owner. Examples include the unauthorized removal of financial records from a corporate office, medical records from a hospital, student records from a college registrar, backup tapes from a storage facility, and historically significant documents from an archival repository.[35] A broader definition recognizes unauthorized copying as a form of information theft that deprives the rightful owner of exclusive use of the information.[36] Unauthorized copying through computer hacking or by an organization's own employees is the most common form of information theft for electronic data and documents where the objective is access to specific content rather than malicious destruction of information. Information theft by copying, which leaves the original information in place, is much more difficult to detect than outright removal of the information. Whether original information or copies are involved, information theft is one of the oldest forms of malicious information loss. The motives for widely publicized information thefts have ranged from political activism to espionage,[37] but information theft is typically motivated by other considerations—the elimination of embarrassing documents from personnel files, identity theft, or misappropriation of proprietary information, for example.[38] In some cases, employees have stolen personnel records to support discrimination claims or other legal actions against their employers.[39]

Vulnerability Assessment

Malicious actions pose significant, widespread, and unpredictable threats to information. Depending on the circumstances, statistics suggest that the frequency of malicious actions is either on the rise or, after years of increasing, stable at a high level:

- Anti-virus companies encounter tens of thousands of new malware applications daily.[40] According to AV-TEST, an independent research institute for IT security, there were over 900 million malicious and potentially unwanted applications for all operating system platforms in 2019, a 100 percent increase in five years.[41] According to Kapersky Lab, a global cybersecurity company, 30 percent of computers were subjected to at least one malware attack in 2018, the latest year for which statistics were available.[42]
- Since 1919, there have been more than nine thousand riots, general strikes, and other civil disorder events worldwide.[43] Since colonial times, the United States has experienced thousands of riots and protests involving the illegal use of force by aggrieved groups.[44] Since 2010, there have been at least thirty such incidents, including violent demonstrations in Ferguson, Missouri; St. Louis, Missouri; Oakland, California; Portland, Oregon; and Charlottesville, Virginia.
- The Uppsala Conflict Data Program, which compiles data on organized violence, has noted a significant increase in the number and intensity of

armed conflict in the second decade of the twenty-first century.[45] At any given time, warfare resulting in death and destruction is ongoing in multiple countries. Recent sites of armed conflict include Afghanistan, Iraq, Israel, Kashmir (on the border between Pakistan and India), Libya, Niger, Nigeria, Somalia, South Sudan, Syria, Ukraine, and Yemen. The destructive impact of armed conflict on the world's archives and libraries is widely recognized and well documented.[46] Much less information is available about damage to or destruction of business records.

- According to the Global Peace Index, global peacefulness and safety and security measures have deteriorated since 2008, largely due to terrorism and internal conflict. In 2018, 104 countries reported increased terrorist activity.[47] According to the Global Terrorism Database maintained by the National Consortium for the Study of Terrorism and Responses to Terrorism (START), there were 1,922 successful terrorist acts in the United States between 1970 and 2016. START reported that, despite a decrease in terrorist attacks in 2017, "terrorist violence remains extraordinarily high compared to historical trends."[48]

- Identity theft, the fraudulent acquisition of personal information, through computer hacking or other unauthorized access, is a leading motivation for information theft. According to a report by Javelin Strategy & Research, a digital financial advisory firm, there were 16.7 million victims of identity theft in 2017.[49] Annual identity theft reports submitted to the Federal Trade Commission increased by 500 percent from 2001 to 2018.[50] According to a 2016 survey by the Bureau of Justice Statistics, a unit of the U.S. Department of Justice, 10 percent of the US population over age 15 were victims of identity theft during the prior twelve months, an increase of 7 percent from 2014.[51]

- Mobile computing and communication devices, which may contain significant business information, are more likely to be stolen than their stationary counterparts. According to widely cited statistics, a laptop computer is stolen every fifty-three seconds in the United States, and one in six users will have a laptop, tablet, or smartphone stolen, lost, or damaged within a twelve-month period. Where organizations allow employees to use their own mobile devices for business purposes, data and documents are unlikely to be protected by encryption, malware detection software, or other security mechanisms.[52] Because the Health Insurance Portability and Accountability Act (HIPAA) requires regulated entities to notify patients about data breaches, thefts of devices and media that contain medical records have been widely reported.[53]

- In a 2009 survey of four hundred senior information technology employees in the United States and United Kingdom by Cyber-Ark Software, a global security firm, over 40 percent of the respondents indicated that they would take financial reports, research and development plans, privileged password lists, and other proprietary information with them if they were fired. In a 2018 survey by Code42, a data loss protection company, of 1,700 business leaders in the United States, United Kingdom, and Germany, 49 percent admitted to taking information from their previous employers. [54]

No organization is immune to information loss through malicious actions, but several factors may increase an organization's vulnerability. Organizations in conflict zones are obviously vulnerable to information loss from warfare. Civil disorder and terrorism are more likely to occur in urban areas than in less populated locations. Malware attacks can affect any organization, but industries that maintain confidential personal information and data about monetary assets—financial services and healthcare, for example—are particularly likely targets. Government agencies and organizations in industries such as defense, energy, and information technology are vulnerable to malware attacks aimed at data theft. Organizations that utilize outdated computer systems and applications may be more vulnerable than those with newer technology components.

Risk Response

Malicious actions that damage, destroy, or steal information are unacceptable and unavoidable. Available security measures cannot eliminate the risk of information loss. An effective mitigation strategy must combine risk transfer with precautionary measures that can reduce an organization's vulnerability to malicious acts.

Risk transfer through insurance coverage can provide partial mitigation of information loss from malicious causes. Most property and casualty insurance policies exclude coverage for damage resulting from hostile acts, including declared or undeclared war, civil war, insurrection, other military action, usurpation of power by armed groups, civil unrest, and vandalism. War risk policies are available, but they are principally intended for ships and aircraft rather than commercial structures. Most property and casualty insurance also excludes coverage for losses resulting from terrorist acts. Terrorism coverage is available as a special addition to commercial property insurance, but some policies exclude loss of electronic data.

Because property and casualty policies are designed to cover physical damage to tangible property, they typically exclude information loss resulting from malicious software. Cyber insurance policies are available for damage, destruction, corruption, alteration, or theft of electronic data caused by a malware attack. These policies cover first-party losses, such as the cost of recovering or repairing lost or damaged data that an organization owns, as well as third-party losses, such as damage claims resulting from loss of customer information, client data, and other electronic data that is maintained by an organization but owned by others.[55] Some policies also reimburse extortion payments associated with ransomware attacks that have been reported to law enforcement. Cyber insurance policies may exclude coverage for malware attacks initiated by a hostile foreign government or terrorist organization. Additional coverage must be purchased for such hostile events.

Insurance coverage for malicious destruction of nonelectronic information is more difficult to obtain. Most property and casualty policies exclude such information losses. Valuable papers and records insurance typically includes an exclusion for war and military actions, including civil insurrection and terrorism.

As with other threats discussed in this chapter, backup copies stored in a secure location are essential for recovery of information that is damaged, destroyed, altered, or otherwise harmed by malicious actions, but an effective mitigation strategy must emphasize prevention of such actions to the extent possible. While the destructive potential of armed conflict, civil unrest, and other geopolitical events can only be mitigated by military or diplomatic interventions, precautions and prudent policies can limit the likelihood of occurrence and adverse impact of other malicious actions.

Passwords and other digital identifiers are supposed to prevent unauthorized access to computer applications that store electronic information, but malware can defeat these protective mechanisms. The following actions, which are widely recommended by information security specialists,[56] can prevent or limit damage, destruction, or alteration of electronic data and documents by malicious software:

- Many organizations have implemented firewalls, intrusion detection systems, spam-filtering software, whitelisting of email addresses, and other security mechanisms to monitor and prevent unauthorized access to computer systems and information by external parties. To protect against malicious actions by insiders, access to computer applications must be strictly controlled based on the principle of least privilege, which restricts employees' access to the minimum information and software functionality necessary to perform assigned duties.
- Anti-malware software provides a critical line of defense against data loss from viruses, worms, trojan horses, and other malicious software. When properly configured, such software will detect, quarantine, and alert an organization's information technology organization to the presence of malicious code. Anti-malware software must be kept up to date in order to identify new forms of malicious software.
- Computer hardware, operating systems, and applications must be kept up to date with the latest security patches. Automatic updates should be ena-

bled whenever possible. Obsolete software should be removed from servers, desktop computers, and mobile computing devices.

- Employees must be instructed not to open suspicious emails or to click on suspect links or attachments. Where a suspicious email may have a legitimate business purpose, the sender should be contacted to confirm that it is safe to open. Employees should also be strongly cautioned about installing browser plug-ins, executing macro scripts in popular office productivity applications, and accessing unsecured shared files, all of which are common vectors for malware penetration and propagation.
- Application whitelisting should be implemented to prevent installation and execution of unauthorized programs. Suspicious web sites and file types should be blacklisted.

Physical security measures are essential to protect nonelectronic information as well as electronic data that is stored on magnetic tapes or other offline media:

- To prevent vandalism and theft, storage areas for documents and offline data should be consolidated in as few locations as possible. Centralized storage areas are easier to secure than decentralized ones. A building that includes record storage areas must have appropriate perimeter security at all times.
- File rooms, record centers, archival repositories, and other storage areas should be limited to a single supervised entrance that is locked when unattended. Access must be restricted to authorized persons who have specific, verifiable business reasons for entering areas where information is stored. To the extent possible, users should be supervised while they are in the record storage area, and containers should be inspected to detect theft. These precautions should be applied to all users, regardless of their position within the organization.[57]
- Janitorial services in record storage areas must be supervised. Record storage areas should never be included in building tours.
- Circulation control records should be kept for every document, file, or other information carrier removed from a storage area. For each transaction, the circulation control records should identify the items that were removed, the authorized borrower, the time and date of removal, the locations to which the items were taken, and the date and time when the items were returned.
- It is very difficult to protect information that is maintained in employees' work areas. A clean desk policy, while difficult to enforce, is recommended. Documents should not be left unattended on work surfaces or in open view on computer screens. All information should be put away and computer applications closed at the end of the workday.

ACCIDENTAL INFORMATION LOSS

An accident is an unforeseen or unplanned occurrence that has unintended effects, which may include damage, destruction, or other loss of information. Accidental information loss can result from human errors or technological malfunctions. Broadly defined, *human error* is the opposite of correct performance of a task or operation, an unintentional mistake.[58] A technological malfunction is a failure of equipment or software that results in loss of information.

Human error has long been recognized as a frequent cause of inadvertent destruction or loss of useful information.[59] Examples of human error include but are not limited to:

- deleting database records, computer files, or email messages that need to be kept;
- redacting or overwriting modifying portions of documents during editing;
- discarding paper records, photographic negatives, and other physical records that need to be kept;
- filing paper records or digital documents in the wrong folder;
- assigning misleading or meaningless names to computer files and folders;
- placing paper folders in the wrong filing cabinet or drawer;
- losing mobile devices, data portable storage devices, or paper records that have been removed from the workplace;
- damaging office documents, engineering drawings, and other paper records through frequent or careless handling; and
- spilling liquids on paper records.

These errors may result from carelessness, fatigue, improper training, defective instructions, failure to follow proper procedures, a mismatch of capabilities and requirements, or other factors.

Technological malfunctions that result in information loss may be due to defective or incompatible hardware components, material fatigue, hardware obsolescence, inadequate maintenance, power surges, overheating, or physical damage from vibrations, shock, environmental contaminants, or water damage from leaking pipes, windows left open during a rainstorm, or accidentally activated fire sprinklers. Unsaved information will be lost during sudden power outages or an improper computer shutdown. Information recorded on magnetic media may be accidentally erased by exposure to magnetic fields.[60] Damage from equipment malfunction is usually associated with electronic information, but it can also apply to paper records; improperly installed shelving can collapse and damage paper records, for example, or the automatic feeder of a photocopier or fax machine can mangle documents. Software failures are many and varied. Software defects that can cause information loss include programming errors, inadequate testing, incompatibility with other software, and improper computer shutdowns.[61]

Compared to natural and manmade disasters, which can destroy entire data centers and record storage facilities, human errors and technological malfunctions typically affect a smaller quantity of information per incident, but the consequences can be significant. Human errors may accidentally delete data and documents that must be kept to comply with legal and regulatory requirements. Unintentional deletion or modification of database records, computer files, email messages, or office documents can expose an organization to court-ordered sanctions for failure to preserve information that is relevant for litigation, government investigations, or other legal proceedings. Inadvertent loss or destruction of specific data or documents can increase the time and effort required for transaction processing, accounting, customer service, marketing, project management, and other information-dependent business operations.

Vulnerability Assessment

Surveys conducted by business researchers confirm that loss of information through human error or technological malfunction has a high likelihood of occurrence in organizations of all types and sizes. Among frequently cited examples, a 2010 survey of two thousand participants in a variety of organizations in seventeen countries found that 27 percent of respondents traced information loss to human error, while 29 percent cited technological malfunction as the cause of their most recent information loss.[62] In a 2014 survey of 453 small and medium-size business in the United States and Canada, 79 percent of respondents reported a major information technology failure in the previous two years.[63] According to a 2013 survey of sixty-seven data centers in various industries in the United States, human error accounted for 22 percent of unplanned system outages, while technology malfunctions, including failure of computing equipment and uninterruptible power systems, were responsible for 28 percent.[64] A 2018 survey of information professionals in 414 companies in the United Kingdom found that human error accounted for 26 percent of data losses, while hardware malfunctions and software failures accounted for 27 percent and 23 percent, respectively.[65]

In a widely publicized incident, the original digital files for the Pixar film "Toy Story 2" were accidentally deleted in 2012 when someone entered an incorrect operating system command.[66] In 2017, a similar error deleted a database maintained by GitLab, the operator of an open source code collaboration platform.[67] Most cases of accidental information loss through human error are less dramatic. Ignoring system prompts, an employee fails to save changes before closing a file. Significant messages are inadvertently deleted during mailbox cleanup. Office staff must hunt through filing cabinets looking for a misplaced folder or through a hard disk directory looking for a vaguely named file created by a former employee. Older engineering drawings that predate computerized design are torn and faded from years of frequent, often careless handling.

The likelihood of technological failure increases as computing devices age. A 2019 survey of seven hundred business technology buyers found that 57 percent needed to upgrade end-of-life equipment,[68] a leading contributor to technological malfunctions. Annualized failure rates for servers range from 5 percent in the first year of operation to 13 percent for a five-year old device.[69] Studies of hard disk reliability indicate annualized failure rates ranging from 2 percent to 6 percent, with high rates during the initial year due to factory defects and after three years of use due to general wear and tear.[70] Unlike computer hardware, which becomes less reliable over time, software may have defects from the time it was developed. Additional defects may be introduced by periodic modifications. Software size and complexity increases vulnerability to programming errors, system incompatibilities, corruption, and other risks. Small and medium-size organizations are more vulnerable to hardware and software malfunction than large data centers, which have personnel and expertise to address problems and minimize the impact of technology failures.

Risk Response

Because human error and technological malfunction are inevitable, risk avoidance is not a realistic mitigation strategy for accidental information loss. An organization might conceivably avoid human error by automating the business processes that create, collect, store, or retrieve information, but a transition from paper to electronic recordkeeping will increase an organization's exposure to technological failure, which may or may not be more controllable than human error.

Risk transfer is a mitigation option for accidental loss of electronic information. Some property and casualty insurance policies provide coverage for recovery or reconstruction of electronic data or documents that are damaged or destroyed by technological failures, subject to monetary limits. Additional coverage can be purchased separately through electronic data loss insurance, but accidental destruction of electronic information by employee actions is usually excluded. Most commercial liability policies specifically exclude accidental loss of electronic information that an organization maintains on behalf of others. Electronic data liability coverage for such situations can be purchased separately. To be covered, however, damage to electronic data must be accompanied by damage to tangible property—that is, technological failure must damage the computing equipment on which the lost data was processed and stored. Risk transfer is not an option for accidental loss of information contained in paper records. Valuable papers and records insurance policies usually exclude damages that result from employee errors in processing, copying, or handling paper documents.

Human errors and technology failures can be minimized, but they cannot be eliminated. An organization must accept some risk of accidental information loss at a level greater than zero. An effective risk mitigation plan must focus on reducing human errors and technology malfunctions to their irreducible minimum:

- As with other adverse events, backup copies are essential to limit accidental loss of information. Regular backup of computer files provides reasonable prospects for recovery of databases, digital documents, and other electronic content, but—unless real-time backup is implemented—backup copies only permit restoration of lost information as of the last backup operation. Training of information workers is necessary to prevent loss of information from failure to save work in progress, accidental overwriting of computer files, accidental editing of file names, filing digital documents in the wrong folder or hard disk directory, and other mistakes that occur between backup operations.
- Training should focus on procedures and precautions that are likely to prevent accidental damage, destruction, or other loss of electronic and nonelectronic information. This emphasis on error prevention should be combined with error-management concepts, which view human errors as learning opportunities that can ultimately avoid repetition of mistakes. [71]
- Mistakes must be accepted as an inevitable part of day-to-day work. Penalizing mistakes inhibits open communication, which is essential for effective error management. Error-prevention initiatives should concentrate on the business processes in which errors arise, not on the employees who made the mistakes. Prevention and correction of human errors and technological failures that lead to information loss is ultimately a management responsibility. [72]
- Human errors and technological malfunctions that result in information loss must be reported as soon as they are detected so that action can be taken to minimize the negative impact. [73]
- Computer processing and storage devices should be replaced at regular intervals to avoid age-related malfunctions that can damage or destroy information. Computer processing and storage devices should be protected against damage from overheating, power surges, static electricity, dust, debris, and vibrations.
- Information should be processed in a clean, safe environment with appropriate temperature, humidity, and ventilation. To eliminate the possibility

of damage through spillage, liquids should be prohibited in areas where paper or electronic information is handled.

FIRE

As an information risk, fire combines the attributes of threats discussed in preceding sections, and it has the same adverse impact. Fire may have an accidental origin in human error or technological malfunction. It may result from warfare, civil insurrection, terrorism, vandalism, or other malicious actions. It may follow a natural disaster; fires sometimes occur in the wake of a hurricane or earthquake, for example. Wildfires, which may be caused by lightning strikes, are often categorized as natural disasters, but most wildfires are caused by human carelessness, technological malfunctions, or arson. [74]

In a typical year, there are about 500,000 nonresidential structure fires in the United States. About 24 percent of these fires occur in commercial structures, including office buildings, schools, and other buildings that may house information. Apart from damage caused by wildfires, most fires in commercial structures originate from cooking equipment (about 30 percent), electrical equipment (12 percent), and heating equipment (11 percent). These three causes account for about 30 percent of property damage in commercial structure fires. Intentional fires account for 10 percent of nonresidential fires but 20 percent of property damage. [75]

Property damage—including destruction of records needed for business operations, regulatory compliance, historical preservation, and other purposes—is an obvious consequence of a building fire. [76] The temperature in a building fire can exceed 1,700 degrees Fahrenheit. Most paper documents maintained in offices or warehouse storage will ignite at 450 to 480 degrees Fahrenheit, subject to variations in the composition and density of the paper. [77] Once ignition occurs, a burning document will be destroyed quickly unless the fire is extinguished. Even then, information contained in parts of the document will likely be unreadable. Documents not destroyed by fire may be damaged by water from building sprinklers or fire hoses.

Compared to paper records, electronic information recorded on magnetic disks and tapes can withstand higher temperatures, but they can still be damaged or destroyed by fire. Magnetic effects decrease with temperature and will disappear completely at temperatures exceeding 1,400 degrees Fahrenheit. [78] At those high temperatures, information will be erased and unrecoverable. Other magnetic media components will be damaged at lower temperatures. Magnetic tape cartridges, for example, will begin to melt at 200 degrees Fahrenheit. Hard drives are easily damaged by heat. Circuit boards will ignite at low temperatures. Disk platters that resist burning will warp.

Even if a fire is extinguished quickly, smoke and soot can render a hard drive inoperable and information unrecoverable.

Vulnerability Assessment

A fire-risk assessment identifies and evaluates fire hazards in specific circumstances.[79] The assessment is based on two considerations: the probability of occurrence of a fire and the magnitude of the consequences should a fire occur. As a cause of information loss, a building fire is a highly destructive event with a low probability of occurrence. This is especially the case with office buildings, which are rarely destroyed by fire despite the presence of cooking appliances, electrical wiring, heating equipment, and other significant risk factors.[80] Office buildings contain combustible paper files as well as computers, monitors, printers, and other electrical devices that can start a fire or catch fire that originates elsewhere, but office building fires are typically confined to a small area and extinguished before extensive information loss occurs. In 2017, the latest year for which statistics were available at the time of this writing, none of the large-loss fires in the United States involved office buildings or extensive information loss.[81]

Fires in data centers and record storage warehouses, two structures that house large quantities of information, have destroyed paper documents and electronic records. The most highly publicized examples have involved government and commercial record centers that contained large quantities of paper records.[82] These fires have been few in number but highly destructive. In 1973, a fire in a government-operated storage facility in St. Louis destroyed many records of discharged military personnel.[83] Between 1996 and 2015, fires destroyed paper records in commercial storage facilities in New Jersey, Pennsylvania, London, Ottawa, Buenos Aires, and New York City. The records—which presumably had sufficient legal, operational, or historical value to warrant continued retention for a fee—belonged to companies, government agencies, hospitals, and other organizations. The fires were widely reported in newspapers, on web sites, and in other sources.[84] While alarming, these record center fires were unusual occurrences. While record centers are filled with combustible materials and have high ceilings that encourage the rapid propagation of flames, warehouse-type record storage facilities represent a very small percentage of structure fires.[85] Most record storage facilities have never had a fire. While several million boxes have been destroyed in record center fires, hundreds of millions of boxes are housed in commercial storage facilities at any given time.

In any given year, data center fires outnumber record center fires, but they receive less notoriety, possibly because information loss is limited by backup copies, which do not exist for most of the paper documents stored in record centers. Even without information loss, data center fires can have a significant adverse impact on an organization's business operations. In 2009, a data center fire in Seattle disrupted e-commerce for thousands of web sites, and a data center fire in Boston disrupted trading by financial services companies. In 2014, there were three data center fires in Iowa within an eight-month period. In 2015, fires damaged operational data centers in Milan, Belfast, and Baton Rouge, as well as an Amazon data center under construction in Virginia. In 2018, a data center fire disrupted Internet connectivity in North Texas. In 2018, fire disrupted service at a multitenant data center in Boston, while loud sounds emitted by a gas-based fire suppression system destroyed hard drives at a Swedish data center. In 2019, fire disrupted banking operations at a data center in Minnesota.[86]

Risk Response

Risk avoidance is not a viable mitigation strategy for fire-related loss of information. Fire hazards can be minimized but not completely eliminated in workplaces where information is created, collected, stored, or used. Destruction or damage by fire is always a possibility for information that is recorded on combustible media. Avoidance strategies merely trade one risk for another. An organization can avoid loss of information in a record center fire by not sending its inactive records to offsite storage, but that will not make the records less combustible in the place where they are kept. Compared to on-premises storage in closets, basements, or empty rooms, properly configured record centers take greater precautions against fires. Similarly, an organization can reduce its vulnerability to business interruption by replacing paper recordkeeping with digital processes, but computers and electronic information can be damaged or destroyed in a building fire.

Risk transfer through insurance is an important mitigation strategy for information loss due to fire. Some property and casualty insurance policies provide limited coverage for recovery or reconstruction of records destroyed by fire. A valuable papers and records policy is necessary for a major loss. Such policies cover the cost to repair or replace paper records that are stored in specified locations, which may include a commercial record center as well as an organization's own business offices.

Valuable papers and records insurance is advisable for records stored by commercial providers. Contracts for offsite record storage typically provide a nominal payment for loss or destruction of records while in the custody of a commercial provider. This provision is treated as insurance coverage and is included, at no additional cost, in the storage and service rates charged by a record center operator. By signing the contract, the customer presumably accepts this amount as sufficient compensation for loss. Most contracts further state that the commercial storage provider will not be liable for the cost of recreating lost records, for lost profits or revenues, or for any other consequential or incidental damages based on tort, contract, or any other legal theory unless the loss or damage resulted from the storage provider's failure to exercise reasonable care that would have prevented the loss or damage.

Valuable papers and records policies typically exclude electronic information. Electronic data loss insurance can be purchased for recovery or reconstruction of electronic information that is damaged or destroyed by fire as well as costs associated with interruption of computer operations following a fire. Most commercial liability policies specifically exclude accidental loss of electronic information that an organization maintains on behalf of others. Electronic data liability coverage for such situations can be purchased separately. To be covered, damage to electronic data must be accompanied by damage to the computing equipment on which the lost data was processed and stored.

Recognizing the low probability of occurrence for a building fire, an organization may be willing to accept a fire risk at a level greater than zero in some circumstances.[87] Risk acceptance should be supported by prevention measures and precautionary practices specified in standards issued by the National Fire Protection Association:[88]

- Backup copies are critical for successful recovery or reconstruction of information damaged by fire. Regular backup of computer files provides reasonable prospects for recovery of databases, digital documents, and other electronic content. Paper records are less likely to have backup copies.
- Office buildings, data centers, record storage facilities, and other structures that house information must comply fully with applicable fire codes and ordinances, which typically mandate heat and smoke detectors, fire alarms connected to a local fire department, portable fire extinguishers, standpipes and hoses, and automatic sprinkler systems or other fire suppression systems.
- Flammable, combustible, and explosive materials must be prohibited in areas where information is created, collected, stored, or used.
- Prompt detection of flaming fires or smoldering events is the first step in any fire-control system. Heat and smoke detectors must be installed in information storage and work areas and tested regularly for proper operation. Sensors should be installed to detect overheating of power supplies, data cables, and data center components that may run hot enough to ignite insulating material.
- Boiler rooms, generators, battery chargers, gasoline-powered devices, and related equipment must be separated from information storage areas by four-hour firewalls.
- Raised flooring in data centers should be inspected for combustible debris and cleaned regularly.

- Mission-critical information or historically significant archival records should be stored in properly constructed fire-resistant vaults and safes, which provide additional protection against a total burnout.
- Fire and smoke barriers should separate data centers and record storage areas from break rooms where coffee makers, microwave ovens, and other electrical appliances may be installed.
- Data centers, record storage facilities, and other buildings that house information should not be located in close proximity to factories, highway ramps, parking structures, or other external fire hazards where flammable or combustible materials are present or accidents involving fuels are likely to occur. Buildings that store information should be located in an area served by a trained fire department.
- Electronic information should be stored apart from large quantities of paper records, which pose a greater fire hazard.
- To prevent arson, access controls, intrusion detection, surveillance systems, and other physical security measures should be implemented in data centers and record repositories.
- Data centers, record storage facilities, and other buildings that house information should be inspected periodically by a licensed fire-protection engineer.

SUMMARY OF MAJOR POINTS

- Information can be damaged or destroyed by natural disasters, malicious actions, accidents, or fire. These risks vary in their likelihood of occurrence and their consequences, which can range from minimal to devastating.
- Compared to other risks, natural disasters have a low likelihood of occurrence, but their consequences for information-dependent operations and activities can range from disruptive to catastrophic. Insurance coverage is available for recovery or reconstruction of information destroyed by a natural disaster. Organizations located in areas where natural hazards are rare or infrequent may be willing to accept a low level of risk.
- Malicious actions pose significant, widespread, and unpredictable threats to information. Depending on the circumstances, information loss may be the intended outcome or incidental result of a malicious action. Statistics suggest that the frequency of malicious software attacks, armed conflict, civil insurrections, vandalism, and information theft is either on the rise or, after years of increasing, stable at a high level. Risk transfer through insurance coverage can provide partial mitigation of information loss from malicious causes.

- Malicious software, information theft, human error, and technological malfunctions are common and unavoidable risks, but precautionary measures and prudent policies can limit their likelihood of occurrence and adverse impact.

- Given the low probability of occurrence for a building fire, an organization may be willing to accept a fire risk at a level greater than zero provided that fire-prevention measures and precautionary practices are implemented. Insurance coverage provides compensation, within limits, for recovery or reconstruction of information lost due to fire.

- Regardless of cause, the ability to recover lost information depends on the availability of backup copies, which are routinely produced for electronic information but are less common for paper documents.

NOTES

1. G. Woo, *Calculating Catastrophe* (London: Imperial College Press, 2011); M. Jouini and L. Ben Arfa Rabal, "Classification of Security Threats in Information Systems," *Procedia Computer Science*, 32 (2014): 489–96, https://doi.org/10.1016/j.procs.2014.05.452.

2. ISO 15489-1:2016, *Information and Documentation—Records Management—Part 1: Concepts and Principles* includes risk assessment and protection of records among the requirements for records management operations. See also ANSI/ARMA 5-2010, *Vital Records Programs: Identifying, Managing, and Recovering Business Critical Records.* Business continuity is covered by many international standards, including ISO 22301:2012, *Societal Security—Business Continuity Management Systems—Requirements*; ISO 22313:2012, *Societal Security—Business Continuity Management Systems—Guidance;* ISO 22316:2017, *Security and Resilience—Organizational Resilience—Principles and Attributes*; ISO/TS 22331:2018, *Security and Resilience—Business Continuity Management Systems—Guidelines for Business Continuity*; and ISO 27031:2011, *Information Technology—Security Techniques—Guidelines for Information and Communication Technology Readiness for Business Continuity.*

3. The Stafford Act (42 U.S.C. § 5122), the statutory authority for most federal disaster response activities, uses the phrase "natural catastrophe" to denote any event that "causes damage of sufficient severity and magnitude to warrant major disaster assistance." The ISO 37100:2016 standard, *Sustainable Cities and Communities—Vocabulary*, defines a natural disaster as a "natural event such as flood, earthquake, or hurricane that causes great damage or loss of life."

4. The Saffir-Simpson scale, for example, defines five categories of hurricanes based on sustained winds with potential damage ranging minimal to catastrophic. The Richter magnitude scale defines ten categories of earthquakes with potential damage ranging from negligible to total destruction. The Enhanced Fujita scale defines six categories of tornadoes with potential damage ranging from light to incredible. A Tsunami Intensity Scale defines twelve categories with potential damage ranging from none to completely devastating. See R. Blong, "A Review of Damage Intensity Scales," *Natural Hazards* 29, no. 2 (2003): 57–76, https://doi.org/10.1023/A:1022960414329.

5. Munich Re's NatCatSERVICE provides free online access to a database of global natural disasters from 1980 to the present: https://natcatservice.munichre.com.

6. M. Gall et al., "The Unsustainable Trend of Natural Hazard Losses in the United States," *Sustainability* 3, no. 11 (2011): 2157–81, https://doi.org/10.3390/su3112157. Hurricanes, flooding, coastal hazards, and severe weather accounted for 74 percent of the total monetary losses. Geological hazards accounted for 12 percent, but this figure is misleading because earthquakes, tsunamis, volcanic eruptions, landslides, and avalanches occur less frequently than meteorological and hydrological hazards.

7. Among the earliest reported examples, fires that followed the San Francisco earthquake of 1908 destroyed official records maintained in government buildings. R. C. Harrison, "A City without Records," *The American Lawyer* 16, no. 3 (1908): 155–65, https://heinonline.org/HOL/LandingPage?handle=hein.journals/amlyr16&div=58&id=&page=&t=1557779137. In the first half of the twentieth century, American diplomatic and consular records were destroyed by earthquakes in Managua, Valparaiso, Tokyo, and Yokohama, according to M. B. Colket Jr., "The Preservation of Consular and Diplomatic Post Records of the United States," *American Archivist* 6, no. 4 (1943): 193–205, https://americanarchivist.org/doi/pdf/10.17723/aarc.6.4.814531u652m31086. In 1973, the Saint John River flood damaged many government records in Fredricton, New Brunswick. M. Beyea, "Records Management: The New Brunswick Case," *Archivaria*, no. 8 (1979): 61–77.

8. Among the many examples that might be cited, a complete loss of electrical power in the Los Angeles basin rendered computers inoperative after the 1994 Northridge earthquake. D. Todd et al., *1994 Northridge Earthquake: Performance of Structures, Lifelines, and Fire Protection Systems, NIST Special Publication 862.* (Gaithersburg, MD: National Institute of Standards and Technology, 1994), www.nist.gov/publications/1994-northridge-earthquake-performance-structures-lifelines-and-fire-protection-systems. According to a hearing before the Committee on Small Business and Entrepreneurship of the U.S. Senate, Hurricane Katrina destroyed real estate records maintained by local governments and banks in the gulf area in 2005, making it difficult to prove property ownership and process loan applications. See Senate Hearing 109-408, The Impact of Hurricane Katrina on Small Business, September 22, 2005, www.govinfo.gov/content/pkg/CHRG-109shrg26763/html/CHRG-109shrg26763.htm.   The Asian tsunami of 2005 destroyed land records in Aceh, North Sumatra, and Sri Lanka. O. Brown and A. Crawford, *Addressing Land Ownership after Natural Disasters: An Agency Survey,* (Winnipeg, Manitoba: International Institute for Sustainable Development, 2006), www.iisd.org/pdf/2006/es_addressing_land.pdf. In March 2011, a magnitude 9.0 earthquake followed by a forty-meter tsunami destroyed official records maintained in local government repositories and disrupted email service in eastern Japan, as reported by K. Kinoshita et al., "Technologies and Emergency Management for Disaster Recovery—with Focus on the Great East Japan Earthquake," *IEICE Transactions on Communication*, E95-B, no. 6 (2012): 1911–14, https://doi.org/10.1587/transcom.E95.B.1911. Flooding after Superstorm Sandy reportedly damaged approximately ten thousand cubic feet of case files and other records maintained by the Federal Bureau of Investigation at a storage facility in New Jersey. https://archive.org/stream/HurricaneSandyDamageAssessmentsOnRecordKeeping/1216811-0_-_062-HQ-A2561116_SER_2_-Section_001_djvu.txt.

9. *Small Business Credit Survey: Report on Disaster-Affected Firms*, issued by the Federal Reserve Banks of Dallas, New York, Richmond, and San Francisco in 2018, www.insurancejournal.com/app/uploads/2018/04/Federal-Reserve-Report-on-Disaster-Affected-Firms.pdf.

10. Ready Business Hurricane Toolkit, www.fema.gov/media-library/assets/documents/152381. See also N. S. Lam et al., "Predictors of Business Return in New Orleans after Hurricane Katrina," *PLoS One* 7, no. 10 (2012): e47935, https://doi.org/10.1371/journal.pone.0047935; D. Webb and S. Gilbert, *A Literature Review of Disaster-Induced Business Interruption and an Exploratory Analysis of the Effects of the 2004 Atlantic Hurricane Season on Florida Establishments at the Zip Code Level. NIST Technical Note 1932* (Gaithersburg, MD: National Institute of Standards and Technology, November 2016).

11. D. Wilhite, "Drought as a Natural Hazard: Concepts and Definitions," in *Drought: A Global Assessment*, ed. D. Wilhite (London: Routledge, 2000), 3–18, http://digitalcommons.unl.edu/droughtfacpub/69.

12. A. Ricciardi et al., "Should Biological Invasions Be Managed as Natural Disasters?" *BioScience* 61, no. 4 (2011): 312–17, https://doi.org/10.1525/bio.2011.61.4.11, emphasizes biological infestations that threaten human, animal, and plan life rather than information.

13. In 1989, a geomagnetic storm caused a widespread blackout in Quebec and other electrical disruption in North America as well as damage to orbiting satellites. See J. Kappernman and V. Albertson, "Bracing for the Geomagnetic Storms," *IEEE Spectrum* 27, no. 3 (1990): 27–33, https://doi.org/10.1109/6.48847. Damage caused by an asteroid impact in Siberia in 2013 is

discussed by O. Popova et al., "Chalyabinsk Airburst, Damage Assessment, Meteorite Recovery, and Characterization," *Science* 342, no. 6162 (2013): 1069–73, https://doi.org/10.1126/science.1242642.

14. On the role of return period estimates in risk assessment, see K. Emanuel and T. Jagger, "On Estimating Hurricane Return Periods," *Journal of Applied Meteorology and Climatology* 49, no. 5 (2010): 837–44, https://doi.org/10.1175/2009JAMC2236.1; E. Gumbel, "The Return Period of Flood Flows," *Annals of Mathematical Statistics* 12, no. 2 (1941): 163–90, www.jstor.org/stable/2235766; B. Fernandez and J. Salas, "Return Period and Risk of Hydrologic Events. I: Mathematical Formation," *Journal of Hydrologic Engineering* 4, no. 4 (1999): 297–307, https://doi.org/10.1061/(ASCE)1084-0699(1999)4:4(297); P. Ward et al., "How Are Flood Risk Estimates Affected by the Choice of Return-Periods?" *Natural Hazards and Earth System Sciences* 11, no. 12 (2011): 3181–95, https://doi.org/10.5194/nhess-11-3181-2011.

15. The so-called encounter probability of a disaster with a given annual return period occurring within a specified number of years is determined by a binomial distribution calculation using the following formula: $Pe=1-[1-(1/T)]n$, where Pe is the encounter probability, T is the return period, and n is the number of years. Thus, the probability of a disaster with a 100-year return period (T) occurring within the next twenty years (n) is $1-[1-(1/100)],20$ which works out to 18.2 percent. Various web sites provide free access to binomial probability calculators that are easy to use.

16. www.nhc.noaa.gov/climo/#returns. See also B. Kelm et al., "Spatiotemporal Patterns and Return Periods of Tropical Storm and Hurricane Strikes from Texas to Maine," *Journal of Climate* 20, no. 14 (2007): 3498–3509, https://doi.org/10.1175/JCLI4187.1.

17. The highest wind ever recorded in New York City was in 1954, when Hurricane Hazel gusted up to 113 miles per hour. The estimated return rate for a category 3 or higher storm in New York City is seventy-four years. By that estimate, New York City may experience a devastating hurricane before 2040. In 2012, Hurricane Sandy, a category 1 storm with sustained winds of 80 miles per hour and gusts up to 100 miles per hour, caused widespread flooding and property damage in New York City. Computer operations were disrupted by power outages. Various archival repositories reported damage to historically significant records. See "MARAC Members Respond to SuperStorm Sandy," *Mid-Atlantic Archivist* 42, no. 3 (2013): 8–12, https://archive.org/details/midatlanticarchi4232unse/page/n5.

18. D. Giardini et al., "The GSHAP Global Seismic Hazard Map," *Annals of Geophysics* 42, no. 6 (1999): 1225–30, https://doi.org/10.4401/ag-3784.

19. B. D. Rinard Hinga, *Ring of Fire: An Encyclopedia of the Pacific Rim's Earthquakes, Tsunamis, and Volcanoes* (Santa Barbara, CA: ABC-CLIO, 2015).

20. T. Rikitake, "Recurrence of Great Earthquakes at Subduction Zones," *Tectonophysics* 35, no. 4 (1976): 335–62, https://doi.org/10.1016/0040-1951(76)90075-5, estimates recurrence intervals at 27 to 132 years for high-magnitude earthquakes, but other sources dispute those estimates.

21. https://earthquake.usgs.gov/hazards/hazmaps/

22. J. B. Eisner et al., "Daily Tornado Frequency Distributions in the United States," *Environmental Research Letters* 9, no. 2 (2014): 1–5, https://doi.org/10.1088/1748-9326/9/2/024018.

23. C. Meyer et al, "A Hazard Model for Tornado Occurrence in the United States," *Climate Variations and Forecasting (Joint with the Sixteenth Conference Probability and Statistics and the Thirteenth Symposium on Global Change and Climate Variations)*, Session J3.6. (2000), www.nssl.noaa.gov/users/brooks/public_html/papers/meyeretal.pdf.

24. T. Coleman and P. Dixon, "An Objective Analysis of Tornado Risk in the United States," *Weather and Forecasting*, 29, no. 2 (2014): 366–76, https://doi.org/10.1175/WAF-D-13-00057.1.

25. As an example, 45 C.F.R. § 164.308, which implements the Health Insurance Portability and Accountability Act, requires regulated entities and their business associates to establish and implement procedures to create and maintain "retrievable exact copies" of electronic protected health information. As specified in 21 C.F.R. § 211.68 and volume 4, annex 11 of Rules Governing Medicinal Products in the European Union, pharmaceutical companies must maintain backup copies of drug manufacturing data. FINRA Rule 4730, issued by the Financial

Industry Regulatory Authority, mandates data backup and recovery capabilities for all mission-critical information systems. According to 19 C.F.R. § 163.5, businesses that import merchandise into the customs territory of the United States must create backup copies of all information required by customs laws and regulations. In the United States, federally regulated financial institutions are required to have backup copies of electronic data. Banking laws and regulations in other countries have similar requirements.

26. A 2013 survey by AVG Technologies, a provider of Internet security and antivirus products, found that more than half of small and midsize business in the United States and United Kingdom do not perform daily backups: www.silicon.co.uk/workspace/small-businesses-data-loss-131887.

27. A 2014 survey of five hundred organizations with fewer than one hundred employees by Carbonite, a provider of cloud-based backup services, found that less than 35 percent send their backup data to an offsite location on a daily basis: www.slideshare.net/Carbonite/carbonite-stateofbackupebook

28. Various studies assess the risk of natural disasters in specific locations. Examples include M. Dilley et al., *Natural Disaster Hotspots: A Global Risk Analysis* (Washington, DC: World Bank Hazard Management Unit, 2005), http://documents.worldbank.org/curated/en/621711468175150317/pdf/344230PAPER0Na101official0use0only1.pdf; *The Global Risks Report 2019, Fourteenth Edition* (Geneva: World Economic Forum, 2019), www3.weforum.org/docs/WEF_Global_Risks_Report_2019.pdf; *World Risk Report 2017* (Berlin: Bundis Entwicklung Hilft, 2017), https://reliefweb.int/report/world/world-risk-report-2017; L. Sundermann et al., *Mind the Risk: A Global Ranking of Cities Under Threat from Natural Disasters* (Zurich: Swiss Reinsurance Company, 2013), https://reliefweb.int/sites/reliefweb.int/files/resources/Mind%20the%20risk_A%20global%20ranking%20of%20cities%20under%20threat%20from%20natural%20disasters.pdf.

29. A 2017 survey of ninety organizations by Forrester Research found that the median distance between original and backup sites was seventy-four miles. S. Balaouras, "The State of Disaster Recovery Preparedness 2017," *Disaster Recovery Journal* 30, no. 1 (2017): 9–18, https://drj.com/images/surveys_pdf/forrester/2017-Forrester-Survey.pdf. In a 2014 report, Gartner Inc., a business research and advisory company, recommended a sixty-mile separation. Report GOO257751, *How to Identify the Best Data Center Locations for Disaster Recovery*, January 10, 2014, www.gartner.com/en/documents/2648117.

30. For a categorization of malware-related events that disrupt computer operations, see C. Harry and N. Gallagher, *Classifying Cyber Events: A Proposed Taxonomy* (College Park, MD: University of Maryland Center for International and Security Studies, 2018), www.cissm.umd.edu/sites/default/files/Cyber-Taxonomy-101918.pdf.

31. This definition is adapted from D. Caldara and I. Matteo, *Measuring Geopolitical Risk, International Finance Discussion Papers No. 1222* (Washington, DC: Board of Governors of the Federal Reserve System, 2018), www.federalreserve.gov/econres/ifdp/files/ifdp1222.pdf.

32. This definition is adapted from "How Is the Term 'Armed Conflict' Defined in International Humanitarian Law?" International Committee of the Red Cross, opinion paper, March 2008, www.icrc.org/en/doc/assets/files/other/opinion-paper-armed-conflict.pdf.

33. There is no universally accepted definition of *terrorism*, but most scholars agree on these characteristics. See F. Cooper, "Terrorism: The Problem of Definition Revisited," *American Behavioral Scientist* 44, no. 6 (2001): 881–93, https://doi.org/10.1177/00027640121956575; B. Jenkins, *The Study of Terrorism: Definitional Problems* (Santa Monica, CA: Rand Corporation, 1980), www.rand.org/pubs/papers/P6563.html; M. Czinkota, "Terrorism and International Business: Conceptual Foundations," in *Terrorism and the International Business Environment: The Security-Business Nexus*, ed. G. Suder (Northampton, MA: Edward Elgar Publishing, 2004), 43–57, https://doi.org/10.4337/9781845420772.00013.

34. As defined in 18 U.S.C. § 2151 et seq., sabotage is closely linked to national defense and destruction of fortifications and war material. It is treated as a crime against the government, whereas terrorism is considered a crime against people or property.

35. This section deals with information theft as a form of information loss. The previous chapter discussed situations where an organization may have unintended possession of infor-

mation that properly belongs to another party. A later chapter will discuss information that is stolen with the intent of disclosing it to others.

36. For a discussion of this issue, see M. Tigar, "The Right of Property and the Law of Theft," *Texas Law Review* 62, no. 6 (1984): 1443–75, https://scholarship.law.duke.edu/cgi/viewcontent.cgi?article=5870&context=faculty_scholarship.

37. In US history, infamous perpetrators of espionage-related theft have included Major John Andre, who was arrested in possession of stolen papers obtained from Benedict Arnold; Alger Hiss, who reportedly had his wife copy classified documents by retyping them; Aldrich Ames, a CIA officer turned double agent who gave originals and copies of classified documents to his KGB handlers; Jonathan Pollard, a government intelligence analyst who delivered hundreds of classified documents to Mossad; and Robert Hanssen, an FBI agent who sold thousands of classified documents to the KGB. Well-known perpetrators of information theft motivated by political activism include Daniel Ellsberg, whose photocopies of the so-called Pentagon Papers were subsequently published by the *New York Times*; Edward J. Snowden, who copied and leaked classified information about the National Security Agency's global surveillance activities; and Julian P. Assange, whose WikiLeaks organization published classified documents about the Iraq war and other matters.

38. In the United States, theft of government records is a crime, as specified in 18 U.S.C. §§ 641, 1506, and 2071. The Computer Fraud and Abuse Act (18 U.S.C. § 1030) criminalizes unauthorized retrieval of information from a government computer or financial records from a financial institution. The Economic Espionage Act of 1996 (18 U.S.C. § 1832) prohibits unauthorized removal, downloading, or reproduction of trade secrets. Many states have adopted a version of the Uniform Trade Secrets Act, which prohibits theft of trade secrets. Under the Identity Theft and Assumption Deterrence Act (18 U.S.C. § 1028), identity theft for purposes that violate federal law is a crime. Every state has a law that criminalizes identity theft. Other countries have similar laws that prohibit information theft.

39. In *O'Day v. McDonnell Douglas Helicopter Co.*, 79 F.3d 756 (9th Cir. 1996), for example, the plaintiff, having been denied a promotion, entered his supervisor's office after hours and copied documents that he thought might be useful for his discrimination claim: https://caselaw.findlaw.com/az-supreme-court/1006795.html. In *Vannoy v. Celanese Corp.*, No. 09-1118, 2011 DOLSOX LEXIS 68 (ARB Sept. 28, 2011), an employee removed confidential and sensitive documents to support a disclosure under the IRS Whistleblower Rewards Program. www.employmentlawgroup.com/wp-content/pdf/09_118.SOXP_.pdf. In *Quinlan v. Curtiss-Wright Corp.*, 204 N.J. 239 (N.J. Dec. 2, 2010), the plaintiff was fired for copying hundreds of documents to support her claim of widespread sex discrimination: www.courtlistener.com/opinion/2556532/quinlan-v-curtiss-wright-corp.

40. U. Bayer et al., "A View on Current Malware Behaviors," in *LEET '09 Proceedings of the Second USENIX Conference on Large-Scale Exploits and Emergent Threats: Botnets, Spyware, Worms, and More* (Berkeley, CA: USENIX Association, 2009), 1–8, http://static.usenix.org/events/leet09/tech/full_papers/bayer/bayer.pdf.

41. www.av-test.org/en/statistics/malware.

42. Kapersky Security Bulletin 2018, https://securelist.com/kaspersky-security-bulletin-2018-statistics/89145.

43. D. Braha, "Global Civil Unrest: Contagion, Self-Organization, and Prediction," *PLoS One* 7, no. 10 (2012): e48596, https://doi.org/10.1371/journal.pone.0048596, analyzed the records of civil unrest in 170 countries from 1919 to 2008 but found no pattern in time or geography. D. Sasikala and K. Premalatha, "Social Network Analysis for Prediction of Civil Unrest: A Review," *International Journal of Pure and Applied Mathematics* 119, no. 16 (2018): 4389–95, https://acadpubl.eu/hub/2018-119-16/2/457.pdf, reviews the literature that analyzed social media to predict civil unrest, noting a variety of approaches.

44. P. Gilje, *Rioting in America* (Bloomington: Indiana University Press, 1996).

45. T. Pettersson and P. Wallensteen, "Armed Conflicts, 1946-2014," *Journal of Peace Research* 52, no. 4 (2015): 536–50, https://doi.org/10.1177/0022343315595927; T. Pettersson and K. Eck, "Organized Violence, 1989–2017," *Journal of Peace Research* 55, no. 4 (2018): 535–47, https://doi.org/10.1177/0022343318784101.

46. H. van der Hoeven and J. van Albada, *Memory of the World: Lost Memory—Libraries and Archives Destroyed in the Twentieth Century* (Paris: General Information Programme and UNISIST, United Nations Educational, Scientific and Cultural Organization, 1996); I. Filippov, "Destruction of Archives and Historical Science," in *Identity and Loss of Historical Memory* (Bern: Peter Lang, 2017), 7–14; A. Riedlmayer, "Erasing the Past: The Destruction of Libraries and Archives in Bosnia-Herzegovina," *Review of Middle East Studies* 29, no. 1 (1995): 7–11, https://doi.org/10.1017/S0026318400030418; H. Wood, "The Destruction of the Public Records: The Loss to Irish History," *Studies: An Irish Quarterly Review* 11, no. 43 (1922): 363–78; D. Cox, "National Archives and International Conflicts: The Society of American Archivists and War," *American Archivist* 74, no. 2 (2011): 451–81, https://doi.org/10.17723/aarc.74.2.42332g3h5p685w87; B. Montgomery, "The Rape of Kuwait's National Memory," *International Journal of Cultural Property* 22, no. 1 (2015): 61–84, https://doi.org/10.1017/S0940739115000053; P. Nugent, "Battlefields, Tools, and Targets: Archives and Armed Conflict," *Provenance, Journal of the Society of Georgia Archivists* 23, no. 1 (2005): 39–55, https://digitalcommons.kennesaw.edu/cgi/viewcontent.cgi?article=1075&context=provenance.

47. *Global Peace Index 2019: Measuring Peace in a Complex World.* (Sydney: Institute for Economics & Peace, 2019), http://visionofhumanity.org/app/uploads/2019/06/GPI-2019-web003.pdf.

48. E. Miller, *Background Report: Global Terrorism in 2017* (College Park, MD: National Consortium for the Study of Terrorism and Responses to Terrorism, 2018), www.start.umd.edu/pubs/START_GTD_Overview2017_July2018.pdf. START's Global Terrorism Database is searchable at www.start.umd.edu/gtd/search/?back=1&casualties_type=b&casualties_max=&start_year=1970&start_month=1&start_day=1&end_year=2016&end_month=12&end_day=31&criterion1=yes&criterion2=yes&criterion3=yes&dtp2=some&success=no&country=217&count=100.

49. A. Pascual et al., *2018 Identity Fraud: Fraud Enters a New Era of Complexity* (Pleasanton, CA: Javelin Strategy & Research, 2018), www.javelinstrategy.com/coverage-area/2018-identity-fraud-fraud-enters-new-era-complexity.

50. *Computer Sentinel Network Data Book 2018* (Washington, DC: Federal Trade Commission, 2019), www.ftc.gov/system/files/documents/reports/consumer-sentinel-network-data-book-2018/consumer_sentinel_network_data_book_2018_0.pdf.

51. E. Harrell, *Victims of Identity Theft, 2016, NCJ 251147* (Washington, DC: Bureau of Justice Statistics, 2019), www.bjs.gov/content/pub/pdf/vit16.pdf.

52. Z. Tu et al., "Learning to Cope with Information Security Risks Regarding Mobile Device Loss or Theft: An Empirical Examination," *Information & Management* 52, no. 4 (2015): 506–17, https://doi.org/10.1016/j.im.2015.03.002; Z. Tu and Y. Yuan, "Coping with BYOD Security Threat: From Management Perspective," Emergent Research Forum Paper presented at the Twenty-First Americas Conference on Information Systems (AMCIS), 2015, https://pdfs.semanticscholar.org/4572/a09c1f609f828c6c25183f39ca928874778d.pdf?_ga=2.228257757.1103046221.1560522746-1616480029.1532633155.

53. Among the many examples that might be cited, two laptops containing health information were stolen from an office at AvMed Health Plans, a healthcare provider in South Florida, in 2009. In that year, fifty-seven hard drives were stolen from a data storage closet at a call center operated by Blue Cross Blue Shield of Tennessee, which subsequently paid a $1.5 million penalty to settle alleged HIPAA violations. In 2011, GRM Information Management, a record storage provider based in New Jersey, reported the theft of data tapes containing health records from an unlocked delivery van. In the same year, unencrypted backup tapes containing patient information were reported missing from a storage cabinet at Nemours Foundation, a pediatric healthcare provider, and SAIC, a government contractor, reported that backup tapes containing health information were taken from an employee's car while they were being transported between federal facilities as part of required backup procedures. In 2012, Howard University Hospital notified patients that their medical data was stolen from a laptop that was left unattended in a contractor's car. In the same year, a Howard University employee was arrested for stealing patient information in order to sell it. In 2013, Advocate Medical Group, the largest health system in Illinois, reported that four laptops containing unencrypted health information were stolen from an administrative office. In 2017, Sutter Health, a Northern

California healthcare provider, reported that paper documents containing personal health information were stolen from an employee's locked car. Sutter Health had previously reported the theft of a computer containing patient data in 2011.

54. 2009 Trust, Security & Passwords Survey, CyberArk Software Inc., July 2009, www.tomsnetworking.de/uploads/media/Cyber-Ark_Snooping_Survey_2009_FINAL.pdf. In a follow-up survey of 820 information technology professionals, almost half of the respondents indicated that they would take some information with them if they were fired. Global Trust, Security & Passwords Survey, CyberArk Software Inc., June 2012, www.dit.co.jp/products/cyberark/pdf/2012Cyber-Ark_TrustSecurityPasswordReport.pdf. Two-thirds of the participants in the Code42 survey said that the work they perform for their employer belongs to them, despite company policies to the contrary. https://on.code42.com/go/content-data-exposure-report-g.

55. For a discussion of cyber insurance coverage, see S. Romanosky et al., "Content Analysis of Cyber Insurance Policies: How Do Carriers Price Cyber Risk?" *Journal of Cybersecurity* 5, no. 1 (2019): tyz002, https://doi.org/10.1093/cybsec/tyz002.

56. See, for example, M. Souppaya and K. Scarfone, *Guide to Malware Incident Prevention and Handling for Desktops and Laptops, NIST Special Publication 800-83* (Gaithersburg, MD: National Institute of Standards and Technology, 2013), https://nvlpubs.nist.gov/nistpubs/SpecialPublications/NIST.SP.800-83r1.pdf.

57. A high position of authority is no guarantee of trustworthiness. In 2003, Sandy Berger, formerly the national security advisor in the Clinton administration, removed classified documents from the National Archives reading room, allegedly by concealing the documents in his clothing. See "Sandy Berger's Theft of Classified Documents: Unanswered Questions, Staff Report of the U.S. House of Representatives Committee on Oversight and Government Reform," January 9, 2007, https://fas.org/irp/congress/2007_rpt/berger.pdf.

58. The Oxford English Dictionary defines an error as "something incorrectly done through ignorance or inadvertence." The lack of intention is an essential characteristic. J. Cebula et al., *A Taxonomy of Operational Cyber Security Risks, Version 2, Report CMU/SEI-2014-TN-006* (Pittsburgh, PA: Software Engineering Institute, Carnegie-Mellon University, May 2014), https://resources.sei.cmu.edu/library/asset-view.cfm?assetid=91013, distinguishes errors, which are incorrect actions by individuals without knowledge of correct procedures, from mistakes, which are incorrect actions by individuals with knowledge of the correct procedures. In either case, the action is unintentional. Many studies of human error focus on accident prevention in manufacturing, transportation, engineering, healthcare, or other fields. See, for example, J. Reason, *Human Error* (Cambridge: Cambridge University Press, 1990); S. Dekker, *The Field Guide to 'Human Error'* (Boca Raton, FL: CRC Press, 2014); B. Strauch, *Investigating Human Error: Incidents, Accidents, and Complex System, Second Edition* (Boca Raton, FL: CRC Press, 2017); T. Kletz, *An Engineer's View of Human Error* (Boca Raton, FL: CRC Press, 2001); T. Muschara, *Risk-Based Thinking: Managing the Uncertainty of Human Error in Operations* (New York: Routledge, 2018).

59. The relationship of human error and information loss is discussed in many publications, including M. Sumner, "Information Security Threats: A Comparative Analysis of Impact, Probability, and Preparedness," *Information Management* 26, no. 1 (2009): 2–12, https://doi.org/10.1080/10580530802384639; K. Loch et al., "Threats to Information Systems: Today's Reality, Yesterday's Understanding," *MIS Quarterly* 16, no. 2 (1992): 173–86, https://doi.org/10.2307/249574; T. Muhrtala and M. Ogundeji, "Computerized Accounting Information Systems and Perceived Security Threats in Developing Economies: The Nigerian Case," *Universal Journal of Accounting and Finance*, 1, no. 1 (2013): 9–18, www.hrpub.org/journals/article_info.php?aid=168; T. Hayale and H. Abu Khadra, "Investigating Perceived Security Threats of Computerized Accounting Information: An Empirical Research Applied on Jordanian Banking Sector," *Journal of Economic and Administrative Sciences* 24, no. 1 (2008): 41–67, https://doi.org/10.1108/10264116200800003; E. Davis, "Perceived Risks and Threats to Accounting Information Systems," *Review of Business Information Systems (RBIS)* 1, no. 4 (1997): 13–24, https://doi.org/10.19030/rbis.v1i4.5507; C. Wood and W. Banks Jr., "Human Error: An Overlooked but Significant Information Security Problem," *Computers & Security*, 12, no. 1 (1993): 51–60, https://doi.org/10.1016/0167-4048(93)90012-T.

60. While magnetic fields are commonly encountered in offices, schools, libraries, or other places where magnetic media are stored or used, the dangers posed by accidental erasure are generally overrated. To erase recorded information, a stray magnetic field must be in close contact with the medium to be erased. See S. Geller, *Care and Handling of Computer Magnetic Storage Media, NBS Special Publication 500-1-1* (Washington, DC: National Bureau of Standards, 1983); W. Saffady, "Stability, Care and Handling of Microforms, Magnetic Media, and Optical Disks," *Library Technology Reports* 33, no. 6 (1997): 609–751.

61. T. Huckle and T. Neckel, *Bits and Bugs: A Scientific and Historical Review of Software Failures in Computational Science* (Philadelphia: Society for Industrial and Applied Mathematics, 2019); S. Sherer, *Software Failure Risk: Measurement and Management* (New York: Springer Science+Business Media, 1992).

62. The survey was conducted by Kroll Ontrack, a company that provides data recovery, computer forensics, and related technology-driven services. In 2005, 11 percent of respondents reported losing information through human errors, and 56 percent reported data loss due to technological malfunction: www.prweb.com/releases/2010/07/prweb4293604.htm.

63. The survey was conducted for Axcient, a cloud-based recovery service provider, by Dimensional Research, a technology market research company. Respondents in 69 percent of companies believed mid-level IT staff accountable for data loss resulting from a system failure: https://axcient.com/wp-content/uploads/2014/11/Axcient-SMB-Backup-and-Recovery-Survey-Report-2014.pdf.

64. The survey was conducted by Poneman Institute, a technology research company, for Emerson Network Power, a provider of equipment and services to data centers. Emerson Network Power was acquired by Vertiv in 2016: www.ponemon.org/local/upload/file/2013%20Cost%20of%20Data%20Center%20Outages%20FINAL%2012.pdf.

65. The survey, titled Data Health Check 2018, was conducted by Databarracks, a company that specializes in business continuity and data recovery services: www.databarracks.com/resources/data-health-check-2018.

66. The lost content was eventually reconstructed with considerable effort and difficulty, but the film itself was ultimately reworked for reasons unrelated to the accidental deletion. For more information, see https://thenextweb.com/media/2012/05/21/how-pixars-toy-story-2-was-deleted-twice-once-by-technology-and-again-for-its-own-good, or the short video "Studio Stories: The Movie Vanishes" at www.youtube.com/watch?v=7l8B16Y7Sp0.

67. The GitLab database reported contained information about five thousand projects. Some of the deleted data was unrecoverable: https://about.gitlab.com/2017/02/10/postmortem-of-database-outage-of-january-31.

68. The survey was conducted by Spiceworks, an online community and marketplace for technology industry professionals: www.spiceworks.com/marketing/state-of-it/report.

69. www.statista.com/statistics/430769/annual-failure-rates-of-servers.

70. E. Pinheiro et al., "Failure Trends in a Large Disk Drive Population," in *Proceedings of the Fifth USENIX Conference on File and Storage Technologies* (Berkeley, CA: USENIX, 2007), 17–28, http://static.googleusercontent.com/media/research.google.com/en//archive/disk_failures.pdf. J. F. Paris et al, *Evaluating the Reliability of Storage Systems, Technical Report No. UH-CS-06-08* (Houston: Department of Computer Science, University of Houston, 2006), https://pdfs.semanticscholar.org/d4df/20eb266f8c5ccc96d9be9ab4cc8613fe8981.pdf?_ga=2.164928767.1716857810.1558799853-1616480029.1532633155. On reasons for hard drive failure, see J. Elerath, "Hard-Disk Drives: The Good, the Bad, and the Ugly," *Communications of the ACM* 52, no. 6 (2009): 38–45, https://doi.org//10.1145/1516046.1516059.

71. N. Keith and M. Frese, "Enhancing Firm Performance and Innovativeness through Error Management Culture," in *The Handbook of Organizational Culture and Climate*, 2nd ed., ed. N. Ashkanasy et al. (Thousand Oaks, CA: SAGE, 2011), 137–49; N. Kieth and M. Frese, "Effectiveness of Error Management Training: A Meta-Analysis," *Journal of Applied Psychology* 93, no. 1 (1993): 59–69, https://doi.org/10.1037/0021-9010.93.1.59; C. van Dyck, "Organizational Error Management Culture and Its Impact on Performance: A Two-Study Replication," *Journal of Applied Psychology* 90, no. 6 (2009): 1228–40, http://dx.doi.org/10.1037/0021-9010.90.6.1228; U. Gronewold et al., "Reporting Self-Made Errors: The Impact of Organizational Error-Management Climate and Error Type," *Journal of Business Ethics* 117, no.

1 (2013): 189–208, https://doi.org/10.1007/s10551-012-1500-6; C. Seifert and E. Hutchins, "Error as Opportunity: Learning in a Cooperative Task," *Human-Computer Interaction* 7, no. 4 (1992): 409–35, http://dx.doi.org/10.1207/s15327051hci0704_3; K. Dahlin et al., "Opportunity, Motivation, and Ability to Learn from Failures and Errors: Review, Synthesis, and Ways to Move Forward," *Academy of Management Annals* 12, no. 1 (2017): 252–77, https://doi.org/10.5465/annals.2016.0049.

72. J. Myszewski, "Management Responsibility for Human Errors," *TQM Journal* 24, no. 4 (2012): 326–37, https://doi.org/10.1108/17542731211247355. An organization may be considered less accountable for errors caused by technological malfunctions than by humans, but this view has no basis in fact. See C. Naquin and T. R. Kurtzberg, "Human Reactions to Technological Failure: How Accidents Rooted in Technology vs. Human Effort Influence Judgments of Organizational Accountability," *Organizational Behavior and Human Decision Processes* 93, no. 2 (2004): 129–41, http://dx.doi.org/10.1016/j.obhdp.2003.12.001.

73. As noted by B. Zhao and F. Olivera, "Error Reporting in Organizations," *Academy of Management Review* 31, no. 4 (2006): 1012–30, https://doi.org/10.2307/20159263, disclosure by the person who made a mistake is often the only way that an organization becomes aware of an error.

74. Wildfire statistics are available from the National Interagency Fire Center at www.nifc.gov/fireInfo/fireInfo_statistics.html.

75. B. Evarts, *Fire Loss in the United States During 2017* (Quincy, MA: National Fire Protection Association, 2018), www.nfpa.org/News-and-Research/Data-research-and-tools/US-Fire-Problem/Fire-loss-in-the-United-States; R. Campbell, *U.S. Structure Fires in Office Properties* (Quincy, MA: National Fire Protection Association, 201), www.nfpa.org/-/media/Files/News-and-Research/Fire-statistics-and-reports/Building-and-life-safety/osoffices.ashx?la=en.

76. Other consequences identified in *NFPA 551: Guide for the Evaluation of Fire Risk Assessments* (Quincy, MA: National Fire Protection Association, 2019) include human losses, environmental damage, loss of image, loss of community confidence, and loss of structures and objects with heritage significance. NFPA codes and standards are available for viewing at no charge at www.nfpa.org/docinfo. ISO 23932:2018, *Fire Safety Engineering—General Principles* lists safety of life, conservation of property, continuity of operations, protection of the environment, and preservation of heritage as fire-safety objectives.

77. J. Borch et al., *Handbook of Physical Testing of Records*, 2nd ed. (Boca Raton, FL: CRC Press, 2001), 406.

78. Permanent magnetization is lost when a given medium is heated to its Curie point, which is named for Pierre Curie, who discovered the disruptive effect of temperature on magnetism. The Curie point of a given magnetic disk or tape depends on the medium's recording material. Magnetic properties are restored when the medium cools, but previously recorded information will be lost.

79. Fire risk assessment principles and concepts are covered in various international standards, including ISO 16732-1:2012, *Fire Safety Engineering—Fire Assessment—Part 1: General*; ISO 16732-2:2012, *Fire Safety Engineering—Fire Assessment—Part 2: Example of an Office Building*; ISO 13943:2008, *Fire Safety—Vocabulary*; ISO 16733-1:2015, *Fire Safety Engineering—Selection of Design Fire Scenarios and Design Fires—Part 1: Selection of Design Fire Scenarios*; ISO 16730-1:2015, *Fire Safety Engineering—Procedures and Requirements for Verification and Calculation Methods—Part 1: General*; and ISO 23932-1:2018, *Fire Safety Engineering—General Principles—Part 1: General.*

80. D. Yung, *Principles of Fire Risk Assessment in Buildings* (Chichester, UK: John Wiley and Sons, 2008), 90–91, estimates the frequency of office building fires in any given year at 0.00012 fires per square meter of floor area. Where sprinklers are installed, there is a greater than 90 percent probability that an office building fire will be extinguished or brought under control before occupants or property are endangered. See also A. M. Hasofer et al., *Risk Analysis in Building Fire Safety Engineering* (London: Routledge, 2007); J. Watts Jr. and M. Kaplan, "Fire Risk Index for Historic Buildings," *Fire Technology* 37, no. 2 (2001): 167–80, https://doi.org/10.1023/A:1011649802894; B. Meachan et al., "Building Fire Risk Analysis," in *SFPE Handbook of Fire Protection Engineering*, ed. M. Hurley (New York: Springer,

2016), 2941–91, https://link.springer.com/chapter/10.1007/978-1-4939-2565-0_75; Y. Kobayashi and H. Nozaki, "A Statistical Method to Evaluate Fire Risks in Non-Residential Buildings in Japan," in *Fire Safety Science—Proceedings of the Eighth International Symposium*, ed. D. Gottuk and B. Lattimer (Washington, DC: International Association for Fire Safety Science), 341–52, http://iafss.org/publications/fss/8/341/view/fss_8-341.pdf; G. Lougheed, "Expected Size of Shielded Fires in Sprinklered Office Buildings," *ASHRAE Transactions* 103, pt. 1 (1997): 395–410, https://pdfs.semanticscholar.org/016f/8e830a8acd0e074acd2ea4caf8c5808c8331.pdf.

81. Of twenty large-loss fires in 2017, ten involved apartment buildings, four occurred in manufacturing facilities, two occurred in industrial warehouses, and one fire each occurred in a high school, a hospital, a country club, and an automobile dealership: S. Badger, *Large-Loss Fires in the United States 2017* (Quincy, MA: National Fire Protection Association, 2018), www.nfpa.org/-/media/Files/News-and-Research/Fire-statistics-and-reports/US-Fire-Problem/osLargeLoss.pdf.

82. Some record centers also store backup data tapes, archival data tapes, video recordings, and other electronic media as well as microfilm and other photographic films, but paper records occupy the majority of space in most facilities.

83. W. Stender and E. Walker, "The National Personnel Records Center Fire: A Study in Disaster," *American Archivist* 37, no. 4 (1974): 521–49, www.archives.gov/files/st-louis/military-personnel/NPRC_fire_a_study_in_disaster.pdf.

84. T. Miller, *Sprinklered Records Storage Facility*, *USFA-TR-107* (Washington, DC: U.S. Fire Administration, 1996), www.usfa.fema.gov/downloads/pdf/publications/tr-106.pdf?utm_source=website&utm_medium=pubsapp&utm_content=Sprinklered%20Records%20Storage%20Facility%20%20(Chicago,%20IL%20-%20October%201996)&utm_campaign=R3D; J. Rothman, "The Many Lives of Iron Mountain," *New Yorker*, October 9, 2013, www.newyorker.com/business/currency/the-many-lives-of-iron-mountain; D. Henriques, "Stored Records Destroyed by Fire," *New York Times*, May 23, 1997, www.nytimes.com/1997/05/23/business/stored-records-destroyed-by-fire-bear-stearns-says.html; L. Mearian, "Iron Mountain Fire in Buenos Aires Kills 9, Destroys Corporate Records," *Computerworld*, February 6, 2014, www.computerworld.com/article/2487415/iron-mountain-fire-in-buenos-aires-kills-9--destroys-corporate-records.html; D. Wiessner, "NYC Warehouse Fire Destroyed Files from 1 Million Court Cases," *Reuters*, March 3, 2015, www.reuters.com/article/us-new-york-documents-fire/nyc-warehouse-fire-destroyed-files-from-1-million-court-cases-idUSKBN0LZ2QE20150303.

85. Overall, structure fires in warehouse-type buildings have declined substantially since 1980, despite significant fire-protection challenges posed by building layouts, ceiling heights, and storage of flammable and combustible items: Richard Campbell, *Structure Fires in Warehouse Properties* (Quincy, MA: National Fire Protection Association, 2016), www.nfpa.org/-/media/Files/News-and-Research/Fire-statistics-and-reports/Building-and-life-safety/oswarehouse.pdf.

86. "Data Center Fires: How Rare Are They?" www.fireline.com/blog/data-center-fires-rare; R. Von Wolffradt, "Fire in Your Data Center: No Power, No Access, Now What," March 20, 2014, www.govtech.com/state/Fire-in-your-Data-Center-No-Power-No-Access-Now-What.html; "NFPA 75 and Fire Protection and Suppression in Data Centers," https://legacy-uploads.ul.com/wp-content/uploads/sites/40/2015/12/NFPA-75-and-Fire-Protection-and-Suppression-in-Data-Centers-white-paper_final.pdf; R. Miller, "Damage from Fisher Plaza Fire: $6.8 million," November 3, 2010, www.datacenterknowledge.com/archives/2010/11/03/damage-from-fisher-plaza-fire-6-8-million; J. Pagliery, "Amazon Data Center on Fire in Virginia," January 9, 2015, https://money.cnn.com/2015/01/09/technology/amazon-data-center-fire; C. Cimpanu, "Loud Sound from Fire Alarm System Shuts Down Nasdaq's Scandinavian Data Center," April 20, 2018, www.bleepingcomputer.com/news/technology/loud-sound-from-fire-alarm-system-shuts-down-nasdaqs-scandinavian-data-center; "Shorting Power Supplies Spark Fire in Downtown Crossing Data Center," June 22, 2018, www.universalhub.com/2018/shorting-power-supplies-spark-fire-downtown; "Fire in Boston Data Center Disrupts Trading Processing," October 13, 2009, www.datacenterdynamics.com/news/fire-in-boston-data-center-disrupts-trading-processing; K. Sweet, "Smoke at Minnesota Data Center Causes Outage for

Wells Fargo Customers," February 7, 2019, www.startribune.com/fire-causes-wells-fargo-customers-to-lose-access-to-accounts/505514282.

87. As evidence of willingness to accept risks, there is no indication that fires in commercial record centers resulted in a loss of customer confidence. Customers who lost records in a fire did not invariably switch to a different storage methodology. Fires in data centers and record storage facilities cease to be newsworthy within a few days of the event. Such fires are initially covered by general news media and trade publications, but follow-up coverage is limited or nonexistent.

88. NFPA 232, *Standard for Protection of Records* (Quincy, MA: National Fire Protection Association, 2017); NFPA 75, *Standard for the Fire Protection of Information Technology Equipment* (Quincy, MA: National Fire Protection Association, 2017). These standards are online at www.nfpa.org/docinfo. The points summarized here are not a substitute for a careful reading of NFPA standards.

Chapter Four

Retention of Information

Retention and destruction of recorded information are critical concerns that must be governed by formalized policies and procedures rather than by the discretion of individual employees or other custodians of the information. A retention schedule identifies information that is maintained by all or part of an organization and specifies the period of time that the information is to be kept. Retention schedules are typically prepared by record managers or information-governance specialists who work with an organization's legal department, compliance officer, department heads, and other stakeholders to ensure that all interests and requirements are addressed. Retention decisions are based on a combination of legal, operational, and scholarly criteria. Permanent preservation is specified for information of scholarly value. Retention decisions based on legal or operational considerations typically apply to nonpermanent information, although some information may have long-term operational value that warrants permanent retention.

Appropriate retention policies and practices for recorded information are important components of an organization's risk management framework. This chapter identifies and discusses the following threats associated with retention and destruction of information:

- failure to comply with laws and regulations that specify minimum or maximum retention periods for information related to particular matters;
- failure to preserve information that is relevant for legal proceedings;
- discarding information that has continuing value (under-retention) or keeping information longer than necessary (over-retention); and
- media instability and obsolescence, which can render information unusable before its retention period elapses.

These threats apply to organizations of all types and sizes. As discussed in the following sections, they can lead to significant adverse consequences, including monetary penalties, court-ordered sanctions, and loss of information of operational or scholarly value.

NONCOMPLIANT RECORDKEEPING

All countries have laws and regulations that prescribe the period of time that certain information must be kept. These laws and regulations, which are collectively characterized as recordkeeping requirements, fall into two broad groups: those that specify minimum retention periods, which can be exceeded for operational purposes or to preserve records of scholarly value, and those that specify maximum retention periods, which mandate the destruction of information when the prescribed time period elapses. Laws and regulations that specify minimum retention periods are far more numerous than those that require destruction of information. Their purpose is to ensure that government agencies will have access to information needed to determine an organization's compliance with laws or regulations to which the information relates. Laws and regulations that specify maximum retention periods are generally intended to ensure timely disposal of data or documents that contain personal information.

Certain recordkeeping laws and regulations apply broadly to organizations of all types and sizes; others are limited to specific industries or business sectors that are subject to regulatory scrutiny. Recordkeeping laws and regulations in the first category specify minimum retention requirements for information related to commonly encountered business functions and operations.[1] Widely cited examples include the following:

- All countries have laws and regulations that specify recordkeeping requirements for business formation and organizational governance. In the United States, the Model Business Corporation Act (MBCA) has been adopted by many states. It specifies permanent retention for minutes of all meetings of a company's shareholders and board of directors as well as for records of all resolutions or other actions taken by committees acting in place of the board of directors.[2] The MCBA specifies a three-year period for financial statements and other written communications sent to a company's shareholders. A corporation must keep its articles of incorporation, bylaws, and amendments to those documents at its principal office. No retention period is specified, but the implication is that business formation records must be kept for the life of the organization. Violations of the MBCA's recordkeeping requirements expose an organization to shareholder litigation and regulatory investigations.

- Many countries have accounting laws, tax codes, or other laws and regulations that specify minimum retention periods ranging from three years to more than ten years for an organization's financial records, including accounting ledgers, financial statements, fiscal audit reports, and supporting documentation, including inventory records, accounts payable and receivable records, and correspondence related to accounting transactions.[3] Failure to comply with these requirements exposes an organization to costly fines and time-consuming audits or other investigations. Some laws also mandate retention of accounting records at a specified location in the country where business is conducted. This is done to ensure the availability of accounting records for tax audits and, in the case of corporations and partnerships, inspection of the records by shareholders and government regulators.
- Many countries have laws and regulations that specify minimum retention periods for employment records. In the United States, employers must keep records of each employee's name, address, date of birth, occupation, rate of pay, and weekly compensation for a minimum of three years as specified in 29 C.F.R. § 1627.3(a). According to Canada Labour Standards Regulations, employers must keep information about hours worked, wages, earnings, and other personnel matters related to individual employees for a minimum of thirty-six months after termination of employment. To comply with the Fair Work Act 2009, Australian employers must retain employee records and pay rosters for a minimum of seven years. Additional retention requirements apply to records that verify an employee's eligibility to work in a given country.[4] Countries that prohibit discriminatory hiring practices require retention of records that document the recruitment and selection process for specific job openings. According to 29 C.F.R. § 1602.14 and 29 C.F.R. § 1627.3(b), nongovernmental employers in the United States must retain hiring records, including employment applications and supporting documentation considered in connection with an advertised job opening, for a minimum of one year from the date of the personnel action to which the records relate.[5]
- All countries have laws and regulations that specify minimum retention periods for records related to import and export of merchandise to and from their customs territory. Examples of such records include import and export authorizations, certificates of origin, invoices, manifests, bills of lading, customs declarations, customs clearances, and claims for refund of taxes, duties, and fees. 19 C.F.R. § 163.4, for example, specifies a minimum retention period of five years for most import and export records required by U.S. Customs and Border Protection. In Canada, import and export records must be retained for six years as specified in the Imported Goods Records Regulations and the Exporters' and Producers' Records

Regulations. In most other countries, the retention period for customs records is five years or less.

Worldwide, thousands of sector-specific laws and regulations mandate minimum retention periods for records maintained by particular types of business entities. Banks, credit unions, broker-dealers, and other financial services companies must retain information about their customers, individual transactions, assets, liabilities, and marketing activities. Insurance companies must retain information about policies and claims. Hospitals, clinics, physicians' offices, and other healthcare providers must retain information about patients. Pharmacies must retain information about the purchase, receipt, dispensing, and disposal of controlled substances. Schools must retain information about students. Law firms must retain information about work performed for clients. Accounting firms must retain records and work papers related to audits of public companies. Drug companies must retain documentation about manufacturing, testing, packaging, labeling, and marketing of pharmaceutical products and medical devices. Food companies must retain records related to ingredients, manufacturing processes, inspection, labeling, and transportation of their products. Manufacturers of certain consumer products must maintain manufacturing and sales information. Airlines, railroads, and other transportation companies must retain information about their equipment, facilities, authorized operators, and maintenance procedures. These sector-specific recordkeeping regulations are not limited to companies and not-for-profit organizations. In many countries, government agencies must comply with record retention requirements specified by archival authorities.[6]

Some laws and regulations mandate the destruction of information after a designated period of time or when a specific event occurs. In some countries, surveillance recordings produced by video devices installed in public spaces must be destroyed within thirty days or less. Many countries mandate the destruction of information about unsubstantiated child abuse investigations, either immediately or after a specified period of time. Privacy and data protection laws limit the retention of personal information. As the most widely publicized example, the European Commission's General Data Protection Regulation (GDPR), which is discussed in different contexts in other chapters, allows a data subject to request the destruction of his or her personal information when it is no longer needed for the purpose for which it was originally collected or when the data subject withdraws consent for processing.[7] When so requested, an organization must erase the personal information without delay unless certain conditions apply.[8] This requirement applies broadly to personnel files, payroll databases, tax records, workplace health and safety records, customer information, shareholder information, student records, patient records, library cardholder records, and many other types of data and documents. Exclusions are provided for reasons related to national security, national defense, public safety, prosecution of criminal offenses, scientific research, and avoidance of ethical breaches by regulated professions. As a complicating factor, erasure requests do not override minimum retention periods that are specified in laws or regulations.

The constitutions of some Latin American countries contain "habeas data" provisions that allow data subjects to request destruction of incorrect information about them.[9] In the United States, which does not have a comprehensive data protection law, the right to be forgotten applies to a limited range of personal information. As specified in 34 C.F.R. § 300.624, public school districts must destroy personal information about special education students at a parent's request when the information is no longer needed to provide educational services to the child. At the state level, the California Consumer Privacy Act of 2018 allows a consumer to request the deletion of personal information maintained by a business and its service providers when the information is no longer needed to complete a transaction or provide goods or services to the consumer, subject to specified exceptions.[10] In most states and localities, criminal case information related to juvenile offenders musts be destroyed after a specified period of time if certain conditions are met. Some other countries have similar laws.

Violation of legally mandated recordkeeping requirements exposes an organization to regulatory investigations and compliance audits, which are time-consuming and may lead to fines, administrative penalties, or, in rare cases, criminal prosecution. In the United States, for example, willful failure to comply with retention requirements for employment records covered by the Fair Labor Standards Act is punishable by fines and imprisonment as specified in 29 U.S.C. § 216. Among the many industry-specific regulations that penalize recordkeeping violations, 19 U.S.C. 1509(g) imposes fines up to $100,000 for willful or negligent failure to comply with retention requirements for certain customs records. 15 U.S.C. §§ 2614-2615 and 19 C.F.R. § 163.6 impose a range of civil and criminal penalties for violation of recordkeeping requirements specified in the Toxic Substances Control Act. 43 C.F.R. § 3161 specifies monetary assessments, civil penalties, and criminal penalties for violations of recordkeeping requirements specified by the Bureau of Land Management's Oil and Gas program. 10 C.F.R. § 21.41 prescribes minimum retention periods ranging from five to fifteen years for records related to maintenance and inspection of facilities that handle nuclear material with criminal penalties for willful noncompliance. The Consumer Financial Protection Bureau imposes penalties up to $10,000 for individual actions and $500,000 for class actions, as specified in 12 C.F.R. § 1002.16, for violations of recordkeeping regulations associated with the Equal Credit Opportunity Act.

Other countries levy similar sanctions for noncompliance with minimum record retention periods. In Canada, for example, the Investment Industry Regulatory Organization imposes fines up to $5 million for violations of the five-year retention rule for transaction documentation, communications, advertisements, and other records related to investment services. In the United Kingdom, the Financial Conduct Authority, which mandates a five-year retention period for investment firm records, imposes a graduated range of penalties for noncompliance, depending on the seriousness of the violation.

Vulnerability Assessment

Recordkeeping noncompliance may be detected during a routine regulatory audit or in the course of an investigation of a suspected violation of the laws or regulations to which the information pertains.[11] The following vulnerabilities contribute to the risk of noncompliance with recordkeeping requirements specified in laws and regulations:

- A regulated entity may not be aware of all applicable recordkeeping requirements. An organization's records manager or information governance specialist, working in cooperation with a compliance officer or legal department, is typically responsible for identifying laws and regulations that specify minimum retention periods, but some organizations do not have in-house records management or compliance expertise. Even for those that do, it can be difficult to keep informed about all applicable legal and regulatory requirements, especially in multinational and transnational organizations that must comply with the laws and regulations of multiple political jurisdictions. Many countries have government-sponsored databases of laws, regulations, ordinance, directives, and other legal instruments that specify retention requirements, but identification of applicable legal mandates requires retrieval expertise and careful examination of legal instruments, many of them irrelevant. To identify a dozen relevant laws or regulations, hundreds must be located, read, and analyzed.
- A regulated entity may not correctly interpret record retention requirements. Recordkeeping laws and regulations can be voluminous, complicated, poorly written, and difficult to understand. Amendments may add complexity and confusion. It may be difficult to determine the specific types of information that must be kept about a given matter. Some laws and regulations merely state that certain records must be kept without specifying a retention period for them. For multinational and transnational organizations, laws and regulations in unfamiliar languages must be translated, which can be difficult and may add ambiguity.
- Legal and regulatory requirements are presumably reflected in an organization's record-retention schedule, assuming that it has one, but many

retention schedules are incomplete, out of date, and difficult to use. [12] Employees may not be able to comply fully with retention requirements due to lack of clear instructions, inadequate staffing, insufficient training, or ineffective supervision. Record custodians and data stewards in some organizational units may not be aware that a retention schedule exists. This is sometimes the case with new employees or those who work in satellite locations or home offices. The progress of record-retention initiatives can be difficult to monitor in large enterprises with complex organizational structures and geographically dispersed business operations. In multinational and transnational organizations, an organization's retention schedule may focus on records maintained at a headquarters location, but business operations in other countries may be subject to different legal and regulatory requirements.

- A regulated entity's business processes and practices may not be conducive to compliance with record-retention laws and regulations. The required information may not be maintained in a single repository. It may be managed by multiple applications, saved in multiple formats, scattered in multiple locations, and controlled by employees who are not aware of an organization's recordkeeping policies.

Risk Response

Noncompliant recordkeeping means that information is destroyed before the minimum time period specified in laws or regulations has elapsed or that information is kept longer than the maximum time period specified in laws or regulations. Risk acceptance, risk avoidance, and risk transfer are not viable mitigation strategies for noncompliance.

Risk acceptance based on a conscious business decision not to comply fully with legal and regulatory recordkeeping requirements is not advisable. Fines for failing to retain or destroy information can add up for persistent noncompliance, and some regulations impose greater penalties for willful violations. Monetary penalties aside, regulatory noncompliance exposes an organization to additional risks that can have an adverse impact on the organization's objectives and performance. Noncompliance with recordkeeping requirements may raise the level of regulatory scrutiny, leading to audits and inspections that can be time-consuming, will likely raise legal costs, and may reveal additional problems that require corrective action. In extreme cases, regulatory authorities may force a noncompliant organization to suspend critical business operations until violations are corrected. Noncompliance also poses risks to an organization's reputation, which can damage business relationships, erode the confidence of investors and other stakeholders, lead to loss of revenue, and make it difficult to recruit and keep qualified employees.

For risk avoidance, the operation or activity that is subject to recordkeeping laws and regulations must be eliminated. This is not a feasible mitigation strategy where the regulated activity is a core component of an organization's business. An organization cannot eliminate recruitment of new employees to avoid keeping applicant records and job descriptions. A company cannot discontinue accounting operations to avoid retention requirements for ledgers, financial reports, and supporting documentation. A bank or brokerage firm cannot eliminate customers to avoid recordkeeping requirements. A healthcare organization cannot eliminate patients to avoid retaining information about them. A pharmaceutical company cannot eliminate new drug products to avoid retention requirements for records related to manufacturing, testing, labeling, and marketing.

Risk transfer through insurance is generally not an option for regulatory violations. Most insurance policies exclude coverage for civil fines and penalties resulting from illegal activity, although insurance coverage may be available for legal fees and other costs associated with government investigations and litigation.

A risk limitation plan that directly addresses the vulnerabilities discussed in the preceding section is the only effective mitigation strategy for noncompliant recordkeeping. An effective limitation plan will reduce the likelihood of regulatory violations:

- An organization's top management and key stakeholders must be committed to compliance. They must understand the importance, purpose, and scope of legal and regulatory requirements and authorize the necessary resources for fully compliant recordkeeping in all organizational units in every location where the organization operates.
- Ignorance of or confusion about recordkeeping requirements is not an acceptable defense for noncompliance. A records manager, information governance officer, compliance specialist, legal researcher, or another qualified employee must be responsible for identifying, analyzing, and interpreting applicable laws and regulations, including any amendments and supplemental guidance documents, that mandate retention or destruction of specific information. This must be done for all national and subnational jurisdictions where an organization operates. If necessary, records management consultants, legal researchers, or compliance specialists should be hired to supplement internal expertise.
- As the key component in a risk limitation plan, an organization must have a comprehensive, up-to-date record-retention schedule that accurately reflects legal and regulatory requirements in all locations where the organization operates. The retention schedule must be distributed to all departments or other organizational units where records are kept. An organization's records manager, information governance officer, or other qualified

employee must work closely and cooperatively with departmental stake-holders to ensure that recordkeeping requirements are well understood, to address questions and concerns raised by record custodians and data ste-wards, and to ensure that implementation issues and problems are appropriately resolved.

- In most organizations, individual departments are responsible for implementing the retention schedule for data or documents in their custody or under their supervisory control. All departmental employees will require a basic understanding of the organization's retention policies and requirements. Appropriate training must be provided to record custodians and data stewards. Clearly written specifications and operating procedures must be prepared for use as training materials. Organizational units should be given a due-diligence checklist or similar quality-control mechanism to ensure that all record-retention and -destruction tasks have been properly completed.

- Regular or unscheduled audits of selected organization units should be conducted to confirm compliance with recordkeeping requirements. Such audits may be performed by a records manager, by an information govern-ance officer, or by a compliance-oriented organizational unit, such as internal audit or quality assurance. Compliance problems and corrective actions should be discussed with departmental stakeholders, with a follow-up to confirm compliance. Continuing problems should be referred to executive management for resolution.

FAILURE TO PRESERVE EVIDENCE

In the absence of a law, regulation, or contractual obligation that specifies recordkeeping requirements, an organization can retain or discard informa-tion according to its own policies, practices, and criteria, which may take the information's continuing operational usefulness or scholarly value into ac-count. As a notable exception, an organization involved in a lawsuit, govern-ment investigation, arbitration, or other legal proceeding has a duty to pre-serve data or documents, including video and audio recordings, that may be relevant for a party's claims or defenses. This preservation duty encompasses relevant information in the organization's possession as well as information the organization has entrusted to agents, experts, attorneys, insurance compa-nies, accountants, cloud-based service providers, record storage companies, or other third parties. In the United States, the preservation duty is supported by both case law and legal statutes.[13] Comparable obligations apply in some other countries, including Canada, the United Kingdom, Ireland, Australia, and New Zealand.

The duty to preserve evidence applies to legal proceedings that are reasonably anticipated as well as to those that have been formally initiated. It may be triggered by a written threat of legal action, receipt of a demand letter that asserts a legal claim, a formal complaint, a notice of regulatory investigation, a subpoena for information, a credible verbal threat to sue, a prelitigation discussion, a workplace accident or injury, or another event that may lead to a legal proceeding. Alternatively, a litigant may file a motion for a preservation order if destruction of relevant information is feared. Regardless of circumstances, organizations involved in legal proceedings are not obligated to keep all recorded information in their possession. The preservation duty is limited to data and documents that are or could be relevant for a legal dispute or government investigation, but relevance for future lawsuits or investigations is always a possibility for certain types of recorded information. Examples include technical reports and test results related to product design, manufacturing, and safety; contracts and related correspondence that specify terms and conditions that must be fulfilled; performance evaluations and other personnel records that document the circumstances in which employees were promoted, demoted, or dismissed; and medical records that document a patient's diagnosis and treatment.

Risks associated with the preservation duty emerge in the context of pretrial discovery, the investigative phase of litigation when the opposing parties can request information from one another to help them prepare for trial. Parties involved in legal proceedings must comply with such requests fully and in a timely manner. Failure to provide the requested information, including potentially incriminating evidence, can have serious consequences, particularly if the information was destroyed, lost, damaged, or altered without a satisfactory explanation. Such destruction or withholding of information can lead to charges of spoliation—the intentional or negligent failure to preserve evidence that is relevant for a pending or reasonably foreseeable legal proceeding.[14] If it is determined that information was destroyed to hamper the opposing party, a court may hold the spoliating party accountable by ordering sanctions. At a minimum, the court may award attorneys' fees and costs to the nonspoliating party. Other possibilities include a more severe monetary penalty; an adverse inference instruction, in which a jury is allowed to infer that the destroyed information was harmful to the party that destroyed it; a default judgment that ends the litigation in favor of the opposing party; and, in extreme cases, criminal penalties for obstruction of justice. In some states, the nonspoliating party can also initiate a negligence claim for monetary damages for destruction of evidence that significantly harms its case.

Through the end of the twentieth century, spoliation sanctions addressed the failure to preserve paper records. In 1984, a federal court issued a default judgment against an aircraft manufacturer for intentionally destroying documents that might be harmful in product liability litigation.[15] In 1987, a court issued a default judgment for willful and flagrant destruction of documents by a corporate officer who lied about the destruction during his testimony.[16] In 1989, a court ordered a significant monetary penalty against a chemicals manufacturer for destruction of documents in an employment discrimination case.[17] In 1997, a federal judge imposed a $1 million fine on a large insurance company for haphazard and uncoordinated document-retention practices that denied plaintiffs potential evidence in a class-action lawsuit.[18]

Twenty-first-century spoliation cases have focused on intentional or negligent destruction of electronic information. In a widely cited employment discrimination case heard between 2003 and 2005, a court issued an adverse inference instruction and awarded the plaintiff reimbursement of costs for an employer's deliberate destruction of relevant information contained in emails and backup tapes.[19] In a 2003 securities fraud case, a defendant was found to have altered the electronic text of a message to conceal illegal stock-trading activity, which led to a prison sentence.[20] In 2009, a court granted an adverse inference instruction for spoliation of evidence resulting from failure to preserve voicemail.[21] In a 2011 dispute, a court imposed a fine and awarded attorneys' fees against a defendant who used a disk-wiping program in violation of a status quo order that prohibited destruction of certain electronic documents while litigation was pending.[22] In a 2011 intellectual property case, a court awarded a default judgment for deliberate destruction of information by throwing one laptop off a building and driving a vehicle over a second laptop.[23] In a 2012 antitrust lawsuit, a court fined the defendant because one of its top executives had instructed employees to delete emails related to the company's competitive practices.[24] In 2016, an adverse inference instruction was issued against a medical devices company for failing to prevent the destruction of text messages requested by the opposing party. That action was ultimately reversed, but the court did allow the parties to present evidence to the jury regarding destruction of the text messages and their likely relevance.[25] In a 2016 trademark-infringement case involving intentional alteration of emails prior to producing them in response to the defendants' discovery request, the court barred the plaintiffs from using the altered emails, which would have been favorable to them. The court also ordered the plaintiff to pay the defendants' attorney fees and court costs.[26] In the most widely publicized case involving failure to preserve evidence, Arthur Andersen LLP, a public accounting firm, was found guilty of obstructing justice in 2002 for destroying large quantities of paper and electronic records related to its audits of Enron Corporation, a utility and services provider engaged in fraudulent accounting practices.[27]

Vulnerability Assessment

When legal proceedings are likely, imminent, or ongoing, an organization must identify and suspend destruction of relevant information to avoid a spoliation charge. The following vulnerabilities increase the risk that an organization will be unable to comply with this preservation duty:

- An organization may not have an established business process for identifying relevant information and for sending a written preservation directive, variously described as a legal hold notice or a litigation hold notice, to employees, department heads, computer system managers, data stewards, or other employees that may have relevant information in their custody or under their supervisory control.
- A legal hold notice may be too narrow to satisfy preservation requirements. The organizational unit responsible for the preservation process, usually an in-house legal department possibly working with external counsel, may fail to identify all possible categories of relevant information or likely custodians of relevant data or documents. Relevant information that is overlooked may be discarded in the regular course of business before its omission is discovered and a revised hold notice is issued.
- An organization may fail to anticipate legal proceedings relating to a specific matter and, consequently, wait too long to initiate the preservation process, with a resulting delay in sending a legal hold notice to employees or departments that are responsible for compliance. Depending on the length of the delay, data or documents that contain relevant information may be discarded or deleted in the regular course of business prior to receipt of the preservation notice.[28]
- The organizational unit responsible for the preservation process may not follow up with individual employees or departments that receive a legal hold notice to confirm that they have read it, to be sure that they recognize the importance of preserving relevant information and understand what is expected of them, to answer questions that may arise during implementation, to address issues and concerns that may require clarification or modification of the legal hold notice, and to monitor and enforce compliance while legal proceedings are ongoing.[29]
- A legal hold may remain in effect for weeks, months, or even years. For legal proceedings of long duration, the organizational unit responsible for the preservation process may not issue periodic reminders or otherwise reconfirm the continued validity of a legal hold notice. New employees, in particular, may not be aware of preservation requirements for relevant records that they inherit from their predecessors. Even experienced employees may mistakenly assume that longstanding legal matters have been

resolved and that destruction of data or documents with elapsed retention periods can be resumed.

- If an organization is involved in parallel litigation, in which a dispute generates multiple lawsuits, or in simultaneous lawsuits and government investigations with some overlap, a given set of data or documents may be covered by multiple hold notices, which can be difficult to coordinate and track. In a large organization, these legal proceedings may be handled by different teams of in-house attorneys or external law firms who may be geographically dispersed and do not communicate effectively with one another. If one of the legal proceedings is resolved and its hold notice rescinded, a department may mistakenly discard information that remains subject to legal holds for other matters.

- An organization's information-management processes and practices may pose preservation challenges. Potentially relevant data and documents may be maintained in multiple repositories, managed by multiple applications, saved in multiple formats, and scattered in multiple locations. Paper records may be stored in offices or off-premises in warehouse locations operated by commercial providers or by an organization itself. Electronic information may be saved on an organization's network servers, in its email system, on personal computers, by cloud-based services, on mobile devices, on social media platforms, on backup tapes or other offline media stored on premises or offsite, in personal email or text-messaging accounts, or even in employees' homes. In some cases, relevant information may be held by an organization's contractors, agents, business partners, or other third parties. Relevant information may also be held by former employees over whom the organization has no control and limited influence.

- Regardless of its storage location and format, an organization's information repositories may not be organized and indexed in a manner that permits the identification of all data or documents that must be preserved. Relevant and irrelevant information may be co-mingled within a given data repository or document collection, making it difficult to identify information that must be kept and isolate it from information that is eligible for disposal. In the case of email, for example, some mailbox owners create topical folders that contain messages pertaining to specific projects, events, activities, business functions, or other matters, while others leave all messages in their inbox, which combines significant business communications with transitory messages, personal messages, and unsolicited junk mail.

- Rather than collecting and copying relevant information from multiple sources for storage in a secure, centralized repository intended exclusively for preservation of evidence related to a specific legal proceeding, an organization may leave the information in place where it is subject to intentional or accidental deletion, damage, or modification.

Risk Response

Compliance with discovery requests for information in paper or electronic form is a time-consuming process. The requested information must be identified, retrieved from its storage location, reviewed for relevance and privileged content, copied to establish a reliable chain of custody, catalogued and assigned control numbers, and submitted to the opposing party in an agreed-upon format. Errors can occur at any stage in the process. An incomplete response is possible, which raises the suspicion of destruction of evidence that may have helped the opposing party. As discussed in preceding sections, an organization's failure to preserve information that is relevant for litigation, government investigations, or other legal proceedings may lead to spoliation charges, which can have adverse consequences. Spoliation sanctions have increased in recent years and are likely to continue to do so.[30] Acceptance of spoliation risk is not an advisable mitigation strategy. Risk avoidance and risk transfer are possible but have significant limitations. The most effective mitigation strategy consists of a risk limitation plan based on a comprehensive legal hold process.

Risk acceptance may be based on either or both of the following beliefs: (1) destruction or alteration of relevant information is unlikely to be detected by a court or government investigator unfamiliar with an organization's recordkeeping practices; (2) if spoliation of evidence is somehow detected, it may not be subject to the most severe penalties, which are typically reserved for flagrant violations where destruction of relevant information is attributable to bad faith rather than ignorance or negligence. It is difficult to endorse this risk mitigation strategy. Legal commentators have long acknowledged the possibility, even the likelihood, of undetected destruction of relevant information.[31] In some cases, spoliation was only revealed when a litigant's employees testified that they were instructed by their superiors to destroy relevant information or when backup copies showed that relevant data or documents were destroyed despite a preservation order.[32] Given the huge quantity of paper and electronic information that an organization creates and maintains and the many locations where information is kept, the chances of being detected destroying or concealing relevant information during litigation or a government investigation appear to be less than 100 percent, but how much less cannot be determined. Even if there is no chance of detection, an in-house attorney or external counsel cannot condone a mitigation strategy that accepts spoliation risk, because such a strategy represents a serious breach of rules of professional conduct.[33]

Spoliation risks can be avoided by not destroying any information at all. This is accomplished by issuing a very broad legal hold when litigation or government investigation appears likely. This avoidance strategy will preserve any data or documents that might conceivably contain relevant information, but the retention of huge quantities of records in anticipation of discovery orders is not practical and introduces its own risks. In most situations, a small percentage of an organization's records have evidentiary value.[34] A broad approach to preservation will require costly storage of many irrelevant records, which must be kept until legal proceedings are fully resolved, even if their retention periods elapse in the meantime.

Further, the needless preservation of large quantities of records can increase the time and effort required to respond to discovery requests. The greater the quantity of records that must be identified, retrieved, and reviewed for relevance and privilege, the longer the process will take. A broad preservation strategy can also give the opposing party access to large quantities of email messages, text messages, drafts, preliminary reports, meeting notes, and other documents that may contain poorly phrased, ill-considered, incomplete, or inaccurate statements, which can be misinterpreted, cited out of context, or otherwise used in a potentially damaging manner.[35] Finally, needless retention of large quantities of data and documents will increase an organization's exposure to third-party preservation orders and discovery requests for legal proceedings in which the organization is neither a claimant nor a defendant. Such requests can be time-consuming and costly to fulfill for legal matters in which an organization has no direct interest.

Transfer of spoliation risk to an insurance carrier is possible in a limited set of circumstances. Courts have held that a general liability carrier is not required to defend an insured party in a spoliation-of-evidence action.[36] Spoliation insurance is available as enhanced liability coverage for unintentional destruction, alteration, or loss of property that serves as material evidence in litigation. Such policies protect the insured against third-party claims that allege spoliation of evidence. Spoliation insurance is intended for law firms, accounting firms, document storage facilities, cloud-based computing services, engineering firms, architectural firms, and other organizations that handle evidence entrusted to them by clients or other parties.[37] Spoliation coverage values lost evidence as the adjudicated damages determined by a court rather than as its replacement value.

Limitation of spoliation risks depends on prompt, decisive preservation action through a formal legal hold process that temporarily suspends destruction of data and documents that may be relevant for legal proceedings.[38] Destruction will not resume until all legal matters are fully resolved and the legal hold is rescinded. Legal holds are typically issued by an organization's legal department or other legal counsel. The responsible legal team must take the following steps to address vulnerabilities that contribute to spoliation risk:

- Initiate the legal hold process as soon as an organization becomes aware of a possible legal proceeding. This may occur when the organization receives a summons or complaint. More likely, however, the legal hold process will be triggered by a pre-litigation dispute, repeated inquiries about a particular matter, or other circumstances that suggest that legal proceedings can be reasonably anticipated.

- Work with business process owners, department heads, the organization's records manager or information governance officer, and other knowledgeable persons to identify the types of records to be covered by a legal hold as well as the individual employees who are likely to have relevant records in their custody and who must receive a legal hold notice. The information technology unit must be consulted to identify computer systems that store and process specific information covered by a legal hold notice. The legal team responsible for the hold process must become familiar with the purpose and scope of these computer systems. Site visits may be needed to examine departmental recordkeeping practices.

- Issue a written legal hold notice that instructs record custodians and data stewards to immediately suspend destruction of data and documents covered by the legal hold notice and to cancel or defer any actions, such as software upgrades or replacements, that may render relevant records unretrievable or unusable. At a minimum, the hold notice must describe the legal matters for which the records are deemed relevant, list the types of data and documents that are covered by the legal hold notice, explain the organization's legal obligation to preserve relevant information until the legal hold is rescinded, and provide contact information for record custodians and data stewards who have questions, need assistance, or want additional information about the legal hold.

- Request an immediate written acknowledgment from each record custodian or data steward who receives the legal hold notice. An escalation letter should be sent to nonrespondents, emphasizing the risks associated with noncompliance and requesting immediate acknowledgment of the legal hold. If the escalation letter does not elicit a response, the record custodian's supervisor should be contacted.

- Communicate directly with record custodians and data stewards to confirm that they have read the legal hold notice and understand what is expected of them. This can be accomplished through individual interviews, group training sessions, telephone calls, or other means. The responsible legal team must maintain continuing communication and interaction with record custodians and data stewards as long as the hold is in effect.

- Issue revised hold notices as warranted. As legal proceedings progress, it may be necessary to change the scope of a hold—to add specific types of data or documents or to increase the time span for information that must be preserved. Written acknowledgment must be obtained from record custodians and data stewards who receive revised hold notices.

- Issue periodic reminders to record custodians and data stewards to inform them that a legal hold remains in effect. Written acknowledgments should be obtained for all reminders, with escalation notices sent to nonrespondents. Failure to receive a written acknowledgment may indicate issues and concerns, such as a change in record custodians or data stewards in a given department. New employees, in particular, will need to be informed about legal holds that took effect before they were hired. Some organizations establish a compliance portal as a single source for up-to-date information about legal holds and required actions.
- Coordinate holds for parallel legal proceedings. Before a legal hold is officially rescinded and resumption of destruction is authorized, the responsible legal team must confirm that data and documents are not subject to ongoing holds for other matters.
- Create a secure repository for relevant information. Rather than retaining relevant information in place, data or documents that are subject to a legal hold should be collected, copied, and transferred into a secure, centralized repository for preservation that is under the direct supervision and control of an organization's legal team. Access to the repository should be strictly limited to those directly involved in the legal proceedings. This will support a legally acceptable chain of custody and greatly decrease the likelihood that relevant information will be intentionally or accidentally destroyed, damaged, or altered while a legal hold is in effect.
- Document every stage of the legal hold process. The documentation must include information about the scope, content, dates, and recipients for each legal hold in sufficient detail to demonstrate that the organization has acted in good faith to preserve relevant information and has implemented a trustworthy process to fulfill its preservation duty.

UNDER-RETENTION AND OVER-RETENTION

As discussed in a preceding section, recordkeeping laws and regulations specify minimum and maximum retention periods for certain types of information. Where information may be needed for litigation or other legal proceedings, minimum retention periods are typically based on statutes of limitations, which specify the period of time that an organization can sue or be sued for breach of contract, personal injury, property damage, or other alleged offenses.[39] Legal requirements aside, operational retention decisions focus on records that are needed for administrative continuity, management planning and decision-making, transaction processing, customer service, marketing, and other day-to-day activities. Operational retention periods must also address the interests of stakeholder groups, including an organization's owners, governing body, customers, business partners, or, in the case of government records, the public. Scholarly retention decisions identify records that warrant permanent preservation for research by historians, political scientists, sociologists, economists, demographers, and others involved in scholarly pursuits. Determination of scholarly value may also consider the interests of genealogists, market trend analysts, private investigators, and others who are not necessarily scholars but are nonetheless involved in research that requires access to information.

Regardless of criteria, retention decisions predict the useful life of the information that specific records contain and, in the case of non-permanent records, establish a future date when the information can be destroyed. As with any prediction, errors can occur. Under-retention—discarding records that have continuing value—and over-retention—retaining records longer than necessary—can have significant adverse consequences.

As discussed in a preceding section, under-retention can lead to fines and penalties for noncompliance with laws and regulations that prescribe minimum retention periods for specific information. Short retention periods can also pose problems during the discovery phase of litigation when an opposing litigant requests information that has been destroyed. In theory, the inability to comply with discovery orders is explainable if the requested information was destroyed prior to the start of litigation in conformity with an organization's formalized retention policies and practices, but merely having a retention policy is not an ironclad defense against spoliation charges. To be legally defensible, an organization's retention periods must be reasonable for the types of information involved and the business operations that the information supports.[40]

Some organizations want to dispose of recorded information as soon as the minimum time periods specified in laws and regulations elapse, but that approach can have negative operational consequences. Older records may be useful long after the matters to which they relate have ended. Closed project files may be consulted when planning similar or related projects or when abandoned projects are reactivated. A former employee's personnel records may be consulted to obtain information about prior performance if the employee is considered for rehiring. Invoices, purchase orders, and other records for completed procurement transactions may be consulted when additional quantities of a previously purchased item are required; to identify the supplier, model number, or cost of a previously purchased item; or when questions arise about warranty provisions for a previously purchased item. Terminated contracts may be useful as models for future contracts and agreements with the same party or for similar purposes. Closed case files may be consulted when a new case involves the same parties, similar legal issues, or similar legal theories. Closed case files may also contain motions, pleadings, interrogatories, and other documents that are useful as models when developing similar materials for new cases. Test results, quality assurance reports, and other records related to products must be retained as long as the products are sold and often longer because discontinued products may remain at customer sites for years after being withdrawn from the market.

In these and other instances, destruction of information with continuing value can impede planning and decision-making, disrupt customer service, delay product development, and otherwise obstruct business activities. Productivity will suffer as time and labor are spent trying to reconstruct lost information. Certain records have continuing operational value that warrants multidecade or permanent retention. Examples include intellectual property records, student transcripts maintained by academic institutions, and deeds, mortgages, birth and death certificates, marriage licenses, and court records maintained by government agencies.

Pervasive under-retention can also have a negative impact on preservation of information of scholarly value. Some records that do not need to be kept for legal reasons and that have short-term operational value may contain information that is significant for an organization's own history or for researchers working on scholarly topics. In the United States, for example, 29 C.F.R. § 1904.33(a) specifies a five-year retention period for reports of workplace injuries and illnesses mandated by the Occupational Safety and Health Administration. These records may be consulted when questions or concerns arise about an accident or other incident. Their operational value diminishes as those issues are resolved, but the records may contain information of interest to occupational health researchers, workplace safety analysts, ergonomic specialists, labor economists, statisticians, and others interested in the cause, prevention, and consequences of workplace accidents and incidents. Similarly, 26 C.F.R. § 1.6001-1 requires organizations to retain records that establish the income, deductions, and credits reported in income tax returns for as long as their contents are relevant for tax assessment—usually three years after a return was filed or due but as long as six years in some circumstances. Previously filed tax returns have operational value for tax planning, when filing an amended return; when property is sold; when operating losses, unused deductions, or unused credits from a prior year are carried forward; and when tax deductions, depreciation allowances, tax credits, goodwill amortization, and other tax benefits are subject to recapture. These situations are typically resolved within a limited time frame, but income tax returns have been cited as primary sources in scholarly studies by economists, accountants, public policy analysts, historians, social scientists, and other researchers.[41]

Over-retention—specifically, the needless retention of inactive records with no continuing value—is the problem that brought records management to prominence as a professional discipline. The earliest records management initiatives emphasized timely disposal of obsolete records in government agencies and large corporations, citing the negative impact of over-retention

on the cost of federal government operations.[42] When stored in office buildings, large quantities of inactive paper records occupy costly floor space and
fill up filing cabinets, forcing the purchase of additional record-storage
equipment, which will require more space as new records are generated.
Moving older records from offices to warehouse storage will reduce but not
eliminate those costs. In-house record storage facilities must be properly
constructed, equipped, maintained, staffed, supervised, and protected from
fire, unauthorized access, and other dangers. Commercial record centers are
often less expensive to own and operate than in-house facilities, but monthly
storage charges will add up for records that are retained longer than necessary. For records that are sent to a commercial storage provider without
defined destruction dates, monthly charges will continue indefinitely.

The proliferation of databases, digital documents, digitized images, and
other electronic information requires increasing quantities of computer storage, but—compared to paper documents—over-retention of electronic information does not have the same adverse impact on storage costs. While the
cost to store paper records will continue to increase over time, the cost of
computer storage has fallen steadily for decades and is likely to continue to
do so. Documents that originate digitally can be stored on hard drives for a
small fraction—perhaps 1 percent or less—of the cost to store their paper
counterparts.[43] Even if the cost of storage equipment is increased by a factor
of 3 to 8 to account for the total cost of ownership,[44] the storage cost for large
quantities of computerized information is a minor concern. Nonetheless, no
organization wants to squander its computer storage budget on obsolete information. While hard drive capacities have increased, so have the storage
demands of data intensive computer applications, such as geographical information systems, digital asset-management systems, and data mining applications that operate on large data sets.

Storage cost aside, over-retention of electronic information can have an
adverse impact on computer performance. All computing devices operate
most efficiently within certain capacity limits. As the volume of saved information increases, the efficient operation of servers will be compromised, and
backup operations, especially full backups, become more difficult to complete in a timely manner. In extreme cases, backup operations, which are
typically performed at night, may extend into business hours. In addition,
replacement of computer equipment and software will be complicated by the
burdensome migration of large quantities of obsolete information. Over-retention can also have a negative impact on the performance of computer
software. As database size increases, response time will increase, and additional memory or processing power may be necessary to maintain an acceptable level of performance. With email client software, certain operations—
such as opening messages, periodic checking for new messages, searching
for specific messages, and sorting messages—will execute more slowly as

the quantity of messages increases. With their increased uploading and downloading requirements, large attachments can degrade system performance and overwhelm an organization's networking infrastructure.

In addition to its operational impact, over-retention can violate laws and regulations that establish maximum retention periods for specific information. While some of those laws apply to a limited range of situations and information, data minimization requirements specified in data protection violations prohibit over-retention by many organizations. Since the European Union's General Data Protection Regulation took effect in May 2018, companies that do business in the European Union have been fined for failure to implement appropriate retention periods for personal information.[45]

Finally, over-retention can increase the time and effort required to respond to discovery orders. Before information is delivered to the requesting party, nonresponsive records must be identified and removed. If this is not done, the opposing party may gain access to drafts, preliminary reports, notes taken at meetings, and other documents that contain inaccurate information or ill-considered statements. This content might be misinterpreted, cited out of context, or otherwise presented to the court in a damaging manner.

Vulnerability Assessment

The following vulnerabilities contribute to the risk of under-retention or over-retention of information:

- An organization may not be aware of retention requirements contained in recordkeeping laws and regulations. A compliance officer or legal department is typically responsible for identifying laws and regulations that affect specific business operations, but some organizations do not have in-house compliance expertise. Even for those that do, it can be difficult to keep informed about all applicable legal and regulatory requirements, especially in multinational and transnational organizations that operate in multiple political jurisdictions.
- An organization's business processes and practices may not be conducive to compliance with retention requirements. Records may be scattered in multiple locations or managed by multiple applications. Database applications may lack retention functionality.
- Retention policies may not be implemented uniformly across all business units in every location where the organization operates. Information pertaining to specific matters may be destroyed prematurely by some departments or in some geographic locations and kept longer than necessary in other circumstances.
- Legal retention decisions are based on fact. Assuming diligent research to identify applicable laws and regulations, there is limited scope for error.

Operational retention decisions, by contrast, depend on the judgment of knowledgeable persons. A fundamental records management assumption is that the principal users of information—usually employees in the departments or other business units that create and maintain the information—are qualified to determine its operational value based on their knowledge of and experience with their organization's business processes, activities, and objectives, but stakeholders may disagree about the future business value of specific information. Such disagreements may be resolved by over-retention, which some stakeholders may consider less risky than under-retention. Information that is retained longer than necessary can be destroyed at any future time when no longer needed, but information that is destroyed too soon can never be recovered.

• Determination of scholarly value, sometimes described as archival appraisal, requires specialized knowledge about the scholarly disciplines and research activities for which particular records may be useful. Many archivists have advanced academic degrees in a subject discipline, such as history or public administration, as well as training in archival management or library science. Government agencies, which may be required by law to preserve records of scholarly value, have trained archivists on staff, as do many universities, cultural institutions, and other not-for-profit organizations. While the scholarly potential of business archives has been recognized for decades,[46] few corporations, partnerships, and other for-profit entities are committed to preservation of their records for scholarly research. In the absence of expert guidance, permanent retention may be limited to records that document a business's formation and perhaps a few key moments in its history. Other records of scholarly value will not be preserved.

Risk Response

Risks associated with under-retention and over-retention of information cannot be avoided. Record retention is not an exact science. Despite diligent legal research and in-depth examination of operational and scholarly requirements, the retention period selected for a given type of information may be shorter or longer than necessary. Legal and regulatory requirements may be misinterpreted. The future operational need for specific information cannot be predicted with certainty. Information of scholarly value may be overlooked. Under-retention and over-retention can be minimized, but they cannot be completely eliminated.

Risk transfer through insurance coverage is not a mitigation option for under-retention or over-retention of information. An organization cannot purchase insurance coverage to mitigate the adverse impact of retaining records longer or shorter than necessary. Errors and omissions insurance, which can protect records management consultants and others against claims of incorrect retention advice, is available for professional liability only.

Acceptance of under-retention or over-retention based on a conscious decision not to comply fully with minimum or maximum retention periods specified in laws and regulations is not advisable. Noncompliance exposes an organization to fines and penalties, but acceptance of under-retention and over-retention is a common approach to risk mitigation for retention decisions based on scholarly and operational criteria. In the absence of an archival program, many businesses and some nongovernmental organizations are willing to accept under-retention of information of scholarly value. Where there is disagreement about the continued operational value of specific information, decision-makers may be willing to accept some degree of over-retention, preferring to err on the side of keeping as a safeguard against premature destruction of information that may be needed in an uncertain future.

Over-retention is an inherent characteristic of so-called "big bucket" schedules, a modern approach to retention that groups records in broad categories corresponding to an organization's major activities, business functions, or work processes. All records in a given category are assigned the longest retention period required by any record in that category. In the process, some records may be retained longer than necessary, but this over-retention is accepted in the interest of simplicity. Big bucket schedules are typically easier to understand and update than traditional retention schedules based on granular lists of records, each with its own retention period.[47]

As part of a risk mitigation strategy, an organization can take the following steps to limit under-retention and over-retention of recorded information:

- An effective risk limitation strategy begins with legal compliance. A qualified organizational unit must be responsible for identifying, analyzing, and interpreting laws and regulations that specify minimum and maximum retention periods. This must be done for all national and subnational jurisdictions where an organization operates. If necessary, external compliance specialists should be hired to supplement internal expertise.
- Recordkeeping laws and regulations establish baseline retention periods that set boundaries for under-retention and over-retention. Laws and regulations that specify minimum retention requirements prohibit under-retention. These minimum retention periods should be the starting point for retention decisions. Increases based on operational or scholarly criteria must be justified. Laws and regulations that specify maximum retention periods cannot be overridden by operational or scholarly considerations. Particular attention should be given to compliance with data protection and privacy laws that prohibit over-retention of personal information.

- Statutes of limitations are useful reference points for retention of information that may be relevant for legal proceedings. Organizations are not obligated to retain information for the entire time periods specified by statutes of limitations, but it is widely considered prudent to do so. Retention decisions based on statutes of limitations will prevent under-retention of accounting information, hiring records, personnel records, building maintenance records, product safety records, and other data and documents that may be needed for civil litigation or government investigations. Retention decisions based on applicable statute of limitations can also limit over-retention. If information without continuing operational or scholarly value is kept solely to support possible legal actions, a retention period that exceeds the applicable statute of limitations serves no purpose.
- Operational retention periods for specific records are typically negotiated through meetings or other consultations with knowledgeable employees who use the records to fulfill their assigned work responsibilities. To limit under-retention and over-retention, operational retention decisions should be based on the use history of specific types of information. The experience of knowledgeable employees, for example, may confirm that mechanical and electrical drawings contain information that is essential for ongoing building maintenance, that closed contract files are useful for preparation of new contracts or contract amendments, or that closed investigative case files for security incidents do contain information that is relevant for subsequent investigation of similar incidents. On the other hand, the experience of knowledgeable persons may indicate that certain records that are being retained because they might be needed in the future have not been consulted in many years.
- Review of the prevailing retention practices of other organizations can provide a useful benchmark for determination of under-retention and over-retention. Many examples of retention schedules are available at the web sites of government agencies, academic institutions, and other organizations with well-developed records management programs.
- Organizations that do not have a formal archival program should consider hiring an archival consultant or other expert to help identify data and documents that warrant permanent preservation for scholarly research.

MEDIA INSTABILITY AND OBSOLESCENCE

Information is as usable as the medium on which it is recorded. Like all physical objects, information storage media are subject to decay. Instability is caused by progressive degradation of an information storage medium's original physical or chemical properties, which may result from characteristics of the medium itself or from damage attributable to external conditions and events, such as inappropriate environmental conditions, careless handling, or improperly adjusted equipment. The stable life of an information storage medium is the period of time that it will remain usable for recording of new information or retrieval of previously recorded information. For this discussion, the ability to read information recorded on a given medium is more important than recording stability. Like the natural and human-induced disasters discussed in the preceding chapter, media instability damages recorded information. Unlike the sudden devastation caused by violent weather or a building fire, however, media instability is the end result of accumulating noncritical defects that ultimately reach a failure point. The impact, while less dramatic than mass destruction by a single catastrophic event, is nonetheless significant for information-dependent legal compliance, business operations, and scholarly research.

Stability estimates for information storage media are based on knowledge of the physical and chemical properties of a given medium, accelerated aging tests, and, where possible, observation of historical media. Taken together, these factors have established reasonable estimates of life expectancy for paper, photographic films, and electronic storage media:

• The stable life of paper varies inversely with its acidic content. Acid—which may be introduced during the papermaking process, absorbed from the environment, or generated spontaneously during aging—is the catalyst for chemical reactions that undermine paper's stability.[48] Paper made from chemical wood pulp or mechanical pulp are acidic and will deteriorate over time. The pH values for these papers range from 4.0 to 6.5. By contrast, papers manufactured from rag fibers have pH values above 7.0. The pH range for permanent papers is 7.5 to 10. Such papers are sometimes described as "acid free." To be considered permanent, paper must include an alkaline reserve that neutralizes acid generated from natural aging or atmospheric pollution. According to the ISO 9706:1994 standard, *Information and Documentation—Paper for Documents—Requirements for Permanence,* permanent paper will remain chemically and physically stable over long periods of time and "will undergo little or no change in properties that affect its use."[49] The ANSI/NISO Z39.48 standard, which focuses on paper for libraries and archives, defines *permanence* as the ability to last "at least several hundred years without significant deterioration under normal use and storage conditions."[50] ASTM D 3290, *Standard Specification for Bond and Ledger Papers for Permanent Records,* which has been withdrawn without a replacement but remains useful, cites an estimated life expectancy of one thousand years for papers with pH values ranging from 7.5 to 10.0, one hundred years for paper with pH values ranging from 6.5 to 7.5, and fifty years for papers with pH values of 5.5 to 6.5.[51] A technical report issued by the National Information Standards

Organization specifies temperature and humidity ranges for paper records intended for permanent preservation.[52]

- Decades of scientific research confirm the chemical and physical stability of photographic media.[53] ISO 18901:2010, *Imaging Materials—Processed Silver-Gelatin-Type Black-and-White—Films—Specifications for Stability* specifies the stability characteristics of silver-gelatin photographic films, the type used in amateur, professional, and microfilm cameras, in motion picture cameras, and by medical and nonmedical x-ray devices. The estimated life expectancy is five hundred years for silver-gelatin photographic films with polyester base materials, the most common type, and one hundred years for older silver-gelatin photographic films with cellulose triacetate base materials. In each case, the film must be manufactured, processed, and stored in conformity with pertinent standards, including ISO 18911:2010, *Imaging Materials—Processed Safety Photographic Film—Storage Practices*, which specifies the maximum temperature and acceptable relative humidity for extended-term (permanent) and medium-term (minimum of ten years) storage.[54] Other standards specify a life expectancy of one hundred years for nonsilver photographic films, which are used primarily for microfilm duplication.[55]

- Magnetic media have dominated data, video, and audio storage since the 1960s. Compared to paper and photographic films, magnetic storage media have shorter life spans. Hard drives, which currently dominate computer storage, are inherently unstable; information recorded on them is continuously vulnerable to damage from hardware malfunctions, which become increasingly likely as equipment ages.[56] Discussion of media stability is most relevant for magnetic tapes, the only removable magnetic medium that remains in wide use. Anecdotal evidence based on operational experience with older magnetic tapes suggests the possibility of multi-decade stability,[57] but many research reports confirm the time-dependent degradation of magnetic media.[58] ISO 18923:2000, *Imaging Materials—Polyester Base Magnetic Tape—Storage Practices* specifies medium-term storage conditions for information to be retained for a minimum of ten years and extended-term storage conditions for information of permanent value, but that standard does not state or imply that magnetic tapes have permanent keeping properties. ISO 18933:2012, *Imaging Materials—Magnetic Tape—Care and Handling Practices for Extended Usage*, emphasizes precautions necessary to protect magnetic tapes from damage and decay. Optical storage offers the potential for longer lifetimes than magnetic media. Various manufacturers have claimed lifetime estimates ranging from seventy-five to two hundred years, but the increased capacity, improved performance characteristics, and lower cost of hard drives have relegated optical disks to niche applications.[59]

Whether paper documents, photographic films, or electronic records are involved, media instability has a direct impact on retention of information. Risk arises when the retention requirement for information is greater than the estimated life span of the medium on which the information is recorded. Stability threats are time-dependent. Unless a given medium has manufacturing defects, instability risk is low when information is initially recorded, but it increases with age. Media deterioration is a significant threat to continued readability of information that warrants long retention or permanent preservation for operational reasons or scholarly value. Even information that is needed for six to ten years after initial recording, a common retention range for many business records, may be damaged by media instability. Information to be retained for five years or less is generally unaffected.

Media instability is not the only limiting factor for long-term retention of electronic information and photographic films. While information contained in paper records can be read without access to special equipment or computer applications, all electronic storage media and certain photographic storage media have significant hardware dependencies for viewing and printing or recorded information. Continued access to databases, digital documents, and other computer-processible information also depends on the availability of compatible software. If compatible equipment or software is not available, a given storage medium will be rendered obsolete, and the information it contains will be effectively lost.

The service life of computer storage equipment is typically shorter than the stable life span of media intended for use in such equipment. Hard drives, which do not use removable storage media, are usually replaced within three to five years, as previously discussed. While magnetic tapes and optical disks may resist deterioration for a decade or longer, few magnetic tape or optical disk drives are engineered for a useful life longer than ten years, and most will be replaced by new products within a shorter time. The replacement models often support higher-capacity recording media than their predecessors. To preserve the usability of previously recorded information, successor products may offer backward compatibility—that is, they can read media recorded by older devices. There is no guarantee, however, that a manufacturer of computer storage devices will continue such backward compatibility in all future products. In fact, the history of computer storage technology suggests that backward compatibility provides a bridge between two or three generations of equipment. Eventually support for older storage media is phased out. As an additional complication, backward compatibility does little, if anything, to address the readability of discontinued storage media for which no replacement products are available. [60]

Unlike computing, microfilm technology is not subject to continuing innovation that will render existing information unusable, and microfilm viewing and printing devices have long service lives. Libraries, archives, and other organizations often use microfilm equipment that was purchased more than ten years ago. These factors suggest that media obsolescence is unlikely, but no microfilm viewing or printing device will remain in service indefinitely. Never popular with users, microfilm technology has been steadily supplanted by electronic document imaging. Rather than replacing their aging microfilm equipment, many organizations have digitized their existing microfilm and microfiche collections for online retrieval, display, and printing.

For databases, digital documents, and other computer-processable information, problems of hardware dependence are compounded by software compatibility and file format issues. All computer applications are designed to read and process information that is recorded in specific file formats. As their default operating mode, most computer applications record information in a proprietary file format that is designed to be read and processed by that application and, in some cases, by other compatible applications. By contrast, information recorded in nonproprietary file formats can be read and processed by multiple applications, which may be more widely available than their proprietary counterparts. Regardless of file format, software may be released in improved versions that cannot read information recorded in predecessor formats. Successive releases of a given application may offer backward compatibility with earlier versions, but such backward compatibility may not reliably preserve all information recorded in an older file format. In any case, backward compatibility is rarely supported in perpetuity. Media that contain information recorded in a discontinued file format will ultimately become obsolete.[61]

Vulnerability Assessment

An organization may have one or more of the following vulnerabilities that exposes it to retention risks associated with media instability or obsolescence:

- Most new information originates in electronic form and much of it is being retained that way, usually on hard drives with limited services lives. In some cases, this information cannot be converted to other media or new file formats without prohibitively high cost or significant loss of functionality.
- While permanent paper is widely available, many business documents are created on papers with acidic content and shorter life spans. This is often the case, for example, with papers used in photocopiers and printers. Documents produced by those devices account for a high percentage of all business records.[62]

- International standards specify environmental conditions for long-term or permanent preservation of paper and photographic films, but those conditions are only encountered in vault-type storage environments where temperature and humidity are tightly controlled. If an organization stores permanent paper records or properly processed photographic films in an office or a warehouse without proper environmental controls, it does not have a complete archival system for permanent preservation of information.[63]

- Magnetic tapes are widely used for backup copies of active information and for offline retention of older information that is "archived" from large databases. These magnetic tapes are often stored in warehouses where the temperature and humidity do not comply with environmental requirements specified in international standards. This poses little risk for backup tapes, which are typically replaced at short intervals, but tapes that contain archived data will deteriorate over time.

- The estimated life span of an electronic medium begins with its manufacturing date, not the date that information was recorded on it. In some organizations, information with continuing operational value is recorded on recycled backup tapes or other previously recorded media with partially elapsed life spans.

- Information in paper, photographic, or electronic form can be damaged in use. There is no such thing as a stable working copy in any medium. Lifetime estimates apply exclusively to storage copies that are referenced as little as possible.

- For organizations that retain information on microfilm, it is increasingly difficult to find suitable replacements for viewing and printing devices. The selection of available microfilm products has decreased steadily since the 1990s, and equipment to display or print certain older microfilm formats has been discontinued.

Risk Response

Risk avoidance is not a practical mitigation option for information loss due to media instability or obsolescence. Organizations have no control over the discontinuation of hardware or software that can read information recorded on specific storage media or in a particular file format. No technology can remain in service indefinitely. If enough time passes, any given storage medium or file format will become obsolete. Similarly, all information storage media are subject to time-dependent deterioration, but the rate of aging differs from one medium to another. Information might be converted from a storage medium with limited stability properties and a rapid aging rate—magnetic media, for example—to a storage medium, such as paper or microfilm, with more stable physical and chemical characteristics and a slower aging rate. At a time when many organizations are trying to transition from paper to digital recordkeeping to improve the efficiency of information-dependent business operations, there is unlikely to be much enthusiasm for a risk mitigation strategy that requires printing or microfilm recording of large quantities of data or documents that originate in electronic form merely to gain a longevity advantage. As an added complication, conversion from electronic to nonelectronic storage to avoid stability or obsolescence risks will likely introduce other risks, including high labor and material costs for printing, microfilming, and verification of conversion; greater costs to store paper records; high cost to purchase microfilm retrieval devices, which are more expensive than computing equipment and available from fewer suppliers; and inadvertent omission of information, inadequate quality control for paper or microfilm copies, and other conversion errors.

Risk transfer is not a mitigation option for loss of information due to media instability or obsolescence. Valuable papers and records insurance policies provide coverage for documents and photographic films that are damaged or destroyed by natural disasters or human-induced catastrophes, such as a destructive storm or a building fire. Their terms and conditions do not appear to include loss of information caused by time-dependent degradation of paper or photographic media. Valuable papers and records coverage typically excludes damage to electronic information. Most policies specifically exclude any loss due to electrical or magnetic injury, disturbance, or erasure of magnetic recordings. Insurance coverage is not available for loss of information due to media obsolescence.

Because time-dependent deterioration or discontinuation of information storage media is inevitable, some degree of risk acceptance is necessary or even advisable. Acceptance of media instability or obsolescence without further precautions or actions is a viable risk mitigation strategy for data and documents that will be retained for five years or less. During that time period, deterioration of paper, photographic films, or electronic media or discontinuation of compatible equipment or software is unlikely to result in information loss. Acceptance is possible but riskier for information that will be retained for six to ten years. For information to be retained longer than ten years, and for very valuable information that will be retained for a shorter period, a risk acceptance strategy must include a data migration process that periodically copies information onto new storage media and/or converts information to a new file format to ensure continued usability. [64]

Data migration frequency is determined by the stable life expectancy of a given information storage medium or by the estimated service life of compatible hardware or software. Migration must be completed before the estimated life span or service life elapses. For an information storage medium with an estimated stable life of ten years, for example, data migration will likely be performed at seven- or eight-year intervals to avoid information loss resulting from accumulated defects at the end of the estimated life span. Where the anticipated service life of equipment required to read information recorded on a given storage medium is five years, data migration will likely be performed at three- or four-year intervals. Once the data migration interval is determined, the number of required iterations will depend on the retention period for information recorded on a given storage medium. If information with a ten-year retention period is stored on a medium that requires seven- or eight-year migration intervals, two iterations will be required.

For information of permanent operational or scholarly value, periodic recopying of information onto new storage media is a perpetual obligation that requires a future commitment of labor and economic resources of uncertain availability. This criticism of data migration is most often associated with electronic information storage media, which have relatively short life expectancies, but migration will ultimately be required for every information storage medium. In the case of information recorded on permanent paper or properly processed photographic film, however, the interval between data migrations may be a century or longer, although such media must be inspected periodically for changes that may affect usability.

To supplement a risk acceptance strategy, an organization should consider the following steps to limit information loss resulting from media instability or obsolescence:

- Media quality affects media stability. An organization should purchase high-quality paper, photographic film, and electronic storage media that conforms to specifications presented in international standards. Brand-name storage media from known manufacturers are typically subjected to tightly controlled manufacturing and quality control processes. Off-brand products may be made from inferior materials.
- Prior to use, paper, photographic films, and electronic media should be stored under temperature and humidity conditions specified by the manufacturer. These specifications are much less stringent than environmental requirements for media that contain recorded information.
- Previously recorded electronic media may be suitable for backup copies, but they should not be used for long-term storage of important information.
- To provide the greatest protection against the possibility of defective media, two copies should be made of media containing information of long-term or permanent value. At least one of the copies should be stored under environmental conditions specified in international standards. Where appropriate storage facilities are not available in-house, commercial providers offer environmentally controlled vault space.

- All information storage media are imperiled by use. Working copies of information storage media should be handled with care. Storage copies should be handled as little as possible.
- Long retention periods will require multiple data migration intervals to maintain the usability of recorded information when the life span of a given storage medium elapses. To reduce data migration requirements, over-retention should be avoided.
- To reduce data migration requirements, information should be saved on media or in file formats that are likely to resist obsolescence. Older magnetic tape formats should be avoided, for example. To the extent possible, nonproprietary or widely used proprietary file formats should be used for digital data and documents. The PDF/A format should be considered for digital documents with long retention periods.
- To preserve the readability of digital content over time, file conversion software and services can accommodate databases, word-processing documents, spreadsheets, presentations, document images, digital photographs, computer-aided design files, geo-reference files, audio recordings, and video recordings in a wide variety of formats, including many formats that are discontinued or rarely encountered.[65]

SUMMARY OF MAJOR POINTS

- Many laws and regulations specify minimum retention periods for information related to particular matters. A smaller group of laws and regulations mandate the destruction of specific information when a prescribed time period elapses. Failure to comply with these legally mandated record-keeping requirements exposes an organization to regulatory investigations and compliance audits, which may lead to fines, administrative penalties, or, in rare cases, criminal prosecution.
- Organizations involved in litigation, government investigations, or other legal proceedings have a duty to preserve relevant information. If such information is destroyed, a court can impose significant sanctions. Dozens of legal cases confirm these adverse consequences. The most effective mitigation strategy consists of a risk limitation plan based on a comprehensive legal hold process.
- Some organizations want to dispose of recorded information as soon as the minimum time periods specified in laws and regulations elapse, but that approach can have negative operational consequences. Pervasive under-retention can also have a negative impact on preservation of records of scholarly value.
- Needless retention of obsolete information increases the cost of record-keeping, degrades the performance of computer applications, increases the

time and effort required to respond to discovery orders, and can violate laws and regulations that establish maximum retention periods for specific information.

- Media instability and obsolescence have a direct impact on retention of information. Risk arises when the retention period for information is greater than the estimated life span of the medium on which the information is recorded or when the information can no longer be read by available equipment or software.

NOTES

1. Worldwide, tens of thousands of laws and regulations specify record-retention requirements. For more detailed information about recordkeeping requirements in specific countries, see W. Saffady, *U.S. Record Retention Requirements: A Guide to 100 Commonly-Encountered Record Series* (Overland Park, KS: ARMA International, 2018); W. Saffady, *Legal Requirements for Electronic Records Retention in Western Europe* (Overland Park, KS: ARMA International, 2014); W. Saffady, *Legal Requirements for Electronic Records Retention in Eastern Europe* (Overland Park, KS: ARMA International, 2014); and W. Saffady, *Legal Requirements for Electronic Records Retention in Asia* (Overland Park, KS: ARMA International, 2015).

2. The MCBA has been issued in successive editions by the Committee on Corporate Laws of the Section of Business Law of the American Bar Association. The full text is available at www.americanbar.org/content/dam/aba/administrative/business_law/corplaws/2016_mbca.authcheckdam.pdf. Business formation and organizational governance laws in other countries have similar recordkeeping requirements for an organization's foundation documents and meeting minutes. See, for example, the Canada Business Corporations Act (https://laws-lois.justice.gc.ca/eng/acts/c-44), the United Kingdom Companies Act 2006 (www.legislation.gov.uk/ukpga/2006/46/pdfs/ukpga_20060046_en.pdf), the French Code de Commerce (www.legifrance.gouv.fr/affichCode.do?cidTexte=LEGITEXT000005634379), the Swiss Code of Obligations (www.admin.ch/opc/en/classified-compilation/19110009/index.html), the Companies Law of the People's Republic of China (www.fdi.gov.cn/1800000121_39_4814_0_7.html), and the Japanese Companies Act (www.japaneselawtranslation.go.jp/law/detail/?id=2035&vm=2&re=).

3. W. Saffady, *Retention of Accounting Records: A Global Survey of Laws and Regulations* (Palmyra, NJ: ARMA International Educational Foundation, 2019), http://armaedfoundation.org/wp-content/uploads/2019/06/AIEF-Research-Paper-Retention-Global-Accounting.pdf, covers retention requirements in two hundred countries and dependent territories.

4. In the United States, Employment Eligibility Verification Form I-9 must be retained for three years after an employee's hiring date or one year after termination of employment, whichever is later, as specified in 8 C.F.R. § 274a.2. In the United Kingdom, copies of passports or other documents that verify an employee's eligibility to work must be retained for two years following termination of employment, as specified in *An Employer's Guide to Right to Work Checks* (London: Home Office, 2018), https://assets.publishing.service.gov.uk/government/uploads/system/uploads/attachment_data/file/720858/29_06_18_Employer_s_guide_to_right_to_work_checks.pdf.

5. State and local government agencies and certain federal government contractors must retain employment applications and related records for two years, as specified in 29 C.F.R. § 1602.31 and 41 C.F.R. § 60-1.12, respectively. State and local laws may specify additional retention requirements for certain hiring records. In New York City, for example, the Stop Credit Discrimination in Employment Act (Local Law 37 of 2015) prohibits the use of an applicant's credit history when making hiring decisions, but exemptions are allowed for specific positions, such as jobs that require bonding or a security clearance. Employers must keep records related to exempt positions—including the reason for the exemption, the names and

contact information for all applicants, and a copy of each applicant's credit history—for five years from the date that the exemption was used.

6. In the United States, the National Archives and Records Administration has retention authority over records maintained by federal government agencies. State archival agencies have similar retention authority over state and local government records. In some countries, archival agencies have the authority to mandate permanent preservation of historically significant records of nongovernmental entities, a concept that dates from the Russian Revolution. See P. Grimsted, "Lenin's Archival Decree of 1918: The Bolshevik Legacy for Soviet Archival Theory and Practice," *American Archivist* 45, no. 4 (1982): 429–43, www.americanarchivist.org/doi/pdf/10.17723/aarc.45.4.tjn5811686q4u0r1; P. Grimsted, "Soviet Archival Organization and the National Documentary Legacy in Estonia, Latvia, and Lithuania," *Journal of Baltic Studies* 9, no. 3 (1978): 195–202, https://doi.org/10.1080/01629777800000211; J. Nalen, "Private Archives in China," *Libri: International Journal of Libraries and Information Studies* 52, no. 4 (2007): 241–62, https://doi.org/10.1515/LIBR.2002.241; X. An et al., "Reinventing the Concept of the State Archival Fond in China," *Archives and Manuscripts* 42, no. 2 (2014): 146–50, https://doi.org/10.1080/01576895.2014.911673.

7. A data subject's "right to be forgotten" is specified in Article 17 and Recitals 65 and 66 of the GDPR. See https://gdpr-info.eu/recitals/no-65. Examples of the many articles that discuss this concept include C. Bartolini and L. Siry, "The Right to Be Forgotten in the Light of Consent of the Data Subject," *Computer Law & Security Review* 32, no. 2 (2016): 218–37, https://doi.org/10.1016/j.clsr.2016.01.005; C. Rees and D. Heywood, "The 'Right to Be Forgotten' or the 'Principle That Has Been Remembered,'" *Computer Law & Security Review* 30, no. 5 (2014): 574–78, https://doi.org/10.1016/j.clsr.2014.07.002; A. Bunn, "The Curious Case of the Right to Be Forgotten," *Computer Law & Security Review* 31, no. 5 (2015): 336–50, https://doi.org/10.1016/j.clsr.2015.03.006; K. Bryrum, "The European Right to Be Forgotten: A Challenge to the United States Constitution's First Amendment and to Professional Public Relations Ethics," *Public Relations Review* 43, no. 1 (2017): 102–11, https://doi.org/10.1016/j.pubrev.2016.10.010; M. Ambrose, "Speaking of Forgetting: Analysis of Possible Non-EU Responses to the Right to Be Forgotten and Speech Exception," *Telecommunications Policy* 38, no. 8–9 (2014): 800–811, www.dhi.ac.uk/san/waysofbeing/data/citizenship-robson-ambrose-2014.pdf; J. Townend, "Data Protection and the 'Fight to Be Forgotten' in Practice: A UK Perspective," *International Journal of Legal Information* 45, no. 1 (2017): 28–33, www.cambridge.org/core/journals/international-journal-of-legal-information/article/data-protection-and-the-right-to-be-forgotten-in-practice-a-uk-perspective/CA6EF1DA15B5C39525DFF0142DF2D2D0; L. Bode and M. Jones, "Do Americans Want a Right to Be Forgotten? Estimating Public Support for Digital Erasure Legislation," *Policy & Internet* 10, no. 3 (2018): 244–63, https://doi.org/10.1002/poi3.174; A. Vavra, "The Right to Be Forgotten: An Archival Perspective," *American Archivist* 81, no. 1 (2018): 100–111, https://doi.org/10.17723/0360-9081-81.1.100; and P. Korenhof et al., "Timing the Right to Be Forgotten: A Study into 'Time' as a Factor in Deciding about Retention or Erasure of Data," in *Reforming European Data Protection Law*, ed. S. Gutwirth et al. (Heidelberg: Spring, 2015), 171–201.

8. Some erasure requests have involved personal information indexed by Internet search engines. In *NT1 and NT2 v. Google LLC* (April 13, 2018), for example, the England and Wales High Court ordered Google to de-list search results referring to the previous criminal conviction of a businessman, referred to anonymously as NT2, who claimed that the search results were inaccurate, irrelevant, and of no public interest. In the same case, however, the court rejected a similar request by a public figure, referred to as NT1, because the information was considered to be of public interest. For a detailed discussion of the case by Columbia University's Global Freedom of Expression initiative, see https://globalfreedomofexpression.columbia.edu/cases/nt1-nt2-v-google-llc. As cited in *Harper's Magazine* 339, no. 2035 (December 2019): 9, 12, https://harpers.org/blog/2019/12/?post_type=archive, Google has received 3.3 million requests to delete search results related to specific individuals under the GDPR's right to be forgotten. Examples include information about data subjects who escaped from a mental hospital, falsified documents, took money from elderly people, was in posses-

sion of child pornography, murdered a close family member, and published a news article about Google's decision to delist a news article.

9. M. Gonzalez, "Habeas Data: Comparative Constitutional Interventions from Latin America against Neoliberal States of Insecurity and Surveillance," *Chicago-Kent Law Review* 90, no. 2 (2015): 641–68, https://scholarship.kentlaw.iit.edu/cklawreview/vol90/iss2/10/?utm_source=scholarship.kentlaw.iit.edu%2Fcklawreview%2Fvol90%2Fiss2%2F10& utm_medium=PDF&utm_campaign=PDFCoverPages.

10. The Act amends Division 3, Part 4 of the California Civil Code commencing with § 1798.05, https://leginfo.legislature.ca.gov/faces/billTextClient.xhtml?bill_id =201720180AB375. See also L. de la Torre, "A Guide to the California Privacy Act of 2018," November 2018, at https://papers.ssrn.com/sol3/papers.cfm?abstract_id=3275571; C. Barrett, "Are the EU GDPR and the California CCPA Becoming the De Facto Global Standards for Data Protection," *Scitech Lawyer* 15, no. 3 (Spring 2019): 24–29, www.americanbar.org/groups/science_technology/publications/scitech_lawyer/2019/spring/are-eu-gdpr-and-california-ccpa-becoming-de-facto-global-standards-data-privacy-and-protection; Elizabeth Harding et al., "Understanding the Scope and Impact of the California Consumer Privacy Act of 2018," *Journal of Data Protection & Privacy* 2, no. 3 (2019): 234–53, www.ingentaconnect.com/content/hsp/jdpp/2019/00000002/00000003/art00007.

11. The most widely publicized recordkeeping violations have involved financial service companies. Among the many examples that might be cited, five brokerage firms were fined a combined $825 million by the SEC, NYSE, and NASD for failing to comply with recordkeeping requirements related to preservation of email communications (Securities Exchange Act Release No. 46937, Administrative Proceeding File No. 3-10957, *In the Matter of Deutsche Bank Securities, Inc., Goldman, Sachs & Co., Morgan Stanley & Co. Incorporated, Salomon Smith Barney Inc., and U.S. Bancorp Piper Jaffray Inc.,* December 3, 2002, www.sec.gov/litigation/admin/34-46937.htm). Three brokerage firms were fined $375 million and received a censure and cease and desist order for willful recordkeeping violations (Securities Exchange Act Release No. 8538, Administrative Proceeding File No. 3-11818, *In the Matter of Banc of America Capital Management, LLC, BACAP Distributors, LLC, and Banc of America Securities, LLC,* February 9, 2005, www.sec.gov/litigation/admin/33-8538.htm). A brokerage firm was fined $1.25 million for failure to preserve audio recordings as required by SEC regulations (Securities Exchange Act Release No. 83650, *In the Matter of BGC Financial, L.P.,* July 17, 2018, www.sec.gov/litigation/admin/2018/34-83650.pdf). A hedge fund was fined $4.25 million for causing prime brokers to violate recordkeeping rules (Securities Exchange Act Release No. 75445, Administrative Proceeding File No. 3-16686, *In the Matter of OZ Management, LP,* July 14, 2015, www.sec.gov/litigation/admin/2015/34-75445.pdf).

12. Records managers and other information professionals have long recognized problems associated with retention schedules. A 2001 report prepared for the U.S. National Archives and Records Administration, the source of many records management innovations, noted that scheduling concepts were poorly understood by federal employees; that many significant records, including most electronic records, were unscheduled; that some significant records were improperly scheduled; and that some agency retention schedules were out of date (SRA International, *Report on Current Recordkeeping Practices within the Federal Government* [Arlington, VA: SRA International, 2001], www.archives.gov/files/records-mgmt/faqs/pdf/report-on-recordkeeping-practices,pdf).

13. Some recordkeeping laws and regulations include a requirement to preserve information that is relevant to regulatory investigations or enforcement actions even if legally mandated retention periods elapse before those matters are resolved. As specified in 29 C.F.R. § 1602.14, for example, an employer must preserve all employment records that are relevant for a charge of discrimination or action brought by the Equal Employment Opportunity Commission or the US attorney general until final disposition of the charge or action.

14. ISO/IEC 27050-1:2016, *Information Technology—Security Techniques—Electronic Discovery—Part 1: Overview and Concepts*, defines *spoliation* as the "act of allowing a change to or destruction of electronically stored information where there is a requirement to keep it intact." The definition is equally applicable to paper records. Spoliation is explained and analyzed in hundreds of legal publications. Examples that treat various aspects of the topic

include M. Koesel and T. Turnbull, *Spoliation of Evidence: Sanctions and Remedies for Destruction of Evidence in Civil Litigation*, 3rd ed. (Chicago: American Bar Association, 2014); P. Oot, ed., *Spoliation* (Washington, DC: Electronic Discovery Institute, 2019); A. KohSweeney et al., *Spoilation in the Electronic Age* (Washington, DC: Bureau of National Affairs, 2015); G. Joseph, *Sanctions: The Federal Law of Litigation Abuse*, 4th ed. (Newark, NJ: LexisNexis, 2008); J. Gorelik et al., *Destruction of Evidence* (New York: Aspen Publishers, 1989); R. Tucker, "The Flexible Doctrine of Spoliation of Evidence: Cause of Action, Defense, Evidentiary Presumption, and Discovery Sanction," *University of Toledo Law Review* 27, no. 1 (1995): 67–84, https://ideaexchange.uakron.edu/ua_law_publications/216; J. Kinsler and A. MacIver, "Demystifying Spoliation of Evidence," *Tort & Insurance Law Journal* 34, no. 3 (1999): 761–83, www.jstor.org/stable/25763303; P Kerkorian, "Negligent Spoliation of Evidence: Skirting the Suit within a Suit Requirement of Legal Malpractice Actions," *Hastings Law Journal* 41, no. 4 (1990): 1077–1109, https://repository.uchastings.edu/cgi/viewcontent.cgi?article=3010&context=hastings_law_journal; C. Adams, "Spoliation of Electronic Evidence: Sanctions versus Advocacy," *Michigan Telecommunications and Technology Law Review* 18, no. 1 (2011): 1–59, https://repository.law.umich.edu/cgi/viewcontent.cgi?article=1024&context=mttlr; A. Spencer, "The Preservation Obligation: Regulating and Sanctioning Pre-Litigation Spoliation in Federal Court," *Fordham Law Review* 79, no. 5 (2011): 2005–34, https://pdfs.semanticscholar.org/0152/5ab55dfbe04fc3a7f393728a0cbe46daf9c0.pdf; R. Durrant, "Spoliation of Discoverable Electronic Evidence," *Loyola Los Angeles Law Review* 38, no. 4 (2005): 1803–34, https://digitalcommons.lmu.edu/cgi/viewcontent.cgi?referer=https://www.google.com/&httpsredir=1&article=2486&context=llr; S. Huang and R. Muriel, "Spoliation of Evidence: Defining the Ethical Boundaries of Destroying Evidence," *American Journal of Trial Advocacy* 22, no. 1 (1998/1999): 191, https://heinonline.org/HOL/LandingPage?handle=hein.journals/amjtrad22&div=12&id=&page=; L. Kindel and K. Richter, "Spoilation of Evidence: Will the New Millennium See a Further Expansion of Sanctions for Improper Destruction of Evidence?" *William Mitchell Law Review* 27, no. 1 (2000): 687–711, https://open.mitchellhamline.edu/cgi/viewcontent.cgi?article=1731&context=wmlr; M. Curtin, "The Duty to Preserve Social Media Evidence," *Quinnipiac Law Review* 35, no. 4 (2017): 791–97, www.quinnipiaclawjournals.com/content/dam/qu/documents/sol/law-journals1/law-review/volume-35/consolidated-pdf/quinnipiac-law-review-volume-35-issue-4.pdf.

15. *Carlucci v. Piper Aircraft Corp.*, 102 F.R.D. 472 (S.D. Fla. 1984), https://casetext.com/case/carlucci-v-piper-aircraft-corporation. On the importance of record retention for product liability lawsuits, see T. Kastetter, "Quality Concepts and Litigation: The Role of Record-Keeping in Products Liability Litigation in the USA," *Management Decision* 37, no. 8 (1999): 633–43, https://doi.org/10.1108/00251749910291604.

16. *Telectron, Inc. v. Overhead Door Corp.*, 116 F.R.D. 107 (S.D. Fla. 1987), https://casetext.com/case/telectron.

17. *Capellupo v. FMC Corp.*, 126 F.R.D. 545, 547 (D. Minn. 1989), https://casetext.com/case/capellupo-v-fmc-corporation.

18. *In re Prudential Ins. Co. of A. Sales Prac. Litigation*, 169 F.R.D. 598 (D.N.J. 1997), https://casetext.com/case/in-re-prudential-ins-co-of-a-sales-prac-litigation.

19. *Zubulake v. UBS Warburg LLC*, 220 F.R.D. 212, 217 (S.D.N.Y. 2003), https://casetext.com/case/zubulake-v-ubs-warburg-llc-5.

20. *Securities and Exchange Commission v. Martha Stewart and Peter Bacanovic*, 03-CIV-4070 (NRB) (S.D.N.Y.), www.sec.gov/litigation/complaints/comp18169.htm.

21. *Vagenos v. LDG Financial Services, LLC*, 2009 WL 5219021 (E.D.N.Y., Dec. 31, 2009), https://casetext.com/case/vagenos-v-ldg-financial-services.

22. *TR Investors, LLC v. Genger*, 2009 WL 4696062 (Del. Ch. Dec. 9, 2009), https://law.justia.com/cases/delaware/court-of-chancery/2009/130800-1.html.

23. *Daynight, LLC v. Mobilight, Inc*, 2011 UT App 28, www.courtlistener.com/opinion/2359629/daynight-llc-v-mobilight-inc/.

24. *GN Netcom, Inc. v. Plantronics, Inc.*, No. 18-1287 (3d Cir. 2019), www2.ca3.uscourts.gov/opinarch/181287p.pdf.

25. *NuVasive, Inc. v. Madsen Med., Inc.*, no. 13CV2077, 2016 WL 305096 (S.D. Cal. Jan. 26, 2016), https://casetext.com/case/nuvasive-inc-v-madsen-med-inc-3. In a widely publicized incident, Tom Brady, quarterback for the New England Patriots, was suspended by the National Football League for failing to provide his personal cell phone for a nonjudicial investigation involving intentional deflating of footballs in a championship game. Brady had reportedly instructed his assistant to destroy the phone.

26. *CAT3 LLC v. Black Lineage, Inc*, No. 14 CIV.5511 (AT)(JCF), 2016 WL 154116 (S.D.N.Y. Jan. 12, 2016), www.americanbar.org/content/dam/aba/publications/litigation_news/ Cat3-Black-Lineage-1.pdf.

27. *United States v. Arthur Andersen LLP*, 374 F.3d 281 (5th Cir. 2004), https://case-text.com/case/us-v-arthur-andersen-llp. Andersen's conviction was reversed in 2005, but many of its leading clients withdrew their business after the criminal charges were announced. Andersen closed its public accounting operation in 2002. For a discussion, see *Indicting Corporations Revisited: Lessons of the Arthur Andersen Prosecution* (Irvine, CA: American College of Trial Lawyers, 2004), www.actl.com/docs/default-source/default-document-library/newsroom/ indicting_corporations_revisited_lessons_of_the_arthur_anderson _prosecution_2005.pdf?sfvrsn=4; J. Arber, "Obstruction of Justice in the Digital Age: Defining the Actus Reus of 18 U.S.C. §§ 1512(c) and 1519," *Columbia Science & Technology Law Review* 18, no. 2 (2016): 220–58, www.stlr.org/download/volumes/volume18/Arber.pdf; M. Brown and P. Weiner, "Digital Dangers: A Primer on Electronic Evidence in the Wake of Enron," *Litigation* 30, no. 1 (2003): 24–30, www.jstor.org/stable/2976039; B. Toffler and J. Reingold, *Final Accounting: Ambition, Greed and the Fall of Arthur Andersen* (New York: Broadway Books, 2003), K. Eichenwald, *Conspiracy of Fools: A True Story* (New York: Broadway Books, 2005).

28. *In EPAC Techs., Inc. v. HarperCollins Christian Publ'g, Inc.*, No. 3:12-cv-00463 (M.D. Tenn. Mar. 29, 2018), https://casetext.com/case/epac-techs-inc-v-harpercollins-christian-publg-inc, a long delay in communicating a legal hold notice led to the destruction of 750,000 email messages and attachments, which were purged on a regular schedule. The court criticized the defendant harshly but only imposed minor sanctions.

29. *In United States of America v. Volkswagen AG*, No 16-CR-20394 (E.D. Michigan), www.justice.gov/opa/press-release/file/924436/download, employees reportedly interpreted an announcement of an impending legal hold notice as a suggestion to destroy potentially incriminating documents before the hold notice took effect.

30. Courts awarded sanctions in 230 of 401 cases involving motions relating to discovery of paper or electronic documents prior to January 1, 2010. In most of the cases, the sanctions involved failure to preserve evidence, sometimes combined with delay or misrepresentation about the completeness of response to a discovery request. D. Willoughby Jr. et al., "Sanctions for E-Discovery Violations: By the Numbers," *Duke Law Journal* 60, no. 4 (2010): 790–863, https://scholarship.law.duke.edu/cgi/viewcontent.cgi?article=1487&context=dlj.

31. While no studies measure the frequency of undetected spoliation, a 1980 survey of 180 civil litigators concluded that "it would be difficult to exaggerate the pervasiveness of evasive practices or their adverse impact . . . on civil discovery." The study noted that over 60 percent of the interviewees complained about some form of evasion. W. Brazil, "Civil Discovery: Lawyers' Views of Its Effectiveness, Principal Problems and Abuses," *American Bar Foundation Research Journal* 5, no. 4 (1980). 789–902, https://scholarship.law.berkeley.edu/cgi/view-content.cgi?referer=https://www.google.com/&httpsredir=1&article=1320&context=facpubs. See also C. Nesson, "Incentives to Spoliate Evidence in Civil Litigation: The Need for Vigorous Judicial Action," *Cardozo Law Review* 13, no. 4 (1991): 793–805, https://heinonline.org/ HOL/LandingPage?handle=hein.journals/cdozo13&div=42&id=&page= , which reports that 50 percent of litigators believe spoliation to be either a frequent or a regular problem; D. Nance, "Hear No Evil, See No Evil: On Professor Nesson's Claims about Evidence Suppression," *Cardozo Law Review* 13, no. 4 (1991): 809–15, https://scholarlycommons.law.case.edu/cgi/ viewcontent.cgi?referer=https://www.google.com/&httpsredir=1&article=1287&con-text=faculty_publications; T. Spencer, "Do Not Fold, Spindle or Mutilate: The Trend towards Recognition of Spoliation as a Separate Tort," *Idaho Law Review* 37, no. 1 (1993): 37–65; On the possibility of undetected destruction or alteration of medical records, see A. Casamassima,

"Spoliation of Evidence and Medical Malpractice," *Pace Law Review* 14, no. 1 (1994): 235–99, https://digitalcommons.pace.edu/cgi/viewcontent.cgi?article=1381&context=plr; A. Hoffman and S. Sanbar, "Spoliation: Record Retention, Destruction, and Alteration," in American College of Legal Medicine, *Medical Malpractice Survival Handbook* (Philadelphia: Mosby, 2007), 45–54.

32. In a 2010 case involving a breach of contract claim, the court noted that the defendant's destruction of laptops containing relevant information would have gone undetected had the plaintiffs not made a diligent examination of information produced during discovery. The missing information was subsequently found on backup media (*Harkabi v. Sandisk Corp.*, 08 Civ. 8203 [WHP] [S.D.N.Y. Aug. 23, 2010], www.ediscoverylaw.com/2010/08/27). In another 2010 case, the court issued an adverse inference instruction against the plaintiff because over two thousand documents contained on a backup disk were found to be missing from a laptop computer that was subject to a preservation order (*Orbit One Communications, Inc. v. Numerex Corp.*, 271 F.R.D. 429 [S.D.N.Y. 2010], https://casetext.com/case/orbit-one-communications-3). In a famous instance of evidence recovered from backup media, Col. Oliver L. North, a National Security Council staff member during the Reagan administration, believed that he had deleted email messages in 1986 related to the clandestine sale of arms to Iran and the subsequent diversion of funds to the anti-communist Contra rebels in Nicaragua, but the messages were saved on backup tapes, which were subsequently used as evidence in a Congressional investigation. These events are recounted in M. Byrne, *Iran-Contra: Reagan's Scandal and the Unchecked Abuse of Presidential Power* (Lawrence: University Press of Kansas, 2014). The destruction of information was not limited to email. In widely publicized testimony during Congressional hearings on the Iran-Contra affair, North's secretary, Fawn Hall, alleged that he instructed her to destroy or alter other documents. Summarizing their record-retention procedure, Ms. Hall noted, "We shred everything." B. Woodward, *Veil: The Secret Wars of the CIA 1981–1987* (New York: Simon and Schuster, 1987), 501.

33. Destruction of relevant information or other actions that unlawfully obstruct another party's access to evidence is prohibited by Rule 3.4 of the Model Rules of Professional Conduct issued by the American Bar Association. According to Rule 1.16, an attorney must refuse or withdraw from representation of a client where such representation will result in a violation of the rules of professional conduct. www.americanbar.org/groups/professional_responsibility/publications/model_rules_of_professional_conduct/model_rules_of_professional_conduct_table_of_contents.

34. A study of discovery requests found that the ratio of pages provided to an opposing party to pages that the receiving party actually used as exhibits in litigation exceeds 1,000 to 1. In 2008, an average of 4.98 million pages of documents were produced in response to discovery orders in major cases that went to trial, but the average number of pages actually used as documentary evidence was less than 4,775 per case. See Lawyers for Civil Justice, Civil Justice Report Group, and U.S. Chamber Institute for Legal Reform, "Litigation Cost Survey of Major Companies," for presentation to the Committee on Rules of Practice and Procedure, Judicial Conference of the United States, 2010 Conference on Civil Litigation, Duke Law School, May 10–11, 2010, www.uscourts.gov/sites/default/files/litigation_cost_survey_of_major_companies_0.pdf.

35. As an effective risk avoidance strategy, an organization should strive to reduce the quantity of information it creates and emphasize the importance of clarity and accuracy when writing email messages, reports, and other documents. See A. Maskin, "The Next Step in Creating a Culture of Risk Avoidance: Avoid the Creation of Harmful Internal Documents," ABA Section of Litigation 2012 Corporate Counsel CLE Seminar, February 16–19, 2012, www.weil.com/~/media/files/pdfs/maskin-taking-away-pltfs-ex-a.pdf.

36. *Essex Insurance Co. v. Wright*, 371 Ill. A 3d 437, 862 N.E.2d 1194 (1st Dist. 2007), https://casetext.com/case/essex-insurance-co-v-wright; *Lincoln Ins. Co. v. Home Emer. Services, Inc.*, 812 So. 2d 433 (Fla. Dist. Ct. A 2002), www.courtlistener.com/opinion/1790903/lincoln-ins-co-v-home-emergency-services-inc.

37. See J. Nicholson, "Plus Ultra: Third-Party Preservation in a Cloud Computing Paradigm," *Hastings Business Law Journal* 8, no. 1 (2012): 191–219, https://repository.uchastings.edu/cgi/viewcontent.cgi?article=1074&context=hastings_business_law_journal.

38. For a detailed discussion of legal holds, see the Sedona Conference, "Commentary on Legal Holds, Second Edition: The Trigger & the Process," *Sedona Conference Journal* 20 (2019) 341–414, https://thesedonaconference.org/publication/Commentary_on_Legal_Holds; A. Ziegler and E. Rojas, *Preserving Electronic Evidence for Trial* (Cambridge, MA: Syngress, 2016); M. Luoma and V. Luoma, "Litigation Holds: Past, Present, and Future Directions," *Journal of Digital Forensics, Security, and Law* 10, no. 1 (2015): 57–68, https://doi.org/10.15394/jdfsl.2015.1198; B. Harris and J. Jablonski, "Grasping Legal Holds: What Organizations Need to Know," *Information Management* 44, no. 5 (2010): 20–24, 50.

39. As an example, retention periods for accounting records are often based on the statute of limitations for contract-related litigation in locations where an organization operates. Similarly, retention periods for hiring records may be based on the statute of limitations for civil litigation related to employment discrimination.

40. In *Lewy v. Remington Arms Co.*, 836 F.2d 1104 (8th Cir., 1988), the defendant, a firearms manufacturer, was unable to produce customer complaint records that it had reportedly destroyed after three years pursuant to its established retention practices, but the court found that such a short retention period "may be sufficient for documents such as appointment books or telephone messages, but inadequate for documents such as customer complaints." https://casetext.com/case/lewy-v-remington-arms-co-inc. In *Broccoli v. Echostar Communications Corp.*, 229 F.R.D. 506 (D. Md. 2005), the court criticized the defendant for its "extraordinary" email-retention policy, which deleted the contents of sent-items folders after twenty-one days and all emails of former employees thirty days after termination. https://casetext.com/case/broccoli-v-echostar-communications-corp.

41. Form 990, in particular, has been used in studies of charitable giving, fundraising effectiveness, the impact of governance on donations, and the financial performance, expense allocations, revenue diversification, and efficiency of non-profit entities. See, for example, N. Feng et al., "Using Archival Data Sources to Conduct Nonprofit Accounting Research," *Journal of Public Budgeting, Accounting & Financial Management* 26, no. 3 (2014): 458–93, https://doi.org/10.1108/JPBAFM-26-03-2014-B004; K. Froelich et al., "Financial Measures in Nonprofit Organization Research: Comparing IRS 990 Return and Audited Financial Statement Data," *Nonprofit and Voluntary Sector Quarterly* 29, no. 2 (2000): 232–54, https://journals.sagepub.com/doi/pdf/10.1177/0899764000292002; T. Gordon et al., "The Quality and Reliability of Form 990 Data: Are Users Being Misled?" *Academy of Accounting and Financial Studies Journal* 11, no. 1 (2007): 27–49, www.bauer.uh.edu/jmeade/articles/Academy of Acctg Government Not Profit Sp_2007.pdf; E. Freisenhahn, "Nonprofits in America: New Research Data on Employment, Wages, and Establishments," *Monthly Labor Review* 139, no. 2 (2016): 1–12, www.bls.gov/opub/mlr/2016/article/pdf/nonprofits-in-america.pdf.

42. In the United States, the Cockrell Committee (1887–1889), the Keep Commission (1905–1909), and the two Hoover Commissions (1947–1949 and 1953–1955) criticized the retention of unnecessary records by federal government agencies. Early records management initiatives—such as the General Records Disposal Act of 1939, the Records Disposal Act of 1943, and the Federal Records Act of 1950—authorized the destruction of federal government records when no longer needed. See O. Kraines, "The Cockrell Committee, 1887–1889: First Comprehensive Congressional Investigation into Administration," *Western Political Quarterly* 4, no. 4 (1951): 583–609, https://doi.org/10.2307/443156; H. Pinkett, "The Keep Commission, 1905–1909: A Rooseveltian Effort for Administrative Reform," *Journal of American History* 52, no. 2 (1965): 297–312; https://doi.org/10.2307/1908809; R. Krauskopf, "The Hoover Commissions and Federal Recordkeeping," *American Archivist* 21, no. 4 (1958): 371–99, www.jstor.org/stable/40289737; H. Angel, "Federal Records Management since the Hoover Commission Report," *American Archivist* 16, no. 1 (1953): 13–26, https://americanarchivist.org/doi/pdf/10.17723/aarc.16.1.j26707451005wxp0.

43. At the time this book was written, prices for a 1 terabyte external hard drive with a USB interface had fallen below $50. For network installations with high reliability requirements, a terabyte of direct-attached, fault-tolerant disk storage could be purchased for less than $400. At that price, the cost to store twelve thousand pages of word-processing documents totaling about 36 megabytes is a fraction of a cent. By contrast, twelve thousand pages will fill a four-drawer filing cabinet that costs about $300 and occupy floor space valued at upwards of $150 per year.

44. The total cost of ownership (TCO) for computer storage encompasses the purchase price of storage devices plus all direct and indirect costs associated with the use and maintenance of those devices. Examples include, but are not limited to, the cost of installation, testing, and deployment; charges for repairs and maintenance contracts; labor costs for operation and technical support; the cost of floor space and utilities; data backup and disaster recovery costs; and administrative overhead costs. For organizations that outsource their computing operations, the TCO includes a reasonable markup for the supplier's profit. Industry analysts agree that the TCO for storage devices is a multiple of the purchase price of the devices themselves, but estimates of that multiple range broadly from 3 to 8. A 2001 Gartner Group report estimated that acquisition costs for storage components account for 20 percent of the TCO, which equates to a TCO multiple of 5. Examples of the many publications on TCO concepts include L. Ellram, "Total Cost of Ownership," *International Journal of Physical Distribution and Logistics Management*, 25, no. 8 (1995): 4–23, https://doi.org/10.1108/09600039510099928; L. Ellram and S. Siferd, "Total Cost of Ownership: A Key Concept in Strategic Cost Management," *Journal of Business Logistics* 19, no. 1 (1998): 55–84, www.academia.edu/956539/Total_cost_of_ownership_a_key_concept_in_strategic_cost_management_decisions; B. Ferrin, "Total Cost of Ownership Models: An Exploratory Study," *Journal of Supply Chain Management* 38, no. 2 (2002): 18–29, https://doi.org/10.1111/j.1745-493X.2002.tb00132.x; B. Kirwin and L. Mieritz, *Defining Gartner Total Cost of Ownership*, December 8, 2005, www.gartner.com/en/documents/487157/defining-gartner-total-cost-of-ownership; J. David et al., "Managing Your Total IT Cost of Ownership," *Communications of the of the ACM* 45, no. 1 (2002): 101–6, https//doi.org/10.1145/502269.502273; M. Walterbusch et al., "Evaluating Cloud Computing Services from a Total Cost of Ownership Perspective," *Management Research Review* 36, no. 6 (2013): 613–38, https://doi.org/10.1108/01409171311325769.

45. In 2018, the Danish Data Protection Agency fined a taxi company 1.2 million kroner for over-retention of customer information in violation of the General Data Protection Regulation. Data retention issues were cited as one of the GDPR violations for which Google was fined €50 million by CNIL, the French data protection authority, in 2019. CNIL also fined a real estate company €400,000 for over-retention of personal data about prospective tenants. Over-retention was one of the offenses for which a Lithuanian company was fined €61,500. In the United Kingdom, the Information Commissioner's Office cited poor data retention practices as one of the offenses for which Equifax was fined £500,000.

46. O. Holmes, "The Evaluation and Preservation of Business Archives," *American Archivist* 1, no. 4 (1938): 171–85, www.americanarchivist.org/doi/pdf/10.17723/aarc.1.4.p2x3r56677tj4423; G. Saretzky, "North American Business Archives: Results of a Survey," *American Archivist* 40, no. 4 (1977): 413–19, www.americanarchivist.org/doi/pdf/10.17723/aarc.40.4.e3553491v54j7607; D. Smith, "An Historical Look at Business Archives," *American Archivist* 45, no. 3 (1982): 273–78, https://americanarchivist.org/doi/pdf/10.17723/aarc.45.3.c7q713vn64q7lu78; E. Adkins, "The Development of Business Archives in the United States: An Overview and a Personal Perspective," *American Archivist* 60, no. 1 (1997): 8–33, https://doi.org/10.17723/aarc.60.1.qk640m762t10g348; I. Deserno, "The Value of International Business Archives: The Importance of the Archives of Multinational Companies in Shaping Cultural Identity," *Archival Science* 9, nos. 3–4 (2009): 215–25, https://link.springer.com/article/10.1007/s10502-009-9106-1; and A. Turton, ed., *The International Business Archives Handbook: Understanding and Managing the Historical Records of Business* (New York: Routledge, 2017). The Society of American Archivists provides an online directory of corporate archives in the United States and Canada at www2.archivists.org/groups/business-archives-section/directory-of-corporate-archives-in-the-united-states-and-canada-introduction.

47. W. Saffady, *Records Management Experience with Big Bucket Retention: A Status Report* (Pittsburgh, PA: ARMA International Education Foundation, 2018), http://armaedfoundation.org/wp-content/uploads/2018/08/AIEF-Research-Paper-Saffady-Big-Buckets-2018-081518.pdf. Over-retention was not an impediment for interviewees in organizations covered by this study, which was based on interviews with records managers who have implemented big-bucket retention schedules. No interviewees reported resistance to the possibility that some records may be retained longer than necessary. Rather than being troubled by over-retention,

some interviewees noted that stakeholders in their organizations viewed long retention favorably.

48. The role of acid in deterioration of paper has been recognized for decades. See, for example, A. Kimberley and A. Emley, *A Study of the Deterioration of Book Paper in Libraries, Bureau of Standards Miscellaneous Publication No. 140* (Washington, DC: U.S. Government Printing Office, 1933), https://nvlpubs.nist.gov/nistpubs/Legacy/MP/nbsmiscellaneouspub140.pdf; W. Barrow and R. Sproull, "Permanence in Book Papers," *Science* 129, no. 3356 (1959): 1075–84, www.doi.org/10.1126/science.129.3356.1075; W. Hollinger Jr., "The Chemical Structure and Acid Deterioration of Paper," *Library Hi Tech* 1, no. 4 (1984): 51–57, https://doi.org/10.1108/eb047525; J. Arney et al., "The Influence of Deacidification on the Deterioration of Paper," *Journal of the American Institute for Conservation* 19, no. 1 (1979): 34–41, https://doi.org/10.1179/019713679806028959; C. Shahani and W. Wilson, "Preservation of Libraries and Archives," *American Scientist* 75, no. 3 (1987): 240–51, www.jstor.org/stable/27854604; H. Carter, "The Chemistry of Paper Preservation: Part 1. The Aging of Paper and Conservation Techniques," *Journal of Chemical Education* 73, no. 5 (1996): 417–20, https://doi.org/10.1021/ed073p417; H. Carter, "The Chemistry of Paper Preservation: Part 4. Alkaline Paper," *Journal of Chemical Education* 73, no. 5 (1996): 417–20, https://doi.org/10.1021/ed074p508; N. Gurnagul et al., "The Mechanical Permanence of Paper: A Literature Review," *Journal of Pulp and Paper Science* 19, no. 4 (1993): 160–66, www.researchgate.net/profile/Norayr_Gurnagul/publication/260124879_The_mechanical_permanence_of_paper_a_literature_review/links/55c3654608aea2d9bdc0d4be/The-mechanical-permanence-of-paper-a-literature-review.pdf; C. Shahani and G. Harrison, "Spontaneous Formation of Acids in the Natural Aging of Paper," *Studies in Conservation* 47, sup. 3 (2002): 189–92, https://doi.org/10.1179/sic.2002.47.s3.039.

49. According to ISO 11108:1996, *Information and Documentation—Archival Paper—Requirements for Permanence and Durability*, archival papers are more durable versions of permanent papers. They must be strong enough to resist tearing and tolerate folding.

50. ANSI/NISO Z39.48-1992 (R2009), *Permanence of Paper for Publications and Documents in Libraries and Archives* (Baltimore, MD: National Information Standards Organization, 2010), https://groups.niso.org/apps/group_public/download.php/13464/Z39-48-1992_r2009.pdf.

51. The ASTM standard notes that definitive lifetime values are not possible because there are many variables in the manufacturing, storage, and use of paper, but the relationship of lifespan to pH values is well established. https://civilengineersstandard.com/wp-content/uploads/2018/12/D-3290.pdf.

52. W. Wilson, *Environmental Guidelines for Storage of Paper Records, NISO TR01-1995*. (Bethesda, MD: NISO Press, 1995), www.niso.org/sites/default/files/2017-08/tr01.pdf. See also ISO/TR 19815:2018, *Information and Documentation—Management of the Environmental Conditions for Archive and Library Collections*.

53. Among the many examples that might be cited: B. Scribner, *Summary Report of Research at the National Bureau of Standards on the Stability and Preservation of Records on Photographic Film* (Washington, DC: U.S. Government Printing Office, 1939), www.govinfo.gov/app/details/GOVPUB-C13-99b52b79c268b5c38f429bef2887e0fa; G. Eaton, "Preservation, Deterioration, Restoration of Photographic Images," *Library Quarterly* 40, no. 1 (1970): 85–98, https://doi.org/10.1086/619814; K. Hendriks, "The Preservation of Photographic Records," *Archivaria*, no. 5 (1977/1978): 92–100, https://archivaria.ca/index.php/archivaria/article/viewFile/10568/11416; A. Ram and J. McCrea, "Stability of Processed Cellulose Ester Photographic Films," *SMPTE Journal* 97, no. 6 (1988): 474–83, https://doi.org/10.5594/J02945; P. Adelstein and J. McCrea, "Stability of Processed Polyester Base Photographic Films," *Journal of Applied Photographic Engineering* 7, no. 6 (1981): 160–67; P. Adelstein et al., "Stability of Photographic Film: Part VI— Long-Term Aging Studies," *SMPTE Journal* 111, no. 4 (2002): 136–43, https://doi.org/10.5594/J11563; A. Ram, "Archival Preservation of Photographic Films—a Perspective," *Polymer Degradation and Stability* 29, no. 1 (1990): 3–29, https://doi.org/10.1016/0141-3910(90)90019-4; D. Norris and J. Gutierrez, eds., *Issues in the Conservation of Photographs* (Los Angeles: Getty Conservation Institute, 2010).

54. See also ISO 18918, *Imaging Materials—Processed Photographic Plates—Storage Practices,* which defines medium-term and extended-term storage of silver-gelatin photographic plates, precursors of photographic films that may be stored in archives, libraries, or other repositories. ISO 18934:2011, *Imaging Materials—Multiple Media Archives—Storage Environment,* suggests temperature and humidity guidelines for storage areas that contain a variety of recording media. Stability tests to confirm that silver-gelatin film is processed in a manner compatible with permanence are specified in ISO 18917:1999, *Photography—Determination of Residual Thiosulfate and Other Related Chemicals in Processed Photographic Materials—Methods Using Iodine-amylose, Methylene Blue and Silver Sulfide.* Stability of color films is covered by ISO 18909:2006, *Photography—Processed Photographic Colour Films and Paper Prints—Methods for Measuring Image Stability.* Manufacturing requirements for silver-gelatin films are covered by ISO 18906:2000, *Imaging Materials—Photographic Films—Specifications for Safety Film.*

55. ISO 18905:2002, *Imaging Materials—Ammonia-Processed Diazo Photographic Film—Specifications for Stability,* and *ISO 18912:2002, Imaging Materials—Processed Vesicular Photographic Film—Specifications for Stability.* ISO 18919:1999, *Imaging Materials—Thermally Processed Silver Microfilm—Specifications for Stability,* specifies a 100-year life expectancy for dry silver films, which were formerly used in computer-output microfilm recorders.

56. The life span of electronic information on a hard drive is effectively limited by the device's reliable service life, which is usually three to five years. Most hard drives are replaced and their contents migrated to new devices within that time frame. On the stability of solid-state memory as an alternative to hard drives, see B. Schroeder et al., "Flash Reliability in Production: The Expected and the Unexpected," in *FAST '16: Proceedings of the 14th USENIX Conference on File and Storage Technologies* (Berkeley, CA: USENIX Association, 2016), 67–80, https://www.usenix.org/system/files/conference/fast16/fast16-papers-schroeder.pdf.

57. Some audio and video tapes created decades ago remain playable today, albeit with impaired quality. Computing facilities have likewise successfully retrieved information from magnetic tapes that have been in storage for more than a decade. S. Geller, *Care and Handling of Computer Storage Media, NBS Special Publication 500-101* (Washington, DC: National Bureau of Standards, 1983), https://archive.org/details/carehandlingofco5001gell/page/n1, and L. E. Smith et al., *Prediction of the Long-Term Stability of Polyester-Based Recording Media* (Gaithersburg, MD: National Bureau of Standards, 1986), https://nvlpubs.nist.gov/nistpubs/Legacy/IR/nbsir86-3474.pdf, reported that some magnetic tapes can remain useful for up to twenty years.

58. Computer, video, and audio information recorded on magnetic tapes are vulnerable to accidental erasure by magnetic fields of sufficient strength. Information recorded on magnetic tapes can be damaged by migration of recorded signals from one layer of tape to another. Recorded information is also imperiled by changes in the physical and chemical characteristics of a given tape. The most significant physical changes result from media wear and improper media handling. The physical and chemical characteristics of magnetic media are adversely affected by improper storage environments. Scientific studies have recognized these problems for decades. See W. Saffady, "Stability, Care and Handling of Microforms, Magnetic Media and Optical Disks," *Library Technology Reports* 33, no. 6 (1997): 609–751. ISO/TR 17797:2014, *Electronic Archiving—Selection of Digital Storage Media for Long Term Preservation,* reviews stability problems of magnetic tapes and other electronic media.

59. Environmental conditions for storage of optical disks are presented in ISO 18925:2013, *Imaging Materials—Optical Disc Media—Storage Practices.* See also ISO 18983:2014, *Imaging Materials—Optical Discs—Care and Handling for Extended Storage*; ISO/IEC 10995:2011, *Information Technology—Digitally Recorded Media for Information Interchange and Storage—Test Method for the Estimation of the Archival Lifetime of Optical Media*; ISO 18926:2012, *Imaging Materials—Information Stored on Magneto-Optical (MO) Discs—Method for Estimating the Life Expectancy Based on the Effects of Temperature and Relative Humidity*; ISO 18927:2013, *Imaging Materials—Recordable Compact Disc Systems—Methods for Estimating the Life Expectancy Based on the Effects of Temperature and Relative Humidity*; ISO/TR 10255, *Document Management Applications—Optical Disk Storage Technology, Management and Standards;* ISO/IEC 29121:2018, *Information Technology—Digitally Recorded*

Media for Information Interchange and Storage—Data Migration Method for Optical Disks for Long-Term Data Storage.

60. For a compendium of obsolete computer storage media, see https://obsoletemedia.org/data.

61. The many publications that discuss this problem include J. Rothenberg, *Ensuring the Longevity of Digital Documents* (Santa Monica, CA: RAND, 1999), www.clir.org/wp-content/uploads/sites/6/ensuring.pdf; G. Lawrence et al., *Risk Management of Digital Information: A File Format Investigation* (Washington, DC: Council on Library and Information Resources, 2000), https://files.eric.ed.gov/fulltext/ED449802.pdf; D. Pearson and C. Webb, "Defining File Format Obsolescence: A Risky Journey," *International Journal of Digital Curation* 3, no. 1 (2008): 90–106, https://doi.org/10.2218/ijdc.v3i1.44; R. Graf and S. Gordea, "A Risk Analysis of File Formats for Preservation," in *iPRES 2013: Proceedings of the 10th International Conference on Preservation of Digital Objects* (Lisbon: Biblioteca Nacional de Portugal, 2013), 178–92, http://purl.pt/24107/1/iPres2013_PDF/iPres2013-Proceedings.pdf; A. Williamson, "Strategies for Managing Digital Content Formats," *Library Review* 54, no. 9 (2005): 508–13, https://doi.org/10.1108/00242530510629515; and C. Arms and C. Fleischhauer, "Digital Formats: Factors for Sustainability, Functionality, and Quality," in *Archiving 2005 Final Program and Proceedings* (Springfield, VA: Society for Imaging Science and Technology, 2005), 222–27, http://memory.loc.gov/ammem/techdocs/digform/Formats_IST05_paper.pdf.

62. Archival collections, as well as very old business files maintained by companies, government agencies, or other organizations, may contain photocopies produced on unstable papers by reprographic technologies, such as the dual-spectrum process and the electrofax process, that are no longer in use. The definitive treatment of obsolete copying processes is W. Hawken, *Copying Methods Manual* (Chicago: American Library Association, 1966), a reference work that is long out of print but still useful for identifying unstable photocopies. See also R. Binkley, *Manual on Methods of Reproducing Research Materials: A Survey Made for the Joint Committee on Materials for Research of the Social Science Research Council and the American Council of Learned Societies* (Ann Arbor: Edwards Brothers, 1936).

63. In the early 1960s, microscopic aging spots, termed "redox blemishes" were discovered on silver-gelatin microfilms that had been in storage for two to twenty years. The microfilm had been processed in a manner compatible with prevailing standards for permanence, but the blemishes were caused by improper storage conditions, which led to oxidation of image silver. With acetate-based photographic films, improper storage conditions also contributed to "vinegar syndrome," a chemical degradation process characterized by a vinegar-like smell. These problems have been discussed in many publications, including C. McCamy and C. Pope, "Current Research on Preservation of Archival Records on Silver-Gelatin Type Microfilm in Roll Form," *Journal of Research of the National Bureau of Standards: A. Physics and Chemistry* 69A, no. 5 (1965): 385–95, https://nvlpubs.nist.gov/nistpubs/jres/69A/jresv69An5p385_A1b.pdf; C. McCamy et al., "A Survey of Blemishes on Processed Microfilm," *Journal of Research of the National Bureau of Standards: A. Physics and Chemistry* 73A, no. 1 (1969): 79–99, https://nvlpubs.nist.gov/nistpubs/jres/73A/jresv73An1p79_A1b.pdf; R. Henn and D. Wiest, "Microscopic Spots in Processed Microfilm: Their Nature and Prevention," *Photographic Science and Engineering* 7, no. 5 (1963): 253–61; N. Allen et al., "Degradation of Historic Cellulose Triacetate Cinematographic Film: The Vinegar Syndrome," *Polymer Degradation and Stability* 19, no. 4 (1987): 379–87, https://doi.org/10.1016/0141-3910(87)90038-3; A. Ram et al., "The Effects and Prevention of the Vinegar Syndrome." *Journal of Imaging Science and Technology* 38, no. 3 (1994): 249–61.

64. ISO 13008:2012, *Information and Documentation—Digital Records Conversion and Migration Process*, defines *conversion* as a change in file format and *migration* as the movement of records from one computer platform to another without changing the format. ISO/TR 18492:2005, *Long-Term Preservation of Electronic Document-based Information*, discusses data migration as an aspect of "media renewal." According to ISO 14721:2012, *Space Data and Information Transfer Systems—Open Archival Information System (OAIS)—Reference Model*, digital migration creates a new archival implementation that preserves the full content of information. This definition encompasses bit-to-bit copying of information onto new media of the same type (refreshment) or a different type (replication). For a discussion of data

migration in the context of digital preservation, see M. Factor et al., "The Need for Preservation Aware Storage," *ACM SIGOPS Operating Systems Review* 41, no. 1 (2007): 19–23, http://citeseerx.ist.psu.edu/viewdoc/download?doi=10.1.1.470.7042&rep=rep1&type=pdf.

65. Most file-conversion applications produce target files in a narrower range of widely encountered formats. Common choices are PDF or PDF/A for digital documents, JPG for digital photographs, MP3 for audio recordings, and MP4 for video recording. A database is typically converted into the file format required by a specific database application. This is usually done in the context of a database upgrade or replacement. Full file conversion preserves all content of the original source file, including metadata, embedded objects, hyperlinks, and macros or scripts. This is usually the preferred approach for lifecycle management of digital content. For other purposes, some file-conversion applications can alter a source file—producing a digital images from a word-processing file, converting a color photograph to a grayscale image, or splitting a single PDF file into multiple pages, for example.

Chapter Five

Retrieval and Disclosure of Information

In the course of their work, companies, government agencies, and not-for-profit organizations search for and disseminate information about people, organizations, events, initiatives, activities, transactions, and other matters. Information retrieval and disclosure are ordinary and necessary aspects of most business operations, but they can expose an organization to significant risks. This chapter identifies and discusses threats, consequences, and risk mitigation options associated with the following aspects of information retrieval and disclosure:

- failure to retrieve information needed for a given purpose;
- unintended disclosure of information through metadata mining;
- failure to comply with laws and regulations that mandate disclosure of information;
- failure to prevent unauthorized disclosure of information;
- failure to comply with laws and regulations that prohibit cross-border transfer of information; and
- failure to comply with data breach notification laws and regulations.

The risks discussed in this chapter apply to information in all formats in organizations of all types and sizes. As discussed in the following sections, they can lead to significant adverse consequences, including fines, civil litigation, reputational damage, and criminal prosecution. Risks associated with information retrieval and disclosure are generally unacceptable. Some of them are unavoidable, but their adverse effects can be prevented, limited, or, in some cases, transferred.

Chapter 5

INFORMATION RETRIEVAL FAILURE

Information retrieval is the process of searching for and obtaining access to data, paper records, engineering drawings, word-processing files, spreadsheets, email messages, web pages, social media posts, or other information resources. The retrieval process, which has been widely studied by librarians and other information specialists, begins with an information need for which a search strategy is formulated. The information need is driven by the purpose for which the information will be used. The purpose may relate to business transactions, administrative tasks, medical care, educational services, scientific experiments, legal cases, scholarly research, personal activities, or other matters. The desired information may range from simple facts that answer straightforward questions to detailed documents that must be carefully studied.[1]

The person who performs a search may be the information seeker or a trained intermediary acting on the information seeker's behalf, which is a common search scenario in scientific, medical, and business libraries. The information seeker may provide a precise description of desired information—the name and address of the customer who placed a particular order, for example, or email messages sent to a particular person on a specified range of dates. In more complicated search scenarios, the desired information may be described more broadly—customer complaints about reported defects in a specific product, research about the effectiveness of a specific medical treatment, knowledgeable opinions about the uniqueness of an invention, social media posts related to a particular event, and so on. Regardless of topic, the information seeker or intermediary must develop a retrieval strategy that determines the search method to be used and the repository where the desired information can presumably be found. The information may be located by browsing through a collection of data or documents or by searching for specific words, phrases, or numeric values in data, documents, and their associated metadata, which will be defined more fully later in this chapter. The desired information may be found in computer databases or data warehouses; in digital documents saved on cloud-based servers, network drives, desktop computers, or mobile devices; in paper records stored in file rooms and warehouses; or in other electronic or non-electronic repositories.

Retrieval failure occurs when the information needed for a given purpose cannot be located. Depending on the circumstances, a given search may fail to retrieve any information, or it may retrieve information that is irrelevant, insufficient, unreliable, or otherwise unable to satisfy the information need. Retrieval failure differs from the information losses discussed in chapter 3. The desired information has not been destroyed or damaged; it is available but cannot be found.

Retrieval failure occurs for a variety of reasons. The information seeker's need may not be adequately conceptualized or clearly articulated. The information seeker's description of the desired information and the purpose for which it is needed may be too general or too detailed. The search strategy, which is essentially an estimate of the characteristics of the desired information and the location where it can be found, may be faulty. The information seeker may be unfamiliar with available information resources and may consequently select the wrong repository to search. The information seeker may not systematically search all relevant collections of data or documents. Useful information resources may be overlooked. Incorrect search terms may be used. The search duration may be too brief to identify all relevant information. The information repository may be poorly organized or inadequately indexed. The information itself may have typographical errors, misspellings, inaccuracies, inconsistencies, omissions, or other defects that prevent reliable retrieval. For retrieval of database records and digital documents, search interfaces may be difficult to use. Retrieval procedures may require specialized subject knowledge or search skills that an untrained information seeker does not possess.

Information is useless if it cannot be retrieved when needed. Retrieval failure can have significant adverse consequences for an organization's efficiency and effectiveness:

- Retrieval failure wastes time and effort. A survey by Deloitte and Touche in the 1990s found that managers spend an average of three hours per week looking for paper records that have been misfiled, mislabeled, or lost.[2] A 2004 survey of US companies by IDC, a market intelligence advisory company, found that knowledge workers spend 3.5 hours per week searching for but not finding information.[3] A 2012 survey by IDC found that knowledge workers in the United Kingdom, France, and Germany spend almost two hours per work searching for but not finding documents.[4]
- Retrieval failure can disrupt transaction processing, customer service, marketing, project management, and other information-dependent business operations. If as-built drawings cannot be located, an organization will not be able to maintain or repair its facilities. If medical test results cannot be located, a hospital or clinic will not be able to provide effective patient care. If customer account information cannot be located, a financial services company will not be able to answer questions about specific transactions. If property appraisal and inspection reports cannot be located, a bank will not be able to process mortgage applications. If repair estimates cannot be located, an insurance company will not be able to process damage claims. In all of these cases, the resulting delays can

damage an organization's reputation, result in lost business, or, in some instances, cause harm.

- If existing data or documents cannot be located, information may need to be reconstructed from other sources or, in extreme cases, recreated from scratch by redoing work. This will involve time, effort, and expense, assuming that it can be done at all.
- If retrieval failure involves data or documents that are subject to discovery orders for litigation or government investigations, an organization will be exposed to fines, penalties, or other sanctions for being unable to produce the requested information.[5] It can be difficult to explain a failure to retrieve data or documents that were not destroyed in the regular course of business when their retention periods elapsed. Retrieval failure may be misinterpreted as insufficient diligence in responding to a discovery request, as a failure to abide by a preservation order, or as an attempt to conceal evidence. Where retrieval failure involves data or documents that are needed to support an organization's own claims or defenses, information may be substituted from secondary sources, which may not carry the same weight as the data or documents that could not be located.

Vulnerability Assessment

Ideally, a retrieval operation will locate all relevant database records or documents without retrieving any irrelevant ones, but that objective is unattainable. Five decades of academic research studies acknowledge the high likelihood that a given search will fail to retrieve all information that is relevant for a given purpose.[6] The following commonplace circumstances increase an organization's vulnerability to retrieval failure:

- In many organizations, essential information about customers, employees, products, financial accounts, and other matters is scattered in multiple databases, which were developed in isolation for processing by specific applications. Information maintained by these application-specific databases may vary in content and format. Some data values may be inaccurate or out-of-date or incomplete—a customer's address may have changed, for example, or customer information may not include a cell phone number or email address. Multiple application-specific databases may have different billing addresses, shipping addresses, or contact persons for the same customer. A given database record may have missing data elements, improperly formatted data, misspellings, inconsistent abbreviations, and other problematic content.
- While databases, by definition, have a defined structure, document repositories may be poorly organized and difficult to search. Shared network drives and file rooms may be unsupervised and lack rules for creating and

labeling files and folders. In the absence of a structured file plan that defines categories into which documents will be grouped, topical and chronological folders may be intermingled within a given disk directory or filing cabinet. Folders may have vague titles and confusing abbreviations that do not accurately identify their contents. Some folders may be labeled with the names of former employees. Some disk directories and filing cabinets have a miscellaneous folder for documents that do not appear to belong in other folders. Boxes of paper records may be sent to warehouse storage without listing their contents. When searching for information about a particular matter, these inadequately differentiated folders and boxes must be opened and examined to determine whether they are relevant, a time-consuming process that may not successfully retrieve desired information. In the absence of clear naming guidelines, new folders may be created for documents that might be appropriately filed in existing folders, thereby scattering related documents in multiple locations that must be individually searched.

- Inadequate indexing is a leading cause of retrieval failures. If information is not properly indexed, it will be difficult or impossible to retrieve when needed.[7] Indexing is based on the premise that the contents of documents or database records can be adequately represented by descriptive labels (index values) that serve as searchable surrogates. Index values for names, dates, and numeric identifiers may be quickly and easily extracted from documents or database records being indexed, but subject indexing requires intellectual analysis to determine words or phrases that represent the content of a given document or database record. Inaccurate, inconsistent, or limited selection of subject terms can render information unretrievable.[8] Publishing companies, scholarly associations, and other organizations that produce bibliographic databases typically hire subject specialists and/or persons with indexing training or experience. They may utilize thesauri, lists of subject headings, lists of previously used index terms, and other tools that can improve indexing quality. In many organizations, however, index terms are selected by the creators or recipients of documents, and indexing aids are rarely used.[9]
- With manual indexing, the number of subject terms assigned to a database record or document is typically limited to those that represent major concepts. Consequently, a retrieval operation may fail to retrieve database records or documents that treat a given subject tangentially. This failure is acceptable where the information seeker wants highly relevant data or documents that deal with a particular subject, but it is a significant shortcoming for patent searches, legal discovery, scholarly research, and other situations where the information seeker needs a comprehensive search. Full-text indexing, a computerized indexing method, addresses this limitation by automatically generating index entries for most of the nouns,

verbs, and other significant words contained in a database record or document. With full-text indexing, retrieval operations can locate database records or documents that treat specific topics peripherally, but many irrelevant items, which must be individually examined, are likely to be retrieved.

- Retrieval operations respond to information needs, which vary in scope, specificity, complexity, and clarity of expression. With a little training, most searchers can successfully perform simple retrieval operations based on names, dates, numeric identifiers, and other straightforward parameters. More complex information needs involve searches for data or documents pertaining to particular subjects, projects, events, transactions, or other matters, which may be described in vague terms or otherwise poorly articulated. Such information needs can only be addressed by complicated retrieval strategies that are prone to failure. They may require searches of multiple information resources using commands with Boolean operators, relational expressions, term truncation, wildcard symbols, proximity operators, and other functionality that requires training and experience.

Risk Response

Risk transfer is not a viable mitigation strategy for retrieval failure. Insurance is not available for adverse business outcomes, reputational damage, or other negative impacts that may result from failure to retrieve information. Insurance coverage for valuable books and papers is intended for hardcopy records that are destroyed by specified perils, such as a building fire or natural disaster. They do not cover documents that are undamaged but cannot be located. In any case, such policies typically exclude databases, digital documents, and other electronic information. Insurance is available as enhanced liability coverage for unintentional destruction, alteration, or loss of property that serves as material evidence in litigation. Such policies protect the insured against claims that allege spoliation of evidence, as defined in chapter 4, but it is not clear whether or to what extent spoliation insurance covers data or documents that cannot be retrieved.

Risk avoidance is not a mitigation option for retrieval failure. Straightforward retrieval operations involving clearly identifiable data or documents—sometimes described as "known item" searches—have a high likelihood of success, assuming that the required information exists and the correct repository is searched. Some level of retrieval failure is unavoidable, however, for information needs that involve complicated subject searches or that require comprehensive identification of all relevant data or documents. A broad search strategy that emphasizes retrieval of all relevant data or documents will necessarily retrieve some irrelevant information, which must be read, evaluated, and rejected. In such searches, irrelevant data and documents may vastly outnumber relevant information. A narrowly focused search can minimize irrelevant information but will likely fail to retrieve all relevant information, possibly missing some data or documents that are more useful than those that were retrieved.[10] When an information need is conceptualized, the information seeker must decide which type of retrieval failure (not enough relevant information or too much irrelevant information) is acceptable.

While information seekers must accept retrieval failure in some situations, procedures and technologies can limit the vulnerabilities discussed in the preceding section:

- Because the strategy and method for a given retrieval operation are based on an information need, the information seeker's objectives and desired outcome should be clarified and assessed before retrieval begins. This is essential where searching will be performed by someone other than the information seeker. In particular, the inevitable trade-off between relevant and irrelevant retrieval results should be explained to the information seeker to encourage realistic expectations about the outcome of a search. As retrieval operations progress, the information seeker should be encouraged to reevaluate the original information need and make any necessary modifications.

- To address retrieval failures resulting from poor data quality, master data management is an information technology initiative that creates and maintains a master data hub as uniform replacement for application-specific databases.[11] As discussed in a preceding chapter, the master data hub collects and consolidates existing data about specific matters. As part of the consolidation process, data-cleaning tools identify conflicting data, missing data elements, improperly formatted data, misspellings, inconsistent abbreviations, and other problems that can have a negative impact on retrieval operations. The objective is a high-quality information resource that will support reliable retrieval.

- An organization's records management procedures and recordkeeping practices should emphasize coherent organization of physical and electronic files. Each document repository should have a structured file plan that defines topical or other categories into which documents will be grouped. Labeling guidelines should be developed for physical and electronic folders. In office file rooms, all cabinets, drawers, and shelves should be clearly labeled to identify their contents. Boxes of records that are sent to offsite storage should be properly inventoried and labeled. To the extent possible, shared drives should be purged of obsolete content in order to facilitate retrieval of digital documents or other information with continuing value. Alternatively, such information should be moved to a managed repository maintained by an electronic content-management application or a records management application.

- Even with a well-designed file plan in place, time-consuming browsing through folder contents may be necessary to identify pertinent documents within a folder. Document indexing can address this problem, but an index must be carefully planned and properly executed. The identification of appropriate indexing parameters or categories is an essential first step. If a document is not indexed by a given parameter, it cannot be retrieved by that parameter. Special attention should be given to indexing depth—the number of indexing parameters to be utilized for a given document repository. For subject retrieval, greater indexing depth facilitates identification of relevant items, but it also increases the retrieval of irrelevant items.

- Federated search is an enabling technology for any retrieval operation that requires comprehensive search functionality. A federated search performs retrieval operations on multiple content repositories simultaneously. It simplifies retrieval operations by providing a single point of access to dispersed content.[12] Federated searches can encompass structured or unstructured information. Searchable content repositories can be internal or external. Some federated search platforms create and maintain a unified index to multiple content sources. Others formulate a search query and pass it in an appropriate format to individual content sources, which have their own indexes. Access to specific repositories and individual content items within a repository is determined by predefined user privileges, which can be specified or denied for individuals or groups.

- Predictive coding technology combines linguistic analysis with statistical calculations to identify digital documents that are likely to be relevant for a given information need. In its most widely publicized use, predictive coding provides an automated alternative to manual review of documents for court-order discovery for legal proceedings.[13] Predictive coding algorithms estimate (predict) the likelihood that a given digital document comes within the scope of a discovery order and identify those that appear to be relevant, but the technology is not limited to legal documents. It can support relevance determinations for a wide range of documents.

- Employees and other persons authorized to retrieve data or documents from a database, content-management system, file room, or other information repository should be trained to perform searches that will satisfy their information needs. For computer-based systems, this will involve learning basic commands that initiate retrieval operations and, where appropriate, advanced functions that can fine-tune a search.

METADATA MINING

According to ISO/IEC 11179-1:2015, *Information Technology—Metadata Registries (MDR)—Part 1: Framework*, metadata is "data that defines and describes other data." Other standards and publications have adopted similar definitions that characterize metadata as data about data or, more broadly, information about information, or, more meaningfully, information about an information resource.[14] Metadata content may describe an information resource's purpose, technical characteristics, structure, or formatting. It may specify who created the resource, who is authorized to access it, or who has accessed it in the past. It may indicate how the resource can be used, how long it is to be kept, or how it will be preserved.[15] Metadata may be entered manually or automatically derived from a database, document, digital photograph, or other information resource with which it is associated. It may be created at the same time as the information resource to which it relates or at a later time.

Metadata is usually associated with computer databases, digital documents, and other electronic information, but it may apply to any information resource in any format. Examples of nonelectronic metadata include a label on a file folder, the title block of an engineering drawing, and the legend of a graph that indicates the meaning of data values. A nonelectronic information resource may have electronic metadata—an online library catalog contains metadata pertaining to the books and other items in a library's collection, for example. Less commonly, an electronic information resource may have nonelectronic metadata, as when a handwritten or printed list identifies persons who are authorized to access a specific database.

Metadata standards have been developed for various types of information resources, including bibliographic materials, web content, statistical data, geolocation data, and healthcare records.[16] Where business records are involved, a broad definition of *metadata* must include deletions, additions, corrections, comments, and other information that may be attached to or embedded in databases, word-processing files, spreadsheets, digital photographs, and other electronic content. This metadata, which is often hidden from view, can pose significant risks if it is unintentionally revealed when documents are distributed to or shared with others. For example:

- In the United Kingdom in 2003, the prime minister's office posted an intelligence report about Iraq as a word-processing file on the No. 10 Downing Street website without removing metadata, which indicated that the report was largely plagiarized from a graduate student's dissertation rather than written by UK intelligence agencies. Portions of the report were subsequently quoted by US secretary of state Colin Powell in an address to the United Nations.[17]
- In 2005, examination of tracked changes in the word-processing file of an article submitted to the *New England Journal of Medicine* showed that Merck had edited information about cardiovascular risks associated with its popular anti-inflammatory drug Vioxx (rofecoxib). In a separate inves-

tigation, analysis of metadata revealed that manuscripts related to clinical trials of rofecoxib were written by unacknowledged authors and subsequently attributed to academically affiliated investigators without disclosing financial support from the pharmaceutical industry.[18]

- In 2005, a United Nations report on the murder of Rafik Hariri, a former Lebanese prime minister, mentioned a plot by unnamed government officials. Metadata revealed that the names of the officials had been deleted from the final version even though Secretary-General Kofi Annan had promised not to alter the report before submitting it to the Security Council.[19]

- In the United States, a suspect in a series of armed robberies in 2011 was convicted on the basis of cell phone metadata that indicated he was in the vicinity of the robberies. The metadata was obtained under the Stored Communications Act (18 U.S.C. §§ 2701 et seq.), which does not require a warrant.[20]

- In 2012, geolocation metadata included in a photograph posted by *Vice* magazine led to the arrest of John McAfee, a software developer who had fled to Guatemala after being named as a person of interest in the murder of his neighbor in Belize.[21]

These examples confirm the threat and potentially adverse consequences of "metadata mining," the process of searching through and analyzing metadata to obtain additional information from a digital document or other information resource. For mining purposes, metadata is itself treated as data. Historians, archivists, librarians, and others who work with electronic data and documents have long acknowledged the research value of metadata and the importance of preserving it as an information resource. In litigation involving objections to proposed destruction of email messages and their associated metadata by US government agencies after the messages have been printed for retention, the court recognized the importance of preserving metadata about transmission and reception of email under the Federal Records Act.[22]

While it can support a variety of research projects and scholarly inquiries, metadata mining is widely and controversially associated with extraction of embedded information from documents obtained through legal discovery.[23] The Federal Rules of Civil Procedure, which apply to civil litigation in federal courts, do not specifically address the discoverability of metadata, but Rule 34(b) gives a requesting party the right to specify the format in which electronically stored information will be provided unless the responding party raises a valid objection.[24] This permits the requesting party to ask for information in native file formats, which include metadata, rather than PDF or TIFF versions.

In this context, metadata mining can give an opposing party access to useful information that might otherwise be unobtainable. It can identify individuals who created, reviewed, edited, or commented on a document. It can uncover deleted passages as well as sections that have been cut and pasted from other documents. It can reveal whether a document has been backdated or modified to conceal problematic content. According to most legal ethics opinions, an attorney who transmits electronic documents in response to a discovery request must take reasonable steps to remove metadata that may inadvertently expose a client's secrets and confidences. The same ethical opinions do not prohibit an attorney from using embedded metadata in electronic documents received from an opposing party, provided the documents were obtained in a lawful and ethical manner.[25]

While metadata mining raises questions and concerns about protection of personal, confidential, and privileged information,[26] it is increasingly recognized as a useful tool that can be a decisive factor in litigation. In a 2016 case, metadata on a flash drive indicated that a defendant accused of misappropriating proprietary information had retained copies of documents containing his former employer's trade secrets.[27] In a 2017 case involving whistleblower retaliation, the defendant claimed that an employee who revealed a potential violation of federal and state laws was fired for poor job performance, but metadata associated with the employee's most recent performance evaluation indicated that it was actually created a month after he was terminated.[28] In a 2018 case, a plaintiff provided copies of digital photographs that she claimed depicted the condition of her apartment several days after an allegedly warrantless search by the police, but examination of the photographs' metadata indicated that they were taken two years after the incident.[29] In medical malpractice cases, metadata in electronic medical records can be used to profile a physician's work habits, while metadata associated with medical images can be used to track a physician's viewing of the images.[30]

Vulnerability Assessment

The threats and consequences discussed in preceding sections are not limited to attorneys and litigants. Inadvertent exposure of metadata can have a negative impact on any organization or person who distributes word-processing files, spreadsheets, digital photographs, or other electronic information to others. A consultant's report may contain passages that were cut and pasted from reports prepared for previous clients; a contractor's proposal may include deletions indicating that lower prices were considered but rejected; a professor's manuscript submitted to a scholarly journal may contain comments and corrections made by colleagues; a college applicant's essay may include additions or corrections that were made by the student's parents or friends. The following vulnerabilities contribute to risks associated with metadata mining:

- Employees may not be aware of metadata that is embedded in the digital documents they create. Documents may be shared with others without considering the advisability of sharing the embedded metadata, which may be invisible to the user but extractable by others.
- Some metadata is generated automatically by applications that create word-processing files, spreadsheets, and other digital documents. Examples include the name of the person who most recently saved a document, the date and time the document was created, the date and time the document was most recently modified, and the date and time the document was last printed, as well as statistical information about the document's size and grammatical characteristics. Email systems automatically generate metadata about a sender's location, the receiver's location, and the route that a given message traveled. Digital cameras automatically generate metadata about the date and time a photograph was created, the device that took the photograph, the camera settings, and the geographic coordinates of the location where the photograph was taken.
- With many applications that generate digital documents, users have the option of entering metadata that may be useful for internal control purposes. Examples include details about the document's originator, keywords, and descriptive comments. When a document is shared with others, this metadata may be useful in unintended ways.[31]
- Employees may routinely activate the "track changes" function when creating word-processing files, spreadsheets, or other digital documents, thereby generating metadata that contains information about additions, deletions, or other editing activity.
- When reviewing a document written by another person, an employee may append comments intended solely for the author or for other internal reviewers without considering how a wider audience might interpret and react to the comments.
- Word-processing files may contain hidden text that is suppressed when a document is displayed or printed. Spreadsheets may contain hidden rows, columns, cells, and formulas. This is often done for practical reasons—to reduce the size of a printed document or to provide an uncluttered document display that excludes some detailed information. These hidden elements are easily overlooked when documents are distributed to others, but they may include personal or proprietary information that should not be shared.

Risk Response

Transfer, avoidance, and acceptance are not viable mitigation strategies for risks associated with metadata mining. Insurance is not available for adverse legal outcomes, reputational damage, or other negative impacts that may result from unintentional exposure of metadata. Metadata mining can be avoided by printing or faxing documents instead of sharing the digital versions with external parties, but that is not a practical alternative for legal discovery or other situations where large quantities of documents are involved. Given the adverse consequences of unintended metadata exposure, passive acknowledgment that documents may contain problematic metadata is not advisable. For documents requested by the opposing party in litigation, such risk acceptance is certainly not a permissible approach for an attorney who is obligated to act in a client's best interests.

While embedded metadata can pose significant problems when inadvertently disclosed, complete elimination of metadata from digital documents is neither practical nor advisable. Basic metadata, such as the name of a document's author and the date it was created, is necessary and useful for document identification and internal control. Information about additions, deletions, and other editing activity is necessary to track a document's development and explain its contents. Embedded comments are essential for collaborative document production. The only effective mitigation strategy limits risk by minimizing or removing metadata from digital documents before sending them as email attachments, posting them on a website, or otherwise sharing them with external parties. This process, which is described as metadata scrubbing or metadata stripping, can be accomplished in several ways:

- As a matter of policy, employees should be instructed to minimize the entry of metadata when creating a document. The "track changes" function and comment insertion should be limited to collaborative document preparation and deactivated otherwise.
- To the extent possible, automatic generation of metadata without user involvement should be disabled. Location tracking by digital cameras and smartphones, for example, should be deactivated unless the geographic information is essential for some purpose.
- Word-processing files, spreadsheets, digital photographs, or other digital documents can be shared with others in a file format, such as PDF or TIF, that accurately preserves a document's content and appearance but does not include all metadata contained in the original source file. In particular, the PDF and TIF formats will not preserve additions, deletions, comments, hidden content, or other metadata generated by editing operations. This approach to metadata removal is not acceptable, however, for legal discovery, where the opposing party requests documents in their native file formats and a valid objection cannot be raised.
- Metadata can be removed from digital documents by using scrubbing software that may be integrated into the application that generated the documents or purchased separately. Metadata can be removed when individual documents are shared with external parties. Alternatively, metadata

scrubbing software can process batches of multiple documents. Some scrubbing software can process documents in a wide range of file formats. The user selects the specific metadata elements to be removed. If desired, documents can be converted to the PDF format following metadata removal. Tools that operate on email servers will automatically remove metadata from email attachments before they are sent.

• To avoid problems, employees should be trained to use scrubbing tools to remove metadata from the final versions of documents in the regular course of business. Note, however, that metadata removal is not an option for documents that are considered relevant for litigation. Such documents, which are typically subject to a legal hold, must be preserved in their original formats because the opposing party may request documents with metadata intact.

MANDATORY INFORMATION DISCLOSURE

Many countries have laws and regulations that mandate the disclosure of information maintained by government agencies, companies, and not-for-profit organizations. Mandatory disclosure applies in the following circumstances:

• Freedom-of-information laws mandate public access to information maintained by government agencies, subject to exclusions related to criminal law enforcement, national security, and foreign intelligence. Under the Freedom of Information Act (5 U.S.C. § 552), the public can request information held by US government agencies. State laws require disclosure of public records maintained by state and local government agencies. In Canada, the Access to Information Act (R.S.C., 1985, c. A-1) provides public access to information held by federal government institutions. Canadian provinces have their own laws that cover provincial and local government information. Many other countries have freedom-of-information and open-government laws passed or pending.[32]

• Various laws and regulations require disclosure of information to law enforcement, regulatory authorities, or other government agencies when certain events occur.[33] Among the many examples that might be cited, anti-money-laundering and anti-terrorism laws and regulations require banks, investment firms, and other financial service companies to report suspicious financial transactions. Regulatory authorities require publicly traded companies to disclose information about their financial condition or certain corporate events. In the United States, federal contractors must report overpayments by the government. In many countries, pharmaceutical companies must disclose information to regulatory authorities about adverse events that occur during clinical trials of unapproved drugs, biological products, and medical devices. To protect public health and welfare, healthcare providers and clinical laboratories must disclose information related to certain infectious diseases. Many countries have laws that require healthcare providers, educators, social workers, caregivers, and others to report suspected maltreatment of children, the disabled, the elderly, or other vulnerable persons.

- In many countries, organizations must tell data subjects, on request, about information that is collected and maintained about them. In member states of the European Union, data subjects have the right to be told about their personal information, as specified in Article 15 of the General Data Protection Regulation. Some other countries have data protection and privacy laws with similar disclosure mandates. In the United States, which does not have omnibus data protection legislation, federal and state laws mandate disclosure of personal information to data subjects in specific situations. Healthcare providers must disclose medical information to patients. Schools, higher educational institutions, and state educational agencies must allow students and their parents to inspect and review educational records maintained about them. Consumer credit companies must give data subjects information about their credit worthiness. Web site operators and online services must tell parents about personal information that is collected about their children under age 13.[34]

- Some laws and regulations require organizations to disclose information to the public about certain events or activities. These legal requirements differ from mandated disclosure in response to specific requests. Many countries have laws that require registered companies to disclose certain information about their officers and finances to the public.[35] Some countries have "right to know" laws that mandate disclosure of information about health hazards to which the public may be exposed. Workplace right-to-know laws require organizations to inform their employees about workplace hazards.[36] In some countries, property owners, real estate developers, and others who are planning commercial or residential construction projects must publicly disclose information about the purpose, scope, and characteristics of proposed projects. In some countries, government agencies must publicly disclose information about sex offenders.

- Many countries have laws that require an organization to disclose information requested by government officials for use in a civil or criminal investigation. Most disclosures are made in response to a court order that specifies the information to be provided. In the United States, for example, the Antitrust Civil Process Act (P.L. 87-664) authorizes the U.S. Department of Justice to serve a civil investigative demand on a company where an antitrust violation is suspected. Several countries have laws that require disclosure of cryptographic keys to law enforcement for forensic investigations or evidence in legal proceedings. Similarly, the USA PATRIOT Act (P.L. 107-56) allows the Federal Bureau of Investigation to apply for a court order for "books, records, papers, documents, and other items" related to investigations of international terrorism.

Noncompliance with mandatory disclosure requirements exposes an organization to fines, penalties, civil litigation, and, in extreme cases, criminal prosecution. Violations of financial disclosure regulations are closely associated with criminal activity and incur the largest penalties. These violations are among the most significant monetary risks discussed in this book. Multi-million-dollar sanctions have been reported.[37] By contrast, civil penalties for nonfinancial disclosure violations rarely exceed several thousand dollars, although some infractions, such as the failure to report child abuse when mandated by law, are misdemeanors—or, for repeat violations, felonies—in some locations.

Vulnerability Assessment

The following vulnerabilities contribute to the risk of noncompliance with information-disclosure mandates specified in laws and regulations:

- A regulated entity may not be aware of information-disclosure requirements. An organization's compliance officer or legal department is typically responsible for identifying laws and regulations that affect specific business operations, but some organizations do not have in-house compliance expertise. Even for those that do, it can be difficult to keep informed about all applicable legal and regulatory requirements, especially in multinational and transnational organizations that operate in multiple political jurisdictions.
- A regulated entity may not correctly interpret information-disclosure requirements. Laws and regulations can be voluminous, complicated, poorly written, and confusing. It can be difficult to determine the specific types of information that must be disclosed about a given matter. This is particularly the case with new disclosure laws and regulations, which often require clarification by their originating agencies as issues arise. Amendments introduced over time to address specific issues and concerns may add complexity and confusion.
- Organizational units responsible for information disclosure may not be able to respond to legal and regulatory mandates in the required timeframe due to lack of clear instructions, inadequate staffing, insufficient training, or ineffective supervision. The progress of compliance initiatives can be particularly difficult to monitor in large enterprises with complex organizational structures and geographically dispersed business operations.

• Disclosure efforts may be impeded by the retrieval failures discussed in a preceding section. Information that is subject to disclosure may be lost, damaged, or otherwise difficult to locate in the required time frame.

Risk Response

As noted above, failure to comply with information-disclosure requirements can have significant adverse consequences. Risk mitigation alternatives are limited. Risk acceptance based on a conscious business decision not to comply fully with legal and regulatory requirements is not an effective mitigation strategy. Fines and other civil penalties can be substantial, and criminal prosecution is possible for some offenses. Regulatory noncompliance exposes an organization to additional risks that can have an adverse impact on the organization's objectives and performance. Noncompliance may raise the level of regulatory scrutiny, leading to audits and inspections that can be time-consuming. Civil actions and criminal prosecution for compliance failure will involve high legal costs. Noncompliance also poses risks to an organization's reputation, which can damage business relationships, erode the confidence of investors and other stakeholders, lead to loss of revenue, and make it difficult to recruit and keep qualified employees.

Risk avoidance is only possible if the regulated activity that is subject to information disclosure is eliminated. This is not a viable mitigation strategy where the regulated activity is a core component of an organization's business. A bank cannot eliminate customers to avoid compliance with disclosure requirements for suspicious transactions. A school cannot stop maintaining educational records in order to avoid disclosure requirements for student information. A healthcare provider cannot stop maintaining patient records in order to avoid disclosing them when requested. Some disclosure mandates, such as providing public records in response to freedom-of-information requests, are nonnegotiable.

Risk transfer through insurance is generally not an option for criminal violations. Most insurance policies exclude coverage for civil fines and penalties resulting from illegal activity, although insurance coverage may be available for legal fees and other costs associated with government investigations and litigation.

A risk limitation plan that addresses the vulnerabilities discussed in the preceding section is the only viable mitigation strategy for regulatory risks associated with information-disclosure requirements. An effective limitation plan depends on thorough preparation and systematic execution to reduce the likelihood of risk events:

• An organization's top management and key stakeholders must be committed to regulatory compliance. They must understand the importance, purpose, and scope of legal requirements and authorize the necessary resources for fully compliant information disclosure.

- Ignorance of or confusion about information-disclosure requirements is not an acceptable defense for noncompliance. A qualified organizational unit must be responsible for identifying, analyzing, and interpreting laws and regulations, including any amendments and supplemental guidance documents, that mandate information disclosure. This must be done for all national and subnational jurisdictions where an organization operates. If necessary, external compliance specialists should be hired to supplement internal expertise.

- Information disclosure must be a managed initiative. A qualified employee must be responsible for planning, organizing, executing, and controlling the disclosure process. Many government agencies appoint a freedom-of-information officer, for example, who has principal responsibility for disclosure requests. The responsible employee must be familiar with the business activities and operations to which the information relates. The responsible employee will determine the staffing, technology support, consulting expertise, and other resources needed to fulfill information disclosure mandates within the required timeframe.

- To ensure compliance and achieve a manageable focus, the scope and intended outcome of an information-disclosure initiative must be clearly defined. The specific information needed to satisfy legal requirements must be determined, and disclosure should be strictly limited to that information. All information must be carefully reviewed for correctness and completeness prior to disclosure. Irrelevant or unnecessary information must be excluded.

- Databases, document repositories, and other records that may contain required information must be identified and evaluated for relevance, reliability, accessibility, and usability. To the extent possible, concerns about data formats, legacy applications, information stored offsite, and other matters should be anticipated and assessed. Organizational units that have relevant information resources in their custody or under their supervisory control must be made aware of disclosure requirements. Their advice and assistance will be needed to address questions and problems that arise during the disclosure process.

- Employees responsible for responding to information-disclosure requests must be trained to perform the work correctly and completely. Clearly written specifications and operating procedures must be prepared for use as training materials. The operating procedures must address problems—such as missing, poorly organized, or unusable information—that may arise during the disclosure process. Employees should be given a due-diligence checklist or similar quality-control mechanism to ensure that all information-disclosure tasks have been properly completed.

UNAUTHORIZED INFORMATION DISCLOSURE

A preceding chapter discussed risks associated with collection and possession of nonpublic information, which is broadly defined as information that is not available to the general public. The term encompasses personal information about identifiable individuals as well as information of a confidential nature about an organization's strategic plans, financial condition, innovations, business operations, and other proprietary matters. Many countries have laws and regulations that prohibit disclosure of nonpublic information unless appropriate authorization is obtained or other conditions apply. Data protection and privacy laws, the most frequently cited examples, prohibit the unauthorized disclosure of personal information maintained by companies, government agencies, not-for-profit entities, and other organizations:

- According to the General Data Protection Regulation, the most widely publicized data protection law, organizations that operate in EU member states must protect personal information against unauthorized processing, which is defined broadly to include unauthorized disclosure by transmission, dissemination, or other means that make the information available. A data subject has the right to object to disclosure of his or her personal information in some situations. As discussed in a later section, the GDPR also imposes restrictions on cross-border transfer of personal information.
- Some European countries that are not EU member states and several dozen countries in Asia, the Middle East, Africa, and Latin America have adopted data protection laws that are modeled on the GDPR's predecessor, Directive 95/46/EC, which included similar restrictions on unauthorized disclosure of personal information.[38]
- In the United States, unauthorized disclosure of personal information is prohibited by multiple laws and regulations. The Privacy Act of 1974 (5 U.S.C. § 552a) limits disclosure of personal information maintained by US government agencies. Privacy laws with similar restrictions apply to personal information maintained by state and local government agencies.[39] The federal government and some states have laws and regulations that deal with disclosure of specific categories of personal information, including medical information,[40] customer information maintained by financial institutions,[41] customer data,[42] student records,[43] records that identify library users,[44] records related to video rentals,[45] court records,[46] information about licensed drivers of motor vehicles,[47] information about children collected by web site operators and online services,[48] and personal information held by electronic communication providers and remote computing service providers.[49]
- In Canada, the Privacy Act regulates the disclosure of personal information by federal government agencies, while provincial laws specify priva-

cy-protection requirements for government records in their jurisdictions. The Personal Information Protection and Electronic Documents Act (PI-PEDA) is the Canadian federal law that regulates disclosure of personal information by private-sector organizations.[50] It prohibits disclosure of personal information without the data subject's knowledge or consent, subject to exceptions.[51]

- Like Canada, Australia has a combination of federal and state legislation that regulates disclosure of personal information. At the federal level, the Australian Privacy Act of 1988 presents privacy principles that apply to commonwealth agencies, certain private-sector companies and not-for-profit organizations, and all private healthcare providers. The law does not apply to government agencies in Australian states and territories, which have their own data protection legislation.[52]
- In New Zealand, the Privacy Act of 1993 applies to all governmental and nongovernmental entities. Subject to limited exceptions, its core principles require authorization by the data subject for disclosure of personal information.[53]

Other laws and regulations prohibit or severely restrict disclosure of nonpersonal information of a confidential or sensitive nature in specific situations. The U.S. Criminal Code, for example, contains various prohibitions against disclosure of classified or dangerous information.[54] As discussed in other chapters, unauthorized disclosure or other misappropriation of trade secrets is prohibited by law in the United States and other countries. Organizations often use non-disclosure agreements, which are legally enforceable contracts, to restrict the dissemination of strategic plans, competitive intelligence, financial information, and other confidential business information that is shared with others. Many countries have insider trading laws that prohibit the unauthorized disclosure of nonpublic information about the plans or financial condition of a publicly traded company where such disclosure could confer a financial advantage related to the purchase or sale of the company's stock. Laws and rules of conduct prohibit certain professions from disclosing nonpersonal information they acquire in the course of their work.[55] In some countries, banks and other financial institutions are prohibited from disclosing nonpublic supervisory information unless authorized by regulatory authorities.[56]

   Violations of laws and regulations that prohibit unauthorized disclosure of nonpublic information expose an organization to fines, penalties, civil litigation, and, in extreme cases, criminal prosecution. The most punitive sanctions involve unauthorized disclosure of personal information that is protected by data protection and privacy laws. Fines are based on the nature of the infringement, the willfulness of the violation, actions taken to mitigate the damage to data subjects, and other factors. For intentional GDPR violations where there is no attempt to mitigate the damage or cooperate with national data protection authorities, fines can total up to €20 million, but even fines for lower-level infractions can exceed €1 million. In the United States, penalties for unauthorized disclosure of protected health information in violation of the HIPAA privacy rule range from $100 to $50,000 per incident up to a maximum of $25,000 to $1.5 million per year. Banks and other financial institutions can be fined up to $100,000 per violation for noncompliance with data protection provisions of the Gramm-Leach-Bliley Act. Fines for violations of other US privacy regulations typically range from $1,000 to $2,500 per incident.

In Canada, fines for noncompliance with PIPEDA's disclosure prohibitions can reach CAD$100,000. In Australia, fines for violations can reach AUS$10 million for serious or repeat offenders. In addition to incurring fines, an organization can be sued for unauthorized disclosure of nonpublic information, including violations of non-disclosure agreements or misappropriation of trade secrets. Violations of criminal code prohibitions on unauthorized disclosure of classified or dangerous information are punishable by imprisonment.

Vulnerability Assessment

All organizations create, collect, and maintain some personal or nonpersonal information that is subject to disclosure prohibitions or restrictions. The following vulnerabilities contribute to the risk of noncompliance with laws and regulations that prohibit or restrict disclosure of nonpublic information:

- An organization may not be aware of applicable information-disclosure prohibitions or restrictions. An organization's compliance officer or legal department is typically responsible for identifying laws and regulations that affect specific business operations, but some organizations do not have in-house compliance expertise. Even for those that do, it can be difficult to keep informed about all applicable laws and regulations that prohibit or restrict information disclosure, especially in multinational and transnational organizations that operate in multiple political jurisdictions.
- A regulated entity may not correctly interpret disclosure prohibitions or restrictions for nonpublic information. Laws and regulations can be voluminous, complicated, poorly written, and confusing. Some disclosure prohibitions are subject to multiple exceptions and exclusions that require expert interpretation. Even then, it can be difficult to determine the specific types of information that can and cannot be disclosed about a specific matter. This is particularly the case with new laws and regulations, which often require clarification by their originating agencies as issues arise.

Amendments introduced over time to address specific issues and concerns may add complexity and confusion.

- Organizational units that maintain personal information may not have systematic business processes in place to obtain disclosure authorizations or refusals from data subjects.
- Unintentional noncompliance with prohibitions on unauthorized disclosure may be due to lack of clear instructions, insufficient training, or ineffective supervision. Compliance can be particularly difficult to monitor in large enterprises with complex organizational structures and geographically dispersed business operations.
- Unauthorized disclosure is a possible consequence of unauthorized access to nonpublic information by employees or external parties, such as computer hackers or other malicious actors.

Risk Response

Unauthorized disclosure of nonpublic information can have significant adverse consequences, but risk mitigation alternatives are limited. Risk acceptance based on a conscious business decision not to comply fully with legal and regulatory prohibitions or restrictions on disclosure of nonpublic information is not an advisable mitigation strategy. Fines and other civil penalties can be substantial, and criminal prosecution is possible for some offenses. Regulatory noncompliance exposes an organization to additional risks that can have an adverse impact on the organization's objectives and performance. Noncompliance may raise the level of regulatory scrutiny, leading to audits and inspections that can be time-consuming. Civil actions and criminal prosecution for compliance failure will involve high legal costs. Unauthorized disclosure of nonpublic information also poses risks to an organization's reputation, which can damage business relationships, erode the confidence of investors and other stakeholders, lead to loss of revenue, and make it difficult to recruit and keep qualified employees.

Disclosure of data or documents that contain nonpublic information is an ordinary and necessary aspect of many business operations and activities. Where personal information is involved, the risk of unauthorized disclosure can be avoided completely by obtaining written consent from every data subject, but this may not be practical or possible in every situation. For personal information related to ongoing business operations and activities, consent could be requested at the time the information is collected, but written consent will be difficult or impossible to obtain for disclosure of personal information contained in legacy data and documents. Identifying, locating, and contacting those data subjects would be a time-consuming and costly undertaking that is unlikely to be completely successful. [57]

For nonpersonal information and personal information for which consent cannot be obtained, risk avoidance is only possible if all information disclosure is prohibited, which is not a viable mitigation strategy, or if operations or activities that involve nonpublic information are eliminated, which is not an option where the operations or activities are core components of an organization's business. An insurance company cannot stop selling property and casualty coverage to avoid unauthorized disclosure of customer information. A school cannot stop enrolling students to avoid unauthorized disclosure of personal information contained in educational records. A healthcare provider cannot stop creating medical records to avoid unauthorized disclosure of protected health information. A pharmaceutical company cannot stop creating laboratory notebooks to avoid unauthorized disclosure of trade secrets. A publicly traded company cannot prohibit decision-makers' access to strategic plans and other nonpublic information to avoid the possibility that it may be used for insider trading.

Risk transfer through data breach insurance can be a viable component of an organization's mitigation plan. If unauthorized disclosure of nonpublic information results from an employee's mistake, technological malfunction, or unauthorized access by malicious actors, data breach insurance will cover costs associated with breach notification and post-breach crisis management, such as setting up a call center to answer questions about the breach and providing credit-monitoring services for affected individuals.[58] These costs are covered on a no-fault basis. The amount of coverage is determined by policy limits. A data breach insurance policy may also cover some costs associated with civil litigation, but coverage is generally excluded for civil fines and penalties resulting from legal or regulatory noncompliance. Insurance coverage may be available for legal fees and other costs associated with government investigations and litigation resulting from unauthorized disclosure of nonpublic information.

A risk limitation plan that addresses the vulnerabilities discussed in the preceding section is an important component of a mitigation strategy for regulatory risks associated with unauthorized disclosure of nonpublic information. An effective limitation plan depends on thorough preparation and systematic execution to reduce the likelihood of risk events:

- An organization's top management and key stakeholders must be committed to regulatory compliance. They must understand the importance, purpose, and scope of legal requirements and authorize the necessary resources for effective control of nonpublic information.
- Ignorance of or confusion about information-disclosure prohibitions or restrictions is not an acceptable defense for noncompliance. A qualified organizational unit must be responsible for identifying, analyzing, and interpreting laws and regulations, including any amendments and supple-

mental guidance documents, that prohibit information disclosure. This must be done for all national and subnational jurisdictions where an organization operates. If necessary, external compliance specialists should be hired to supplement internal expertise. To avoid overly broad interpretations of laws and regulations, particular attention should be paid to exceptions and exclusions that may permit disclosure of nonpublic information in specific circumstances.

- Information disclosure must be tightly controlled. A qualified employee must have designated responsibility for the disclosure process in each organizational unit that creates, collects, or maintains nonpublic information. The responsible employee must be familiar with the business activities and operations to which the information relates and the applicable legal and regulatory prohibitions and restrictions on disclosure. The responsible employee will determine the staffing, technology support, consulting expertise, and other resources needed to comply with legal and regulatory requirements.

- An organization must have an effective process for obtaining and documenting disclosure authorizations or refusals from data subjects for every business process, operation, or activity that creates, collects, or maintains personal information.

- Databases, document-management applications, network drives, cloud-based services, mobile devices, file rooms, and other repositories that may contain nonpublic information must be identified and evaluated to determine whether and to what extent disclosure restrictions apply. The evaluation should encompass nonpublic information maintained by legacy applications and inactive records stored in offsite locations.

- Organizational units that have nonpublic information in their custody or under their supervisory control must be made aware of disclosure prohibitions. Employees responsible for information disclosure must be trained to perform the work correctly and completely. Clearly written specifications and operating procedures for obtaining disclosure authorizations and releasing information must be prepared for use as training materials. Employees should be given a due-diligence checklist or similar quality-control mechanism to ensure that all information-disclosure tasks have been properly completed.

- Appropriate security measures must be implemented to prevent unauthorized access to databases, document collections, and other repositories that contain nonpublic information.

CROSS-BORDER DATA TRANSFER

Cross-border data transfer is a variant form of information disclosure in which data or documents are sent from one political jurisdiction to another for storage, retention, processing, or other purposes. Cross-border data transfer may involve data, digital documents, or other electronic information that is transferred online, or paper records, photographic media, or removable computer media that are transferred physically. In most cases, the sending and receiving jurisdictions are sovereign states or self-governing dependent territories.

Cross-border transfer of information can occur in any organization, but it is most important for multinational and transnational companies and not-for-profit organizations, including charities, religious groups, universities, and cultural institutions that operate in multiple countries. Such organizations must be able to transfer information between countries. Some multinational and transnational organizations want to use centralized servers or cloud-based computing services for enterprise-wide information sharing. If an organization closes a branch office or field location in a given country, it must be able to transfer databases, digital documents, and paper records to a different country for retention or to maintain continuity of operations.

Many countries have laws or regulations that prohibit or restrict cross-border data transfer in specific circumstances.[59] Most data protection laws prohibit transfer of personal information to countries that lack an adequate level of protection unless the data subject consents to the transfer. This prohibition applies to database records, digital documents, or other electronic information that may be transferred from a branch office or field location in one country to servers operated by an organization's centralized information technology unit or a cloud-based storage provider in another country. The prohibition also applies to paper records and other physical storage media, including backup or archival tapes that may be transferred to a commercial storage provider or an in-house record-storage facility in another country. Exceptions may be made if the transfer is mandated by a contract that is in the interest of the data subject, the transfer involves information that is publicly available, the transfer is mandated by legal proceedings, or the transfer is judged to be in the national interest.

Adequate protection is typically defined as the same level of data protection provided for personal information in the originating country. Where personal information originates in a member state of the European Union, for example, it can be transferred to any other EU member state or to countries that are members of the European Economic Area. As prescribed in the General Data Protection Regulation, the European Commission may designate other countries, dependent territories, and international organizations that offer an adequate level of protection. These adequacy decisions are reviewed at four-year intervals, at which time they may be renewed, amended, or suspended. Alternatively, cross-border transfer of personal information within a company or group may be based on binding corporate rules, which are subject to approval by the European Commission. The binding corporate rules must comply with GDPR requirements and provide mechanisms for ensuring compliance. Other transfer arrangements are also possible.[60]

Personal information aside, some countries have laws that prohibit the cross-border transfer of specific types of information for litigation or investigative purposes. These laws, which are collectively described as "blocking statutes," impede or prevent the collection of evidence for use in legal proceedings outside of the country where the information is sought. As an example, Article 271 of the Swiss Criminal Code prohibits gathering of evidence for legal proceedings by a foreign authority on Swiss territory. The French blocking statute (Law no. 80-538) prohibits the disclosure of commercial, financial, or technical information for use in legal or administrative proceedings outside of France unless the disclosure is ordered by a French court. Similar laws in other countries prohibit compliance with foreign discovery orders that may infringe on national sovereignty or security.[61]

Many countries have laws and regulations that mandate in-country retention of specific types of information, accounting information being the most common example. These laws do not generally prohibit cross-border transfer of copies of information. Their purpose is to ensure the availability of information that may be needed for tax audits, shareholder examination, or other purposes. Some laws allow databases, digital documents, and other electronic records to be stored in another country provided that they are immediately accessible when requested by government officials or other stakeholders. As a variant form of blocking statute, laws in some political jurisdictions prohibit the transfer of specific information to other political jurisdictions, including jurisdictions in the same country, for storage or other purposes. As an example, the Ontario Business Records Protection Act (R.S.O. 1990, c. B.19) prohibits the removal of business records from Ontario unless the records are being sent from a branch office or subsidiary in Ontario to a head office or parent company located elsewhere. In Quebec, the Business Concerns Records Act (CQLR c. D-12) has similar provisions.[62] These laws apply to copies as well as original records.

Noncompliance with legal prohibitions on cross-border transfer of personal information are subject to the same sanctions as other violations of data protection laws. Depending on the circumstances, large monetary penalties may be imposed. Civil litigation is also possible. Noncompliance with a blocking statute is a criminal violation punishable by fines or imprisonment.

Vulnerability Assessment

The following vulnerabilities can impede compliance with laws and regulations that prohibit or restrict cross-border transfer of information:

- An organization may not be aware of prohibitions or restrictions on cross-border data transfer. While restrictions on transfer of personal information have been widely publicized, blocking statutes and laws that mandate in-country retention of information are not as well known. An organization's compliance officer or legal department is typically responsible for identifying laws and regulations that affect specific business operations, but some organizations do not have in-house compliance expertise. Even for those that do, it can be difficult to keep informed about all applicable laws and regulations that prohibit or restrict cross-border data transfer in every location where an organization operates.

- A regulated entity may not correctly interpret prohibitions or restrictions on cross-border data transfer. Some disclosure prohibitions are subject to multiple exceptions and exclusions that require expert interpretation and legal advice. This is particularly the case with new laws and regulations, which often require clarification by their originating agencies as issues arise. Amendments introduced over time to address specific issues and concerns may add complexity and confusion. For GDPR compliance, the European Commission reviews the data protection status of non-EU countries and may prohibit information transfers to a country that was previously considered acceptable.

- An organization may not have systematic business processes in place to obtain written consent from data subjects for cross-border transfer of personal information.

- Unintentional noncompliance with prohibitions on cross-border data transfer may be due to lack of clear instructions, insufficient training, or ineffective supervision. An employee who is unaware of applicable prohibitions might send an email attachment that contains personal information to a co-worker in another country in violation of a data protection law. Similarly, an employee located in a foreign country might send data or documents needed for litigation to a company's US headquarters in violation of a blocking statute. Compliance with cross-border prohibitions on information transfer can be particularly difficult to monitor in large enterprises with complex organizational structures and geographically dispersed business operations.

- Unauthorized cross-border data transfer is a possible consequence of unauthorized access to information by employees or external parties, such as computer hackers or other malicious actors.

Risk Response

Failure to comply with laws and regulations that prohibit or restrict cross-border data transfer can have significant adverse consequences. As with unauthorized disclosure requirements discussed in the preceding section, risk mitigation options are limited.

Risk acceptance based on a conscious business decision not to comply fully with legal and regulatory prohibitions or restrictions on cross-border data transfer is not an advisable mitigation strategy. Fines and other civil penalties can be substantial, and criminal prosecution is possible for some offenses. As discussed in preceding sections, noncompliance also exposes an organization to regulatory, economic, and reputational risks that can have an adverse impact on the organization's objectives and performance.

Risk transfer through insurance is generally not an option for criminal violations. Most insurance policies exclude coverage for civil fines and penalties resulting from illegal activity, although insurance coverage may be available for legal fees and other costs associated with government investigations and litigation resulting from cross-border transfer of information in violation of a data protection or blocking statute.

Where personal information is involved, the risk of illegal cross-border data transfer can be avoided completely by obtaining written consent from data subjects. Where this is not practical or possible, data protection regulations provide various alternative arrangements, such as binding corporate rules or privacy agreements, for cross-border transfer of information within an organization or to an external entity. No comparable arrangements are available for prohibitions imposed by blocking statutes.

The following measures can reduce the likelihood of risk events associated with cross-border data transfer:

- As with all risks discussed in this chapter, an organization's top management and key stakeholders must be committed to regulatory compliance. They must understand the importance, purpose, and scope of legal requirements and authorize the necessary resources for effective control of nonpublic information.
- Ignorance of or confusion about prohibitions or restrictions on cross-border data transfer is not an acceptable defense for noncompliance. A qualified organizational unit must be responsible for identifying, analyzing, and interpreting laws and regulations, including any amendments and supplemental guidance documents, that prohibit such transfers. This must be done for all national and subnational jurisdictions where an organization operates. If necessary, external compliance specialists should be hired to supplement internal expertise. To avoid overly broad interpretations of laws and regulations, particular attention should be paid to exceptions and

exclusions that may permit disclosure of cross-border transfer of information in specific circumstances.

- Cross-border transfer of information must be tightly controlled. A qualified employee must have designated responsibility for such transfers in each organizational unit. The responsible employee must be familiar with the business activities and operations to which the information relates and the applicable legal and regulatory prohibitions and restrictions on cross-border data transfer. The responsible employee will determine the staffing, technology support, consulting expertise, and other resources needed to comply with legal and regulatory requirements.
- An organization must have an effective process for obtaining and documenting authorizations or refusals from data subjects for cross-border transfer of personal information.
- User permissions for databases, document-management applications, network drives, cloud-based services, mobile devices, file rooms, and other repositories must be reviewed to determine whether and to what extent they violate prohibitions on cross-border transfer of information. Employees should be prohibited from accessing data or documents that contain personal information when traveling in countries that do not offer an acceptable level of data protection.
- Employees who communicate or collaborate with co-workers in other countries must be given clear guidance about the circumstances in which cross-border transfer of information is permissible or prohibited.
- Appropriate security measures must be implemented to prevent unauthorized cross-border access to databases, document collections, and other information repositories.

DATA BREACH NOTIFICATION

Broadly defined, a data breach is an accidental or unlawful disclosure of personal or confidential information, which may be stolen, viewed, copied, distributed, used, altered, or destroyed by an unauthorized person.[63] Data breaches may involve unauthorized access to databases, digital documents, or other electronic information; theft of paper documents, removable storage devices and media, or mobile computing devices; or other incidents that involve potential misuse of personal information. A data breach may be discovered by a breach-detection tool, an employee, a data subject, or a third party, such as a person or organization that received personal or confidential information for which a breach is suspected.

The following discussion is limited to data breaches that involve personal information for which breach notification is required by laws and regulations. A data breach could involve other types of confidential or sensitive information, including trade secrets, proprietary financial data, strategic plans, and information about an organization's critical infrastructure. Those data breaches are not subject to notification requirements.

Data protection laws typically require organizations to implement technical and organizational measures to safeguard personal information and prevent unauthorized access. When a data breach involving personal information occurs, an increasing number of laws and regulations mandate formal notification to regulatory authorities and the affected data subjects.[64] For example:

- In the United States, all fifty states, the District of Columbia, Puerto Rico, Guam, and the Virgin Islands have enacted data breach notification laws.[65] These laws apply to all organizations, including government agencies, that operate in a given state or territory. They define the events that constitute a data breach and specify the timing and acceptable methods for a breach notification. Over the last several years, some state laws have broadened the definition of *personal information* and expanded the number of organizations that are subject to breach notification requirements.
- At the federal level, various sector-specific laws and regulations include data breach notification requirements. As an example, the HIPAA breach notification rule (45 C.F.R. §§ 164.400 et seq.) requires covered entities and their business associates to notify the affected data subjects and the secretary of health and human services about any impermissible use or disclosure that compromises the security or privacy of protected health information. Where more than five hundred residents of a state or jurisdiction are involved, prominent media outlets must also be notified.[66] The FTC Health Breach Notification Rule (16 C.F.R. §§ 318 et seq.) specifies requirements for non-HIPAA-covered entities that maintain electronic personal health records.
- According to the Interagency Guidelines Establishing Information Security Standards (12 C.F.R. Part 225, Appendix F), banks and other financial institutions subject to the supervisory authority of the Board of Governors of the Federal Reserve System must notify customers about security incidents that involve unauthorized access to or use of their personal information, including any combination of components that allow someone to access a customer's account. Federally insured credit unions have similar requirements for member notification, as specified in 12 C.F.R. Part 748, Appendix A.
- In Canada, the Digital Privacy Act (S.C. 2015, c. 32) requires prompt and conspicuous notification of data breaches involving unauthorized access to or disclosure of personal information where there is "a real risk of significant harm." Some Canadian provinces have laws that require notification for data breaches within their jurisdictions.

- Articles 33 and 34 of the General Data Protection Regulation mandate notification of data breaches to data subjects and regulatory authorities when a breach "is likely to result in a high risk to the rights and freedoms of natural persons." Notification must be made "without undue delay."
- Several Asian countries have data breach notification requirements that apply to specific sectors, such as financial services. Under the South Korean Personal Information Protection Act, regulators must be notified about data breaches that involve more than ten thousand individuals. In Taiwan, the Personal Information Protection Act specifies that affected individuals must be notified about unauthorized disclosure, theft, or other data breaches.
- Organizations subject to the Australian Privacy of Act 1988 must report all data breaches that may result in serious harm to one or more individuals when remedial action is unlikely to address the risk.

Depending on the location and circumstances, violations of data breach notification requirements are subject to fines and civil litigation.[67] Penalties may be assessed per breach, per violation, per data subject affected, or according to some other measure. Well-known organizations have incurred multimillion-dollar fines.[68] In some states, organizations involved in data breaches may be subject to injunctions that could restrain their business operations, resulting in a loss of revenue. Criminal prosecution is also possible. Equally important, ineffective data breach notification can cause significant reputational damage that will impact future business and, for publicly traded companies, shareholder value.[69]

Vulnerability Assessment

According to the Privacy Rights Clearinghouse, a not-for-profit organization that tracks and analyzes data protection issues, over nine thousand data breaches involving over 10 billion records have been publicly reported since 2005.[70] A 2018 survey conducted for Experian Data Breach Resolution by Ponemon Institute, an information technology and data protection research firm, found that only 36 percent of businesses are prepared to respond to a data breach.[71] The following vulnerabilities can impede compliance with data breach notification requirements:

- An organization's top management and key stakeholders may not fully understand the importance of data breach notification and may not be willing to commit the resources necessary for a fully compliant response that will avoid sanctions and minimize reputational damage.
- Data breach laws and regulations apply to specific political jurisdictions. An organization may not be aware of data breach notification require-

ments in every country, state, province, or territory where it operates. An organization's compliance officer or legal department is typically responsible for identifying laws and regulations that affect specific business operations, but some organizations do not have in-house compliance expertise. Even for those that do, laws and regulations that mandate data breach notifications are subject to periodic modification, which makes it difficult to keep informed about the latest requirements.

- An organization may not correctly interpret data breach notification requirements. Some notification laws and regulations are subject to exceptions and exclusions that require expert interpretation and legal advice. Amendments may broaden the scope of notification requirements, alter the timeframe for response, or make other changes that impose new mandates or add complexity and confusion.

- Globally, data breaches are increasingly frequent, but for any given organization, they are rare occurrences. When a breach occurs, most organizations are unable to draw on previous experience with notification requirements.

- Laws and regulations typically mandate notification soon after a data breach is detected—a few days after detection in some cases—but an organization that has not previously experienced a data breach may not have a systematic process in place for compliance within the required timeframe in all political jurisdictions where a breach may occur.

- As previously discussed in chapter 3, malicious actors pose significant, widespread, and unpredictable threats to information. Many data breaches begin with unauthorized access to an organization's computer systems. Passwords and other digital identifiers are supposed to prevent unauthorized access to computer applications that store electronic information, but malware can defeat these protective mechanisms.

Risk Response

Noncompliance with data breach notification laws will have significant adverse consequences. Fines and other civil penalties can be substantial, reputational damage is likely, and criminal prosecution is possible for some offenses. Risk avoidance and risk transfer are possible in some situations. Risk acceptance based on a conscious business decision not to comply fully with notification mandates is not an advisable mitigation strategy.

Data breach notification requirements are not negotiable. Risk of noncompliance is only avoidable if an investigation determines that a given data breach is outside the scope of notification mandates. Some laws and regulations exclude smaller organizations and waive notification requirements where a reasonable investigation determines that a data breach caused no harm to data subjects—if the data breach involved personal information that is encrypted, redacted, or otherwise unusable or unreadable, for example.[72] Some laws and regulations include a "good faith" exception for unintentional disclosure of personal information to an employee or agent of an organization where the disclosure does not result in unauthorized use, disclosure, or retention of the information.

Some insurance companies offer data breach policies that cover data breach notification costs within specified policy limits. A given policy may also cover the cost to retain security experts to investigate the breach, public relations consultants to address reputational damage following data breach notification, and call center teams to handle customer questions following data breach notification. Some policies provide coverage for civil litigation resulting from a data breach. As a mitigation option, data breach insurance is limited to costs associated with the notification process. It does not cover fines, penalties, or other sanctions that may result from noncompliance with breach notification requirements.

Implemented alone or as an adjunct to insurance coverage, the following actions can limit the risk of noncompliance with data breach notification requirements:

- An organization's top management and key stakeholders must be committed to compliance with data protection laws in general and data breach notification requirements in particular. They must understand the importance, purpose, and scope of notification requirements and authorize the necessary resources.
- Ignorance of or confusion about breach notification requirements is not an acceptable defense for noncompliance. A qualified organizational unit must be responsible for identifying, analyzing, and interpreting statutory obligations, including any amendments and supplemental guidance documents, that specify, clarify, or interpret data breach notification requirements. This must be done for all national and subnational jurisdictions where an organization operates. If necessary, external compliance specialists should be hired to supplement internal expertise.
- Data breach notification must be a managed initiative. A qualified employee at an appropriate level of authority must be responsible for planning, organizing, executing, controlling, and monitoring the notification process, including any investigations and risk assessments that determine whether a given breach causes sufficient harm to warrant notification. The responsible employee must be familiar with the type of information involved in a given breach, the business activities and operations to which the breach relates, and the risks that the breach poses.
- The employee responsible for breach notification should form a response team with appropriate experience and expertise. Legal, compliance, security, public relations, information technology, records management, and

other departmental stakeholders must be involved. The project team will determine the staffing, technology support, consulting expertise, and other resources needed to fulfill the notification mandate within the required timeframe and will oversee the process through completion.

- To ensure compliance and achieve a manageable focus, a breach notification's scope and content must be clearly defined. The data subjects and regulatory authorities to be notified, the timeframe for response, and the notification method(s) must be determined. Notifications to data subjects must clearly explain the nature of the breach and the corrective actions or other steps that organization will take to mitigate the adverse impact. If media notification is required, public relations staff or crisis communication consultants should be involved. [73]

- Staff assigned to a breach notification initiative must be trained to perform the work correctly and completely. Written operating procedures must be prepared. Staff should be given a due-diligence checklist or similar quality-control mechanism to ensure that all notification-related tasks have been properly completed.

SUMMARY OF MAJOR POINTS

- Information is useless if it cannot be retrieved when needed. Retrieval failure can have adverse consequences for an organization's efficiency and effectiveness. It wastes time and effort, can disrupt information-dependent business operations, and may require costly reconstruction of information. Where data or documents are subject to discovery orders for litigation or government investigations, retrieval failure exposes an organization to fines, penalties, or other sanctions.

- Metadata mining is the process of searching through and analyzing metadata to obtain additional information from a digital document or other information resource. Inadvertent exposure of metadata can have a negative impact on anyone who distributes word-processing files, spreadsheets, digital photographs, or other electronic information to others. In litigation, metadata mining can give an opposing party unintended access to potentially problematic information that might otherwise be unobtainable.

- Many countries have laws and regulations that mandate the disclosure of information maintained by government agencies, companies, and not-for-profit organizations. Noncompliance with mandatory disclosure requirements exposes an organization to fines, penalties, civil litigation, and criminal prosecution.

- Many countries have laws and regulations that prohibit disclosure of non-public information unless appropriate authorization is obtained or other conditions apply. Violations expose an organization to fines, penalties, civil litigation, and criminal prosecution. The most punitive sanctions involve unauthorized disclosure of personal information that is protected by data protection and privacy laws.

- Many countries have laws or regulations that prohibit or restrict cross-border data transfer in specific circumstances. Most data protection laws prohibit transfer of personal information to countries that lack an adequate level of protection. Some countries have blocking statutes that prohibit the cross-border transfer of specific types of information for litigation or investigative purposes.

- When a data breach involving personal information occurs, an increasing number of laws and regulations mandate formal notification to regulatory authorities and the affected data subjects. Violations of data breach notification requirements are subject to fines and civil litigation.

NOTES

1. Examples of the large and varied literature on information needs include R. Taylor, "Question-Negotiation and Information Seeking in Libraries," *College & Research Libraries* 29, no. 3 (1968): 178–94, https://crl.acrl.org/index.php/crl/article/view/12027/13473; J. O'Connor, "Some Questions Concerning Information Need," *American Documentation* 19, no. 2 (1968): 200–203, https://doi.org/10.1002/asi.5090190216; R. Derr, "A Conceptual Analysis of Information Need," *Information Processing & Management* 19, no. 5 (1983): 273–78, https://doi.org/10.1016/0306-4573(83)90001-8; C. Kuhlthau, "Inside the Search Process: Information Seeking from the User's Perspective," *Journal of the American Society for Information Science* 42, no. 5 (1991): 361–71; T. Wilson, "Human Information Behavior," *Human Information Behavior* 3, no. 2 (2000): 49–55, www.researchgate.net/profile/Tom_Wilson25/publication/270960171_Human_Information_Behavior/links/57d32fe508ae601b39a42875/Human-Information-Behavior.pdf; I. Ruthven, "The Language of Information Need: Differentiating Conscious and Formalized Information Needs," *Information Processing & Management* 56, no. 1 (2019): 77–90, https://doi.org/10.1016/j.ipm.2018.09.005; L. Lu and Y. Yuan, "Shall I Google It or Ask the Competent Villain Down the Hall? The Moderating Role of Information Need in Information Source Selection," *Journal of the American Society for Information Science and Technology* 62, no. 1 (2011): 133–45, https://doi.org/10.1002/asi.21449; and C. Cole, "A Theory of Information Need for Information Retrieval That Connects Information to Knowledge," *Journal of the American Society for Information Science and Technology* 62, no. 7 (2011): 1215–31, https://doi.org/10.1002/asi.21541.

2. H. Sarantis, *Business Guide to Paper Reduction* (San Francisco: ForestEthics, 2002), https://sustainability.tufts.edu/wp-content/uploads/BusinessGuidetoPaperReduction.pdf.

3. S. Feldman et al., *The Hidden Cost of Information Work* (Framingham, MA: International Data Corporation, 2005), https://vdocuments.mx/the-hidden-costs-of-information-work-2005-idc-report.html.

4. M. Webster, *Bridging the Information Worker Productivity Gap in Western Europe: New Challenges and Opportunities for IT* (Framingham, MA: International Data Corporation, 2005), https://denalilabs.com/static/ProductivityWhitepaper.pdf.

5. Under Rule 37(e) of the Federal Rules of Civil Procedure, sanctions may be ordered if reasonable steps are not taken to preserve lost information, but there is a difference between a document that cannot be located and one that is deliberately withheld. See, for example, *Koon v. Aventis Pharmaceuticals, Inc.*, 367 F.3d 768 (2004), where no sanction was ordered for

failure to produce a document that appeared to be have been accidentally misplaced. www.leagle.com/decision/20041135367f3d76811065.

6. Examples include C. Cleverdon, *Report on the Testing and Analysis of an Investigation into the Comparative Efficiency of Indexing Systems* (Cranfield, England: Aslib, 1962), https://dspace.lib.cranfield.ac.uk/handle/1826/836; C. Cleverdon et al., *Factors Determining the Performance of Indexing Systems, Vol. 1: Design* (Cranfield, England: Aslib, 1966), https://dspace.lib.cranfield.ac.uk/handle/1826/861; C. Cleverdon and M. Keen, *Factors Determining the Performance of Indexing Systems, Vol. 2: Test Results* (Cranfield, England: Aslib, 1966), https://dspace.lib.cranfield.ac.uk/handle/1826/863; F. Lancaster, *Evaluation of the MEDLARS Demand Search Service* (Washington, DC: National Library of Medicine, 1968), http://resource.nlm.nih.gov/0147241; D. Swanson, "Information Retrieval as a Trial-and-Error Process," *Library Quarterly* 47, no. 2 (1977): 128–48, www.jstor.org/stable/4306788; J. Dickson, "An Analysis of User Errors in Searching an Online Catalog," *Cataloging & Classification Quarterly* 4, no. 3 (1984): 19–38, https://doi.org/10.1300/J104v04n03_02; D. Blair and M. Maron, "Effectiveness for a Full-Text Document Retrieval System," *Communications of the ACM* 28, no. 3 (1985): 289–99, https://pdfs.semanticscholar.org/91f7/579e660c139cb971f37f87c2dc0d3c86b9c6.pdf; S. Klugman, "Failures in Subject Retrieval," *Cataloging & Classification Quarterly* 10, nos. 1–2 (1989): 9–35, https://doi.org/10.1300/J104v10n01_03; T. Peters, "When Smart People Fail: An Analysis of the Transaction Log of an Online Public Access Catalog," *Journal of Academic Librarianship* 15, no. 5 (1989): 267–73, https://eric.ed.gov/?id=EJ404249; Y. Tonta, "Analysis of Search Failures in Document Retrieval Systems: A Review," *Public-Access Computer Systems Review* 3, no. 1 (1992): 4–53, http://eprints.rclis.org/9463/; P. Wallace, "How Do Patrons Search the Online Catalog When No One's Looking? Transaction Log Analysis and Implications for Bibliographic Instruction and System Design," *RQ* 33, no. 2 (1993): 239–52, www.jstor.org/stable/20862411; T. Saracevic, "Effect of Inconsistent Relevance Judgments on Information Retrieval Test Results: A Historical Perspective," *Library Trends* 56, no. 4 (2008): 763–83, https://doi.org/10.1353/lib.0.0000.

7. As a famous example of the impact of faulty indexing on information retrieval, a computer search by law enforcement failed to identify Albert DeSalvo as a suspect in the Boston Strangler case because his official criminal file was improperly categorized under breaking and entry rather than as a sex offender. See G. Frank, *The Boston Strangler* (New York: New American Library, 1966), 292. DeSalvo ultimately confessed to a cellmate while under arrest for a different crime.

8. Examples of the many publications on indexing quality include P. Zunde and M. Dexter, "Indexing Consistency and Quality," *American Documentation* 20, no. 3 (1969): 259–67, https://doi.org/10.1002/asi.4630200313; M. Funk and C. Reid, "Indexing Constancy in MEDLINE," *Bulletin of the Medical Library Association* 71, no. 2 (1983): 176–83, www.ncbi.nlm.nih.gov/pmc/articles/PMC227138/; L. Rolling, "Indexing Consistency, Quality and Efficiency," *Information Processing & Management* 17, no. 2 (1981): 69–76, https://doi.org/10.1016/0306-4573(81)90028-5; M. Sievert and M. Andrews, "Indexing Consistency in Information Science Abstracts," *Journal of the American Society for Information Science* 42, no. 1 (1991): 1–6; K. Markey, "Interindexer Consistency Tests: A Literature Review and Report of a Test of Consistency in Indexing Visual Materials," *Library and Information Science Research* 6, no. 2 (1984): 155–77; E. Stubbs et al., "Internal Quality Audit of Indexing: A New Application of Interindexer Consistency," *Cataloging & Classification Quarterly* 28, no. 4 (2000): 53–69, https://doi.org/10.1300/J104v28n04_06; J. Saarti, "Consistency of Subject Indexing of Novels by Public Library Professionals and Patrons," *Journal of Documentation* 58, no. 2 (2002): 49–65, https://doi.org/10.1108/00220410210425403; and H. Olson and D. Wolfram, "Syntagmatic Relationships and Indexing Constancy on a Larger Scale," *Journal of Documentation* 64, no. 4 (2008): 602–15, https://doi.org/10.1108/00220410810884093.

9. Several studies suggest that authors can effectively index their own documents. See, for example, C. Schultz, "Comparative Indexing: Terms Supplied by Biomedical Authors and by Document Titles," *American Documentation* 16, no. 4 (1965): 299–312, https://doi.org/10.1002/asi.5090160405, and V. Diodato, "Author Indexing," *Special Libraries* 72, no. 4 (1981): 361–69, https://eric.ed.gov/?id=EJ254062; Most publishers of bibliographic databases

view author-supplied subject terms as a useful adjunct to their own indexing operations. Motivation is another matter, however; document creators may not appreciate the importance of indexing and may be reluctant to give it their full attention.

10. The traditional measures of retrieval performance, recall and precision, exist in an inverse relationship. Recall measures the percentage of relevant information retrieved by a given search in relation to the total amount of relevant information in a given repository. If a search retrieves sixteen of twenty relevant documents, for example, the recall is 80 percent. Precision, by contrast, measures the amount of relevant information retrieved by a given search as a percentage of the total amount of information, relevant and irrelevant, that is retrieved. If a search retrieves twenty documents of which twelve are judged to be relevant, the precision is 60 percent. As a practical matter, precision can be calculated by sorting through search results to distinguish relevant from irrelevant documents. Recall, by contrast, has conceptual rather than practical significance. It can only be tested under artificial circumstances where the number of documents relevant to a given search is predetermined. A high-recall retrieval operation typically involves a broad selection of search terms, while a high-precision search uses fewer terms. These effects are well documented in information science publications. Examples include V. Raghavan et al., "A Critical Investigation of Recall and Precision as Measures of Retrieval System Performance," *ACM Transactions on Information Systems* 7, no. 3 (1989): 205–29, https://doi.org/10.1145/65943.65945; M. Gordon and M. Kochen, "Recall-Precision Trade-Off: A Derivation," *Journal of the American Society for Information Science* 40, no. 3 (1989): 145–51, https://eric.ed.gov/?id=EJ395519; M. Buckland and F. Gey, "The Relationship between Recall and Precision," *Journal of the American Society for Information Science* 45, no. 1 (1994): 12–19; and T. Usmani et al., "A Comparative Study of Google and Bing Search Engines in Context of Precision and Relative Recall Parameter," *International Journal of Computer Science and Engineering* 4, no. 1 (2012): 21–34, http://citeseerx.ist.psu.edu/view-doc/download?doi=10.1.1.443.7684&rep=rep1&type=pdf.

11. For an explanation of the technology, see A. Berson and L. Dubov, *Master Data Management and Data Governance* (New York: McGraw-Hill, 2011); D. Loshin, *Master Data Management* (Amsterdam: Morgan Kaufmann Publishers, 2008); and A. Dreibelbis et al., *Enterprise Master Data Management: An SOA Approach to Managing Core Information* (Upper Saddle River, NJ: IBM Press, 2008).

12. Federated search technology was initially developed in the 1980s for library retrieval operations involving public access catalogs and bibliographic databases maintained by multiple applications. The applicable standard is ISO 23950, *Information and Documentation—Information Retrieval (Z39.50)—Application Service Definition and Protocol Specification.* In recent years, the market for federated searching has broadened to encompass nonlibrary usage scenarios and business requirements.

13. C. Nasuti, "Shaping the Technology of the Future: Predictive Coding in Discovery Case Law and Regulatory Disclosure Requirements," *North Carolina Law Review* 93, no. 1 (2014): 222–75, http://scholarship.law.unc.edu/cgi/viewcontent.cgi?article=4703&context=nclr; D. Remus, "The Uncertain Promise of Predictive Coding," *Iowa Law Review* 99, no. 4 (2014): 1691–1724, https://ilr.law.uiowa.edu/assets/Uploads/ILR-99-4-Remus2.pdf.

14. ISO 19115-1:2014, *Geographic Information—Metadata—Part 1: Fundamentals*, defines *metadata* as "information about a resource," which is itself defined as an "identifiable asset or means that fulfills a requirement." In the context of records management, ISO 23081-1:2017, *Information and Documentation—Records Management Processes—Metadata for Records—Part 1: Principles*, defines *metadata* as "structured or semi-structured information, which enables the creation, management, and use of records through time and within and across domains." The same definition is presented in ISO 15489-1:2016, *Information and Documentation—Records Management—Part 1: Concepts and Principles.* The Oxford English Dictionary defines *metadata* as "data that describes and gives information about other data." The earliest usage cited by the OED is taken from P. Bagley, *Extension of Programming Language Concepts* (Philadelphia: University City Science Center, 1968), 26, https://apps.dtic.mil/dtic/tr/fulltext/u2/680815.pdf.

15. Publications about metadata, many of them written from a library perspective, include J. Riley, *Understanding Metadata: What Is Metadata, and What Is It For?* (Baltimore: National

Information Standards Organization, 2004), www.niso.org/publications/understanding-metadata-2017; D. Haynes, *Metadata for Information Management and Retrieval: Understanding Metadata*, 2nd ed. (London: Facet Publishing, 2018); M. Zeng and J. Qin, *Metadata*, 2nd ed. (Chicago: ALA Neal-Schuman, 2016); M. Baca, ed., *Introduction to Metadata*, 3rd ed. (Los Angeles: Getty Research Institute, 2016); P. Hider, *Information Resource Description: Creating and Managing Metadata* (London: Facet Publishing, 2018); J. Pomerantz, *Metadata* (Cambridge: MIT Press, 2015); J. Park, ed., *Metadata Best Practices and Guidelines* (London: Routledge, 2012); R. Gartner, *Metadata: Sharping Knowledge from Antiquity to the Semantic Web* (Basel: Springer International, 2016); W. Inmon et al., *Business Metadata: Capturing Enterprise Knowledge* (Burlington, MA: Morgan Kaufmann, 2008); P. Caplan, *Metadata Fundamentals for All Librarians* (Chicago: American Library Association, 2003). For a skeptical view, see D. Butterman, "Is It Time for a Moratorium on Metadata?" *IEEE MultiMedia* 11, no. 4 (October–December 2004): 10–17, https://doi.org./10.1109/MMUL.2004.29; also W. Kim, "On Metadata Management Technology: Status and Issues," *Journal of Object Technology* 4, no. 2 (March–April 2005): 41–47, www.jot.fm/issues/issue_2005_03/column4.pdf.

16. Examples include ISO 15836-1:2017, *Information and Documentation—The Dublin Core Metadata Element Set—Part 1: Core Elements*; ISO 19115:2014, *Geographic Information—Metadata—Part 1: Fundamentals*; ISO 16684-1:2019, *Graphic Technology—Extensible Metadata Platform (XMP)—Part 1: Data Model, Serialization and Core Properties*; ISO 13119:2012, *Health Informatics—Clinical Knowledge Resources—Metadata*; ISO 82045-2:2004, *Document Management—Part 2: Metadata Elements and Information Reference Model*; ISO/IEC 15938-5:2003, *Information Technology—Multimedia Content Description Interface—Part 5: Multimedia Description Schemes*; ISO/TS 20428:2017, *Health Informatics—Data Elements and their Metadata for Describing Structured Clinical Genomic Sequence Information in Electronic Health Records*; ISO/IEC 19788-1:2011, *Information Technology—Learning, Education and Training—Metadata for Learning Resources—Part 1: Framework*; ISO/TR 17948:2014, *Health Informatics—Traditional Chinese Medicine Literature Metadata*; and ISO/TR 19033:2000, *Technical Product Documentation—Metadata for Construction Documentation*, which has been withdrawn but remains useful.

17. R. Aldrich, "Whitehall and the Iraq war: The UK's Four Intelligence Enquiries," *Irish Studies in International Affairs* 16, no. 1 (2005): 73–88, https://warwick.ac.uk/fac/soc/pais/people/aldrich/publications/four.inq.pdf; E. Wilding, *Information Risk and Security: Preventing and Investigating Workplace Computer Crime* (Burlington, VT: Gower Publishing, 2006).

18. Merck ultimately paid $4.85 billion to settle claims by patients injured by Vioxx, as well as $600 million to resolve additional civil claims. Merck also pleaded guilty to federal criminal misdemeanor charges for which it was incurred a fine of $321.6 million. G. Curfman et al., "Expression of Concern: Bombarkier et al., 'Comparison of upper gastrointestinal toxicity of rofecoxib and naproxen in patients with rheumatoid arthritis,'" *New England Journal of Medicine* 353, no. 26 (2005): 2813–14, https://doi.org/10.1056/NEJMe058314; J. Ross et al., "Guest Authorship and Ghostwriting in Publications Related to Rofecoxib: A Case Study of Industry Documents from Rofecoxib Litigation," *JAMA* 299, no. 15 (2008): 1800–1812, https://doi.org/10.1001/jama.299.15.1800.

19. H. Abelson et al., *Blown to Bits: Your Life, Liberty, and Happiness After the Digital Explosion* (Upper Saddle River, NJ: Addison-Wesley, 2008), www.bitsbook.com/wp-content/uploads/2008/12/B2B_3.pdf.

20. An appeal based on a violation of the defendant's fourth amendment rights, which prohibits unreasonable searches and seizures, was rejected, but that decision was reversed by the U.S. Supreme Court. *United States v. Carpenter*, 819 F.3d 880, 890, 895 (6th Cir. 2016), https://scholar.google.com/scholar_case?case=14626167511079628834; *Timothy Ivory Carpenter v. United States of America*, 585 U.S. ___ (2018), https://supreme.justia.com/cases/federal/us/585/16-402/.

21. K. Albrecht and L. McIntyre, "Psst . . . Your Location Is Showing! Metadata in Digital Photos and Posts Could Be Revealing More Than You Realize," *IEEE Consumer Electronics Magazine* 4, no. 1 (2015): 94–96, https://doi.org/10.1109/MCE.2014.2360059.

22. *Armstrong v. Executive Office of the President*, 1 F.3d 1274 (D.C. Cir. 1993), https://casetext.com/case/armstrong-v-executive-office-of-president-2. D. Bearman, "The Implica-

tions of *Armstrong v. Executive Office of the President* for the Archival Management of Electronic Records," *American Archivist* 56, no. 4 (1993): 674–89, https://americanarchivist.org/doi/pdf/10.17723/aarc.56.4.v4x38681q7217155; C. Pasterczyk, "Federal E-mail Management: A Records Manager's View of *Armstrong v. Executive Office of the President* and Its Aftermath," *Records Management Quarterly* 32, no. 2 (1998): 10–22; P. Schrag, "The Working Papers of Federal Policymaking: Our Vanishing Public History," *The Public Historian* 16, no. 4 (1994): 37–45, www.jstor.org/stable/3378009; C. Meltzer, "More Than Just Ones and Zeros: The Reproducibility of Metadata under the Freedom of Information Act," *I/S: A Journal of Law and Policy for the Information Society* 9, no. 2 (2013): 327–66, https://kb.osu.edu/bitstream/handle/1811/73314/ISJLP_V9N2_327.pdf?sequence=1.

    23. P. Favro, "A New Frontier in Electronic Discovery: Preserving and Obtaining Metadata," *Boston University Journal of Science & Technology Law* 13, no. 1 (2007): 1–25, https://papers.ssrn.com/sol3/papers.cfm?abstract_id=2255160; W. Wescott III, "The Increasing Importance of Metadata in Electronic Discovery," *Richmond Journal of Law and Technology* 14, no. 3 (2008): 1–24, https://scholarship.richmond.edu/cgi/viewcontent.cgi?article=1291&context=jolt.

    24. *Federal Rules of Civil Procedure* (Washington, DC: U.S. Government Publishing Office, 2018), www.law.cornell.edu/rules/frcp. In a widely cited wrongful termination case involving deletion of metadata from spreadsheets provided to the plaintiff in response to a discovery request, the court ruled that electronic documents should be produced as they are maintained in the ordinary course of business with their metadata intact. See *Williams v. Sprint/United Management Co.*, 230 F.R.D. 640 (D. Kan. 2005), https://casetext.com/case/williams-v-sprintunited-management-company-12, and L. Cucu, "The Requirement for Metadata Production under *Williams v. Sprint/United Management Co.*: An Unnecessary Burden for Litigants Engaged in Electronic Discovery," *Cornell Law Review* 93, no. 1 (2007): 221–42, https://scholarship.law.cornell.edu/cgi/viewcontent.cgi?article=3082&context=clr. In a case involving an alleged violation of the Individuals with Disabilities Education Improvement Act, the defendant provided digital documents to the requesting party without metadata despite a clear request for documents in their native format. The defendant, which had known about the request for more than three years while the case was pending, objected to the additional expense of producing the documents in their native format, but the court ordered them to do so "with all metadata attached" within thirty days. See *Morgan Hill Concerned Parents Assn v. Cal. Dept. of Educ.*, No. 2:11-cv-03471-KJM-AC (E.D. Cal. Sep. 18, 2017), https://casetext.com/case/morgan-hill-concerned-parents-assn-v-cal-dept-of-educ-11.

    25. See, for example, American Bar Association Standing Committee on Ethics and Professional Responsibility, Formal Opinion 06-442, Review and Use of Metadata (August 5, 2006), www.americanbar.org/content/dam/aba/publications/YourABA/06_442.authcheckdam.pdf; D. Hricik, "I Can Tell When You're Telling Lies: Ethics and Embedded Confidential Information," *Journal of the Legal Profession* 30, no. 1 (2005–2006): 79–101, www.law.ua.edu/pubs/jlp_files/issues_files/vol30/vol30art04.pdf; C. Thorpe, "Metadata: The Dangers of Metadata Compel Issuing Ethical Duties to 'Scrub' and Prohibit the 'Mining' of Metadata," *North Dakota Law Review* 84, no. 1 (2008): 257–98, https://law.und.edu/_files/docs/ndlr/pdf/issues/84/1/84ndlr257.pdf; A. Perlman, "The Legal Ethics of Metadata Mining," *Akron Law Review* 43, no. 3 (2010): 785–800, https://ideaexchange.uakron.edu/cgi/viewcontent.cgi?referer=www.google.com/&httpsredir=1&article=1149&context=akronlawreview; E. King, "The Ethics of Mining for Metadata Outside of Formal Discovery," *Penn State Law Review* 113, no. 3, 803–40, http://pennstatelawreview.org/articles/113 Penn St. L. Rev. 801.pdf; J. Beckham, "Production, Preservation, and Disclosure of Metadata," *Columbia Science and Technology Law Review* 7, no. 1 (2006): 1–16, http://stlr.org/download/volumes/volume7/beckham.pdf; B. Reznikov, "To Mine or Not to Mine: Recent Developments in the Legal Ethics Debate Regarding Metadata," *Shidler Journal of Law, Commerce and Technology* 4, no. 4 (2008): 1–14, http://digital.law.washington.edu/dspace-law/handle/1773.1/414.

    26. By analyzing metadata stored in over 10 million documents from public web sites, researchers were able to identify authors who collaborated in the creation of a document and match them to their Twitter accounts. The researchers noted that their work raised concerns about the privacy impact of metadata. E. Gessious et al., "Digging up Social Structures from

Documents on the Web," in *2012 IEEE Global Communications Conference (GLOBECOM)* (Anaheim, CA: IEEE, 2012), 744–50 www.cs.ucy.ac.cy/~eliasathan/papers/globecom12.pdf.

27. *Engility Corp v. Daniels*, Civil Action No. 16-cv-2473-WJM-MEH (D. Colo. Dec. 2, 2016), https://casetext.com/case/engility-corp-v-charles-aaron-daniels-rutherford-chip-surber-deployable-tech-solutions-llc.

28. *Walder v. Bio-Rad Laboratories, Inc.*, No. 17-16193, (9th Cir. 2019), https://cases.justia.com/federal/appellate-courts/ca9/17-16193/17-16193-2019-02-26.pdf?ts=1551204121.

29. *Lawrence v. City of New York*, 2018 WL 3611963 (S.D.N.Y. 2018), https://ediscovery.co/wp-content/uploads/2018/08/Lawrence-v.-City-of-New-York_2018-08-13-17_31_56-0400.pdf. When the defendant requested sanctions, the plaintiff claimed that mental illness caused her to provide the misleading photographs.

30. T. McLean et al., "Electronic Medical Record Metadata: Uses and Liability," *Journal of the American College of Surgeons* 206, no. 3 (2008): 405–11, https://doi.org/10.1016/j.jamcollsurg.2007.09.018; T. McLean, "EMR Metadata Uses and E-Discovery," *Annals of Health Law* 18, no. 1 (2009): 75–118, https://lawecommons.luc.edu/cgi/viewcontent.cgi?article=1120&context=annals.

31. Commenting on the National Security Agency's collection of metadata about email messages and telephone calls, Stewart Baker, the NSA's General Counsel, said that "metadata absolutely tells you everything about somebody's life. If you have enough metadata, you don't really need content." Agreeing with this comment, General Michael Hayden, former director of the NSA and the Central Intelligence Agency, stated, "We kill people based on metadata." See D. Cole, "We Kill People Based on Metadata," *NYR Daily (New York Review of Books)*, May 10, 2014, www.nybooks.com/daily/2014/05/10/we-kill-people-based-metadata.

32. Examples include the United Kingdom Freedom of Information Act 2000, the French Law on Free Access to Administrative Documents (Law No. 78-753 of July 17, 1978), the German Freedom of Information Act, the Swiss Freedom of Information Act 2004, the Australian Freedom of Information Act 1982, the New Zealand Official Information Act 1982, the Indian Right to Information Act 2005, the Japanese Law Concerning Access to Information Held by Administrative Organs, the South Korean Act on Disclosure of Information by Public Agencies, and the Liberian Freedom of Information Act 2010. The Council of Europe Convention on Access to Official Documents (Treaty 205), which has been ratified by a subset of member states, recognizes a general right of access to official documents held by public authorities. Publications that discuss freedom of information principles include J. Ackerman and I. Sandoval-Ballesteros, *Administrative Law Review* 58, no. 1 (2006): 85–130, www.jstor.org/stable/40712005; T. Mendel, *Freedom of Information: A Comparative Legal Survey*, 2nd ed. (Paris: UNESCO, 2008), https://law.yale.edu/sites/default/files/documents/pdf/Intellectual_Life/CL-OGI_Toby_Mendel_book_%28Eng%29.pdf; and G. Michener, "FOI Laws around the World," *Journal of Democracy* 22, no. 2 (2011): 145–59, https://muse.jhu.edu/article/427167/summary. The National Freedom of Information Coalition provides links to freedom of information laws in American states: www.nfoic.org/coalitions/state-foi-resources/state-freedom-of-information-laws. For links to European freedom of information laws, see www.access-info.org/uncategorized/12042.

33. These event-based disclosure requirements differ from the periodic filings, reports, or other mandatory submissions for which an organization is required to create or collect information, as discussed in chapter 2.

34. Pertinent federal laws and regulations include the Health Information Portability and Accountability Act of 1996 (P.L. 104-191), the Family Educational Rights and Privacy Act (20 U.S.C. § 1232g), the Fair Credit Reporting Act (15 U.S.C. § 1681), and the Children's Online Privacy Protection Act (15 U.S.C. § 6501).

35. As an example, EU Directive 2009/101/EC mandates public disclosure of a company's incorporation documents, officers, registered office location, annual accounting documents that must be published in accordance with EU directives, and liquidation proceedings. In the United States, companies regulated by the Securities and Exchange Commission must comply with disclosure requirements specified in Regulation S-X (17 C.F.R. Part 210) and Regulation S-K

(17 C.F.R. Part 227). Under Canadian federal law, business corporations must disclose the names and addresses of their directors.

36. Examples of right-to-know laws that are designed to protect the general public include the Emergency Planning and Community Right to Know Act (42 U.S.C. § 11004), which requires chemical manufacturing facilities to immediately notify the public about the accidental release of certain toxic substances, and the Safe Water Drinking Act (42 U.S.C. § 300f), which requires water utilities to notify customers when there is a problem with their drinking water. In the United States, workplace right-to-know requirements are based on the Hazard Communication Standard issued by the Occupational Safety and Health Administration (www.osha.gov/dsg/hazcom). Examples of the many publications that discuss the right-to-know concept include T. Emerson, "Legal Foundations of the Right to Know," *Washington University Law Quarterly* 1976, no. 1 (1976): 1–24, https://openscholarship.wustl.edu/cgi/viewcontent.cgi?article=2625&context=law_lawreview, and M. Baram, "The Right to Know and the Duty to Disclose Hazard Information," *American Journal of Public Health* 74, no. 4 (1984): 380–90, https://ajph.aphapublications.org/doi/pdf/10.2105/AJPH.74.4.385.

37. In the United States, violation of disclosure requirements associated with anti-money-laundering regulations is punishable by fines exceeding $100,000 per incident and up to twenty years in prison. In 2018, Capital One agreed to pay a $100 million penalty for failing to file suspicious activity reports, among other violations. U.S. Bancorp paid $613 million in penalties for failing to disclose suspicious transactions, while Commonwealth Bank of Australia was fined $534 million, the largest civil penalty imposed on any business in Australia, for various violations, including failing to report large transactions as required by law. Danske Bank could incur fines up to $8 billion and face criminal charges for failing to report suspicious transactions exceeding $200 million at its Estonian branch. Compared to these sanctions, penalties for nonfinancial-disclosure violations are little more than a wrist-slap.

38. For a listing of data protection and privacy legislation, see G. Greenleaf, "Global Tables of Data Privacy Laws and Bills," an annual compilation, at www2.austlii.edu.au/~graham.

39. For a survey of privacy laws and regulations, see V. Jones, *Requirements for Personal Information Protection, Part 1: U.S. Federal Law* (Pittsburgh: ARMA International Educational Foundation, 2008), www.armaedfoundation.org/pdfs/FederalPrivacy.pdf, and V. Jones, *Requirements for Personal Information Protection, Part 2: U.S. State Laws* (Pittsburgh: ARMA International Educational Foundation, 2009), www.armaedfoundation.org/pdfs/Requirements_for_Personal_Information_US_States.pdf.

40. The HIPAA Privacy Rule (45 C.F.R §§ 164.500 et seq.) restricts disclosure of individually identifiable health information. It applies to patient records and other personal health information maintained by health plans, health care clearinghouses, health care providers, and their business associates. Disclosure is limited to the minimum amount of information necessary for treatment, payment, or health care operations, such as quality assessments and auditing functions.

41. As specified in 15 U.S.C. §§ 6801 et seq., financial institutions have an "affirmative and continuing obligation" to protect the security and confidentiality of their customers' nonpublic personal information. According to the Financial Services Modernization Act of 1999 (P.L. 106-102), commonly known as the Gramm-Leach-Bliley Act (GLBA), banks, credit unions, securities firms, and other financial institutions must give customers a privacy notice indicating the types of businesses to which their personal information may be disclosed. Customers can refuse to have their personal information shared under certain circumstances.

42. The Fair and Accurate Credit Transaction Act (P.L. 108-159) gives data subjects the option of stopping a company's affiliates from sharing their customer information for marketing purposes. The California Consumer Privacy Act (Cal. Civ. Code §§ 1798.100 et seq.), the most comprehensive and broadly applicable state law that protects consumer information, allows California residents to prohibit sale of their personal information to third parties. It applies to any for-profit entity that does business in California if their annual revenues or data collection activities exceed specified limits.

43. The Family Educational Rights and Privacy Act (20 U.S.C. § 1232g) prohibits unauthorized disclosure of information about students. It requires written permission from students or parents of minor students to release information from educational records to a third party

subject to exceptions specified in 34 C.F.R. § 99.31. This disclosure restriction applies to elementary, secondary, and post-secondary educational institutions and agencies that receive funds from any program administered by the U.S. Department of Education. The restriction is limited to information derived from educational records as defined in the law itself and in 34 C.F.R. § 99.3. Such records may be maintained by an educational institution or by an external party, such as cloud-based service provider, on the educational institution's behalf. Disclosure restrictions do not apply to student information that a school employee may obtain through personal knowledge, observation, or other means. For a summary of FERPA's major provisions, see J. Feder, *The Family Educational Rights and Privacy Act (FERPA): A Legal Overview* (Washington, DC: Congressional Research Service, 2013), www.higheredcompliance.org/wp-content/uploads/2018/10/ CRS_FERPAOverview_2013_11_19.pdf. Similar disclosure requirements are specified in the Individuals with Disabilities Education Act (20 U.S.C. §§ 1401 et seq.). See K. Surprenant et al., *IDEA and FERPA Confidentiality Provisions* (Washington, DC: U.S. Department of Education, 2014), www2.ed.gov/policy/gen/guid/ptac/pdf/idea-ferpa.pdf.

44. The American Library Association provides links to state laws related to privacy and confidential library records. www.ala.org/advocacy/privacy/statelaws. In New York State, for example, personal information about library users is considered confidential and can only be disclosed to the extent necessary for library operations, with consent of the data subject, or pursuant to a court order or statute. As specified in NY C.P.L.R. § 4509, confidentiality extends to information related to circulation of library materials, computer database searches, interlibrary loan transactions, reference inquiries, requests for photocopies of library materials, title reserve requests, and use of audiovisual materials, films, or sound recordings.

45. The Video Privacy Protection Act (18 U.S.C. § 2710) was passed in 1988 after the *Washington City Paper*, an alternative weekly newspaper, published the video rental records of Judge Robert Bork, a Supreme Court nominee. The newspaper obtained the information from a video rental store. The original law prohibited the disclosure of video rental information outside of the ordinary course of business unless written consent was obtained from the data subject at the time of each disclosure. Subsequent amendments, which were supported by Netflix and other entertainment companies, allow disclosure if the data subject provides a blanket written consent. The same provisions apply to video streaming services.

46. Generally, courts decide what information about their proceedings will be available to the public. The National Center for State Courts has compiled a list of laws relating to privacy and public access to court records. www.ncsc.org/topics/access-and-fairness/privacy-public-access-to-court-records/state-links.aspx. Examples of the many publications that discuss privacy issues related to court records include D. Ardia, "Privacy and Court Records: Online Access and the Loss of Practical Obscurity," *Illinois Law Review* 2017, no. 5 (2017): 1387–454, https://pdfs.semanticscholar.org/55c3/1dd28827bfaeb98efabaf345bd5a7a14cc6b.pdf; L. Sudbeck, "Placing Court Records Online: Balancing the Public and Private Interests," *Justice System Journal* 27, no. 3 (2006): 268–85, https://cdm16501.contentdm.oclc.org/digital/collection/tech/id/356; A. Conley and A. Datta, "Sustaining Privacy and Open Justice in the Transition to Online Court Records: A Multidisciplinary Inquiry," *Maryland Law Review* 71, no. 3, 772–847, https://digitalcommons.law.umaryland.edu/cgi/viewcontent.cgi?article=3504&context=mlr; and P. Winn, "Online Court Records: Balancing Judicial Accountability and Privacy in an Age of Electronic Information," *Washington Law Review* 79, no. 1 (2004): 307–321, https://papers.ssrn.com/sol3/papers.cfm?abstract_id=2155282.

47. The Driver's Privacy Protection Act (18 U.S.C. § 2721) prohibits the disclosure of personal information contained in motor vehicle records maintained by state governments without the consent of the data subject, subject to exceptions. Personal information covered by the restriction includes the individual's name, address, driver identification number, telephone number, medical or disability information, social security number, and photograph.

48. The Children's Online Privacy Protection Rule (16 C.F.R. § 312) requires parental consent prior to disclosure of personal information about children under thirteen years of age. See J. Warmund, "Can COPPA Work? An Analysis of the Parental Consent Measures in the Children's Online Privacy Protection Act," *Fordham Intellectual Property, Media and Entertainment Law Journal* 11, no. 1 (2000): 189–216, https://ir.lawnet.fordham.edu/cgi/viewcon-

tent.cgi?referer=www.google.com/&httpsredir=1&article=1212&context=iplj; M. Hersh, "Is COPPA a Cop Out? The Child Online Privacy Protection Act as Proof That Parents, Not Government, Should Be Protecting Children's Interests on the Internet," *Fordham Urban Law Journal* 28, no. 6 (2001): 1831–78, https://ir.lawnet.fordham.edu/cgi/viewcontent.cgi?referer=www.google.com/&httpsredir=1&article=2058&context=ulj; D. Boyd et al., "How the COPPA, as Implemented, Is Misinterpreted by the Public: A Research Perspective," *OSF Preprints*, January 5, 2017, https://doi.org/10.31219/osf.io/yrcxk.

49. Under the Electronic Communications Privacy Act of 1986 (18 U.S.C. §§ 2701 et seq.), telecommunication service providers must not intentionally divulge the contents of any communications they transmit unless the originator or addressee consent to the disclosure or certain other conditions apply. For a discussion of the law, see D. Mulligan, "Reasonable Expectations in Electronic Communications: A Critical Perspective on the Electronic Communications Privacy Act," *George Washington Law Review* 72, no. 6 (2004): 1557–98, https://scholarship.law.berkeley.edu/cgi/viewcontent.cgi?referer=www.google.com/&httpsredir=1&article=3131&context=facpubs, and O. Kerr, "The Next Generation Communications Privacy Act," *University of Pennsylvania Law Review* 162, no. 2 (2014): 373–419, www.jstor.org/stable/24247892.

50. PIPEDA applies to associations, charities, religious groups, advocacy groups, and other not-for-profit organizations to the extent that they engage in commercial activities, such as the sale of membership lists or donor lists. Some Canadian provinces have substantially similar data protection laws take precedence over PIPEDA for disclosure of personal information within their jurisdiction. PIPEDA is the regulatory authority for personal information that flows out of the province or territory to which a given law applies. See L. Austin, "Reviewing PIPEDA: Control, Privacy and the Limits of Fair Information Practices," *Canadian Business Law Journal* 44, no. 1 (2006): 21–53, https://papers.ssrn.com/sol3/papers.cfm?abstract_id=1169162.

51. The exceptions permit disclosure of personal information to collect a debt, to comply with a court order, to respond to a request by a government institution that is authorized to obtain the information in relation to national security or legal matters, or to communicate with the data subject's next of kin, authorized representative, or other person in the event of an emergency. Disclosure restrictions do not apply to information that is produced by a data subject in the course of employment and that is consistent with the purpose for which the information was produced; information that is contained in a witness statement that is necessary for an insurance claim; information that is used for statistical or scholarly purposes, provided that confidentiality is assured and the data subject's consent cannot be obtained; information that is publicly available; or information that was created more than one hundred years ago or twenty years after the death of the data subject.

52. Examples of state and territorial data protection laws include the Privacy and Personal Information Protection Act 1998 (New South Wales), Information Privacy Act 2009 (Queensland), Privacy and Data Protection Act 2014 (Victoria), Information Privacy Act 2014 (Australian Capital Territory), Information Act 2002 (Northern Territory), and Personal Information Protection Act 2004 (Tasmania). B. Srinivas, *A Concise Guide to Various Australian Laws Related to Privacy and Cybersecurity Domains* (Bethesda, MD: SANS Institute, 2015), www.sans.org/reading-room/whitepapers/legal/concise-guide-australian-laws-related-privacy-cybersecurity-domains-36072; *Privacy Guide: A Guide to Compliance with Privacy Laws in Australia* (Melbourne: Justice Connect, 2017), www.nfplaw.org.au/sites/default/files/media/Privacy_Guide_Cth.pdf.

53. See R. Hazell, "Freedom of Information in Australia, Canada and New Zealand," *Public Administration* 67, no. 2 (1989): 189–210, https://doi.org/10.1111/j.1467-9299.1989.tb00721.x; E. Rose, "An Examination of the Concern for Information Privacy in the New Zealand Regulatory Context," *Information & Management* 43, no. 3 (2006): 322–35, https://doi.org/10.1016/j.im.2005.08.002.

54. 18 U.S.C. § 798 prohibits disclosure of classified information in any manner that imperils national security. According to 18 U.S.C. § 842, it is a federal crime to disclose any information pertaining to the manufacture or use of explosive, destructive devices in connection with a violent crime.

55. Most countries have laws or legal precedents that recognize some form of attorney-client privilege for legal advice. Subject to some exceptions, attorneys cannot disclose any confidential communications related to representation of a current or former client without the client's informed consent. In limited circumstances, accountants, tax practitioners, and actuaries may be prohibited from voluntarily disclosing a client's financial or tax-related information without the client's permission, subject to certain exceptions. In the United States, the Uniform Arbitration Act, which has been enacted by many states, allows an arbitrator to issue a protective order prohibiting the disclosure of specific information.

56. See, for example, 12 C.F.R. 4.37, which prohibits disclosure of reports of examinations, supervisory correspondence, investigatory records, or other nonpublic information created, compiled, or issued by the Office of the Comptroller of the Currency.

57. To balance privacy mandates with the interests of archivists, historians, and biographers, some data protection laws limit the period of protection for personal information. The GDPR, for example, does not apply to the personal information of deceased data subjects, although EU member states may have national laws that extend protection to deceased persons. In Denmark, for example, the GDPR prohibition on unauthorized disclosure of personal information lasts for ten years after the death of the data subject. In Italy, GDPR protection can be extended by an agent acting in the interest of a deceased person or where warranted by family considerations. In the United States, the HIPAA privacy rule prohibits unauthorized release of health information for fifty years after the death of the data subject. In Canada, PIPEDA does not apply to personal information that was created more than one hundred years ago or twenty years after the death of the data subject. Most data protection laws permit anonymization or pseudonymization of personal information of protected data subjects for research purposes. For a discussion of the impact of data protection laws on archival practice, see L. Iacovino and M. Todd, "The Long-Term Preservation of Identifiable Personal Data: A Comparative Archival Perspective on Privacy Regulatory Models in the European Union, Australia, Canada, and the United States," *Archival Science* 7, no. 1 (2007): 107–27, https://link.springer.com/article/10.1007/s10502-007-9055-5; P. Henttonen, "Privacy as an Archival Problem and a Solution," *Archival Science* 17, no. 3 (2017): 285–303, https://link.springer.com/article/10.1007/s10502-017-9277-0; L. Corti et al., "Confidentiality and Informed Consent: Issues for Consideration in the Preservation of and Provision of Access to Qualitative Data Archives," *Forum: Qualitative Social Research* 1, no. 3 (2000): art. 7, http://dx.doi.org/10.17169/fqs-1.3.1024.

58. For a discussion of data breach insurance and related types of coverage, see A. Moss and J. Deni, "A User's Guide to Data Breach Insurance Coverage," *Risk Management* 65, no. 3 (2018): 48–51, www.rmmagazine.com/2018/04/02/a-users-guide-to-data-breach-insurance-coverage; M. Eling and W. Schnell, "What Do We Know about Cyber Risk and Cyber Risk Insurance?" *Journal of Risk Finance* 17, no. 5 (2016): 474–91, https://doi.org/10.1108/JRF-09-2016-0122; B. Nieuwesteeg et al., "The Law and Economics of Cyber Insurance Contracts: A Case Study," *European Review of Private Law* 26, no. 3 (2018): 371–420, http://kluwerlawonline.com/abstract.php?area=Journals&id=ERPL2018027.

59. For an overview of cross-border data transfer, see M. Ferracane, *Restrictions on Cross-Border Data Flows: A Taxonomy,* ECIPE Working Paper No. 1 (Brussels: European Center for International Political Economy, November 18, 2017), https://ecipe.org/publications/restrictions-to-cross-border-data-flows-a-taxonomy. Restrictions on cross-border transfer of information are separate and distinct from laws and regulations that prohibit the transfer of specific information to foreign nationals who may be resident in the country where the information originates. In the United States, for example, the Arms Export Control Act (22 U.S.C. §§ 2751 et seq.) and the Export Administration Act (50 U.S.C. §§ 2401 et seq.) prohibit dissemination of certain technical data to a foreign national or an agent of a foreign national who is located in the United States. Violations are punishable by fines and imprisonment.

60. Possibilities include international transfer agreements between the European Commission or EU member states and public authorities in non-EU countries; binding corporate rules that comply with GDPR requirements and provide mechanisms for ensuring compliance; codes of conduct that include enforceable commitments to protect personal information; certifications; and model or ad hoc clauses approved by the European Commission. As its name implies, the EU-U.S. Privacy Shield Framework provides a mechanism for transfer of personal

information from EU member states to the United States, which does not have a national data protection law. Participating US companies must certify their adherence to GDPR-compliant data protection principles issued by the U.S. Department of Commerce. Compliance is enforced by the Federal Trade Commission and other regulatory bodies. The Privacy Shield Framework also limits access to transferred information by law enforcement and national security agencies in the United States. The Swiss-U.S. Privacy Shield Framework provides a comparable mechanism for transfer of personal information from Switzerland to the United States. For a discussion of these transfer arrangements, see D. Bender and L. Ponemon, "Binding Corporate Rules for Cross-Border Data Transfer," *Rutgers Journal of Law & Urban Policy* 3, no. 1 (2006): 154–62, https://heinonline.org/HOL/LandingPage?handle=hein.journals/rutjulp3&div=16&id=&page=; M. Burri, "The Governance of Data and Data Flow in Trade Agreements: The Pitfalls of Legal Adaptation," *UC Davis Law Review* 51, no. 1 (2017): 65–132, https://lawreview.law.ucdavis.edu/issues/51/1/Symposium/51-1_Burri.pdf; M. Wugmeister et al., "Global Solution for Cross-Border Data Transfers: Making the Case for Corporate Privacy Rules," *Georgetown Journal of International Law* 38, no. 2 (2006): 449–98, http://media.mofo.com/docs/pdf/0801CrossBorder.PDF; L. Kong, "Data Protection and Transborder Data Flow in the European Context," *European Journal of International Law* 21, no. 2 (2010): 441–56, https://doi.org/10.1093/ejil/chq025; M. Weiss and K. Archick, *U.S.-EU Data Privacy: From Safe Harbor to Privacy Shield* (Washington, DC: Congressional Research Service, 2016), https://epic.org/crs/R44257.pdf; W. Voss, "European Union Data Privacy Law Reform: General Data Protection Regulation, Privacy Shield, and the Right to Delisting," *Business Lawyer* 72, no. 1 (2016): 221–33, www.researchgate.net/publication/312093729_European_Union_Data_Privacy_Law_Reform_General_Data_Protection_Regulation_Privacy_Shield_and_the_Right_to_Delisting.

61. Examples include the UK Protection of Trading Interests Act 1980 and the Canadian Foreign Extraterritorial Measures Act. Publications that provide background information about blocking statutes include K. Alexander, *Economic Sanctions* (London: Palgrave MacMillan, 2009), esp. 224–57, https://link.springer.com/chapter/10.1057/9780230227286_9; K. Nakata, "The SEC and Foreign Blocking Statutes: Need for a Balanced Approach," *University of Pennsylvania Journal of International Business Law* 9, no. 3, 549–91, www.law.upenn.edu/journals/jil/articles/volume9/issue3/Nakata9U.Pa.J.Int%27lBus.L.549%281987%29.pdf; H. Dahl, "Forum non conveniens, Latin America and Blocking Statutes," *University of Miami Inter-American Law Review* 35, no. 1 (2004): 21–63, https://repository.law.miami.edu/cgi/viewcontent.cgi?referer=www.google.com/&httpsredir=1&article=1189&context=umialr; M. Hoda, "The Aerospatiale Dilemma: Why U.S. Courts Ignore Blocking Statutes and What Foreign States Can Do about It," *California Law Review* 106, no. 1 (2018): 231–61, https://scholarship.law.berkeley.edu/cgi/viewcontent.cgi?article=4394&context=californialawreview; and V. Curran, "United States Discovery and Foreign Blocking Statutes," *Louisiana Law Review* 76, no. 4 (2016): 1142–49; https://digitalcommons.law.lsu.edu/cgi/viewcontent.cgi?article=6583&context=lalrev.

62. These laws were originally designed to counteract the extraterritorial reach of American antitrust legislation, but they also impede discovery of information for litigation initiated in other Canadian provinces. See R. Wisner, "Uniformity, Diversity and Provincial Extraterritoriality· Hunt v. T&N plc," *McGill Law Journal* 40, no. 3 (1995): 759–79, www.canlii.org/t/2bj9.

63. This definition is adapted from ISO/IEC 27040:2015, *Information Technology—Security Techniques—Storage Security*. While data breaches are widely associated with computer security failures, they can involve information in any format. A study of data breach reports from 2009 to 2016 found that the most common type of data breaches in US hospitals involved paper records and photographic films. M. Gabriel et al., "Data Breach Locations, Types, and Associated Characteristics among US Hospitals," *American Journal of Managed Care* 24, no. 2 (2018): 78–84, www.ajmc.com/journals/issue/2018/2018-vol24-n2/data-breach-locations-types-and-associated-characteristics-among-us-hospitals.

64. Examples of the many publications that discuss data breach notifications include C. Garrison and C. Hamilton, "A Comparative Analysis of the EU GDPR to the US's Breach Notifications," *Information & Communications Technology Law* 28, no. 1 (2019): 99–114, https://doi.org/10.1080/13600834.2019.1571473; G. Stevens, *Data Security Breach Notifica-*

tion Laws (Washington, DC: Congressional Research Service, 2012), http://dev.journalistsresource.org/wp-content/uploads/2012/04/R42475.pdf; R. Peters, "So You've Been Notified, Now What? The Problem with Current Data Breach Notification Laws," *Arizona Law Review* 56, no. 4 (2014): 1117–1202, www.arizonalawreview.org/pdf/56-4/56arizlrev1171.pdf; J. Joerling, "Data Breach Notification Laws: An Argument for a Comprehensive Federal Law to Protect Consumer Data," *Washington University Journal of Law & Policy* 32, no. 1 (2010): 467–88, https://openscholarship.wustl.edu/cgi/viewcontent.cgi?referer=&httpsredir=1&article=1087&context=law_journal_law_policy; P. Schwartz and E. Janger, "Notification of Data Security Breaches," *Michigan Law Review* 105, no. 5 (2007): 913–84, https://repository.law.umich.edu/cgi/viewcontent.cgi?article=1474&context=mlr; R. Sullilvan and J. Maniff, "Data Breach Notification Laws," *Economic Review* 101, no. 1 (2016): 65–85, www.kansascityfed.org/~/media/files/publicat/econrev/econrevarchive/2016/1q16sullivanmaniff.pdf; and D. Lesemann, "Once More unto the Breach: An Analysis of Legal, Technological, and Policy Issues Involving Data Breach Notification Statutes," *Akron Intellectual Property Journal* 4, no. 2 (2010): 203–37, www.uakron.edu/dotAsset/1139182.pdf.

65. The National Conference of State Legislatures has complied a state-by-state list of security breach legislation with links to individual laws. See www.ncsl.org/research/telecommunications-and-information-technology/security-breach-notification-laws.aspx. See also *Data Breach Notification in the United States and Territories*, a report on state laws issued by the Privacy Rights Clearinghouse, www.privacyrights.org/blog/data-breach-notification-united-states-and-territories.

66. As required by the Health Information Technology for Economic and Clinical Health (HITECH) Act (42 U.S.C. 139w-4(0)(2)), the Department of Health and Human Services posts a list of data breaches that were reported by health care providers, health plans, and health care clearinghouses within the preceding twenty-four months and are currently under investigation by the Office for Civil Rights as well as older breach reports. The listed incidents include unauthorized disclosure, theft, hacking, or other incidents involving paper, photographic, and unencrypted electronic records. See https://ocrportal.hhs.gov/ocr/breach/breach_report.jsf.

67. For a discussion of lawsuits related to data breaches, see D. Solove and D. Citron, "Risk and Anxiety: A Theory of Data-Breach Harms," *Texas Law Review* 96, no. 4 (2018): 737–86, https://texaslawreview.org/risk-and-anxiety/; and C. Rust, "Against the Wind: Have We Accepted Data Breach as an Inevitability?," *Northern Kentucky Law Review* 43, no. 1 (2016): 87–104, https://chaselaw.nku.edu/content/dam/chase/docs/lawreview/v43/nklr_v43n1.pdf.

68. Widely publicized examples include Equifax, British Airways, Uber, Marriott International, Yahoo, Tesco Bank, and Target.

69. In a 2011 survey of senior-level executives in the United States by Ponemon Institute, respondents estimated that a data breach involving confidential customer information would diminish the value of an organization's brand by more than 20 percent and that it would take an average of eight months to restore the organization's reputation. www.databreachtoday.com/whitepapers/ponemon-institute-study-reputation-impact-data-breach-w-540-dynamic-popup; www.centrify.com/media/4772757/ponemon_data_breach_impact_study_uk.pdf. K. Gatzlaff and K. McCullough, "The Effect of Data Breaches on Shareholder Wealth," *Risk Management and Insurance Review* 13, no. 1 (2010): 61–83, https://doi.org/10.1111/j.1540-6296.2010.01178.x found that data breaches have a negative and statistically significant effect on the stock price of publicly traded companies. See also I. Confente et al., "Effects of Data Breaches from User-Generated Content: A Corporate Reputation Analysis," *European Management Journal* 37, no. 4 (2019): 492–504, https://doi.org/10.1016/j.emj.2019.01.007; and S. Chatterjee et al., "Reacting to the Scope of a Data Breach: The Differential Role of Fear and Anger," *Journal of Business Research* 101 (2019): 183–93, https://doi.org/10.1016/j.jbusres.2019.04.024. A 2017 survey by Ponemon Institute of 113 publicly traded companies in the United Kingdom found that their stock price declined by an average of 5 percent immediately following disclosure of a data breach.

70. Healthcare providers and medical insurance services account for more than half of reported data breaches in recent years. For statistics and a searchable database of data breaches, see www.privacyrights.org/data-breaches.

71. *Sixth Annual Study: Is Your Company Ready for a Big Data Breach?* www.experian.com/data-breach/2019-data-breach-preparedness.html?ecd_dbres_blog _sixth_annual_preparedness_study.

72. M. Burdon et al., "Encryption Safe Harbours and Data Breach Notification Laws," *Computer Law & Security Review* 26, no. 5 (2010): 520–34, https://doi.org/10.1016/ j.clsr.2010.07.002.

73. On the importance of language in data breach notifications, see A. Jenkins et al., "All That Glitters Is Not Gold: The Role of Impression Management in Data Breach Notification," *Western Journal of Communication* 78, no. 3 (2014): 337–57, https://doi.org/10.1080/ 10570314.2013.866686; J. Veltsos, "An Analysis of Data Breach Notifications as Negative News," *Business Communication Quarterly* 75, no. 2 (2012): 192–207, https://doi.org/10.1177/ 1080569912443081; S. Jackson, "How Readable Are Data Breach Notifications?" *Computer Fraud & Security* 2019, no. 5 (2019): 6–8, https://doi.org/10.1016/S1361-3723(19)30051-X.

Chapter Six

Ownership of Information

Broadly defined, *ownership* is the legal right to possession of property, which is itself broadly defined as something that belongs to someone.[1] Property may be tangible or intangible. Information has both properties. It can be memorized or shared verbally without any tangible manifestation, but it has a physical existence and can become someone's property when it is recorded on paper, photographic, or electronic media. This chapter identifies and discusses the following threats to ownership of recorded information:

- challenges to and infringement of an organization's intellectual property rights;
- the impact of the work-for-hire doctrine on ownership of information;
- loss of ownership of trade secrets through disclosure; and
- data portability laws and regulations that give data subjects certain ownership rights to personal information about them.

These threats and their associated vulnerabilities and consequences apply to recorded information in all formats and media, including databases, digital documents, paper records, photographs, and social media content. As discussed in the following sections, threats to ownership of information have a high likelihood of occurrence, but their adverse effects can be prevented, limited, or, in some cases, transferred.

INTELLECTUAL PROPERTY RIGHTS

Intellectual property is the product of original thought. The World Intellectual Property Organization (WIPO)—a self-funding agency of the United Nations that serves as a global forum for intellectual property policies, services, information, and cooperation—defines *intellectual property* as the result of "intellectual activity in the industrial, scientific, literary and artistic fields."[2] Intellectual property rights are rules and privileges that govern the ownership and exploitation of an organization's intellectual property. As a variant form of private property rights, intellectual property rights have the dual purpose of encouraging writing, research, invention, artistic expression, and other activities that create information while allowing the information's owner to control and profit from it. A creator's right to benefit from ownership of intellectual property is affirmed in Article 27 of the Universal Declaration of Human Rights, which was issued by the United Nations General Assembly in 1948.[3] While original thought, the basis for intellectual property, is intangible, intellectual property rights protect their tangible manifestations.[4]

The World Intellectual Property Organization divides intellectual property rights into two categories: (1) copyright, which gives the creator of a work the exclusive right to reproduce, publish, perform, translate, or adapt it,[5] and (2) rights that protect industrial property.[6] The latter includes patents, which grant an exclusive right to commercialize an invention; trademarks and trade names, which distinctively identify an organization and its products or services; industrial designs, which pertain to the aesthetic or ornamental aspects of a product, handicraft, or other item; and geographical indications, which distinctively identify products that originate in a specific location.[7]

To serve the public's interest in the availability of information, intellectual property rights are limited in scope and duration. According to the territoriality principle, intellectual property rights are only protected by law in the country or region where they have been granted.[8] Intellectual property laws are strongest in countries with well-developed economies and a long history of innovation. Certain countries have weak or nonexistent intellectual property protection.[9]

Intellectual property rights are also time-limited. The period of protection for specific types of intellectual property varies from country to country. The copyright period for most works ranges from fifty to one hundred years after the death of the author. For works of corporate, anonymous, or pseudonymous authorship, the copyright period ranges from fifty to seventy-five years from the date of publication or creation in most countries.[10] Protection periods for industrial property are shorter. In most countries, the protection period for patents is twenty years from the date a patent application for a given invention was filed, although some countries provide shorter terms of protection for certain types of inventions.[11] Protection periods for industrial designs range from fifteen to twenty-five years from the date of the award. Geographical indications are usually protected for a ten-year period, which can be renewed indefinitely. In most countries, trademarks are protected for a five-year period, which can be renewed indefinitely.

An organization's ownership of intellectual property rights may be threatened by challenges or unauthorized use by competitors, collaborators, or other parties:

- A patent or industrial design application may be challenged by someone who claims to be the actual inventor or a co-inventor.
- The patentability of an invention might be disputed because the invention is not sufficiently novel when compared to similar products that are already in existence or not sufficiently useful for its intended purpose to qualify for a patent award. The disputing party may allege fraud in a patent application, such as failure to disclose the existence of inventions with comparable characteristics, incorrect claims, or other intentional misrepresentation. These issues can be raised while a patent application is being evaluated or, more problematically, after a patent has been issued.[12] Even if a disputed patent is not invalidated, it may be limited in a way that diminishes its value.
- Copyright challenges are less common than patent disputes because copyright protection takes effect automatically and immediately when original information is fixed (recorded) in tangible form on paper, photographic, or electronic media.[13] Formal registration is not necessary for copyright protection. Copyright registration is not supported in many countries, and it is voluntary in others. National copyright offices, where they exist at all, merely record copyright claims. They do not evaluate copyright applications.[14]
- Originality is a requirement for copyrightability. The copyright registration process does not question the originality of a work submitted for registration, but the originality and copyrightability of the work may be challenged in court by someone who claims authorship of the work or incorporation of content from a previously copyrighted work.
- Infringement is a violation of an organization's intellectual property rights. Copyright infringement is the reproduction, publication, adaptation, translation, or performance of a work protected by copyright without the permission of the copyright owner, who may be the work's creator or another person or organization to which the copyright has been assigned. Patent infringement is the unauthorized production, sale, distribution, or other use of a patented invention for commercial purposes while patent protection is in effect. Design infringement involves a comparable violation involving the visual appearance of a protected industrial design. The more general and broadly useful the scope of a patent or industrial design, the greater the number of potential infringers.[15]
- Cloud computing poses challenges for control of an organization's intellectual property. A cloud service provides online access to computer resources for processing, retrieval, publication, distribution, retention, or

other use of digital content, which is stored on servers operated by the cloud service provider.[16] Depending on the services offered, customers can upload data, documents, images, or other content to a cloud platform for storage, retrieval, or distribution.[17] Alternatively, applications implemented on a cloud platform may be used to create digital content.[18] Ownership rights to cloud content are determined by intellectual property laws and contract provisions.[19] Cloud service providers disavow ownership of digital content that is uploaded to their computing platforms or created by customers using their online applications, but their terms of service may authorize certain actions that are customarily associated with ownership.[20] All cloud providers require customers to grant them a license to host, store, use, and reproduce their intellectual property for purposes of providing services, which are rarely specified in detail. Some cloud service providers also require a worldwide license that allows them to modify, publish, or create derivative works, such as translations and adaptations, from a customer's intellectual property. In some cases, the license to use the customer's intellectual property remains in effect after the customer stops using the cloud service.[21]

- A cloud service provider can delete or deny an organization access to its own intellectual property when an account is delinquent, when a customer is suspected of infringing or misappropriating another organization's intellectual property, or for any other breach of the provider's terms of service.[22] If a cloud service provider ceases operation, customers will have an opportunity to download their intellectual property or transfer it to another cloud service, assuming they are given prior notice of the provider's closure, but some providers have closed down with very short notice to customers.[23] In that case, an organization's intellectual property may be temporarily or permanently inaccessible.

- The largest cloud service providers operate global networks of data centers. In most cases, the cloud service provider determines the storage location for customer content, which may be in a foreign country. Storage in a foreign country may expose an organization's content to intellectual property laws that differ from those in the country where the content originated. In the worst case, cloud content may be stored in a country where intellectual property protection is weak or absent. Storage in a foreign country may also violate laws and regulations that require in-country retention, or prohibit cross-border transfer of specific information, as discussed in the preceding chapter.

Failure to address these threats can have damaging consequences for ownership of intellectual property. Governments grant intellectual property rights that apply in specific political jurisdictions, but owners of intellectual property are responsible for enforcing their rights.[24] Successful challenges to an organization's ownership of intellectual property can result in invalidation or revocation of patent awards and copyright registrations. Legal action is often necessary to protect and enforce intellectual property rights, but civil litigation, arbitration, mediation, or other legal proceedings can be time-consuming and costly, especially in complicated cases that involve multiple infringements or foreign political jurisdictions. According to a 2009 survey commissioned by the American Intellectual Property Law Association, average litigation costs for patent infringement cases in the United States exceeded $3 million where the amount in dispute was less than $25 million and approached $6 million where the amount in dispute exceeded $25 million.[25]

From an accounting perspective, intellectual property rights protect intangible assets with anticipated benefits.[26] Any threats to those rights can degrade an organization's financial performance, damage its reputation, and harm its competitive position. For some organizations, intellectual property is more valuable than real property, physical plant, and equipment, the principal forms of tangible property.[27] In for-profit entities, invalidation or revocation of intellectual property rights can have a negative impact on a company's market valuation. Challenges and infringement of intellectual property rights are likely to be closely scrutinized when an organization seeks collateral-based financing, during negotiations for joint ventures and strategic alliances, and as part of due diligence for mergers and acquisitions. Failure to protect and enforce intellectual property rights can also affect an organization's business relationships. If an organization is unable to protect its own copyrights, patents, and industrial designs, its business partners, suppliers, and other collaborators may be unwilling to grant them licenses to use their intellectual property.

Vulnerability Assessment

According to a 2019 global survey of over 2,300 organizations, 81 percent of respondents identified intellectual property issues as among the ten most important risks their organizations must address; 28 percent of respondents reported that their organizations had experienced a major infringement-related incident involving intellectual property within the past two years. Of those incidents, 69 percent involved challenges to the organizations' intellectual property rights.[28]

Infringement of intellectual property rights is pervasive. While the number of infringement cases is relatively low in relation to the number of issued patents, copyrights, and industrial designs, it is nonetheless substantial. Since 2016, 3,500 to 4,500 patent-infringement cases have been filed annually in US district courts.[29] A 2018 survey found that 37 percent of the software installed on personal computers worldwide is unlicensed. In some regions, unlicensed software exceeds 50 percent of installations.[30]

The following vulnerabilities increase an organization's exposure to intellectual property threats discussed in the preceding section:

- An organization may not have a comprehensive inventory or audit of the intellectual property it owns or an up-to-date review and assessment of its protection status.
- The exposure period for threats to ownership of intellectual property is measured in decades. As previously discussed, copyright ownership is protected for a minimum of fifty years. Depending on authorship and the circumstances of creation, copyright protection for a given work can remain in effect for more than one hundred years. Patents are protected for twenty years from the date an application was filed and industrial designs for fifteen to twenty-five years.
- An organization must be familiar with legal requirements for protection and enforcement of intellectual property rights in every country where it does business or where the protected products may be used. It must also be aware of countries with inadequate intellectual property protection. Multinational and transnational entities with large portfolios of copyrights and industrial property will typically have in-house expertise supplemented by local external counsel to advise about these matters, but small to medium-size enterprises may not be aware of applicable intellectual property laws and regulations.
- Competing companies may engage in research with similar outcomes; the greater the amount of innovation in a particular field, the greater the likelihood of competing patent claims. Research suggests that competing patent claims are likely to arise from inventors working in the same geographic area, the reason being that inventors benefit from the exchange of ideas in a given locality.[31]
- Infringement undermines the economic benefits of intellectual property rights, but it is difficult to detect. Owners of intellectual property can take legal action against infringement, but a comprehensive plan to detect infringers requires an impractical and unaffordable allocation of resources. Competitors' product development, marketing, and distribution activities must be monitored. Products that might infringe a copyright, patent, or industrial design must be identified and closely scrutinized in every country where an organization's intellectual property rights are protected, but evidence of infringement may be difficult to detect in some parts of the world.
- To detect patent infringement, competing products must be purchased and analyzed. Technical specifications, marketing materials, and product manuals must be examined. Reverse engineering of competing products may be required in some cases. Large corporations may be able to do this for key intellectual property in important countries, but systematic monitoring

of intellectual property rights is beyond the capabilities of most small to medium-size organizations. In those organizations, infringements in a given country will be detected by chance, if they are detected at all. [32]

- In the United States, the fair use doctrine permits limited reproduction of copyrighted material for research, parody, commentary, criticism, and news reporting. A fair use determination based on the purpose and character of the use, the nature of the copyrighted work, the amount and substantiality of use, and the impact on the copyrighted work's value as specified in 17 U.S.C. § 107. Because these factors can be difficult to interpret, some instances of fair use verge on infringement. [33]

- While most organizations purchase insurance to protect their most valuable physical property, a smaller percentage have insurance coverage for their intellectual property.

- An organization may not have fully considered the impact of a cloud service provider's terms of service on ownership and control of its content. In particular, the license granted to a cloud service provider may give it broad permission to use a customer's intellectual property for purposes that are described vaguely in the provider's terms of service.

Risk Response

Given variations in intellectual property laws and the difficulty of detecting infringement in every country where an organization's intellectual property rights might be violated, some measure of risk acceptance may be necessary in specific situations. Some organizations focus their enforcement initiatives on those countries where their intellectual property is most likely to be infringed on or where effective legal mechanisms support enforcement actions.

An organization can avoid intellectual property risks associated with cloud computing by declining to use cloud services, but that may not be possible for essential computing applications that are only available in a cloud environment. [34] Over the next several years, most organizations are likely to contract with cloud service providers for information storage, hosted computer applications, social media interactions, email management, and other purposes if they are not already doing so. Social media platforms, in particular, are an important component of many organizations' public relations and marketing strategies. Some measure of risk acceptance is consequently necessary where intellectual property is maintained on cloud platforms.

Because they forfeit or reduce the economic benefits of intellectual property protection, copyright alternatives are not viable risk avoidance options for most organizations. In some countries, the creator of a work can expressly relinquish copyright protection or simply ignore infringements, effectively allowing the work to enter the public domain, which is the ultimate fate of copyrighted works when the period of protection elapses. Proponents argue that this will eliminate significant transaction costs and infringement associated with intellectual property rights, but they recognize the limitations of this approach.[35] Open access, which is principally used for online publishing of scientific research and other scholarly work, eliminates most copyright restrictions along with subscription fees, site licenses, and pay-per-view charges.[36] As a compromise between the all-rights-reserved approach of copyright protection and unrestricted public domain access, a Creative Commons license provides a range of copyright alternatives that allow the creator of a work to waive certain restrictions on reproduction, distribution, performance, and adaptation, subject to specified terms and conditions.[37] The creator of a work might waive copyright restrictions for noncommercial use, for example, or waive copyright restrictions for all but derivative works.

Unlike copyright, intellectual property protection is not automatic for patents and industrial designs. To obtain protection, an invention or industrial design must be registered with national patent offices and evaluated by trained examiners. Public disclosure of the invention or design is an integral aspect of the application process. Infringement of a patent or industrial design can be avoided by keeping an invention or design a trade secret rather than filing an application for protection, but that approach might merely substitute misappropriation for infringement. Ownership risks associated with trade secrets are discussed elsewhere in this chapter.

As noted above, infringement litigation can be expensive for both the owner and the alleged violator of intellectual property rights. Legal costs associated with enforcement of an organization's intellectual property rights are excluded by most commercial general liability insurance policies. For transfer of ownership risks posed by infringement of intellectual property, abatement insurance, also known as enforcement insurance, will reimburse an organization's legal expenses to enforce a copyright, patent, or other intellectual property right, subject to policy limits and deductibles.[38] Intellectual property abatement insurance allows an owner of intellectual property to take aggressive action against infringement. Abatement coverage may also deter infringement by putting potential violators on notice that the owner of intellectual property intends to enforce its rights. If infringement litigation is initiated, the insured party's claims for legal expenses will only be covered if an enforcement action is successful. Policy premiums depend on the amount and type of intellectual property involved. An owner of intellectual property may limit coverage to specific patents, copyrights, or industrial designs that are likely to be infringed.[39] Some enforcement policies also provide coverage for loss of value resulting from legal claims against a patent, copyright, or other intellectual property. Depending on the policy, coverage may include representation that intellectual property rights involved in a merger or acquisition transaction are valid.

A risk mitigation strategy can combine insurance coverage for high-value intellectual property with acceptance for copyrights, patents, and industrial designs that are less likely to be infringed. To limit risk through more effective management and control of its information assets, an organization should have a comprehensive, up-to-date inventory of its intellectual property rights.[40] Sometimes described as an intellectual property catalog, the inventory serves as an authoritative reference source for essential information about each copyright, patent, industrial design, or other item in an organization's portfolio of intellectual property. Information to be included in the inventory includes but is not necessarily limited to:

- the type of intellectual property;
- the responsible organizational unit;
- the name of the author, inventor, or other creator;
- co-ownership agreements;
- the date the intellectual property was created or acquired;
- the method by which the intellectual property rights were obtained (created in-house, acquired through a merger, or ordered through a work-for-hire arrangement, for example);
- the current protection status;
- the patent number, copyright registration number, or other unique identifier;
- renewals, fee payments, or other actions necessary to maintain protection;
- the countries where protection applies;
- the starting and expiration dates for protection;
- the business value of the property;
- limitations on licensing, use, or distribution;
- an assessment of the property's vulnerability to infringement;
- information about past or ongoing litigation; and
- information about loans or other financial arrangement for which intellectual property serves as collateral.

An intellectual property inventory should be reviewed for correctness and completeness on a regular schedule or when events, such as changes in statutory or case law or an impending merger or acquisition, may impact the protection status, valuation, or other characteristics of an organization's intellectual property.

To further limit risk, an intellectual property audit can identify ownership issues and concerns that an organization needs to address.[41] Depending on its objectives, the audit may provide a comprehensive review of an organization's intellectual property rights or an in-depth assessment of specific copyrights or industrial property being evaluated for licensing, sale, transfer of rights, gaps in protection, or other purposes. In either case, an audit can assess the financial value of intellectual property and identify any risk exposure that must be addressed, including the risk of infringing another organization's intellectual property rights. An organization's intellectual property portfolio may be audited as part of due diligence for a merger, acquisition, joint venture, divestiture, bankruptcy filing, or business closure or for a financial transaction for which intellectual property will serve as collateral.

WORK FOR HIRE

The work-for-hire doctrine is a provision of copyright law that addresses the ownership of information created by an organization's employees or by others who perform work for the organization. As defined in 17 U.S.C. § 101, a "work made for hire" is a work prepared by an employee within the scope of his or her employment. Subject to express agreement by the parties involved, *work for hire* also denotes a work that is specially ordered or commissioned by an individual or group. To be considered a work for hire, a commissioned work must fall into one of the following categories: a contribution to a collective work, a part of a motion picture or other audiovisual work, a translation, a supplemental work, a compilation, an instructional text, a test, answer material for a test, or an atlas. Commissioned works are created by independent contractors rather than employees. In either case, the work-for-hire doctrine determines the ownership of information in the context of copyright law.

The work-for-hire doctrine is broadly applicable to any original information that is created by an organization's employees or by others on behalf of the organization as explained below. Examples of original business information include databases that pertain to customers, patients, or students; strategic, analytical, and investigative reports; spreadsheets that contain financial and statistical calculations; media releases, press kits, brochures, and other promotional materials; transcripts of speeches and presentations; drawings and technical specifications for facilities or products; content that an organization posts on its public web site; and business forms and standard contracts developed by an organization.[42]

Under the work-for-hire doctrine, the designated author of a work for copyright purposes is not the person who actually created the work:[43]

- In the most straightforward circumstances, the creator of a database, report, engineering drawing, technical specification, photograph, press release, email message, web page, or other information is a paid employee of an organization, and the information is clearly prepared in the course of the creator's assigned duties. If an application for copyright registration is filed for such information in the United States, the employer is named as the author of the work, unless a different authorial designation is agreed on in a contract or other written agreement.

- Where a database, document, or other business information is created by a consultant, contractor, or other nonemployee hired by an organization, ownership of the information is determined by the circumstances in which the work was created and the relationship between the parties involved. In the United States, the common law of agency determines the relationship between an agent (a consultant or contractor, for example) and a principal (the organization that hires the consultant or contractor).[44] An agent agrees to perform work for a principal, subject to the principal's control. In such cases, the personal interests of the agent are secondary to the principal's interests. A principal-agent relationship exists between an organization and a consultant or contractor if the organization that commissioned a database, report, engineering drawing, or other information specifies how the information will be created, controls the creator's schedule in producing the work, determines the method of payment and tax treatment for the payment, determines whether the consultant or contractor receives employee benefits, and is able to assign further projects to the consultant or contractor beyond the work in question.[45]

- An organization's ownership of specific information may be challenged if some or all of these factors are absent or subject to interpretation or dispute. This is the case with some consulting engagements and contractor relationships. Confusion, legal complications, and risk are also possible where information is created by outsourced employees, leased employees, temporary employees, part-time employees, paid interns, and other contingent workers.[46]

- Application of the work-for-hire doctrine to ownership of information created by certain types of employees—such as college professors, artists-in-residence, and certain clergy—is subject to dispute.[47] In charities, religious groups, and other not-for-profit organizations, information may be created by unpaid board members, volunteers, or student interns who are neither employees nor independent contractors.

Legislative treatment of work for hire varies from country to country.[48] The United States, the United Kingdom, Ireland, the Netherlands, Luxembourg, Japan, Australia, and some other countries have adopted pro-employer ownership rules, subject to some exceptions. In some countries, however, the work-for-hire doctrine is either nonexistent or limited in scope. In Germany, Italy, Belgium, Denmark, Spain, Portugal, and Greece, for example, the employee or independent contractor who created a work is considered its author and owner unless copyright is transferred by written agreement to the employer or organization that commissioned the work. France has adopted the work-for-hire doctrine for work performed by employees but not by independent contractors.

Where an organization operates in multiple countries, national copyright laws may constrain the organization's ability to use data or documents prepared by employees, consultants, or contractors. In particular, some copyright laws prohibit editing, redacting, abridging, or other modification of data or documents without the author's permission. Even where a contractual provision acknowledges that a given work is made for hire, the author may retain a moral right to protect the integrity of the work by prohibiting its modification by others, including the organization that paid for its creation. [49] As discussed in a preceding section, copyright laws confer both economic rights and moral rights. The latter protect the integrity of a work from unauthorized alteration, distortion, or mutilation.

As a legal concept, the work-for-hire doctrine addresses ownership of information in the context of copyright, but it may have implications for other situations, such as ownership of trade secrets or other confidential information that may come up during work performed by an independent contractor but that are unrelated to that work. [50] The work-for-hire doctrine does not apply to patents. Under US patent law, an employer has no rights to an employee's invention except through a written assignment or where the employee was specifically hired to create an invention. [51] In practice, however, these exceptions are customary. If neither exception applies, an employer may still acquire a limited "shop right" to use a patent without payment to the inventor. [52]

Vulnerability Assessment

The work-for-hire doctrine poses risks for ownership of information in every organization that has employees or that commissions the creation of data or documents by independent contractors. The following vulnerabilities increase an organization's risks:

- An organization may not be aware of or correctly interpret work for hire rules, or the absence of such rules, in every country where it operates or commissions the creation of information by independent contractors. An organization's compliance officer or legal department is typically responsible for identifying and interpreting laws and regulations that affect specific business operations, but some organizations do not have in-house compliance expertise. Even for those that do, it can be difficult to keep informed about all applicable legal and regulatory requirements, especially in multinational and transnational organizations that operate in multiple political jurisdictions.

- In the United States, an employer's ownership of information created by an employee in the course of assigned duties is automatic under the work-for-hire doctrine, but that is not the case in some other countries. An organization may not have policies or clauses in employment contracts that clearly assert its ownership rights for information created by employees in every location where the organization operates.

- Consultants, contractors, temporary workers supplied by an employment agency, and volunteers may not be subject to written agreements that address ownership and assignment of copyrights for information they create in the course of their work. In the absence of such an agreement, a consultant, contractor, or other nonemployee may claim entitlement to the information. This risk is greatest where commissioned work performed by a consultant or contractor does not fall into one of the previously listed categories specified in 17 U.S.C. § 101. In such situations, ownership of the commissioned work is not determined by the work-for-hire doctrine.

- Universities, museums, research libraries, and other academic and cultural institutions may not have policies that address the ownership of information created by professors, visiting professors, guest lecturers, curators, artists in residence, composers in residence, writers in residence, and other creative and scholarly workers in the context of the work-for-hire doctrine. Churches, synagogues, and other religious institutions may not have policies that address ownership of sermons, prayers, musical compositions, or other devotional works that clergy or others may prepare for religious services.

Risk Response

Risk acceptance through forfeiture of ownership claims for information produced by an organization's employees or independent contractors is not an advisable mitigation option for issues and concerns related to the work-for-hire doctrine. Risk transfer is possible, but it is not an optimal mitigation strategy. A commercial general liability policy may provide insurance coverage for some costs related to copyright litigation, but covered claims typically relate to infringement of copyright protection rather than to ownership disputes based on the work-for-hire doctrine.

To limit or avoid risks associated with the work-for-hire doctrine, a mitigation strategy should be based on written agreements and policies that affirm an organization's ownership of information created by employees, independent contractors, and others. At a minimum, an organization should take the following steps to address the vulnerabilities discussed in the preceding section:

- An organization should have a written policy that establishes itself as the owner of any information that it creates, commissions, receives, or maintains in relation to its mission, functions, operations, or activities. The policy should state that no employee has any personal or property right to or property interest in such information even though he or she may be named as the creator, recipient, or custodian of them. The ownership policy should encompass information in all formats and media.
- Employees should be clearly told at the time they are hired that any data, documents, or other information they create in the course of their assigned duties will be considered work for hire and that all intellectual property rights to the information will be vested in the employer. All employment contracts should include a clause to that effect, which will be acknowledged in writing by the employee.
- In countries that do not recognize the work-for-hire doctrine, employment contracts should include a clause stating that any data, documents, or other information created by employees in the course of their assigned duties will be considered the employer's property and that intellectual property rights will be vested in the employer to the extent permitted by law.
- Contracts and agreements with independent contractors should include a clause stating that any data, documents, or other information created as deliverables under the contract or agreement are the property of the organization that commissioned the work. The clause should further state that all intellectual property rights to the deliverables are vested in the organization that commissioned the work, excluding any information that is properly considered the intellectual property of the independent contractor or another party. The independent contractor must acknowledge these clauses in writing before beginning the commissioned work.
- Where deliverables created by independent contractors contain information that is properly considered the independent contractor's intellectual property, contracts and agreements should include a clause that grants the organization that commissioned the work a perpetual, royalty-free license to use such information in connection with the deliverables. Where deliverables created by an independent contractor contain information that is protected by intellectual property rights, contracts and agreements should include a clause that requires the independent contractor to indemnify the organization that commissioned the deliverable against any litigation or other legal actions alleging infringement of copyright, misappropriation of trade secrets, or unauthorized use of proprietary information.
- Before they begin work, volunteers, student interns, and other unpaid workers should be clearly told that any data, documents, or other information they create in the course of their assigned duties will be the property of the organization for which the work is performed. Volunteers, student

interns, and other unpaid workers should be asked to sign a statement that relinquishes any claim to intellectual property rights for such information.

• Where warranted, an organization should have a policy that specifies exceptions to the work-for-hire doctrine for designated categories of employees and types of information. A university, for example, may exempt academic writings of professors, even though they are required to publish scholarly work as a condition of tenure and promotion. Similarly, a church or synagogue may exempt sermons, prayers, or other devotional material written by clergy, even though they may be expected to present such material at religious services as a condition of employment. Some scientific organizations may allow researchers to work on their own projects for a specified number of hours per week with the understanding that such projects are exempt from the work-for-hire doctrine.

TRADE SECRETS

Broadly defined, a trade secret is nonpublic intellectual property that gives an organization a competitive advantage or another present or future economic benefit because it involves information that is not generally known.[53] Examples of trade secrets include unpatented inventions, product formulations, undisclosed industrial designs, proprietary research methods or manufacturing processes, computer code, technical data, and proprietary sales or distribution methods. Trade secrets may also include commercial information, such as customer lists, proprietary information about customer requirements, pricing information, marketing plans, and confidential supplier agreements.[54] Even information gained through unsuccessful initiatives, such as a failed scientific experiment or an unfavorable outcome of a market test for a new product, can be considered a trade secret if knowledge of the negative results would be advantageous to a competitor.

To be considered a trade secret, information must have commercial value, cannot be readily ascertainable, and must be protected by reasonable security measures to prevent unauthorized access. Examples of reasonable security include locked doors, locked file rooms, password protection, network encryption, and non-disclosure agreements. A trade secrets is usually recorded on some tangible medium, but this not a requirement. Trade secrets are sometimes equated with "know-how," which is practical knowledge that a person acquires through experience. This is the case in the European Union, where know-how is considered intellectual property provided that it is secret, substantial, and identifiable as such.[55] In other countries, know-how is widely recognized as an economic asset, but it is not necessarily protected by intellectual property rights. As a complicating factor, the line between knowledge acquired during employment and knowledge acquired through education or prior work experience is not always clear.

A previous chapter discussed threats and consequences associated with accidental or intentional collection of trade secrets, which are protected by intellectual property laws.[56] This chapter deals with threats to ownership of trade secrets. Most authorities include trade secrets in the industrial property category of intellectual property.[57] Like patents, industrial designs, trademarks, and geographical indications, trade secrets have potential commercial value, but they differ from other forms of industrial property in one important respect: their property rights are not protected by registration, which requires public disclosure of information about the industrial property in return for the exclusive right to exploit the property for a prescribed period of time. By contrast, trade secret protection is not time-limited, but protection ends when a secret is exposed.

Unlike other forms of industrial property, which are subject to a formal registration and approval process, protection of trade secrets is automatic and takes effect immediately. The owner of a trade secret can stop others from revealing, using, or otherwise misappropriating it, but ownership of a secret is threatened by the following actions or events, which terminate an organization's intellectual property rights in the secret:

- A trade secret may be inadvertently disclosed by someone with knowledge of it. Proprietary information may be imprudently discussed at a meeting, mistakenly distributed with nonconfidential documents, unintentionally left on a desktop, displayed on a computer screen in open view, or revealed in an email that is sent to the wrong recipient. The trade secret may be inadvertently disclosed by an employee, supplier, contractor, intern, or another party who obtained knowledge of the secret in the course of their work for the secret's owner. A trade secret may also be disclosed during pre-trial discovery for legal proceedings.[58] Following such inadvertent disclosure, the trade secret may be shared with others.
- A trade secret may be disclosed by a current or former employee, supplier, contractor, or intern who acquired knowledge of the secret while employed by the secret's owner. Disclosure may occur during a job interview or in the course of performing work for a new employer, even if a non-disclosure agreement is in effect. There is a high risk of this occurring. According to the legal doctrine of "inevitable disclosure," a former employee who takes a job with a competitor will eventually reveal a former employer's trade secrets because the new job will require it.[59] In a widely cited case, a soft drink company asserted that a former employee familiar with the company's sports drinks "cannot help but rely on" the company's trade secrets when making decisions about competing products developed by his new employer. The court agreed that the defendant would require

"an uncanny ability to compartmentalize information" in order to avoid disclosure of his former employer's trade secrets.[60]

- A trade secret may be stolen by bribing, coercing, or deceiving someone with knowledge of the secret or by breaching the electronic or physical security measures that protect the secret from disclosure. As previously discussed in chapter 1, data or documents that contain trade secrets may be copied, memorized, and then reproduced at a later time, or removed outright from their original location by an unauthorized person.[61] Mobile devices that contain trade secrets may be stolen. A trade secret may be stolen directly from its owner or obtained from a third party who acquired it legally or illegally. The thief may be an employee, supplier, contractor, or intern; an agent of a foreign government or a competitor; or a computer hacker or other external party who may be assisted by an insider.[62] Studies confirm that the guilty party is usually an employee, a business partner, or someone else the trade secret owner knows.[63] In any case, the trade secret ends up in the possession of someone who is not authorized to have it.

- If a trade secret is stored on a cloud platform, the cloud service provider may disclose it in response to a subpoena, court order, or warrant from a government agency, law enforcement, or civil litigant.[64] According to their terms of service, some cloud providers will notify the customer when this occurs, but an organization will not have the opportunity to review the content for relevance, privilege, and trade secret status as it would for information stored on its own computers. To prevent this from occurring, an organization can delete cloud content that contains a trade secret, but the content may not be removed from the cloud platform immediately. Delays typically range from 30 to 180 days, during which time trade secrets may be exposed to disclosure in response to a legal process or other events.[65] Cloud service providers may retain backup copies of deleted content for an even longer period of time.[66]

- A trade secret may be discovered by lawful means. A product, computer program, chemical formula, or other object based on a trade secret may be reverse-engineered—that is, deconstructed and analyzed to determine how it was created or how it works—by someone who purchases the object in the open market. Alternatively, a product or other innovation based on a trade secret may be independently invented by someone without knowledge of the secret. The innovation may be subsequently patented by the new inventor, which will confer intellectual property rights on the patent holder and stop the original inventor from using the trade secret. It is also possible that two organizations may simultaneously possess the same trade secret, which they developed independently, but presumably they would not know it unless one of them discloses the secret.

Like other forms of intellectual property, trade secrets are intangible assets with anticipated benefits. A 2010 survey of senior-level decision-makers estimated that trade secrets account for two-thirds of the value of an organization's intellectual property portfolio, but they account for more than 70 percent of value in organizations that provide professional, scientific, and technical services.[67] Estimates of the value of stolen trade secrets range from less than $5 million to more than $26 million.[68]

Loss of trade secrets through disclosure can disrupt an organization's strategic plans, degrade its competitive position, damage its reputation, and reduce its market share, revenue, and profits. These consequences are reflected in damage awards for misappropriation of trade secrets.[69] In for-profit entities, loss of trade secrets can have a negative impact on a company's market valuation. Misappropriation is likely to be closely scrutinized when an organization seeks financing based on trade secrets as collateral, during negotiations for joint ventures and strategic alliances, and as part of due diligence for mergers and acquisitions.

Vulnerability Assessment

Confirming the threats discussed in the preceding section, litigation related to alleged misappropriation of trade secrets has increased significantly in recent years.[70] The following vulnerabilities increase the risk of unauthorized disclosure that will terminate an organization's intellectual property rights to a trade secret:

- An organization may not have a comprehensive inventory or audit of its trade secrets or an up-to-date review and assessment of their protection status.
- Unlike patents and industrial designs, which have a limited threat window defined by the period of protection, the exposure period for threats to ownership of trade secrets is indefinite.
- Extraterritorial enforcement of trade secret protection is complicated. An organization must be familiar with applicable legal requirements in every country where it does business. Large multinational and transnational entities will typically have in-house legal expertise supplemented by local external counsel, but small to medium-size enterprises may not be aware of all applicable laws and regulations.
- Employees may not understand trade secret concepts and may not know which information in their custody or under their supervisory control is considered a trade secret. In particular, employees may be unaware of the trade secret status of customer lists, supplier lists, price lists, and other nontechnical information that supports business transactions rather than research and product development.

- Business partners, contractors, suppliers, and others who gain knowledge of an organization's trade secret may not limit access to the secret by their own employees or properly inform their employees about restrictions on disclosure of the secret.
- Trade secrets may not be reasonably protected by electronic or physical security measures. Access to customer lists, supplier information, and other electronic data and documents that contain trade secrets may not be strictly limited on a need-to-know basis. Database records and digital documents that contain trade secrets may be displayed on computer screens in open view. Paper records that contain trade secrets may not be stored in locked cabinets or in secure file rooms with tightly controlled access. Business plans, technical specifications, research reports, and other paper documents that contain trade secrets may be exposed on employees' desks or in unsupervised work areas.
- Non-disclosure agreements may not be signed by all employees, contractors, suppliers, business partners, or others who may gain knowledge of an organization's trade secrets. Even if they are, a non-disclosure agreement provides imperfect protection against disclosure.[71] To be legally acceptable, a non-disclosure agreement must not be more restrictive than reasonably necessary; it must not prevent an employee or other party from using knowledge gained through experience; and it must expire after a specified period of time.[72] Compliance with disclosure restrictions can be difficult to monitor.
- Employees, contractors, suppliers, business partners, and others who sign non-disclosure agreements may not fully understand the restrictions imposed on them. Long-term employees who signed a non-disclosure agreement along with many other forms at the time they were hired may not recall doing so.
- An organization cannot prevent loss of ownership of a trade secret through reverse-engineering or independent invention of a product that is based on the secret.

Risk Response

Some of the mitigation actions discussed in the preceding section on intellectual property rights are relevant for trade secrets; but unlike patents and industrial designs, which an organization must disclose as part of the protection process, a trade secret is directly threatened by disclosure, which terminates the owner's intellectual property rights. Given the many opportunities for accidental or intentional disclosure of a trade secret by former employees, contractors, suppliers, and others, combined with the possibility of independent invention or disclosure through reverse engineering, some measure of risk acceptance is necessary.

The risk of independent invention can be eliminated by seeking patent protection for a trade secret that involves an invention or industrial design, but patent awards impose a time limit on intellectual property rights that an organization may not consider acceptable.[73] Seeking patent protection for a trade secret will not eliminate violation of an organization's intellectual property rights. It merely substitutes infringement for misappropriation as a cause for legal action. As a further limitation, patent protection is not possible for customer lists, supplier lists, strategic plans, and other trade secrets that are not inventions or may not even be novel.

As with other forms of intellectual property, risk transfer is a viable mitigation option for misappropriation of trade secrets. As discussed above, abatement insurance, also known as enforcement insurance, allows an organization to take aggressive action against alleged violation of intellectual property rights. Insurance coverage may also deter misappropriation by putting potential violators on notice that the owner of a trade secret intends to enforce its intellectual property rights. Abatement insurance will reimburse a trade secret owner's civil litigation expenses, subject to policy limits and deductibles, but claims for legal expenses are only covered if an enforcement action is successful.

To limit risk, an organization should consider the following actions to protect its ownership of trade secrets:

- An organization must have clear written policies and procedures regarding protection of trade secrets. These policies and procedures must be made available by a prominent and convenient method to all employees, contractors, suppliers, business partners, or others who may gain knowledge of a trade secret during the course of their work. The policies and procedures should be reflected in the organization's code of conduct and incorporated into the onboarding process for new employees, contractors, and suppliers.
- As discussed in a preceding section, an organization should have a comprehensive, up-to-date inventory of its intellectual property, including trade secrets. The inventory should be reviewed for correctness and completeness on a regular schedule or when events, such as changes in statutory or case law or an impending merger or acquisition, may impact the protection status, valuation, or other characteristics of trade secrets. To further limit risk, periodic audits of trade secrets can confirm their validity and identify ownership issues that an organization needs to address.
- Department managers should be responsible for ensuring that their employees understand protection requirements for trade secrets contained in data or documents in their custody.
- Non-disclosure agreements must be signed by all employees, contractors, suppliers, business partners, and others who may gain knowledge of a

trade secret by direct means or through second-hand communication about the secret. Non-disclosure agreements should be renewed annually or at other periodic intervals.

- Data or documents that contain trade secrets should be clearly identified and marked as proprietary or confidential. Access must be limited to employees, contractors, suppliers, or others who have a verifiable need to know a trade secret in order to perform specific work for the secret's owner.
- Access to data or documents that contain trade secrets must be controlled and monitored by electronic and physical security measures, such as password protection, encryption, locked cabinets, locked filing areas, sign-in sheets, and log-in lists. In legal actions involving alleged misappropriation, courts require implementation of reasonable security precautions that prevent unauthorized access to and affirm the value of an organization's trade secrets. The security measures must be more restrictive than those for nonsecret information.[74] An organization must be able to demonstrate that affirmative security measures were actually in place at the time a trade secret was misappropriated. Security measures must be audited for effectiveness and compliance.
- Printing, copying, or other reproduction or distribution of data or documents that contain trade secrets must be strictly limited to the minimum number of copies needed for a purpose that is approved by the owner of the secret. The copies should be destroyed after that purpose is fulfilled.
- Employees, contractors, suppliers, business partners, and others should be strongly cautioned against discussing trade secrets in meetings, in speaking engagements, at trade shows, in written publications, or in other public forums.
- Departing employees, contractors, suppliers, and others who may have gained knowledge of an organization's trade secrets must be instructed to delete all confidential or proprietary data or documents from their personally owned computers or mobile devices and return any confidential or proprietary paper records in their possession, including records that employees may maintain in their home offices.[75] Non-disclosure obligations should be reviewed in exit interviews with departing employees and in close-out meetings with contractors, suppliers, and business partners.

DATA PORTABILITY

Data portability is the ability to easily transfer information from one computer system or service to another computer system or service without being required to reenter the data. The transfer might be based on a commonly used data format or on simple, straightforward data transformation using commonly available conversion tools.[76] Broadly defined, data portability can involve any type of data that is transferred between computer systems. In the most common scenarios, data is transferred from a computer system or service to its replacement or from one computer system to another for further processing. Such transfers are initiated for business purposes by the organization that maintains the data. Unless the data is being sold, the transferring organization's ownership and control of the data are not threatened.

That is not necessarily the case where personal data is involved. In some countries, portability of personal information is regulated by national and regional laws. The data transfer process is initiated by the data subject rather than by the data controller—that is, the organization that maintains the data. The data controller must give the data subject a copy of the requested information in an agreed-upon format. The data subject takes possession and ownership of that copy for his or her own purposes, which may include transferring all or part of the data to another party for processing or storage. In limited circumstances, continued ownership of the requested information by the data controller may be affected after the request is fulfilled.

Depending on the circumstances, portability of personal information may be mandated by privacy legislation, by computer protection laws, or by healthcare regulations:

- In the European Union, the right to data portability is an aspect of the broader right to personal privacy and data protection. According to Article 20 of the General Data Protection Regulation, which applies in EU member states, a data subject "shall have the right to receive personal data concerning him or her." According to GDPR Recital 68, this right is designed to strengthen the data subject's "control over his or her own data," the implication being that data subjects own the personal information that organizations maintain about them.[77] Upon request, personal information must be provided to the data subject in a structured, commonly used machine-readable format. A data portability request must be fulfilled "without undue delay," within one month or not more than three months in complex cases. Where feasible, the data subject has the right to request transmission of the data directly to another organization. The right to data portability has significant restrictions. It is limited to data that the organization obtained from the data subject with his or her consent or to data that is necessary for performance of a contract. It does not include anonymized data; personal data that an organization obtains by other means, such as observation, calculation, or analysis; or data that includes information about other data subjects whose rights may be affected by the transfer. As a further limitation, data portability is limited to computer-processible information. Paper records that contain personal information about a data subject are excluded. A data subject takes ownership of personal information provided under the right to data portability, but the ownership rights of the organization that provides the data are only affected if the data subject exercises the right to be forgotten, which allows a data subject to request the destruction of his or her personal information when it is no longer needed for the purpose for which it was originally collected. In that case, the organization must erase the data in its possession when the transfer is completed.

- In some countries, the right to data portability is based on consumer-protection laws. Its purpose is to thwart monopolization of personal data by companies that offer consumer products and services. In the United Kingdom, for example, the Midata initiative gives consumers access to data about their account transactions in a standard file format. A consumer can send the transaction data to a comparison provider for competitive analysis and recommendations regarding alternative service providers. The initiative targets energy companies, banks, insurance companies, credit card issuers, mobile phone services, and other service suppliers that have frequent interactions with consumers.[78] In the United States, the California Consumer Protection Act (Cal. Civ. Code §§ 1798.100 and 1798.130) requires business to provide consumers with their personal information for the preceding twelve-month period in a readily usable format that can be transmitted to an alternative service supplier. In Australia, amendments to the Competition and Consumer Act 2010 introduces a "consumer data right" that enables consumers to obtain information about themselves from banks, energy companies, and other designated sectors of the Australian economy for use as they see fit.[79] The right to data portability under consumer laws does not affect a regulated organization's ownership of the information.

- The GDPR's data portability provisions apply to patient information maintained by physicians, hospitals, and other healthcare providers in EU member states.[80] As with nonmedical information, the right to data portability is limited to personal data that is obtained from the data subject, either directly or indirectly through a medical device, such as a blood pressure monitor. The right to data portability does not encompass diagnoses, treatment plans, physicians' notes, or other data that is based on observation or analysis. In the United States, data portability requirements for protected health information are specified in the Health Insurance Portability and Accountability Act, which gives patients access to their medical records maintained by HIPAA-covered entities, subject to limited exclusions.[81] According to the HIPAA Privacy Rule (45 C.F.R. § 164.524), a HIPAA-covered entity must provide the information in the form and format requested by the data subject if it is readily producible in that form and format. Otherwise, the information must be provided in paper form or in another form agreed to by the covered entity and the data subject.[82] The right to data portability under the HIPAA Privacy Rule does not affect ownership of patient data by covered entities, which must retain their copies of medical records for minimum time periods specified by state laws.[83]

Failure to comply with data portability requirements exposes an organization to fines and penalties. Civil penalties for violations of the HIPAA Privacy Rule range from $100 to $50,000 depending on the severity and willfulness of the violation. GDPR violations are subject to administrative fines levied by data protection authorities in EU member states. As specified in GDPR Articles 83 and 84 and Recitals 148 through 152, the amounts depend on the nature, gravity, willfulness, and duration of the infringement. Maximum penalties can approach €20 million for large-scale violations. Fines for violations of the California Consumer Protection Act range from $2,500 per incident for unintentional violations or $7,500 per incident for willful noncompliance.

Vulnerability Assessment

The following vulnerabilities contribute to risks associated with data portability requirements specified in laws and regulations:

- An organization may not be aware of its data portability compliance obligations in every jurisdiction where it maintains personal data. An organization's compliance officer or legal department is typically responsible for identifying laws and regulations that affect specific business operations, but some organizations do not have in-house compliance expertise.
- An organization may not correctly interpret data portability requirements. In particular, the specific personal information to be included in or excluded from a data portability request may be difficult to determine. This may result in an incomplete response or one that violates the privacy rights of other data subjects who may be identified in documents or depicted in photographs that appear to come within the scope of a data portability request. Compliance may be impeded by comingling and possible confusion of information obtained from a data subject, which is subject to data portability requirements, with information derived from observation, calculation, or inference, which is exempt.
- An organization's business processes and practices may not be conducive to fulfillment of data portability requests. The requested data may not be maintained in a single, easily accessible repository. It may be managed by multiple applications, saved in multiple formats, recorded in multiple languages, and scattered in multiple locations. Small and medium-size organizations may have difficulty providing data in a format requested by a data

subject. Format conversions may introduce errors that were not present in the original data sources.[84]

- When faced with a large number of data portability requests, an organization may not have sufficient staff or technical resources in place to respond within the time period prescribed by law.[85]
- An organization's response to a data portability request may violate other laws by inadvertently disclosing a trade secret or infringing another party's intellectual property rights. Personal information about a data subject may be included in a proprietary list of customers or in a copyrighted document or photograph. Upon receipt of this information, the data subject may transfer it to a different data controller for processing, which will further expose it to unauthorized access and use. These issues are not addressed in laws that provide a right to data portability. It is not clear that the right to data portability takes precedence over trade secret protection or intellectual property law.

Risk Response

A legal right to data portability is a relatively new concept, and fulfillment of data portability requests can be a burdensome addition to an organization's existing operations. Noncompliance can have significant adverse consequences, but risk mitigation options are limited:

- Risk acceptance based on a conscious business decision not to comply fully with data regulatory requirements exposes an organization to costly penalties and possible civil litigation.
- Complete risk avoidance is only possible if collection and maintenance of personal data ceases, which is not a realistic mitigation strategy where such data is critical to an organization's mission or where collection is mandated by laws or regulations. A bank is required by law to collect personal data about account holders. A health care provider cannot eliminate collection of personal data about patients. A profession association cannot eliminate collection of personal data about members. As a form of risk avoidance, an organization could dispose of personal data as soon as legal and operational retention requirements are satisfied. If personal data has continuing research value, it should be anonymized at the earliest opportunity. As noted above, anonymized data is not subject to portability requests.
- Risk transfer through insurance is generally not an option for criminal violations. Most insurance policies exclude coverage for civil fines and penalties resulting from illegal activity, although insurance coverage may be available for legal fees and other costs associated with government investigations and litigation.

- To limit the risk of noncompliance with data portability requirements, an appropriately staffed, properly supervised organizational unit must be responsible for receiving, evaluating, and fulfilling data portability requests. Procedures must be established to respond to requests within prescribed time limits. Staff assigned to the data portability initiative must be trained to perform the work correctly and completely. Knowledgeable persons must be consulted when necessary to identify personal data that was obtained through observation or inference rather than directly from the data subject who submitted the portability request. All responses to data portability requests must be reviewed carefully to confirm that trade secrets are not disclosed, intellectual property rights are not infringed, and the privacy rights of third parties are not violated. Staff should be given a due-diligence checklist or similar quality-control mechanism to ensure that all required tasks have been properly completed. Information technology involvement is necessary to identify databases and other digital repositories that contain the requested data and ensure that it is delivered to the data subject or to a designated third party in a compliant format.

SUMMARY OF MAJOR POINTS

- For some organizations, intellectual property is more valuable than real property, physical plant, or equipment, but an organization's ownership of copyrights, patents, industrial designs, and other intellectual property may be threatened by challenges or unauthorized use by competitors, collaborators, or other parties. Such threats can degrade an organization's financial performance, damage its reputation, and harm its competitive position.
- Infringement of intellectual property rights is pervasive and difficult to detect. Litigation to enforce intellectual property rights can be expensive for both the owner and the alleged infringer.
- A risk mitigation strategy can combine insurance coverage for high-value intellectual property with risk acceptance for copyrights, patents, and industrial designs that are less likely to be infringed. An organization can take additional actions to limit risk, including inventories and audits of intellectual property to assess its financial value and risk exposure.
- To limit or avoid risks associated with the work-for-hire doctrine, a mitigation strategy should be based on written agreements and policies that affirm an organization's ownership of information produced by employees, independent contractors, and others.
- Loss of trade secrets through disclosure can disrupt an organization's strategic plans, degrade its competitive position, damage its reputation, and reduce its market share, revenue, and profits. Unlike patents and in-

dustrial designs, which an organization must disclose as part of the protection process, a trade secret is directly threatened by disclosure. The owner's intellectual property rights terminate when a trade secret becomes generally known.

- Given the many opportunities for accidental or intentional disclosure of a trade secret by former employees, contractors, suppliers, and others, combined with the possibility of independent invention or disclosure through reverse engineering, some measure of risk acceptance is necessary. Enforcement insurance allows an organization to take aggressive action against alleged misappropriation of trade secrets.

- Non-disclosure agreements must be signed by all employees, contractors, suppliers, business partners, and others who may gain knowledge of a trade secret by direct means or through second-hand communication about the secret.

- Data portability may be mandated by privacy legislation, by computer-protection laws, or by health care regulations. Such laws enable data subjects to take possession and ownership of their personal information for their own purposes, which may include transferring all or part of the data to another party for processing or storage. Failure to comply with data portability requirements exposes an organization to fines and penalties.

NOTES

1. A. Bell and G. Parchomovsky, "A Theory of Property," *Cornell Law Review* 90, no. 3 (2005): 531–616, https://pdfs.semanticscholar.org/6136/58614e15c367af85dee0 f4d292a87e5eb454.pdf; B. Bouckaert, "What Is Property," *Harvard Journal of Law and Public Policy* 13, no. 2 (1990): 775–816, https://heinonline.org/HOL/Landing-Page?handle=hein.journals/hjlpp13&div=49&id=&page=.

2. *What Is Intellectual Property, WIPO Publication NO. 450(E)* (Geneva: World Property Organization, 2004), www.wipo.int/edocs/pubdocs/en/intproperty/450/wipo_pub_450.pdf; *WIPO Intellectual Property Handbook: Policy, Law and Use, WIPO Publication No. 489(E)*, (Geneva: World Property Organization, 2004), www.wipo.int/edocs/pubdocs/en/ wipo_pub_489.pdf. As defined in ISO /IEC 21000-19:2010, *Information Technology—Multimedia Framework (MPEG-21)—Part 19: Media Value Chain Ontology*, intellectual property is "any identifiable product of the mind attributable to any person(s) or one or more legal entities that can be represented or communicated physically and protectable by copyright of similar laws." According to ISO/IEC/IEEE 24765:2017, *Systems and Software Engineering Vocabulary*, intellectual property is the "output of creative thought process that has some intellectual or informational value." According to ISO/IEC/IEEE 26511, ISO/DIS 56000, *Innovation Management—Fundamentals and Vocabulary* defines *intellectual property* as the "results of intellectual, industrial, or creative activities that are eligible for protection by law."

3. www.un.org/en/universal-declaration-human-rights. Discussions of the rights and benefits of intellectual property include P. Drahos, *A Philosophy of Intellectual Property* (Acton, Australia: ANU eText, Australian National University, 2016), https://press-files.anu.edu.au/ downloads/press/n1902/pdf/book.pdf; P. Drahos, *A Philosophy of Intellectual Property* (Acton, Australia: ANU eText, Australian National University, 2016), https://press-files.anu.edu.au/ downloads/press/n1902/pdf/book.pdf; J. Hughes, "The Philosophy of Intellectual Property," *Georgetown Law Journal* 77, no. 2 (1988): 330–50, https://heinonline.org/HOL/Landing-Page?handle=hein.journals/glj77&div=19&id=&page=; H. Smith, "Intellectual Property as

Property: Delineating Entitlements in Information," *Yale Law Journal* 117, part 87 (2007): 1742–1822, https://digitalcommons.law.yale.edu/cgi/viewcontent.cgi?referer=www.google .com/&httpsredir=1&article=4048&context=fss_papers; R. Posner, "Intellectual Property: The Law and Economics Approach," *Journal of Economic Perspectives* 19, no. 2 (2005): 57–73, http://doi.org/10.1257/0895330054048704; S. Besen and L. Raskind, "An Introduction to the Law and Economics of Intellectual Property," *Journal of Economic Perspectives* 5, no. 1 (1991): 3–27, www.jstor.org/stable/1942699; M. Carroll, "One Size Does Not Fit All: A Framework for Tailoring Intellectual Property Rights," *Ohio State Law Journal* 70, no. 6 (2009): 1361–434, https://digitalcommons.wcl.american.edu/cgi/viewcontent.cgi?referer=& httpsredir=1&article=1044&context=facsch_lawrev.

4. See R. Schechter and J. Thomas, *Intellectual Property: The Law of Copyrights, Patents and Trademarks* (St. Paul, MN: West Academic Publishing, 2003), especially 1–5.

5. Copyright protection also extends to "related rights," which protect the rights of performers and producers of a creative work independent of the author's rights. See G. Bodenhausen, "Protection of 'Neighboring Rights,'" *Law and Contemporary Problems* 19, no. 2 (1954): 156–71, www.jstor.org/stable/1190485; H. Jehoram, "The Nature of Neighboring Rights of Performing Artists, Phonogram Producers and Broadcasting Organizations," *Columbia-VLA Journal of Law & the Arts* 15, no. 1 (1991): 75–92, https://heinonline.org/HOL/Landing-Page?handle=hein.journals/cjla15&div=18&id=&page=; R. Towse, "The Singer or the Song? Developments in Performers' Rights from the Perspective of a Cultural Economist," *Review of Law and Economics* 3, no. 3 (2007): 745–66, https://doi.org/10.2202/1555-5879.1158. In member states of the European Union, directive 96/9/EC of 11 March 1996, *On the Legal Protection of Databases*, extends copyright protection to databases created by persons or organizations. https://eur-lex.europa.eu/legal-content/EN/TXT/?uri=celex%3A31996L0009.

6. The *Convention Establishing the World Intellectual Property Organization* (the WIPO Convention), which took effect in 1970, lists the following types of intellectual property as protected by intellectual property rights: "literary, artistic and scientific works, performances of performing artists, phonograms and broadcasts, inventions in all fields of human endeavor, scientific discoveries, industrial designs, trademarks, service marks, and commercial names and designations, protection against unfair competition, and all other rights resulting from intellectual activity in the industrial, scientific, literary or artistic fields." https://wipolex.wipo.int/en/text/283854.

7. See *Understanding Industrial Property, Second Edition, WIPO Publication No. 895E* (Geneva: World Intellectual Property Organization, 2016), www.wipo.int/edocs/pubdocs/en/ wipo_pub_895_2016.pdf.

8. A. von Muhlendahl and D. Stauder, "Territorial Intellectual Property Rights in a Global Economy—Transit and Other 'Free Zones,'" in *Patents and Technological Progress in a Globalized World: MPI Studies on Intellectual Property, Competition and Tax Law, Vol. 6*, ed. W. Pyrmont et al. (Berlin: Springer, 2009), 653–73, https://doi.org/10.1007/978-3-540-88743-0_46; A. Peukert, "Territoriality and Extra-Territoriality in Intellectual Property Law," in *Beyond Territoriality: Transnational Legal Authority in an Age of Globalization*, ed. G. Handl et al. (Leiden: Martinus Nijhoff, 2012), 189–228, https://doi.org/10.1163/9789004227095; C. Bradley, "Territorial Intellectual Property Rights in an Age of Globalism," *Virginia Journal of International Law* 37, no. 3 (1997): 504–85, https://scholarship.law.duke.edu/cgi/viewcontent.cgi?article=1982&context=faculty_scholarship; T. Cook, "Territoriality and Jurisdiction in EU IP Law," *Journal of Intellectual Property Rights* 19, no. 4 (2014): 293–97, http:// nopr.niscair.res.in/handle/123456789/29292; M. Trimble, "The Territorial Discrepancy between Intellectual Property Rights Infringement Claims and Remedies," *Lewis & Clark Law Review* 23, no. 2 (2019): 501–52, https://scholars.law.unlv.edu/cgi/viewcontent.cgi?article=2276&context=facpub. Exceptions are limited to certain well-known trademarks. See, for example, J. Darnton, "The Coming Age of the Global Trademark: The Effect of TRIPS on the Well-Known Marks Exception to the Principle of Territoriality," *Michigan State International Law Review* 20, no. 1 (2011): 11–32, https://digitalcommons.law.msu.edu/cgi/ viewcontent.cgi?article=1068&context=ilr; J. Faris, "The Famous Marks Exception to the Territoriality Principle in American Trademark Law," *Case Western Reserve Law Review* 59, no. 2

(2009): 451–89, https://scholarlycommons.law.case.edu/cgi/viewcontent.cgi?article=1811& context=caselrev.

9. Under Section 301 of the Trade Act of 1974 (19 U.S.C. § 2411), the Office of the United States Trade Representative issues an annual report that lists foreign trading partners with inadequate intellectual property protection. https://ustr.gov/sites/default/files/2019_Special_301_Report.pdf.

10. Fifty years after the death of the author is the minimum copyright period stipulated by the Berne Convention for the Protection of Literary and Artistic Works, an international agreement ratified by 177 countries. In the United States, the United Kingdom, member states of the European Union, Switzerland, Norway, Russia, Japan, South Korea, Israel, Australia, and some other countries, the period of copyright protection is seventy years after the death of the author. In the United States, the protection period for corporate, anonymous, or pseudonymous works is ninety-five years from first publication or 120 years from creation, whichever is shorter. Some countries, including the United States, provide longer or shorter protection periods for nonwritten works or for works created before a specified date, which usually corresponds to the date a national copyright law was revised. Perpetual copyright applies to a small number of works in certain countries. The most frequently cited example, the King James version of the Bible, is protected by Crown Copyright in the United Kingdom. See S. Saxby, "Crown Copyright Regulation in the UK—Is the Debate Still Alive?" *International Journal of Law and Information Technology* 13, no. 3 (2005): 299–335, https://doi.org/10.1093/ijlit/eai017; R. Syn, "Copyright God: Enforcement of Copyright in the Bible and Religious Works," *Regent University Law Review* 14, no. 1 (2001): 1–34, www.regent.edu/acad/schlaw/student_life/studentorgs/lawreview/docs/issues/v14n1/Vol. 14, No. 1, 1 Syn.pdf; J. Cohn, "The King James Copyright: A Look at the Originality of Derivative Translations of the King James Version of the Bible," *Journal of Intellectual Property Law* 12, no 2 (2005): 513–38, http://digitalcommons.law.uga.edu/cgi/viewcontent.cgi?article=1343&context=jipl. On the arguments for indefinite copyright protection, see R. Posner and W. Landes, "Indefinitely Renewable Copyright," *University of Chicago Law Review* 70, no. 2 (2003): 471–518, https://chicagounbound.uchicago.edu/cgi/viewcontent.cgi?article=2550&context=journal_articles.

11. The minimum term or protection is twenty years from the date a patent application was filed as stipulated by the Agreement on Trade-Related Aspects of Intellectual Property Rights, the so-called TRIPS agreement, which applies to all members of the World Trade Organization. National laws may provide for shorter-term patents for certain inventions.

12. S. Graham et al., *Post-Issue Patent 'Quality Control': A Comparative Study of US Patent Re-examinations and European Patent Oppositions,* Working Paper 8807 (Cambridge, MA: National Bureau of Economic Research, 2002), www.nber.org/papers/w8807.pdf. Challenged patents can be revoked or limited, but this is not common in the United States. See, for example, E. Rogers, "Ten Years of Inter Partes Patent Reexamination Appeals: An Empirical View," *Santa Clara High Technology Law Journal* 29, no. 2 (2012): 305–67, https://digitalcommons.law.scu.edu/cgi/viewcontent.cgi?article=1559&context=chtlj. For reexamination statistics issued by the U.S. Patent and Trademark Office, see www.uspto.gov/learning-and-resources/statistics/reexamination-information. For patent opposition decisions by the European Patent Office, see www.epo.org/about-us/annual-reports-statistics/annual-report/2017/statistics/searches.html - tab4. In Germany, where patent revocation proceedings are separate from infringement lawsuits, a study of patents tested in court for validity found that 45 percent were determined to be fully invalid and 33 percent partially invalid, principally due to incomplete searches for prior art—a finding that highlights the risk of retrieval failure previously discussed in chapter 4. See J. Henkel and H. Zischka, "How Many Patents Are Truly Valid? Extent, Causes, and Remedies for Latent Patent Invalidity," *European Journal of Law and Economics* 48, no. 2 (2019): 195–239, https://link.springer.com/article/10.1007/s10657-019-09627-4; also C. Ann, "Patent Invalidation and Legal Certainty," in *The Object and Purpose of Intellectual Property,* ed. S. Frankel (Cheltenham, UK: Edward Elgar, 2019), 286–80, https://doi.org/10.4337/9781789902495.00019.

13. In *Cartoon Network LP, LLLP v. CSC Holdings, Inc.,* 536 F.3d 121 (2d Cir. 2008), www.courtlistener.com/opinion/2599/cartoon-network-lp-lllp-v-csc-holdings-inc, the court stated that copyrighted information must be "embodied in a medium . . . such that it can be

perceived, reproduced etc.," and it must remain in that medium for more than a transitory period.

14. Where available, copyright registration may be advantageous in certain situations. In some countries, registration provides *prima facie* evidence of facts related to ownership of a copyrighted work. In the United States, registration with the U.S. Copyright Office is required for infringement litigation in federal court. Registration makes a copyright owner eligible for statutory damages, attorneys' fees, and court costs. See *Copyright Basics,* Circular 1 (Washington, DC: U.S. Copyright Office, 2017), www.copyright.gov/circs/circ01.pdf.

15. J. Lanjouw and M. Schankerman, *Stylized Facts of Patent Litigation: Value, Scope and Ownership,* Working Paper 6297 (Cambridge, MA: National Bureau of Economic Research, 1997), www.nber.org/papers/w6297.pdf. Copyright registration can be refused or canceled if a copyright application was submitted by someone who was not authorized to register the copyright or if the material is not copyrightable, such as a work in the public domain or work created by the US government. See www.dmlp.org/legal-guide/works-not-covered-copyright.

16. ISO/IEC 17788:2014, *Information Technology—Cloud Computing—Overview and Vocabulary,* defines *cloud computing* as a "paradigm for enabling network access to a scalable and elastic pool of shareable physical or virtual resources with self-service provisioning and administration on-demand." It defines a cloud service as "one or more capabilities offered via cloud computing," and a cloud service provider as a "party which makes cloud services available." The National Institute of Standards and Technology defines *cloud computing* as "a model for enabling ubiquitous, convenient, on-demand network access to a shared pool of configurable computing resources." P. Mell and T. Grance, *The NIST Definition of Cloud Computing, Special Publication 800-145* (Gaithersburg, MD: National Institute of Standards and Technology, 2011), https://nvlpubs.nist.gov/nistpubs/Legacy/SP/nistspecialpublication800-145.pdf. See also E. Simmons, *Evaluation of Cloud Computing Services Based on NIST SP 800-145, Special Publication 500-322* (Gaithersburg, MD: National Institute of Standards and Technology, 2018), https://doi.org/10.6028/NIST.SP.500-322. For a summary of the various types of cloud services, see S. Goyal, "Public vs Private vs Hybrid vs Community Cloud Computing: A Critical Review," *International Journal of Computer Network and Information Security* 6, no. 3 (2014): 20–29, www.mecs-press.org/ijcnis/ijcnis-v6-n3/IJCNIS-V6-N3-3.pdf.

17. Such services offer an alternative or supplement to an organization's in-house computing capabilities. They may be operated by global cloud providers, such as Amazon and Microsoft, or by various regional and special-purpose providers, including those that offer cloud-based email and backup services.

18. Examples include cloud-based versions of enterprise resource-management software, customer-relationship-management software, document-management software, and other applications that are also available for on-premises installation; services that offer subscription access to office productivity software, such as Microsoft Office 365 and Google's G Suite, that may or may not have an on-premises counterpart; and social media sites that allow users to post digital content for viewing by others.

19. C. Reed, *Information 'Ownership' in the Cloud,* Queen Mary School of Law Legal Studies Research Paper No. 45/2010 (London: Queen Mary University, 2010), https://papers.ssrn.com/sol3/papers.cfm?abstract_id=1562461; C. Reed, "Information in the Cloud: Ownership, Control, and Accountability," in *Privacy and Legal Issues in Cloud Computing,* ed. A. Cheung and R. Weber (Northampton, MA: Edward Elgar, 2015), 139–59, https://doi.org/10.4337/9781783477074.00014; M. Phelps and M. Jennex, "Ownership of Collaborative Works in the Cloud," *International Journal of Knowledge Management* 11, no. 4 (2015): 35–51, https://doi.org/10.4018/IJKM.2015100103; D. Heaven, "Dark Cloud: How Life Online Has Changed Ownership," *New Scientist* 217, no. 2910 (2013): 34–37, https://doi.org/10.1016/S0262-4079(13)60820-9; C. Marshall and F. Shipman, "Exploring the Ownership and Persistent Value of Facebook Content," in *CSCW '15: Proceedings of the 18th ACM Conference on Computer Supported Cooperative Work & Social Computing* (New York: ACM, 2016), 712–23, https://doi.org/10.1145/2675133.2675203; R. Chow et al., "Controlling Data in the Cloud: Outsourcing Computation without Outsourcing Control," in *CCSW '09: Proceedings of*

the *2009 ACM Workshop on Cloud Computing Security* (New York: ACM, 2009): 85–90, http://markus-jakobsson.com/papers/jakobsson-ccsw09.pdf.

20. As an example, Microsoft's terms of service for Office 365 states that "we don't claim ownership of your content," but a customer must grant Microsoft a "worldwide and royalty-free intellectual property license to use your content, for example, to make copies of, retain, transmit, reformat, display, and distribute" the content. www.microsoft.com/en-us/servicesagreement.

21. Google's terms of service of service require the customer to give Google a worldwide license to "use, host, store, reproduce, modify, create derivative works (such as those resulting from translations, adaptations or other changes we make so that your content works better with our Services), communicate, publish, publicly perform, publicly display and distribute such content." https://policies.google.com/terms?hl=en-US. Facebook's terms of service require the customer to grant a license for all of these operations plus the right to "publicly perform" customer content. www.facebook.com/terms.php. According to Instagram's terms of service, customers grant it a transferable, sub-licensable worldwide license to use any customer content. The license "survives even if you stop using the platform." www.instagram.com/about/legal/terms/api.

22. According to the terms of service for Microsoft Azure services, customer access will be suspended thirty days after notification that a payment is delinquent, that the customer has violated the service's acceptable use policy, or that the customer has failed to respond in a timely manner to a claim of alleged infringement. If the issues are not addressed, customer content will be deleted sixty days thereafter. https://azure.microsoft.com/en-us/support/legal/subscription-agreement. Similarly, Google will suspend customer access to its G Suite service for a material breach of the terms of the agreement and delete the customer's content. https://gsuite.google.com/intl/en_uk/terms/2013/1/premier_terms.html. According to the terms for its AWS cloud service, Amazon may remove or disable access to customer content that infringes or misappropriates the intellectual property rights of a third party. https://aws.amazon.com/service-terms.

23. When Iron Mountain closed its cloud-based storage service in 2011, Nirvanix offered free migration to its cloud service. Nirvanix subsequently filed for bankruptcy protection and discontinued its cloud service in 2013, giving customers twenty-eight days to download their content.

24. For a tutorial introduction to enforcement concepts and methods, see L. Harms, *A Casebook on the Enforcement of Intellectual Property Rights, Fourth Edition,* WIPO Publication No. 791E (Geneva: World Intellectual Property Organization, 2018), www.wipo.int/edocs/pubdocs/en/wipo_pub_791_2018.pdf. See also J. Lanjouw and J. Lerner, *The Enforcement of Intellectual Property Rights: A Survey of the Empirical Literature,* Working Paper 6296 (Cambridge, MA: National Bureau of Economic Research, 1997), www.nber.org/papers/w6296.pdf.

25. W. Towns, "U.S. Contingency Fees—A Level Playing Field?" in *WIPO Magazine,* issue 1 (February 2010): 3–5, www.wipo.int/export/sites/www/wipo_magazine/en/pdf/2010/wipo_pub_121_2010_01.pdf. In *Imperium Ip Holdings (Cayman) Ltd. v. Samsung Elecs. Co.,* No. 14-cv-371, 2018 WL 1602460 (E.D. Tex. Apr. 3, 2018), the court awarded $7 million in attorneys' fees, which exceeded the damages awarded to the plaintiff, but an appeals court subsequently reversed the award. https://casetext.com/case/imperium-ip-holdings-cayman-ltd-v-samsung-elecs-co-19. Litigation costs tend to be lower in other countries. Legal proceedings in France or Germany rarely exceed 25 percent of their US counterparts. *World Intellectual Property Indicators 2018,* WIPO Publication No. 941E/18 (Geneva: World Intellectual Property Organization, 2018), www.wipo.int/edocs/pubdocs/en/wipo_pub_941_2018.pdf.

26. According to *IFRS Standard, IAS 38: Intangible Assets,* issued by the IFRS Foundation, a not-for-profit international organization that develops global accounting standards, an intangible asset is a resource that is controlled by an entity as a result of past events and from which future economic benefits are expected to flow to the entity. An entity controls an intangible asset if it has the power to obtain the future economic benefits and the legal right to restrict access to those benefits by others. Future economic benefits may include revenue, cost savings, or other benefits resulting from use of the asset. www.ifrs.org/issued-standards/list-of-standards/ias-38-intangible-assets.

27. Examples of the many publications on valuation of intellectual property include R. Parr, *Intellectual Property*, 5th ed. (Hoboken, NJ: John Wiley and Sons, 2018); P. Groves, *Intellectual Property Rights and Their Valuation: A Handbook for Bankers, Companies and Their Advisers* (Cambridge, England: Woodhead Publishing, 1997); S. Kamiyama et al., *Valuation and Exploitation of Intellectual Property*, STI Working Paper 2006/5 (Paris: Organization for Economic Cooperation and Development, 2006), https://doi.org/10.1787/307034817055; A. Bismuth, *Intellectual Assets and Value Creation: Implications for Corporate Reporting* (Paris: Organization for Economic Cooperation and Development, 2006), www.oecd.org/corporate/ca/corporategovernanceprinciples/37811196.pdf; D. Samuel, "Intellectual Property Valuation: A Finance Perspective," *Albany Law Review* 70, no. 4 (2007): 1207–25, www.albanylawreview.org/Articles/Vol70_4/70.4.1207-Samuel.pdf; C. Greenhalgh and M. Rogers, "The Value of Intellectual Property Rights to Firms and Society," *Oxford Review of Economic Policy* 23, no. 4 (2007): 541–67, www.jstor.org/stable/23606746; N. Kossovsky, "Fair Value of Intellectual Property," *Journal of Intellectual Property* 3, no. 1 (2002): 62–70, https://doi.org/10.1108/14691930210412863; K. King, "The Value of Intellectual Property, Intangible Assets and Goodwill," *Journal of Intellectual Property Rights* 7, no. 2 (2002): 245–48, http://nopr.niscair.res.in/handle/123456789/4919; H. Wirtz, "Valuation of Intellectual Property: A Review of Approaches and Methods," *International Journal of Business and Management* 7, no. 9 (2012): 40–48, https://pdfs.semanticscholar.org/a9e2/a7a4377ae882031424f3e81c6c2b5a92c257.pdf; M. Bezant, "The Use of Intellectual Property as Security for Debt Finance," *Journal of Knowledge Management* 1, no. 3 (1997): 237–63, https://doi.org/10.1108/EUM0000000004597.

28. www.aon.com/thought-leadership/ponemoninstitutereport.jsp.

29. https://lexmachina.com/resources. From 1978 through 1999, there was a tenfold increase in patent litigation, with much of the increase occurring during the 1990s, especially in new technology areas. See J. Lanjouw and M. Schankerman, *Enforcing Intellectual Property Rights*, Working Paper 8656 (Cambridge, MA: National Bureau of Economic Research, 2001), www.nber.org/papers/w8656.pdf. Over 190,000 individual copyright, patent, and trademark cases were filed in U.S. District Courts from 1994 to 2014. See M. Sag, "IP Litigation in U.S. District Courts: 1994–2014," *Iowa Law Review* 101, no. 3, 1065–1111, https://ilr.law.uiowa.edu/print/volume-101-issue-3/ip-litigation-in-u-s-district-courts-19942014; J. Lanjouw and M. Schankerman, *Enforcing Intellectual Property Rights*, Working Paper 8656 (Cambridge, MA: National Bureau of Economic Research, 2001), www.nber.org/papers/w8656.pdf.

30. https://gss.bsa.org.

31. I. Ganguli et al., *The Paper Trail of Knowledge Spillovers: Evidence from Patent Interference*, Working Paper No. 17-44 (Philadelphia: Research Department, Federal Reserve Bank of Philadelphia, 2017), www.minneapolisfed.org/institute/working-papers/wp18-06.pdf.

32. For an interesting and useful discussion, see A. Leinonen, *Patent Infringement Monitoring* (Helsinki: Department of Commercial Law, Hanken School of Economics, 2011), https://pdfs.semanticscholar.org/3bbb/f2456afde0aa2c5d2d2aedbe9a749cc55823.pdf. On protection of intellectual property in small and medium-size organizations, see R. Blackburn, ed., *Intellectual Property and Innovation Management in Small Firms* (London: Routledge, 2003).

33. In *Campbell v. Acuff-Rose Music, Inc.*, (9-1292), 510 U.S. 569 (1994), which involved a parody of a Roy Orbison song by 2 Live Crew, the District Court and Appeals Court interpreted fair use requirements differently. In finding for the plaintiff, the U.S. Supreme Court ruled that all four factors must be considered in determinations of fair use. www.law.cornell.edu/supct/html/92-1292.ZS.html. Publications that reflect continuing problems of interpreting fair use in the light of the Supreme Court decision include K. Piele, "Three Years after *Campbell v. Acuff-Rose Music, Inc.*: What Is Fair Game for Parodists?" *Loyola of Los Angeles Entertainment Law Review* 18, no. 1 (1997): 75–100, https://digitalcommons.lmu.edu/cgi/viewcontent.cgi?article=1353&context=elr; M. Bunker and C. Calvert, "The Jurisprudence of Transformation: Intellectual Incoherence and Doctrinal Murkiness Twenty Years after *Campbell v. Acuff-Rose Music*," *Duke Law & Technology Review* 12, no. 1 (2014): 92–128, https://scholarship.law.duke.edu/dltr/vol12/iss1/5; Z. Said, "Forward: Fair Use in the Digital Age, and *Campbell v. Acuff-Rose* at 21," *Washington Law Review* 90, no. 2 (2015), 579–96, http://digi-

tal.law.washington.edu/dspace-law/bitstream/handle/1773.1/1457/
90WLR0579.pdf?sequence=1&isAllowed=y; T. Irvin, "If That's the Way It Must Be, Okay: *Campbell v. Acuff-Rose* on Rewind," *Loyola of Los Angeles Entertainment Law Review* 36, no. 2 (2016): 137–69, https://digitalcommons.lmu.edu/cgi/viewcontent.cgi?referer=www.google.com/&httpsredir=1&article=1600&context=elr.

34. A 2019 analysis by Gartner Inc., a research and advisory company, projected exponential growth of public cloud revenue through 2022, as organizations adopt cloud-first and cloud-only computing strategies for new applications. www.gartner.com/en/newsroom/press-releases/2019-04-02-gartner-forecasts-worldwide-public-cloud-revenue-to-g.

35. See, for example, C. Asay, "A Case for the Public Domain," *Ohio State Law Journal* 74, no. 5 (2013): 753–806, https://digitalcommons.law.byu.edu/faculty_scholarship/88.

36. For a discussion of the impact of Open Access, see B. Bjork et al., "Open Access to the Scientific Journal Literature: Situation 2009," *PLoS ONE* 5, no. 6 (2010): e11273, https://doi.org/10.1371/journal.pone.0011273; K. Antelman, "Do Open-Access Articles Have a Greater Research Impact?" *College & Research Libraries* 65, no. 5 (2004): 372–82, https://crl.acrl.org/index.php/crl/article/view/15683/17129; S. Harnad and T. Brody, "Comparing the Impact of Open Access (OA) vs. Non-OA Articles in the Same Journals," *D-Lib Magazine* 10, no. 6 (2004), www.dlib.org/dlib/june04/harnad/06harnad.html; H. Piwawar, "The State of OA: A Large-Scale Analysis of the Prevalence and Impact of Open Access Articles," *PeerJ* 6 (2018): 6:e4375, https://doi.org/10.7717/peerj.4375; J. Willinsky, *The Access Principle: The Case for Open Access to Research and Scholarship* (Cambridge, MA: MIT Press, 2006), http://hdl.handle.net/10150/106529.

37. Examples of the many articles on Creative Commons include A. Goss, "Codifying a Commons: Copyright, Copyleft, and the Creative Commons Project," *Chicago-Kent Law Review* 8, no. 2 (2007): 963–96, https://scholarship.kentlaw.iit.edu/cgi/viewcontent.cgi?article=3609&context=cklawreview; L. Loren, "Building a Reliable Semicommons of Creative Works: Enforcement of Creative Commons Licenses and Limited Abandonment of Copyright," *George Mason Law Review* 14, no. 2 (2007): 271–328, http://georgemasonlawreview.org/wp-content/uploads/2014/03/14-2_Loren.pdf; M. Carroll, "Creative Commons and the New Intermediaries," *Michigan State Law Review* 2006, no. 1 (2006): 45–65, http://digitalcommons.wcl.american.edu/cgi/viewcontent.cgi?article=1039&context=facsch_lawrev&seiredir=1; G. Russi, "Creative Commons, CC-Plus, and Hybrid Intermediaries: A Stakeholder's Perspective," *BYU International Law and Management Review* 7, no. 2 (2011): 102–32, https://digitalcommons.law.byu.edu/cgi/viewcontent.cgi?article=1089&context=ilmr; N. Elkin-Koren, "Exploring Creative Commons: A Skeptical View of a Worthy Pursuit," in *The Future of the Public Domain: Identifying the Commons in Information Law*, ed. L. Guibault and P. Hugenholtz (Alphen aan den Rijn, The Netherlands: Kluwer Law International, 2006), 325–45, https://hewlett.org/library/creative-commons-a-skeptical-view-of-a-worthy-pursuit; M. Kim, "The Creative Commons and Copyright Protection in the Digital Era: Uses of Creative Commons Licenses," *Journal of Computer-Mediated Communication* 13, no. 1 (2007): 187–209, https://doi.org/10.1111/j.1083-6101.2007.00392.x.

38. J. Kumar, "Insurance Coverage in Intellectual Property Litigation," *Journal of Intellectual Property Rights* 13, no. 3 (2008): 234–38, http://nopr.niscair.res.in/handle/123456789/1384; G. Llobet and J. Suarez, "Patent Litigation and the Role of Enforcement Insurance," *Review of Law and Economics* 8, no. 3 (2012), https://doi.org/10.1515/1555-5879.1461; M. Simensky and E. Osterberg, "The Insurance and Management of Intellectual Property Risks," *Cardoza Arts & Entertainment Law Journal* 17, no. 2 (1999): 321–43, https://heinonline.org/HOL/LandingPage?handle=hein.journals/caelj17&div=18&id=&page=; T. Rowe, "Specialty Insurance for Intellectual Property: Additional Security for Owners of Intellectual Property Assets," *DePaul Journal of Art, Technology & Intellectual Property Law* 19, no. 1 (2008): 1–40, https://via.library.depaul.edu/cgi/viewcontent.cgi?article=1117&context=jatip.

39. Examples of the many studies of the likelihood of infringement for intellectual property include C. Chien, "Predicting Patent Litigation," *Texas Law Review* 90, no. 2 (2011): 283–329, https://pdfs.semanticscholar.org/44a6/ad2a0c63594d9ada479a3909732d44a44a22.pdf; T. Cowart et al., "Two Methodologies for Predicting Patent Litigation Outcomes: Logistic Regression versus Classification Trees," *American Business Law Journal* 51, no. 4 (2014):

843–77, https://doi.org/10.1111/ablj.12036; H. Su et al., "Patent Litigation Precaution Method: Analyzing Characteristics of US Litigated and Non-Litigated Patents from 1976-2010," *Scientometrics* 92, no. 1 (2012): 181–95, https://doi.org/10.1007/s11192-012-0716-7; Q. Liu, "Patent Litigation Prediction: A Convolutional Tensor Factorization Approach," in *Proceedings of the Twenty-Seventh International Joint Conference on Artificial Intelligence (IJCAI-18)*, ed. J. Lang (Marina del Rey, California: International Joint conferences on Artificial Intellligence, 2018), 5052–59, www.ijcai.org/proceedings/2018/0701.pdf; K. Moore, "Worthless Patents," *Berkeley Technology Law Journal* 20, no. 4 (2005): 1521–52, http://scholarship.law.berkeley.edu/cgi/viewcontent.cgi?article=1586&context=btlj; M. Sag, "Predicting Fair Use," *Ohio State Law Journal* 73, no. 1 (2012): 47–91, https://kb.osu.edu/bitstream/handle/1811/71532/OSLJ_V73N1_0047.pdf.

40. K. Spelman and J. Moss, "The Intellectual Property Inventory: Why Do It?" *Computer Law & Security Review* 10, no. 1 (1994): 22–24, https://doi.org/10.1016/0267-3649(94)90079-5; Y. Benkler, "Intellectual Property and the Organization of Information Production," *International Review of Law and Economics* 22, no. 1 (2002): 81–107, https://doi.org/10.1016/s0144-8188(02)00070-4; K. Jain and V. Sharma, "Intellectual Property Management System: An Organizational Perspective," *Journal of Intellectual Property Rights* 11, no. 5 (2006): 330–33, http://hdl.handle.net/123456789/3595; J. Lis-Gutierrez et al., "Museums and Management of Intellectual Property," *International Journal of Control Theory and Applications* 9, no. 44 (2016): 458–61, www.researchgate.net/profile/Amelec_Viloria2/publication/317370490_Museums_and_Management_of_Intellectual_Property/links/5936e0690f7e9b374c103de2/Museums-and-Management-of-Intellectual-Property.pdf; R. Pantalony, *Managing Intellectual Property for Museums* (Geneva: World Intellectual Property Organization, 2013), www.wipo.int/publications/en/details.jsp?id=166.

41. G. Gouri and K. Jain, "Intellectual Property Audit for Efficient Intellectual Property Management of an Organization," in *2012 Proceedings of PICMET '12: Technology Management for Emerging Technologies* (Piscataway, NJ: IEEE, 2012), 894–906, https://ieeexplore.ieee.org/abstract/document/6304105; T. Rastogi, "IP Audit: Way to a Healthy Organization," *Journal of Intellectual Property Rights* 15, no. 4 (2010): 302–9, http://nopr.niscair.res.in/handle/123456789/10009; P. Ackerman, "Intellectual Property Audit and Management," in *Intellectual Property: Valuation, Exploitation, and Infringement Damages*, 5th ed., ed. R. Parr (New York: John Wiley and Sons, 2018), 352–71, https://doi.org/10.1002/9781119419235.ch23.

42. In *Phoenix Renovation Corp. v. Rodriguez*, 403 F. Supp. 2d 510 (E.D. Va. 2005), www.courtlistener.com/opinion/2349097/phoenix-renovation-corp-v-rodriguez, the court ruled that former subcontractors of a plumbing company had infringed copyright by using the plumbing company's standard contract, a proprietary document with original content that specified the terms and condition for work to be performed for customers. Because the plumbing company's standard contract was not registered with the U.S. Copyright Office at the time of the infringement, the defendants were not liable for statutory damages specified in 17 U.S.C. § 504, but the court did issue a permanent injunction against any future infringements by the defendants. In *Feist Publications, Inc., v. Rural Telephone Service Co*, 499 U.S. 340 (1991), www.law.cornell.edu/copyright/cases/499_US_340.htm, the U.S. Supreme Court ruled that a work must possess some originality and creativity to qualify for copyright protection but the court's opinion, written by Justice Sandra Day O'Connor, noted that "the originality requirement is not particularly stringent" and a "minimal degree of creativity" is sufficient. By those standards, some email messages qualify for copyright protection.

43. For a succinct explanation of the work-for-hire doctrine, see *Circular 30: Works Made for Hire*, issued by the U.S. Copyright Office, www.copyright.gov/circs/circ30.pdf.

44. On the common law principle of agency, see American Law Institute, *Restatement of the Law Third, Agency* (St. Paul, MN: American Law Institute, 2006); H. Bennett, *Principles of the Law of Agency* (Oxford: Hart, 2013); O. Holmes Jr., "Agency," *Harvard Law Review* 4, no. 8 (1891): 345–64, https://en.wikisource.org/wiki/Agency.

45. In *Community for Creative Non-Violence v. Reid* (1989), 490 U.S. 730 (1989), http://cdn.loc.gov/service/ll/usrep/usrep490/usrep490730/usrep490730.pdf, the U.S. Supreme Court listed factors to be considered when differentiating an independent contractor from an employ-

ee. The plaintiff had paid a sculptor to create a statue that depicted the plight of homeless people, but the two parties filed competing copyright applications for the completed work. A district court considered the statue a work for hire, but that determination was reversed by the court of appeals. The Supreme Court's opinion, written by Justice Thurgood Marshall, determined that the sculptor was an independent contractor and the statue was not a work for hire. Factors that differentiate an employee from an independent contractor were refined in *Aymes v. Bonelli*, 980 F.2d 857, 862 (2nd Cir. 1992), https://law.resource.org/pub/us/case/reporter/F2/980/980.F2d.857.82.92-7098.html.

46. L. Turcik, "Rethinking the Weighted Factor Approach to the Employee Versus Independent Contractor Distinction in the Work for Hire Context," *University of Pennsylvania Journal of Labor and Employment Law* 3, no. 2 (2001): 333–53, https://pdfs.semanticscholar.org/d4d4/bf54af391286fca43645196c744327638d29.pdf; A. Polivka, "Contingent and Alternative Work Arrangements, Defined," *Monthly Labor Review* 119, no. 10 (1996): 3–9, www.bls.gov/mlr/1996/10/art1full.pdf; C. Muhl, "What Is an Employee? The Answer Depends on Federal Law," *Monthly Labor Review* 125, no. 1 (2002): 3–11, www.bls.gov/opub/mlr/2002/01/art1full.pdf; M. Bodie, "Participation as a Theory of Employment," *Notre Dame Law Review* 89, no. 2 (2014): 661–726, https://pdfs.semanticscholar.org/b4b6/733df29f869edf35c7a833c5e626a2779b30.pdf; R. Carlson, "Why the Law Still Can't Tell an Employee When It Sees One and How It Ought to Stop Trying," *Berkeley Journal of Employment & Labor Law* 22, no. 2 (2001): 295–368, https://scholarship.law.berkeley.edu/cgi/viewcontent.cgi?article=1301&context=bjell.

47. Some courts have recognized a teacher exception to the work-for-hire doctrine for academic writings. For a sampling of the many publications on this contentious subject, see T. Simon, "Faculty Writings: Are They 'Works Made for Hire' under the 1976 Copyright Act?" *Journal of College and University Law* 9, no. 4 (1983): 485–513, https://eric.ed.gov/?id=EJ279698; R. Dreyfuss, "The Creative Employee and the Copyright Act of 1976," *University of Chicago Law Review* 54, no. 2 (1987): 590–647, https://chicagounbound.uchicago.edu/cgi/viewcontent.cgi?article=4523&context=uclrev; R. VerSteeg, "Copyright and the Educational Process: The Right of Teacher Inception," *Iowa Law Review* 75, no. 2 (1990): 397–407, https://heinonline.org/HOL/LandingPage?handle=hein.journals/ilr75&div=19&id=&page=; L. Lape, "Ownership of Copyrightable Works of University Professors: The Interplay between the Copyright Act and University Copyright Policies," *Villanova Law Review* 37, no. 2 (1992): 223–69, https://digitalcommons.law.villanova.edu/cgi/viewcontent.cgi?referer=www.google.com/&httpsredir=1&article=2776&context=vlr; N. Strauss, "Anything but Academic: How Copyright's Work-for-Hire Doctrine Affects Professors, Graduate Students, and K–12 Teachers in an Information Age," *Richmond Journal of Law & Technology* 18, no. 1 (2011): 1–47, https://scholarship.richmond.edu/cgi/viewcontent.cgi?referer=&httpsredir=1&article=1355&context=jolt; T. Borow, "Copyright Ownership of Scholarly Works Created by University Faculty and Posted on School-Provided Web Pages," *Miami Business Law Review* 7, no. 1 (1999): 149–69, https://repository.law.miami.edu/cgi/viewcontent.cgi?referer=www.google.com/&httpsredir=1&article=1198&context=umblr; L. Leslie, "Application of the Teacher Exception Doctrine to On-Line Courses; Note," *Journal of Legislation* 29, no. 1 (2003): 109–24, https://pdfs.semanticscholar.org/cfb3/6a9ad00839cfc95053f6d5432306a0fd513c.pdf; R. Denicola, "Copyright and Open Access: Reconsidering University Ownership of Faculty Research," *Nebraska Law Review* 85, no. 2 (2006): 351–82, https://digitalcommons.unl.edu/cgi/viewcontent.cgi?article=1115&context=nlr; G. Gertz, "Copyright in Faculty-Created Works: How Licensing Can Solve the Academic Work-for-Hire Dilemma," *Washington Law Review* 88, no. 4 (2013): 1465–93, http://digital.law.washington.edu/dspace-law/bitstream/handle/1773.1/1316/88WLR1465.pdf?sequence=1; P. Hellyer, "Who Owns This Article? Applying Copyright's Work-Made-for-Hire Doctrine to Librarians' Scholarship," *Law Library Journal* 108, no. 1 (2016): 33–54, https://scholarship.law.wm.edu/cgi/viewcontent.cgi?referer=www.google.com/&httpsredir=1&article=1119&context=libpubs.

48. R. Colby, "Works Made for Hire in International Copyright Law," *Loyola of Los Angeles Entertainment Law Review* 3, no. 1 (1983): 87–99, https://pdfs.semanticscholar.org/ef9f/bd61997e79799751740ebeedeb0b02b6057a.pdf.

49. This is the case, for example, in Belgium and Luxembourg, where national copyright laws do not allow authors to transfer their moral right to works they create. For a useful survey of European copyright provisions, see R. Jacobs, "Work-for-Hire and the Moral Right Dilemma in the European Community: A U.S. Perspective," *Boston College International and Comparative Law Review* 16, no. 1 (1993): 29–79, https://lawdigitalcommons.bc.edu/cgi/viewcontent.cgi?article=1318&context=iclr. On the role of moral rights, see M. Gunlicks, "A Balance of Interests: The Concordance of Copyright Law and Moral Rights in the Worldwide Economy," *Fordham Intellectual Property, Media, and Entertainment Law Journal* 11, no. 3 (2001): 601–68, https://ir.lawnet.fordham.edu/cgi/viewcontent.cgi?article=1220&context=iplj.

50. R. Saka, "Confidential Ideas and Independent Contractors: Trade Secret Ownership in the Age of the Hired Gun," *Hastings Business Law Journal* 10, no. 1 (2014): 245–69, https://repository.uchastings.edu/cgi/viewcontent.cgi?article=1044&context=hastings_business_law_journal; S. MacDougall and D. Hurst, "Identifying Tangible Costs, Benefits and Risks of an Investment in Intellectual Capital," *Journal of Intellectual Capital* 6, no. 1 (2005). 53–71, https://doi.org/10.1108/14691930510574663, notes the risks associated with exposing contingent workers to confidential competitive information.

51. J. Simmons, "Inventions Made for Hire," *New York University Journal of Intellectual Property and Entertainment Law* 2, no. 1 (2012): 1–50, https://jipel.law.nyu.edu/wp-content/uploads/2015/05/NYU_JIPEL_Vol-2-No-1_1_Simmons_InventionsMadeForHire.pdf.

52. S. Sandrock, "The Evolution and Modern Application of the Shop Right Rule," *The Business Lawyer* 38, no. 3 (1983): 953–74, www.jstor.org/stable/40686490; W. Hovell, "Patent Ownership: An Employer's Rights to His Employee's Invention," *Notre Dame Law Review* 58, no. 4 (1983): 863–89, https://scholarship.law.nd.edu/cgi/viewcontent.cgi?article=2429&context=ndlr; P. Van Slyke and M. Friedman, "Employer's Rights to Inventions and Patents of Its Officers, Directors, and Employees," *American Intellectual Property Law* 18, no. 2 (1990): 127–54, https://heinonline.org/HOL/LandingPage?handle=hein.journals/aiplaqj18&div=14&id=&page=.

53. As defined in 18 U.S.C. § 1839, trade secrets encompass "all forms and types of financial, business, scientific, technical, economic, or engineering information" that the owner has taken "reasonable measures" to keep secret and that has actual or potential economic value because it is not generally known. Article 39 of the Agreement on Trade-Related Aspects of Intellectual Property Rights specifies the same characteristics for "undisclosed information" that is considered intellectual property. By definition, trade secrets are confidential, but most organizations have other types of confidential information—personal information about employees, suppliers, and customers, for example—that are not considered trade secrets.

54. According to Section 757 of the *Restatement of Torts*, a standard legal source published by the American Law Institute, a trade secret "may consist of any formula, pattern, device or compilation of information which is used in one's business, and which gives him an opportunity to obtain an advantage over competitors who do not know or use it." www.lrdc.pitt.edu/ashley/RESTATEM.HTM. See also F. Cavico, "Business Plans and Strategies as Legally Protected Trade Secrets: Florida and National Perspectives," *University of Miami Business Law Review* 9, no. 1 (2001): 1–66, https://pdfs.semanticscholar.org/0266/d86f08f912715f218c107211456c4ece48e4.pdf.

55. EC Regulation No 316/2014, https://eur-lex.europa.eu/legal-content/EN/TXT/PDF/?uri=CELEX:32014R0316&from=EN. According to Directive 2016/943, the definition of *trade secrets* encompasses know-how along with business information and technical information. https://eur-lex.europa.eu/eli/dir/2016/943/oj.

56. As previously cited in chapter 1, the principal US laws include the Economic Espionage Act of 1996 (18 U.S.C. § 1832), Defend Trade Secrets Act of 2016 (18 U.S.C. § 1836), and the Uniform Trade Secrets Act, which has been adopted by many states. For a discussion of US laws, see S. Sandeen and E. Rowe, *Trade Secret Law Including the Defend Trade Secrets Act of 2016 in a Nutshell* (St. Paul, MN: West Academic Publishing, 2018). Directive 2016/943 of the European Parliament protects trade secrets in EU Member States. In Canada, the United Kingdom, Australia, and some other countries, trade secrets are protected by case law related to breach of confidence, fiduciary duty, or contracts or by laws that prohibit unfair competition.

57. See, for example, C. Fisk, "Working Knowledge, Trade Secrets, Restrictive Covenants in Employment, and the Rise of Corporate Intellectual Property," *Hastings Law Journal* 52, no. 2 (2001): 441–535, https://repository.uchastings.edu/cgi/viewcontent.cgi?article=3432&context=hastings_law_journal; P. David, "Intellectual Property Institutions and the Panda's Thumb: Patents, Copyrights, and Trade Secrets in Economic Theory and History," in *Global Dimensions of Intellectual Property Rights in Science and Technology*, ed. M. Wallerstein et al. (Washington, DC: National Academies Press, 1993), 19–64, www.nap.edu/catalog/2054/global-dimensions-of-intellectual-property-rights-in-science-and-technology; S. Cheung, "Property Rights in Trade Secrets," *Economic Inquiry* 20, no. 1 (1982): 40–53, https://doi.org/10.1111/j.1465-7295.1982.tb01141.x; W. Caenegem, *Trade Secrets and Intellectual Property: Breach of Confidence, Misappropriation and Unfair Competition* (Alphen aan den Rijn, The Netherlands: Kluwer Law International, 2014); C. Graves, "Trade Secrets as Property: Theory and Consequences," *Journal of Intellectual Property Law* 39, no. 1 (2007): 39–89, https://digitalcommons.law.uga.edu/cgi/viewcontent.cgi?referer=www.google.com/&httpsredir=1&article=1292&context=jipl; D. Friedman et al., "Some Economics of Trade Secret Law," *Journal of Economic Perspectives* 5, no. 1 (1991): 61–72, www.aeaweb.org/articles?id=10.1257/jep.5.1.61.

58. In *Smith & Fuller, P.A. v. Cooper Tire & Rubber Co.*, 685 F.3d 486 (5th Cir. 2012), the plaintiff mistakenly copied Cooper Tire's trade secrets and confidential information onto compact discs that were distributed to personal injury lawyers during a conference. https://casetext.com/case/smith-fuller-pa-v-cooper-tire-rubber-co. In *Ideal Aerosmith, Inc. v. Acutronic USA, Inc.*, Civil Action No. 07-1029 (W.D. Pa. Apr. 23, 2008), messages containing trade secrets were inadvertently sent to the wrong email addresses. https://casetext.com/case/ideal-aerosmith-inc-v-acutronic-usa-3. In *Fisher Stoves, Inc. v. All Nighter Stove Works, Inc.*, 626 F.2d 193 (1st Cir. 1980), a confidential dealer list was accidentally left in open view. https://casetext.com/case/fisher-stoves-inc-v-all-nighter-stove-works. In *B.C. Ziegler & Company v. Lawrence P. Ehren*, 141 Wis. 2d 19 (1987), 414 N.W. 2d, forty-eight customer lists sent offsite for disposal were subsequently sold by a scrap paper company. www.courtlistener.com/opinion/1699880/bc-ziegler-co-v-ehren. In *Hoechst Diafoil Co. v. Nan Ya Plastics Corp.*, 174 F.3d 411 (4th Cir. 1999), a protective order required all trade secrets to be filed under seal in response to a discovery motion, but one document describing proprietary technology was inadvertently submitted unsealed and remained in the court's public files. https://casetext.com/case/hoechst-diafoil-co-v-nan-ya-plastics-corp. In *HMS Holdings Corp. v. Arendt*, 18 N.Y.S.3d 579 (N.Y. Sup. Ct. 2015), an inadvertent electronic filing of unredacted documents resulted in public disclosure of trade secrets. https://scholar.google.com/scholar_case?case=4930627301443852159&hl=en&as_sdt=6&as_vis=1&oi=scholarr.

59. Examples of the many publications on the doctrine of inevitable disclosure include S. Lowry, "Inevitable Disclosure Trade Secret Disputes: Dissolutions of Concurrent Property Interests," *Stanford Law Review* 40, no. 2 (1988): 519–44, www.jstor.org/stable/1228823; J. Edelstein, "Intellectual Slavery?: The Doctrine of Inevitable Disclosure of Trade Secrets," *Golden Gate University Law Review* 26, no. 3 (1996): 717–36, https://digitalcommons.law.ggu.edu/cgi/viewcontent.cgi?article=1686&context=ggulrev; J. Koh, "From Hoops to Hard Drives: An Accession Law Approach to the Inevitable Misappropriation of Trade Secrets," *American University Law Review* 48, no. 2 (1998): 271–357, https://digitalcommons.wcl.american.edu/cgi/viewcontent.cgi?article=1317&context=aulr; A. Gill, "The Inevitable Disclosure Doctrine: Inequitable Results Are Threatened but Not Inevitable," *Hastings Communications and Entertainment Law Journal* 24, no. 3 (2002): 403–26, https://repository.uchastings.edu/cgi/viewcontent.cgi?article=1584&context=hastings_comm_ent_law_journal; J. Saulino, "Locating Inevitable Disclosure's Place in Trade Secret Analysis," *Michigan Law Review* 100, no. 5 (2002): 1184–1214, https://repository.law.umich.edu/cgi/viewcontent.cgi?article=1901&context=mlr; E. Rowe, "When Trade Secrets Become Shackles: Fairness and the Inevitable Disclosure Doctrine," *Tulane Journal of Technology and Intellectual Property Law* 7, no. 2 (2005): 169–226, https://scholarship.law.ufl.edu/cgi/viewcontent.cgi?article=1065&context=facultypub; W. van Caenegem, "Inter-Firm Migration of Tacit Knowledge: Law and Policy," *Prometheus* 23, no. 3 (2005): 285–306, https://doi.org/10.1080/08109020500210951; G. Slowinski et al., "Protecting Know-How and Trade Secrets in Collab-

orative R&D Relationships," *Research-Technology Management* 49, no. 4 (2006): 30–38, https://doi.org/10.1080/08956308.2006.11657385; Y. Feldman, "The Expressive Function of Trade Secret Law: Legality, Cost, Intrinsic Motivation, and Consensus," *Journal of Empirical Legal Studies* 6, no. 1 (2009): 177–212, https://doi.org/10.1111/j.1740-1461.2009.01141.x; R. Wiesner, "A State-by-State Analysis of Inevitable Disclosure: A Need for Uniformity and a Workable Standard," *Intellectual Property Law Review* 16, no. 1 (2012): 211–29, http://scholarship.law.marquette.edu/cgi/viewcontent.cgi?article=1187&context=iplr; M. Reder and C. O'Brien, "Managing the Risk of Trade Secret Loss Due to Job Mobility in an Innovation Economy with the Theory of Inevitable Disclosure," *Journal of High Technology Law* 12, no. 2 (2012): 373–449, http://hdl.handle.net/2345/2632; M. Flowers, "Facing the Inevitable: The Inevitable Disclosure Doctrine and the Defend Trade Secrets Act of 2016," *Washington and Lee Law Review* 75, no. 4 (2019): 2207–63, https://scholarlycommons.law.wlu.edu/cgi/viewcontent.cgi?article=4631&context=wlulr.

    60. *PepsiCo, Inc. v. Redmond*, 54 F.3d 1262 (7th Cir. 1995), https://casetext.com/case/pepsico-inc-v-redmond-2. The product lines in dispute were PepsiCo's All Sport drink, which competed with Gatorade, which was developed by Quaker Oats, the defendant's new employer, and a PepsiCo joint venture with Lipton and Ocean Spray, which competed with Quaker Oats' Snapple beverages.

    61. In an extreme example, armed security guards forcibly entered a hotel company's computer room and downloaded proprietary customer and financial information. See *Four Seasons Hotels & Resorts B.V. v. Consorcio Barr, S.A.*, 267 F. Supp. 2d 1269, 1268 (S.D. Fla. 2003), www.courtlistener.com/opinion/2574320/four-seasons-hotels-resorts-bv-v-consorcio-barr-sa.

    62. On the role of industrial espionage in misappropriation of trade secrets, see B. Wimmer, *Business Espionage: Risks, Threats, and Countermeasures* (Waltham, MA: Butterworth Heinemann, 2015); C. Roper, *Trade Secret Theft, Industrial Espionage, and the China Threat* (Boca Raton, FL: CRC Press, 2014); D. Benny, *Industrial Espionage: Developing a Counterespionage Program* (Boca Raton, FL: CRC Press, 2014); R. Mendell, *The Quiet Threat: Fighting Industrial Espionage in America* (Springfield, IL: Charles C. Thomas, 2010); C. Burgess and R. Power, *Secrets Stolen, Fortunes Lost: Preventing Intellectual Property Theft and Economic Espionage in the 21st Century* (Burlington, MA: Syngress, 2008); H. Nasheri, *Economic Espionage and Industrial Spying* (Cambridge: Cambridge University Press, 2005); D. Ben-Atar, *Trade Secrets: Intellectual Piracy and the Origins of American Industrial Power* (New Haven, CT: Yale University Press, 2004); R. Effron, "Secrets and Spies: Extraterritorial Application of the Economic Espionage Act and the TRIPS Agreement," *New York University Law Review* 78, no. 4 (2003): 1475–517, www.nyulawreview.org/wp-content/uploads/2018/08/5_0.pdf.

    63. D. Almeling et al., "A Statistical Analysis of Trade Secret Litigation in Federal Courts," *Gonzaga Law Review* 45, no. 2 (2009): 291–334, www.tradesecretsandemployeemobility.com/files/2014/05/Statistical-Analysis-of-Trade-Secret-Litigation-in.pdf; D. Almeling et al., "A Statistical Analysis of Trade Secret Litigation in State Courts," *Gonzaga Law Review* 46, no. 1 (2010): 57–101, http://blogs.gonzaga.edu/gulawreview/files/2011/01/AlmelingSnyderSapoznikowMcCollumWeader.pdf.

    64. A cloud service provider may be subject to the Stored Communications Act (18 U.S.C. §§ 2701 et seq.), which enables the US government to obtain electronic communications or other customer content. See I. Kattan, "Cloud Privacy Protections: Why the Stored Communications Act Fails to Protect the Privacy of Communications Stored in the Cloud," *Vanderbilt Journal of Entertainment and Technology Law* 13, no. 3 (2011): 616–56, www.jetlaw.org/wp-content/journal-pdfs/Kattan.pdf.

    65. Facebook, for example, may take up to ninety days to remove content that a customer has deleted, and it will not delete content that affects its legal obligations or ability to investigate violations of its terms or policies.

    66. With IBM's cloud service, backup copies of deleted content may be kept until their retention period expires. https://cloud.ibm.com/docs/overview/terms-of-use?topic=overview-terms. Prezi, a cloud service for creating and sharing presentations, retains backup copies of customer content for three years for residents of EEA states and indefinitely otherwise, even if a customer's account is closed. https://prezi.com/terms-of-use/ - toc6.2.

67. Forrester Consulting, *The Value of Corporate Secrets: How Compliance and Collabora-tion Affect Enterprise Perceptions of Risk* (Cambridge, MA: Forrester Research, 2010), www.nsi.org/pdf/reports/The Value of Corporate Secrets.pdf. According to a widely cited source, the estimated value of trade secrets owned by publicly traded companies in the United States was $5 trillion in 2006. Cited in E. Rowe, "Contributory Negligence, Technology, and Trade Secrets," *George Mason Law Review* 17, no. 1 (2009): 1–37, https://scholar-ship.law.ufl.edu/cgi/viewcontent.cgi?article=1060&context=facultypub.

68. G. Reid et al., "What's It Worth to Keep a Secret?" *Duke Law & Technology Review* 13, no. 1 (2015): 116–61, https://scholarship.law.duke.edu/cgi/viewcontent.cgi?article=1273&con-text=dltr.

69. For examples, see E. Rowe, "Snapshot of Trade Secret Developments," *William and Mary Law Review* 60, no. 45 (2019): 45–91, https://wmlawreview.org/sites/default/files/Eliza-beth A. Rowe - Snapshot of Trade Secret Developments.pdf; E. Rowe, "Unpacking Trade Secret Damages," *Houston Law Review* 55, no. 1 (217): 156–98, https://doi.org/10.2139/ssrn.2842325.

70. According to a 2018 study by Lex Machina, a legal analytics company, the number of trade secret cases initiated in US state courts in 2017 was over 30 percent greater than the 2016 total. www.gordonrees.com/Templates/media/files/pdf/Trade_Secret _Litigation_Report_2018.pdf. An analysis by Willamette Management Associates found that the number of federal trade secret cases increased by 14 percent per year from 2001 to 2012. www.willamette.com/insights_journal/16/spring_2016_11.pdf. For examples of cases involv-ing misappropriation of trade secrets, see *The Case for Enhanced Protection of Trade Secrets in the Trans-Pacific Partnership Agreement,* a policy paper prepared by Covington & Burling LLP for the U.S. Chamber of Commerce. www.uschamber.com/sites/default/files/legacy/inter-national/files/Final TPP Trade Secrets 8_0.pdf.

71. As an example, a newspaper article about the bankruptcy of the Forever 21 clothing chain reported statements by former employees speaking "on the condition of anonymity, citing nondisclosure agreements." S. Maheshwari, "One Family Had a Bubble, Then Burst It," *New York Times*, Late Edition, October 26, 2019, B5.

72. See B. Reid, "A Business Review of the Ethics and Law of Non-Disclosure Agree-ments," *Mustang Journal of Business & Ethics* 4 (2013): 72–85, http://mustangjournals.com/MJBE/v4_MJBE_2013.pdf; P. Witman, "The Art and Science of Non-Disclosure Agree-ments," *Communications of the Association for Information Systems* 16 (2005): 260–69, https://aisel.aisnet.org/cais/vol16/iss1/11. On the difficulty of enforcing a non-disclosure agreement, see M. Pagnattaro, "'The Google Challenge': Enforcement of Noncompete and Trade Secret Agreements for Employees Working in China," *American Business Law Journal* 44, no. 4 (2007): 603–37, https://doi.org/10.1111/j.1744-1714.2007.00047.x.

73. On the advantages of trade secrets over patents, see A. Schwartz, "The Corporate Prefer-ence for Trade Secret," *Ohio State Law Journal* 74, no. 4 (2013): 623–68, https://schol-ar.law.colorado.edu/cgi/viewcontent.cgi?article=1680&context=articles.

74. In *Art of Living Found. v. Does 1-10,* Case No. 5:10-cf-05022-LHK (N.D. Cal. May 1, 2012), the court defined *reasonable efforts* to include advising employees about the existence of a trade secret, limiting access on a need-to-know basis, requiring employees to sign confi-dentiality agreements, and keeping secret documents under lock and key. https://casetext.com/case/art-of-living-found-v-does-1-1. In *Dryco, LLC v. ABM Industries, Inc.,* Case No. 07 CV 0069 (N.D. Ill. Oct. 16, 2009), the court disallowed a claim of misappropriation of trade secrets, noting that the plaintiff did not take reasonable steps to prevent others from acquiring or using its proprietary information. It did not require confidentiality agreements or label documents containing trade secrets as confidential. https://casetext.com/case/dryco-llc-v-abm-industries.

75. In *Formfactor, Inc. v. Micro-Probe, Inc.*, No. C10-3095 PJH (N.D. Cal. June 7, 2012), the court rejected a claim of misappropriation of trade secrets by a departing employee because the plaintiff did not ask the employee to sign a nondisclosure agreement, allowed him to retain his contact information when he left the company, allowed him to use his personal email for company business and to backup company data on his own external hard drive, and did not request the return of company data from his home office when he tendered his resignation.

During an exit interview, the departing employee was not asked whether he possessed any company material in his home. https://casetext.com/case/formfactor-inc-v-micro-probe-1.

76. This definition is based on ISO/IEC 17788:2014, *Information Technology—Cloud Computing—Overview and Vocabulary*. Data portability is not equivalent to interoperability—that is, the ability of two systems to process data in the same manner.

77. Data Protection Working Party, Guidelines on the Right to Data Portability rev. 5 April 2017, WP 242 rev.01 Brussels: European Commission, https://iapp.org/media/pdf/resource_center/WP29-2017-04-data-portability-guidance.pdf. Examples of the growing literature on the GDPR right to data portability include P. De Hert et al., "The Right to Data Portability in the GDPR: Towards User-Centric Interoperability of Digital Services," *Computer Law & Security Review* 34, no. 2 (2018): 193–203, https://doi.org/10.1016/j.clsr.2017.10.003; I. Graef et al., "Data Portability and Data Control: Lessons for an Emerging Concept in EU Law," *German Law Journal* 19, no. 6 (2018): 1359–98, https://doi.org/10.1017/S2071832200023075; J. Wong and T. Henderson, "How Portable Is Portable?: Exercising the GDPR's Right to Data Portability," in *UbiComp '18 Proceedings of the 2018 ACM International Joint Conference and 2018 International Symposium on Pervasive and Ubiquitous Computing and Wearable Computers* (New York: ACM, 2018), 911–20, https://doi.org/10.1145/3267305.3274152; H. Ursic, "Unfolding the New-Born Right to Data Portability: Four Gateways to Data Subject Control," *Scripted* 15, no. 1 (2018): 42–69, https://doi.org/10.2966/scrip.150118.42; L. Urquhart et al., "Realising the Right to Data Portability for the Internet of Things," *Personal and Ubiquitous Computing* 22, no. 2 (2018): 317–32, https://doi.org/10.1007/s00779-017-1069-2; K. Ishii, "Discussions on the Right to Data Portability from Legal Perspectives," in *This Changes Everything—ICT and Climate Change: What Can We Do?*, ed. D. Kreps et al. (Cham, Switerland: Springer Nature, 2018), 338–55, https://doi.org/10.1007/978-3-319-99605-9_26; A. Vanberg, "The Right to Data Portability in the GDPR: What Lessons Can Be Learned from the EU Experience?" *Journal of Internet Law* 21, no. 7 (2018): 12–21, http://gala.gre.ac.uk/id/eprint/24255; B. Van der Auwermeulen, "How to Attribute the Right to Data Portability in Europe: A Comparative Analysis of Legislations," *Computer Law & Security Review* 33, no. 1 (2017): 57–72, https://doi.org/10.1016/j.clsr.2016.11.012; A. Vanberg and M. Unver, "The Right to Data Portability in the GDPR and EU Competition Law: Odd Couple or Dynamic Duo," *European Journal of Law and Technology* 8, no. 1 (2017): http://ejlt.org/article/view/546; R. Janal, "Data Portability: A Tale of Two Concepts," *JIPITEC* 8, no. 1 (2017): 59–69, www.jipitec.eu/issues/jipitec-8-1-2017/4532.

78. *Review of the Midata Voluntary Programme* (London: Dept for Business Innovation and Skills, July 2014), https://assets.publishing.service.gov.uk/government/uploads/system/uploads/attachment_data/file/327845/bis-14-941-review-of-the-midata-voluntary-programme-revision-1.pdf. Midata particulation was voluntary when the program began in 2011, but portability of consumer data was incorporated into sections 89 through 91 of the Enterprise and Regulatory Reform Act 2013.

79. S. Esayas and A. Daly, "The Proposed Australian Consumer Right to Access and Use Data: A European Comparison," *European Competition and Regulatory Law Review* 2, no 3 (2018): 187–202, https://doi.org/10.21552/core/2018/3/6.

80. On the implications for healthcare practitioners, see B. McCall, "What Does the GDPR Mean for the Medical Community?" *The Lancet* 391, no. 10127 (2018): 1249–50, https://doi.org/10.1016/S0140-6736(18)30739-6; V. Chico, "The Impact of the General Data Protection Regulation on Health Research," *British Medical Bulletin* 128, no. 1 (2018): 109–18, https://doi.org/10.1093/bmb/ldy038; S. Lurie, "GDPR: Patient Consent and the Law," *Practice Management* 29, no. 5 (2019): 34–37, https://doi.org/10.12968/prma.2019.29.5.34; N. Lea, "How Will the General Data Protection Regulation Affect Healthcare?" *Acta Medica Portuguesa* 31, nos. 7–8 (2018): 363–65, https://doi.org/10.20344/amp.10881; N. Knott, "The General Data Protection Regulation," *FDJ* 9, no. 2 (2018): 54–57, https://doi.org/10.1308/rcsfdj.2018.54; R. Philip, "General Data Protection Regulation (GDPR) and Paediatric Medical Practice in Ireland: A Personal Reflection," *Irish Journal of Medical Science* 188, no. 2 (2019): 721–24, https://doi.org/10.1007/s11845-018-1857-3; European Society of Radiology, "The New EU General Data Protection Regulation: What the Radiologist Should Know," *Insights into Imaging* 8, no. 3 (2017): 295–99, https://doi.org/10.1007/s13244-017-0552-7; S. Edwards,

"Review of a Medical Illustration Department's Data Processing System to Conform General Data Protection Regulation (GDPR) Compliance," *Journal of Visual Communication in Medicine* 42, no. 3 (2019): 140–43, https://doi.org/10.1080/17453054.2019.1594724.

81. As defined in 45 C.F.R. § 160.103, *protected health information* means individually identifiable health information that is maintained in any form or medium by HIPAA-covered entities, which include health plans, health care clearinghouses, and health care providers who transmit any health information in electronic form. As specified in 45 C.F.R. § 164.524, exclusions include psychotherapy notes that are maintained separate from other patient records and information compiled in reasonable anticipation of a civil, criminal, or administrative proceeding.

82. As specified in 45 C.F.R. § 164.502, the right to data portability extends to the personal representative of a recently deceased data subject. The HIPAA Privacy Rule does not apply to data subjects who have been deceased for more than fifty years. The GDPR's right to data portability, like other GDPR provisions, is limited to living data subjects, but some countries have national laws regarding access to medical records of deceased individuals. In the United Kingdom, for example, a deceased patient's personal representative or any person who may have a claim arising out of the patient's death can request access under the Health Records Act 1990, but no right to data portability is provided.

83. On ownership of patient records, see M. Rodwin, "Patient Data: Property, Privacy and the Public Interest," *American Journal of Law & Medicine* 36, no. 4 (2010): 586–818, https://doi.org/10.1177/009885881003600403.

84. A survey of 230 data portability requests sent to data controllers in EU member states found that some organizations failed to comply with the GDPR requirement for data in a "structured, commonly used, and machine-readable" format, which is poorly defined and subject to interpretation. J. Wang and T. Henderson, "The Right to Data Portability in Practice: Exploring the Implications of the Technologically Neutral GDPR," *International Data Privacy Law* 9, no. 3 (2019), https://doi.org/10.1093/idpl/ipz008.

85. A 2018 survey by Talend, a data integration firm, found that 70 percent of 103 companies based in or operating in Europe failed to respond to data portability requests within the one-month time frame specified by the GDPR. www.talend.com/about-us/press-releases/the-majority-of-businesses-are-failing-to-comply-with-gdpr-according-to-new-talend-research.

Index

academic publications, 2
accidental information loss, 62, 76–80
accountability, 4, 93n72
accounting, 50, 135n39, 193, 219n26
adequate protection, 165–166
adverse events, 5, 79
Affordable Care Act, 27
Age Discrimination Act, 43
Americans with Disabilities Act, 43
Ames, Aldrich, 89n37
Andersen LLP, 107, 133n27
Anderson, Jack, 56n12
anti-malware software, 74
anti-trust laws, 39
anti-virus companies, 71
application whitelisting, 75
appraisal, 6
archival collections, 139n62
artificial intelligence, 45
Asia, 171
assessment. *See* vulnerabilities
assets, 1, 13n1–14n2, 20n34
attorney-client privilege, 184n55
audio tapes, 138n57
audit programs, 52, 105, 206
Australia, 29, 40, 160, 171
AVG Technologies, 88n26
AvMed Health Plans, 90n53–91n54
AV-TEST, 71
Axcient, 92n63

backup practices, 94n82; for adverse
    events, 79; for information, 66–67, 83;
    for mission-critical office records,
    68–69; real-time, 68; technology for,
    68; theft and, 74
banks, 31
Berger, Sandy, 91n57
Berger, Warren, 56n12
big bucket schedules, 119
big data, 35, 37–38
biological hazards, 62
Boolean expressions, vii–viii
Brady, Tom, 133n25
Bureau of Land Management, 101
businesses: archival collections for,
    139n62; GDPR for, 117; information
    quality for, 50; Ontario Business
    Records Protection Act, 166;
    processing for, 112; project managers
    in, 31–32; publications, 2; records, 72;
    regulation for, 30, 98; research for, 77;
    risk acceptance for, 168, 213; surveys
    of, 78; unstructured business
    documents, 51

Cadbury, Adrian, 19n27
California Consumer Privacy Act, 34,
    181n42
California Education Code, 34
California Welfare and Institutions Code,
    34

Canada: Canadian Human Rights Act, 43; Digital Privacy Act in, 170; FINTRAC in, 29; noncompliance in, 161; protection in, 166; regulation in, 40, 99, 159

Capability Maturity Model (CMM), 18n24

casualty policies, 73–74

chief risk officer (CRO), 4

children, 34, 55n7

Children's Online Privacy Protection Act (COPPA), 34, 182n48–183n49

circulation control records, 75

civil action, 35, 166

civil disorder, 70, 71

civil penalties, 55n7, 59n31

classified information, 183n54

climatological hazards, 62, 63–64

clinical trials, 27

closed project files, 114–115

cloud computing, 191–192, 195, 218n16–218n18, 226n66; economics of, 221n34; Stored Communications Act for, 150, 226n64

CMM. *See* Capability Maturity Model

codes of conduct, 41–42

coding, 148

collection. *See specific topics*

commercial record centers, 95n87

commercial value, 203–204

Committee of Sponsoring Organizations (COSO), 3, 7

Community for Creative Non-Violence v. Reid, 222n45–223n46

competitive industries, 41, 42, 194, 204–205

compliance: with data portability, 212; with data subjects, 174; with discovery requests, 110; governance and, 6–7; GRC for, 6–7; information and, 63; information quality and, 50; in-house, 29; initiatives for, 158; with legislation, 167; maturity models for, 20n30; OCEG for, 6; officers, 37, 117; for organizations, 19n28–20n29, 29; with regulation, 5, 37; risk acceptance and, 119; risk limitation plans and, 119; threats and, 97–98; timetables for, 32

computer hardware, 74–75, 79, 123

computer viruses, 69

confidential information, 151

consultants, 41, 42

consumers, 34, 57n26–58n27, 211

contract claims, 134n32, 202

contractors, 41, 42, 90n53–91n54, 129n5–130n6, 202, 222n45–223n46

COPPA. *See* Children's Online Privacy Protection Act

copyrights, 191, 194, 195–196, 218n14–218n15; globalization of, 200, 217n10, 224n49; independent invention and, 208; *Phoenix Renovation Corp. v. Rodriguez* for, 222n42; work-for-hire and, 198–199; written agreements with, 201

COSO. *See* Committee of Sponsoring Organizations

Criminal Code, 160

criminal prosecution, 160–161

CRO. *See* chief risk officer

cross-border data transfer, 165–169, 175, 184n59

Curie, Pierre, 93n78

Curie point, 93n78

customers, 31, 135n40, 143–144, 207

CVS Pharmacy, 59n31

Cyber-Ark Software, 72–73, 91n54

damage potential, 62

data: for American Library Association, 182n44; analysts, 35; centers, 81–82, 83, 84; cloud computing for, 191–192; collection, 28, 53, 59n33; copying of, 71; cross-border data transfer, 165–169, 184n59; Danish Data Protection Agency, 136n45; data breach, 163, 169–174, 175, 185n63; data cleaning software, 53; data entry errors, 53; Data Health Check, 92n65; data migration, 126–127, 128, 139n64–140n65; Data Quality Act, 58n27; distribution of, 209; double-keying and, 60n39; from employees, 42–43; erasure requests for, 130n8–131n9; GDPR for, 33; GIS, 51; HIPAA and, 211, 212, 229n82; historical, 64; information and, 58n28; as market research, 40; MDM software for, 53; metadata mining, 148–154; minimization, 35–36; on organized violence, 71–72; physical security for, 75, 209; privacy, 133n25; protection of, 33–34; quality, 49, 147; real-time backup of, 68; requests for, 212–213; resource, 56n11, 177n14; for stakeholders, 37; storage, 109; storage costs of, 36; subjects, 37, 155, 174; surveys on, 50, 59n32; tapes, 94n82; for telecommunication companies, 35; trade secrets in, 209; Uppsala Conflict Data Program, 71–72. *See also specific topics*

databases: document repositories and, 158; electronic information in, 116; Global Terrorism Database, 72; information and, 32, 53; nonpublic documents in, 164; perfect information for, 51–52; records for, 50–51, 76, 124; retrieval from, 144–146; user permissions for, 169

data portability: compliance with, 212; in EU, 210–211; GDPR for, 210–211, 212, 229n84; in HIPAA, 211, 212, 229n82; information ownership and, 209–214; legislation, 213–214, 215; for organizations, 212–213; requests, 229n84; risk response to, 213–214; vulnerabilities with, 212–213. *See also* Health Insurance Portability and Accountability Act

data theft, 38–42

defamatory content, 45–48

defective media, 127

Defend Trade Secrets Act, 39, 224n56

Deloitte and Touche, 143

Department of Health and Human Services, 26, 28, 59n33, 170, 186n66

Department of Justice, 59n31

Department of Labor, 63

Department of Transportation, 28

destruction, of information, 97, 100–101, 110, 134n33

digital content, 128

digital documentation, 152, 153–154

digital identifiers, 74

digital object identifier (DOI), ix

Digital Privacy Act, 170

disaster-prone area, 67

disclosure: of classified information, 183n54; documentation and, 164; for employees, 158, 164; in EU, 180n35–181n36; Family Educational Rights and Privacy Act for, 181n43–182n44; of information, viii; laws, 155–156, 180n33; mandatory information, 154–158; of nonpublic information, 174–175; for organizations, 155–156, 180n33; of personal information, 183n51; of trade secrets, 204–205, 206, 214–215, 225n59–226n60; unauthorized information, 159–164; in U.S., 181n37. *See also specific topics*

discovery requests, 110, 133n30, 134n34, 144

distribution, 209

documentation, 113; authority and, 169; digital, 152, 153–154; disclosure and, 164; metadata and, 150–151; physical security for, 209; PIPEDA, 160; repositories, 144–145, 158; review, 152; of trade secrets, 209

Dodd, Thomas, 56n12

DOI. *See* digital object identifier

double-keying, 60n39

Driver's Privacy Protection Act, 182n47

due-diligence checklists, 32, 105

earthquakes, 85n4, 86n7

economics, 186n66; of cloud computing, 221n34; copyrights and, 195–196; of damage potential, 62; Economic Espionage Act, 38–39, 89n38; of infringement cases, 194; of storage, 116–117, 135n43

Electronic Communications Privacy Act, 183n49

electronic information, 68, 75, 80–81, 83; in databases, 116; fire and, 78–79, 84; life span of, 138n56

electronic records, 123

Ellsberg, Daniel, 89n37

email systems, 45, 75, 131n11, 152

embedded metadata, 153

employees: in competitive industries, 204–205; data from, 42–43; disclosure for, 158, 164; harassment claims from,

43; independent contractors and, 222n45–223n46; information and, 48, 75, 164; information forms for, 35; knowledge of, 169, 209; legal hold notices for, 133n28; management and, 208; in meetings, 209; metadata and, 152; NDAs for, 207, 208–209, 215, 227n71; performance of, 48; privacy legislation for, 47; regulation of, 43; responsibilities of, 173–174; retrieval for, 148; sabotage by, 70; scrubbing tools for, 154; suspicious emails for, 75; track changes for, 152; trade secrets for, 227n74, 227n75–228n76; training for, 57n17; in U.S., 129n4; work-for-hire for, 199, 202; wrongful termination of, 179n24

employment practices liability insurance (EPLI), 44

encounter probability, 87n15

Enron Corporation, 107

enterprise risk management (ERM), 3–5, 12, 13

EPLI. *See* employment practices liability insurance

Equal Credit Opportunity Act, 101

erasure requests, 130n8–131n9

ERM. *See* enterprise risk management

errors, 59n33, 59n37–60n38, 79, 93n72. *See also* humans

espionage, 38–39, 57n15, 89n37, 89n38

essential information, 144

European Union (EU): data portability in, 210–211; Defend Trade Secrets Act for, 39; disclosure in, 180n35–181n36; GDPR for, 33, 36, 100–101, 155, 159, 165–166, 167; information for, 29; international transfer agreements for, 184n60–185n61; regulation in, 43, 117; Treaty on the Functioning of the European Union, 40

evaluation, 6

evidence preservation, 105–113

extraterrestrial hazards, 62, 63–64

extraterritorial enforcement, 206

failure mode and effects analysis (FMEA), 15n15–16n16

Fair and Accurate Credit Transaction Act, 181n42

Fair Information Practice Principles (FIPPS), 33–34, 55n5

Fair Labor Standards Act, 101

fair use doctrine, 195, 220n33–221n34

Family Educational Rights and Privacy Act, 181n43–182n44

Federal Aviation Administration, 28

Federal Emergency Management Agency, 63, 66

Federal Motor Carrier Safety Administration, 28

Federal Rules of Civil Procedure, 150, 175n5–176n6, 179n24

Federal Trade Commission, 58n27, 72

federated searches, 148, 177n12

file conversions, 140n65

file plans, 148

financial institutions, 181n41

financial risk, 23n46

Financial Services Modernization Act, 34

Financial Transactions and Reports Analysis Centre (FINTRAC), 29

FIPPS. *See* Fair Information Practice Principles

fire, 62, 80–84, 85, 86n7, 93n80–94n81, 94n85

firewalls, 74

flooding, 65–66, 85n6

Florida, 34

FMEA. *See* failure mode and effects analysis

Forrester Research, 88n29

France, 29

fraud, 107

freedom-of-information laws, 154, 180n32

General Data Protection Regulation (GDPR), 33, 117; data breaches for, 171; data minimization for, 35, 36; for data portability, 210–211, 212, 229n84; data subjects for, 33; employee information forms for, 35; for EU, 33, 36, 100–101, 155, 159, 165–166, 167; globalization of, 159; limitations to, 184n57; for organizations, 33; personal information for, 35; requirements for, 184n60–185n61

General Motors, 57n15
geographic information systems (GIS), 51
geolocation metadata, 150
geological hazards, 62, 85n6
Geological Survey, 65
geomagnetic storms, 86n13–87n14
geopolitical risk, 69–70
GIS. *See* geographic information systems
GitLab, 77–78, 92n67
GLBA. *See* Gramm-Leach Bliley Act
Global Peace Index, 72
Global Seismic Hazard Assessment
    Program, 65
Global Terrorism Database, 72
Google, vii, 130n8–131n9, 219n21
governance, risk, and compliance (GRC),
    6–7, 13, 17n19, 20n34
government agencies, 26
Gramm-Leach Bliley Act (GLBA), 34
GRC. *See* governance, risk, and
    compliance

Hanssen, Robert, 89n37
harassment claims, 43–44, 57n17, 57n18
Hariri, Rafik, 150
Hawley Committee, 13n1–14n2
hazards, 15n12, 62–63, 85n6, 86n8, 155.
    See also natural disasters
healthcare providers, 186n70
health hazards, 155
Health Informatics, 7
Health Insurance Portability and
    Accountability Act (HIPAA), 181n40,
    229n81; data and, 211, 212, 229n82; for
    information, 72, 87n25–88n26,
    90n53–91n54, 161, 170
hierarchies, 4–5, 18n24
HIPAA. *See* Health Insurance Portability
    and Accountability Act
Hiss, Alger, 89n37
historical data, 64
humans, 8–9, 11–12, 43, 67; human error,
    76–77, 78, 79, 91n59–92n60; human
    rights, 57n16, 57n23, 189–190
hurricanes, 64–65, 86n8, 87n17
hydrological hazards, 62

identity theft, 38–42, 72
ignorance. *See* noncompliance

inactive records, 115–116
inadvertent exposure, 151–152, 153
independent contractors, 202,
    222n45–223n46
independent invention, 208
indexing, 145–146, 176n7
India, 40
industrial property, 204
information: asset management and,
    13n1–14n2; backup practices for,
    66–67, 83; business records, 72;
    classified, 183n54; collection of, viii,
    25–26, 30–32; commercial value of,
    203–204; between competitive
    industries, 41; compliance and, 63;
    confidential, 151; contract claims and,
    134n32; copying of, 109; data and,
    58n28; databases and, 32, 53; data
    collection and, 28; data theft of, 38–40;
    defamatory content, 45–48; deficiency
    of, 1–2; for Department of Health and
    Human Services, 28; for Department of
    Transportation, 28; destruction of, 97,
    100–101, 110, 134n33; disclosure of,
    viii; employee information forms, 35;
    employees and, 48, 75, 164; essential,
    144; for EU, 29; for federal government
    contractors, 27; financial risk and,
    23n46; FIPPS for, 33–34, 55n5;
    flooding and, 65–66; freedom-of-
    information laws, 154; GIS, 51; *Health
    Informatics*, 7; HIPAA for, 72,
    87n25–88n26, 90n53–91n54, 161, 170;
    human error and, 76–77, 91n59–92n60;
    in identity theft, 38; information-
    dependent activities, 49; initiatives for,
    32; insurance for, 74; international
    standards for, ix; in inventory, 197,
    208; in legislation, 161–162; libel, 48;
    litigation and, 110–111; on magnetic
    tapes, 138n57–138n58; management of,
    109; for Medicaid agencies, 27;
    Medicare, 59n33; natural disasters and,
    84; NDAs for, 38; needs, 146;
    nonpersonal, 163; nonpublic, 38, 39,
    40, 41–42, 54, 56n12, 56n14, 174–175;
    objectionable content in, 42–43;
    observation of, 54; obsolete, 116–117,
    128–129; for organizations, 30, 68, 73,

82, 97–98, 115, 124–125; ownership of,
viii, 199, 200; perfect, 51–52; personal,
151, 163, 168, 169–171, 183n51;
Personal Information Protection Act,
171; for pharmaceutical companies, 27;
in Physician Payments Sunshine Act,
27; PIPEDA, 160, 161, 183n50;
planning and, viii, 3, 30; poor quality,
49, 50, 59n32; private content as,
45–46, 48; processing, 79–80;
proprietary, 42, 57n15, 73, 226n61;
quality of, 48–54, 59n36; recovery of,
66, 85; regulation, viii, 26, 29, 44, 50,
54; repositories for, 113; requests, 26;
resource data as, 177n14; retrieval
failure, 142–148; retrieval of, 141, 174;
risk mitigation and, 37, 52–54, 68–69;
of scholarly value, 127; searches for,
142, 147–148; software for, 76;
stability of, 121–124; for state
government agencies, 27–28; statutes of
limitations for, 120; stolen, 39, 56n13;
storage of, 42; surveys on, 72–73;
taxonomic approach for, 10–12; theft,
70–71, 73, 88n35–89n36,
90n53–91n54; threats to, 61–62; in
trade secrets, 224n53; transfer of,
209–210; unnecessary content in, 37;
for unpaid workers, 202–203; in
unstructured business documents, 51;
USA FREEDOM Act for, 55n6;
vulnerabilities with, 29–30, 35–36,
40–41, 43–44, 46–47, 50–51; work-for-
hire and, 189. *See also specific topics*
information disclosure, 174; cross-border
data transfer and, 165–169, 184n59;
data breach notification and, 169–174;
mandatory, 154–158; metadata mining
and, 148–154; for organizations, 141;
retrieval failure and, 142–148;
unauthorized, 159–164; vulnerabilities
with, 144–146, 151–152, 156–157,
161–162, 167, 171–172
information governance, vii, 7
information loss, viii, 61, 62,
88n35–89n36; accidental, 62, 76–80;
from fire, 80–84; malicious, 61, 69–75,
84; from natural disasters, 61, 62–69;
risk mitigation and, 127–128;
vulnerabilities with, 64–67, 71–73,
77–78, 81–82
information ownership, 189, 195–197; data
portability and, 209–214; intellectual
property and, 189–198; trade secrets
and, 203–209; in U.S., 201;
vulnerabilities with, 193–195; work-
for-hire and, 198–203
information retention, 136n47–137n48; for
accounting, 135n39; decisions in,
113–120; evidence preservation and,
105–113; noncompliance and, 98–105;
obsolescence and, 120–128; policies
for, 97–98; regulation of, 128;
schedules for, 131n12; in U.S., 135n42;
vulnerabilities with, 102–103, 108–109,
117–118, 124–125
information retrieval failure, 142–148,
176n7
information technology, viii, 71, 72–73,
148–149
information theft, 70–71, 73,
88n35–89n36, 90n53–91n54
infringement cases, 193, 194–195, 196,
214
in-house compliance, 29
initiatives: big data, 35, 37–38; for
compliance, 158; for information, 32;
management of, 31–32, 158, 173; risk
governance and, 7; risk related, 6; by
United Nations, 65
innovation, 205
insider trading laws, 56n14
instability, of media, 120–128, 129
insurance: casualty policies, 73–74; data
breach, 163, 173; EPLI, 44; HIPAA,
72; for information, 74; litigation and,
48; media liability insurance, 57n24;
medical, 186n70; noncompliance and,
173–174; for organizations, 9–10, 51;
for property, 195; for records, 82–83;
for risk mitigation, 197, 214; risk
transfer and, 12, 31, 36–37, 67–68, 73,
82, 104, 111, 118–119, 126, 157, 168,
213
intellectual property, 107, 115; information
ownership and, 189–198; legislation
for, 195; nonpublic documents and,
203; for organizations, 189, 193, 195,

214; protection of, 196; threats to, 192–193, 194–195; Trade-Related Aspects of Intellectual Property Rights, 217n11; trade secrets as, 206; in U.S., 217n9; WIPO, 189–190, 216n6

Interagency Guidelines Establishing Information Security Standards, 170

International Organization for Standardization, ix

International Risk Governance Council (IRGC), 6

international transfer agreements, 184n60–185n61

Internet filtering software, 45

inventory, 194, 197, 208

investigations, 172–173

investments, 23n46, 102

IRGC. *See* International Risk Governance Council

Iron Mountain, 219n23

janitorial services, 75

Latin American countries, 101

law enforcement, 154

law firms, 100

legal hold notices, 108–109, 111–112, 113, 133n28

legislation: compliance with, 167; data portability, 213–214, 215; freedom-of-information laws, 154; information in, 161–162; for intellectual property, 195; for libel, 46; noncompliance with, 172; privacy, 34, 36–54, 210; recordkeeping laws, 98–100; for regulation, 98, 172, 174; right-to-know laws, 181n36; for trade secrets, 54; in U.S., 159, 170; for work-for-hire, 199–200; in Wyoming, 56n11

Lewy v. Remington Arms Co., 135n40

liability, 57n24, 78–79, 106–107

libel, 46–47, 48

litigation, 106; information and, 110–111; infringement cases, 193, 194–195, 196, 214; insurance and, 48; liability, 106–107; in New York, 57n18; nonpublic information in, 56n12; for organizations, 45, 128; parallel, 109, 113; privacy legislation and, 47;

probability of, 108–109; proprietary information in, 57n15; risk, 46; risk mitigation and, 47; threats and, 206–207; trade secrets in, 225n58, 227n70

Loi Bertrand, 29

magnetic fields, 92n60

magnetic media, 122

magnetic tapes, 125, 138n57–138n58

malfunctions, with technology, 11, 76–77, 78

malicious actors, 172

malicious information loss, 61, 69–75, 84

malicious software, 69, 85

malware attacks, 73

management: employees and, 208; executive, 4; of initiatives, 31–32, 158, 173; in organizations, 37, 45; probability for, 15n15–16n16; quality, 52, 57n25, 57n26–58n27, 59n37–60n38; records, 147; stakeholders and, 31, 104, 157–158, 163, 168, 171, 173

mandatory information collection, 26–32

mandatory information disclosure, 154–158

manual indexing, 145–146

marketing, 40, 52–53

master data management (MDM), 53

maturity models, 4–5, 18n24, 20n30

McAfee, John, 150

MDM. *See* master data management

media, 57n24, 120–128, 129

Medicaid agencies, 27

medical insurance services, 186n70

Medicare, 59n33

meetings, 209

Merck, 149–150, 178n18

metadata mining, 148–154, 174, 179n26–180n27

meteorological hazards, 62

microfilm technology, 123–124, 125

Microsoft, 219n20, 219n22

minimization, of data, 35–37

mission-critical office records, 68–69, 84

mistakes, 79

mobile computing, 72

National Association of Corporate Directors (NACD), 17n19

National Center for State Courts, 182n46

National Fire Protection Association, 83–84

National Oceanic and Atmospheric Administration, 64–65

National Security Agency (NSA), 180n31

National Stolen Property Act, 39

natural disasters, 61; earthquakes, 85n4; geomagnetic storms, 86n13–87n14; information and, 84; probability of, 64, 84, 87n15; risk response for, 67–69; threats of, 62–64; vulnerability assessment for, 64–67

NDAs. *See* non-disclosure agreements

negative risk, 2

New England Journal of Medicine, 149–150

New York, 57n16, 57n18, 57n23, 87n17

New Zealand, 40, 65, 160

noncompliance: with Affordable Care Act, 27; in Canada, 161; civil action for, 35, 166; civil penalties for, 55n7; of data portability legislation, 213–214; defenseless, 31, 104, 158, 163–164, 168–169, 173; with disclosure laws, 156; information retention and, 98–105; insurance and, 173–174; investigations for, 172–173; with legislation, 172; with nonpublic information, 40; of objectionable content, 43; for organizations, 156–157; penalties for, 26–27; regulation of, 28; risk limitation plans for, 214; risk mitigation and, 30–31, 157; risk response and, 103–105; unintentional, 162, 167; vulnerabilities for, 29–30

non-disclosure agreements (NDAs), 38, 40; for employees, 207, 208–209, 215, 227n71; for organizations, 42

nonpersonal information, 163

nonpublic documents, 40, 159, 161–162, 164, 203

nonpublic information, 38, 39; disclosure of, 174–175; insider trading laws and, 56n14; in litigation, 56n12; noncompliance with, 40; for organizations, 40; regulation of, 54;

unauthorized collection of, 41–42

NSA. *See* National Security Agency

objectionable content, 42–45

obsolescence, 120–128

obsolete information, 116–117, 128–129

OCEG. *See* Open Compliance and Ethics Group

O'Day v. McDonnell Douglas Helicopter Co., 89n39

Office of Management and Budget (OMB), 26

off-site storage, 82–83

of patents, 217n12

Oil and Gas program, 101

OMB. *See* Office of Management and Budget

Ontario Business Records Protection Act, 166

Open Compliance and Ethics Group (OCEG), 6

Open Group, 8

operational objectives, 37

operational retention periods, 113–114, 120

organizations: accountability in, 4, 93n72; asset management for, 1; audit programs for, 105, 206; backup copies for, 66–67; cloud computing for, 195; codes of conduct for, 41–42; in competitive industries, 42; compliance for, 19n28–20n29, 29; COSO, 3; data portability for, 212–213; in disaster-prone areas, 67; disclosure laws for, 155–156, 180n33; email systems in, 45; ERM in, 13; executive management for, 4; firewalls for, 74; GDPR for, 33; governance of, 6–7; harassment claims for, 44; information disclosure for, 141; information for, 30, 68, 73, 82, 97–98, 115, 124–125; information retrieval failure for, 142–148; insurance for, 9–10, 51; intellectual property for, 189, 193, 195, 214; libel for, 46–47; litigation for, 45, 128; management in, 37, 45; NDAs for, 42; noncompliance for, 156–157; nonpublic documents for, 161–162; nonpublic information for, 40; officers for, 20n34; ownership for,

191, 197–198, 207; recordkeeping laws for, 102–103, 128; risk avoidance for, 134n35; risk limitation plans for, 208–209; risk management for, 9; risk mitigation for, 108–109, 119–120; risk oversight for, 12; risk responses for, 10; social media for, 47; storage areas for, 75; strategic objectives for, 5; threats for, 11; training in, 45; unauthorized information disclosure for, 159–160; vulnerabilities for, 12, 64; work-for-hire for, 200–201, 203; written policies for, 202, 208

over-retention, 113–120, 136n47–137n48

ownership, viii, 136n44, 189; exposure period for, 194; of information, viii, 199, 200; for organizations, 191, 197–198, 207; risk acceptance with, 201. *See also* information ownership

paper records, 80–81, 121–122; deterioration of, 137n48; electronic records and, 123; environmental conditions for, 125; permanent paper for, 124

Paperwork Reduction Act, 58n27

parallel litigation, 109, 113

passwords, 72–73, 74, 91n54

patents, 191, 194–195, 208, 217n12

Pearson, Drew, 56n12

PepsiCo, Inc. v. Redmond, 226n60

perfect information, 51–52

permanent magnetization, 93n78

permanent paper, 124

perpetual copyright, 217n10

personal information, 33–35, 151, 163, 168, 210; data breaches and, 169–171; disclosure of, 183n51; Personal Information Protection Act, 171; regulation of, 32–33, 210–212; risk avoidance with, 213; risk response and, 36–38; vulnerability assessment and, 35–36

Personal Information Protection and Electronic Documents Act (PIPEDA), 160, 161, 183n50

pharmaceutical companies, 27, 58n30

Phoenix Renovation Corp. v. Rodriguez, 222n42

physical security, 75, 209

Physician Payments Sunshine Act, 27, 29

PIPEDA. *See* Personal Information Protection and Electronic Documents Act

Pixar, 77–78

political jurisdictions, 171–172

Poneman Institute, 92n64, 186n69

poor quality information, 49, 50, 59n32

positive risk, 2

Powell, Colin, 149

power outages, 86n8

preassessment, 6

predictive coding technology, 148

preservation, of evidence, 105–113

privacy. *See specific topics*

Privacy Acts. *See specific acts*

privacy legislation, 34, 36–54, 210

Privacy Rights Clearinghouse, 171

private content, 45–48

probability, 15n12; of fire, 83, 85, 93n80–94n81; of litigation, 108–109; for management, 15n15–16n16; of natural disasters, 64, 84, 87n15; of risk, 49–50; of technology failure, 77–78; of threats, 3, 8, 62; uncertainty and, 2–3; unpredictable threats and, 71

processing, 37, 79–80, 112

project managers, 4, 31–32

property, 20n34, 73–74, 80, 189–190, 216n6; industrial, 204; insurance for, 195. *See also* intellectual property

proprietary information, 42, 57n15, 73, 226n61

protection, 33–34, 165–166; consumer protection laws, 211; for customers, 207; extraterritorial enforcement and, 206; of health information, 229n81; of intellectual property, 196; National Fire Protection Association, 83–84. *See also specific topics*

public interest, 190

quality control, 32, 51

quality management, 52, 57n25, 57n26–58n27, 59n37–60n38

quantitative analysis, 2–3

racism, 57n18

real-time backup, 68

records: accuracy of, 58n30; businesses, 72; circulation control, 75; closed project files, 114–115; commercial record centers, 95n87; custodians of, 112, 113; customers complaint, 135n40; for databases, 50–51, 76, 124; inactive, 115–116; insurance for, 82–83; management, 147; paper, 80–81; recordkeeping laws, 98–100, 101, 102–103, 104–105, 113–114, 119–120, 128, 131n11, 131n13; regulation and, 105; risk acceptance and, 103

recovery, 66, 85, 92n66

redox blemishes, 139n63

regulation: in Australia, 40; authority in, 170; for businesses, 30, 98; California Consumer Privacy Act for, 34; California Education Code for, 34; California Welfare and Institutions Code for, 34; in Canada, 40, 99, 159; compliance with, 5, 37; of contractors, 129n5–130n6; criminal prosecution for, 160–161; of employees, 43; in EU, 43, 117; in Florida, 34; from government agencies, 26; information, viii, 26, 29, 44, 50, 54; of information retention, 128; Investment Industry Regulatory Organization, 102; of knowledge, 38–41; in Latin American countries, 101; law enforcement and, 154; legislation for, 98, 172, 174; of noncompliance, 28; of nonpublic information, 54; for OMB, 26; of personal information, 32–33, 210–212; of pharmaceutical companies, 58n30; privacy legislation and, 54; of recordkeeping laws, 113–114, 131n13; records and, 105; requirement awareness and, 32; risk avoidance and, 31, 36, 157; risk limitation plans for, 31; scrutiny in, 30–31; of social media, 42–43; of telecommunication companies, 35. *See also* General Data Protection Regulation

religious institutions, 201

repositories, for information, 113

resource data, 56n11, 177n14

Restatement of Torts, 224n53

retention. *See* information retention

retention schedules, 131n12

retrieval, 177n10; from databases, 144–146; efficiency and, 143–144; failure, 142–148; indexing and, 145; of information, 141, 174; metadata and, 149–150. *See also* information disclosure

revised hold notices, 112

RHT. *See* risk homeostasis theory

Richter scale, 85n4

right-to-know laws, 181n36

riots, 71

risk. *See specific topics*

risk acceptance, 9; for businesses, 168, 213; for commercial record centers, 95n87; compliance and, 119; evidence and, 110; for National Fire Protection Association, 83–84; obsolescence and, 127–128; with ownership, 201; records and, 103

risk avoidance, 9, 104, 201; for organizations, 134n35; with personal information, 213; regulation and, 31, 36, 157; risk limitation plans and, 214; risk mitigation and, 125–126, 146–147

risk exposure, 13

risk governance, 6, 7

risk homeostasis theory (RHT), 22n43

risk limitation plans, 10, 31; compliance and, 119; for intellectual property, 197–198; for noncompliance, 214; for organizations, 208–209; recordkeeping laws and, 104–105; risk avoidance and, 214; for vulnerabilities, 143–164

risk management, vii; ERM, 3–5; frameworks for, 8; GRC for, 6–7; history of, 1–2; human action and, 8–9; investments and, 23n46; maturity models for, 20n30; monetary consequences in, 8; for organizations, 9; planning in, ix; surveys of, 15n15–16n16; unrecognized risks and, 13

risk mitigation, 9–10, 13; for fire, 82; human error and, 79; information and, 37, 52–54, 68–69; information loss and, 127–128; insurance for, 197, 214;

litigation and, 47; noncompliance and, 30–31, 157; for organizations, 108–109, 119–120; passwords for, 74; risk avoidance and, 125–126, 146–147; risk transfer and, 78–79, 146; for trade secrets, 207

risk oversight, 12

risk response, 9–10, 13; for accidental information loss, 78–80; for cross-border data transfer, 168–169, 184n59; for data breach notification, 172–174; to data portability, 213–214; for data theft, 41–42; for evidence preservation, 110–113; for fire, 82–84; to information ownership, 195–198; for information quality, 51–54; for malicious information loss, 73–75; mandatory information and, 30–32, 157–158; for metadata mining, 152–154; for natural disasters, 67–69; noncompliance and, 103–105; for objectionable content, 44–45; for obsolescence, 125–128; personal information and, 36–38; for private content, 47–48; retention and, 118–120; for retrieval failure, 146–148; with trade secrets, 207–209; for unauthorized information disclosure, 162–164; to work-for-hire, 201–203

risk taxonomy, 10–12, 13

risk transfer, 9–10; data breach insurance and, 163; insurance and, 12, 31, 36–37, 67–68, 73, 82, 104, 111, 118–119, 126, 157, 168, 213; risk mitigation and, 78–79, 146; with trade secrets, 208

risk treatment, 9–10, 13

sabotage, 70, 88n34

San Francisco earthquake, 86n7

scientific research, 122

scrubbing, of metadata, 153–154

searches, 142, 143, 144–145, 147–148, 177n12

security, 91n57, 164

sentencing commission, 19n28–20n29

Sherman Act, 40

Singapore, 40

Snowden, Edward, 55n6

social media, 42–43, 47

software, 218n18; anti-malware, 74; Cyber-Ark Software, 72–73, 91n54; data cleaning, 53; for information, 76; malicious, 85; MDM, 53; surveillance, 45

solar storms, 63–64

Spiceworks, 92n68

spoliation, 106–107, 110–113, 133n31–134n32

staff, 10, 32, 174

Stafford Act, 85n3

stakeholders, 6, 37; management and, 31, 104, 157–158, 163, 168, 171, 173; responsibilities of, 4, 12

START. *See* Study of Terrorism and Responses to Terrorism

statutes of limitations, 120

stolen information, 39, 56n13

storage, 138n54; areas, 75; commercial, 81; costs, 36; data, 109; devices, 79, 123; economics of, 116–117, 135n43; of information, 42; janitorial services and, 75; media, 126; off-site, 82–83; redox blemishes in, 139n63; Stored Communications Act, 150, 226n64

strategic objectives, 5

strikes, 71

stripping, of metadata, 153–154

structure fires, 94n85

Study of Terrorism and Responses to Terrorism (START), 72

surveillance software, 45

suspicious emails, 75

Switzerland, 166

taxonomic approach, 10–12

TCO. *See* total cost of ownership

technology, 125; anti-malware software, 74; AVG Technologies, 88n26; for backup practices, 68; data cleaning software, 53; digital identifiers, 74; failure, 77–78, 79; for federated searches, 177n12; for file conversions, 140n65; malfunctions with, 11, 76–77, 78; malicious software, 69; MDM software for, 53; microfilm, 123–124; mobile computing, 72; predictive coding, 148; quality control and, 51; surveillance software, 45; in United

Kingdom, 72–73
telecommunication companies, 35
terrorism, 70, 72, 88n33
theft, 74, 75; identity, 38–42, 72;
    information, 70–71, 73, 88n35–89n36,
    90n53–91n54
threats: assessments of, viii–ix; compliance
    and, 97–98; fire, 80; human action as,
    12; inadvertent exposure, 151–152; to
    information, 61–62; information risk as,
    2; to intellectual property, 192–193,
    194–195; litigation and, 206–207;
    metadata mining, 150; of natural
    disasters, 62–64; for organizations, 11;
    probability of, 3, 8, 62; threat agents, 8;
    trade secrets and, 204; unpredictable,
    71; vulnerabilities and, 2, 8–9, 12, 13,
    189
tornadoes, 65
total cost of ownership (TCO), 136n44
Total Quality Management (TQM), 52
Toxic Substances Control Act, 101
TQM. *See* Total Quality Management
Trade-Related Aspects of Intellectual
    Property Rights, 217n11
trade secrets, 203–209, 225n59–226n60;
    Defend Trade Secrets Act, 39, 224n56;
    documentation of, 209; for employees,
    227n74, 227n75–228n76; information
    in, 224n53; legislation for, 54; in
    litigation, 225n58, 227n70; from
    previous employers, 40–41; Uniform
    Trade Secrets Act, 39, 89n38; written
    agreements for, 42
traffic safety research, 22n43
training, 10, 45, 57n17, 79, 174
transaction processing, 143–144
Treaty on the Functioning of the European
    Union, 40
tropical cyclones, 64–65
true statements, 48
Twitter, 179n26–180n27

unauthorized collection, 41–42
unauthorized copying, 71
unauthorized information disclosure,
    159–164
under-retention, 113–120
Uniform Trade Secrets Act, 39, 89n38

unintentional noncompliance, 162, 167
United Kingdom, vii, 13n1–14n2, 72–73,
    149
United Nations, 65, 152, 189–190
United States, vii; CMM in, 18n24;
    Criminal Code, 160; data protection in,
    33–34; disclosure in, 181n37;
    employees in, 129n4; espionage in,
    89n37; fair use doctrine in, 195; FIPPS
    in, 33–34, 55n5; fires in, 80; Geological
    Survey, 65; information ownership in,
    201; information regulation in, 44, 198,
    199; information retention in, 135n42;
    intellectual property in, 217n9;
    legislation in, 159, 170; metadata for,
    152; NSA in, 180n31; OMB in, 26;
    privacy legislation in, 36; sentencing
    commission, 19n28–20n29
unpaid workers, 202–203
unpredictable threats, 71
unrecognized risks, 13
unstructured business documents, 51
Uppsala Conflict Data Program, 71–72
USA FREEDOM Act, 55n6
user permissions, 169

vandalism, 70, 75
Video Privacy Protection Act, 182n45
video tapes, 138n57
violence, 71–72
Vioxx, 149–150, 178n18
vulnerabilities, viii, ix; business risk and,
    11; categorization of, 10–11; with data
    portability, 212–213; with information,
    29–30, 35–36, 40–41, 43–44, 46–47,
    50–51; with information disclosure,
    144–146, 151–152, 156–157, 161–162,
    167, 171–172; with information loss,
    64–67, 71–73, 77–78, 81–82; with
    information ownership, 193–195; with
    information retention, 102–103,
    108–109, 117–118, 124–125; for
    noncompliance, 29–30; for
    organizations, 12, 64; risk avoidance
    for, 9; risk exposure as, 13; risk
    limitation plans for, 143–164; threats
    and, 2, 8–9, 12, 13, 189; with trade
    secrets, 206–207; with work-for-hire,
    200–201

warranties, 10
WIPO. *See* World Intellectual Property
  Organization
word-processing files, 152, 153
work-for-hire doctrine, 198–203, 214

World Intellectual Property Organization
  (WIPO), 189–190, 216n6
written agreements, 42, 112, 201
written policies, 202, 208
wrongful acts, 69
wrongful termination, 179n24

About the Author

William Saffady is a records management and information governance consultant and researcher based in New York City. He is the author of over three dozen books and many articles on information governance, records management, record retention, document storage and retrieval technologies, library automation, and other information management topics. Dr. Saffady received his BA degree from Central Michigan University and his MA, PhD, and M.S.L.S. degrees from Wayne State University. Before establishing his full-time consulting practice, he was a professor of library and information science at the State University of New York at Albany, Long Island University, Pratt Institute, and Vanderbilt University. Dr. Saffady is a fellow of ARMA International, and he is profiled in the *Encyclopedia of Archival Writers, 1515–2015*, a reference work published by Rowman & Littlefield in 2019.